Introducing .NET

D1368705

James Conard
Patrick Dengler
Brian Francis
Jay Glynn
Burton Harvey
Billy Hollis
Rama Ramachandran
John Schenken
Scott Short
Chris Ullman

Wrox Press Ltd.

Introducing .NET

wrox

Published by Wrox Press Ltd,
Arden House, 1102 Warwick Road, Acocks Green,
Birmingham, B27 6BH, UK
Printed in the United States
ISBN 1-861004-89-3

Trademark Acknowledgements

Wrox has endeavored to provide trademark information about all the companies and products mentioned in this book by the appropriate use of capitals. However, Wrox cannot guarantee the accuracy of this information.

Credits

Authors
James Conard
Patrick Dengler
Brian Francis
Jay Glynn
Burton Harvey
Billy Hollis
Rama Ramachandran
John Schenken
Scott Short
Chris Ullman

Technical Reviewers
Richard Anderson
Robert Bazinet
Clive Browning
Robert Chang
Damien Foggon
Mark Harrison
Rob Howard
Leif Kornstaedt
Marc Kuperstein
David Liske
Tim McCarthy
Craig McQueen
Christophe Nasarre
Fredrik Normén
Kent Sharkey
Mark Smith
Robert Taylor

Category Managers
Dominic Lowe
Kirsty Reade

Technical Architects
Sarah Drew
Chris Goode
Devin Lunsford

Technical Editors
Claire Brittle
Ewan Buckingham

Author Agents
Tony Berry
Sarah Bowers

Project Administrator
Jake Manning

Production Coordinator
Pip Wonson

Figures
Shabnam Hussain

Index
Adrian Axinte

Cover
Shelley Frazier

Proof Reader
Fiona Berryman

About the Authors

James Conard

James M. Conard is a Solutions Champion for ePartners, a leading eBusiness solutions provider for emerging middle market companies. At ePartners James is responsible for training and mentoring other developers on Microsoft.NET technologies, as well as defining the development standards and methodologies for the organization. He also consults with middle market companies on how to leverage these technologies to solve real-world business problems. James is a Microsoft Certified Trainer (MCT), Solutions Developer (MCSD) and Systems Engineer (MCSE). He specializes in COM(+), ADO(.NET), XML, SQL Server and related Microsoft.NET technologies from a Visual Basic perspective and has co-authored several books for Wrox Press on these subjects.

Patrick Dengler

Patrick is busily growing Internet startups throughout the "Silicon Forest" area. His interests include building companies by creating frameworks for Internet architectures. He has received several patents in stateless Internet database architectures.

I want to thank my lovely, graceful and beautiful wife Kelly for simply putting up with me. Without her and my family, Devin, Casey and Dexter, I wouldn't be whole.

Brian Francis

Brian Francis is the Technical Evangelist for NCR's Web Kiosk Solutions. From his office in Duluth, Georgia, Brian is responsible for enlightening NCR and their customers in the technologies and tools used for creating Web Kiosk solutions. Brian also uses the tools that he evangelizes in developing solutions for NCR's customers. Brian has developed and deployed multimedia kiosk applications, computer-based training applications, and other advanced user interface prototypes for the past 10 years.

He has worked extensively with Wrox Press as an author and technical reviewer. Some of his projects have included *Professional Active Server Pages* (versions 1.0, 2.0, and 3.0) , *Professional Internet Explorer 4.0* , *Beginning Active Server Pages* (versions 2.0 and 3.0), *ASP Programmers Reference* (version 2.0 and 3.0), *IE5 Programmer's Reference*. Brian is now working on some new books for the .NET platform.

Jay Glynn

Jay started developing software in the late 1980's, writing applications for the Pick operating system in Pick BASIC. Since then he has created applications using Paradox PAL and Object PAL, Delphi, Pascal, C/C++, Java, VBA and Visual Basic. Currently, Jay is a Project Coordinator and Architect for a large insurance company based in Nashville TN. For the past 5 years he has been developing software for pen based computers and more recently ASP and server based systems. When not sitting in front of a keyboard, Jay is busy restoring a house in Franklin TN, playing a round of golf whenever possible and watching Disney movies with his wife and 3 year old son.

Burton Harvey

Burton Harvey is a consultant for Oakwood Systems Group, a Microsoft partner firm that specializes in Web development. An MCSD with a Master's Degree in Computer Science, Burt has over fifteen years' experience using Microsoft development tools, and enjoys architecting software that elegantly fulfills his customers' needs. After speaking at Wrox conferences in Las Vegas and Amsterdam, Burt co-authored *C# Programming: The Public Beta* and *Introducing .NET with the Public Beta*. Although fascinated by all computer topics from electrons to evolutionary computation, Burt's most interested in the object-oriented paradigm, improving the state of software engineering, and finding innovative ways to better human life through computers. He currently resides in Nashville, Tennessee, and can be contacted via e-mail at kbharvey@mindspring.com.

Billy Hollis

Billy Hollis has been developing software for over twenty years. He has written for many technical publications and is a frequent speaker at conferences, including Comdex and the Visual Basic Insiders Technical Summit (VBITS). He is also the author of the book *"Visual Basic 6:Design, Specification, and Objects"*.

Mr. Hollis is General Manager of the Nashville branch of Oakwood Systems Group, a consulting firm based in St. Louis, which specializes in Internet software development with Microsoft technologies. He is also MSDN Regional Director of Developer Relations in Nashville for Microsoft.

Rama Ramachandran

Rama Ramachandran is the Director of Technology with Imperium Solutions, a Microsoft Solution Provider Partner. He is a Microsoft Certified Solution Developer and Site-Builder and designs and develops web and e-commerce applications using .NET, ASP/+, COM, Visual Basic, SQL Server and Windows 2000. He also has extensive experience with building database systems using Visual Basic, Visual InterDev, Access, and FoxPro. Rama is the contributing author *for "Professional ASP Data Access"* and *"Professional Visual InterDev 6 Programming"* (both from Wrox) as well as co-author of four books on Visual Basic from Que Publishing.

Rama is also the ASP Pro at Devx.com where he answers ASP related questions. He teaches Visual Basic and Web Development at Fairfield University as well as at the University of Connecticut. He lives in Stamford, Conn., with his wife Beena and their sons Ashish and Amit. Reach Rama at rama@imperium.com

This book is dedicated to my wife Beena and our miracle babies – Ashish and Amit. A lot of prayers, friends and support enabled us to go through two very difficult pregnancies and we are grateful to our prayer-answering God for their laughing, mischievous, adoring lives. Thanks for being there, Beens. I love you.

John Schenken

John Schenken is a Test Lead at Microsoft in the .NET Frameworks team. John has been at Microsoft for over 4 years. John graduated from Texas A&M University with a Computer Science degree. He joined Microsoft at the time the Visual InterDev was starting development. During his tenure at Microsoft, John has worked on Visual InterDev, NT Option Pack, Microsoft Script Debugger, Visual Basic, and on the .NET Frameworks team.

Scott Short

Scott Short is a consultant with Microsoft Consulting Services. He works mostly with dot-com and telecommunications companies helping architect scalable, available, and maintainable component-based web applications. Before joining Microsoft, he was a software developer for JD Edwards and MCI. When not working with the latest beta software, authoring books, or presenting at developer conferences, Scott enjoys spending time in the Colorado Rocky Mountains skiing, backpacking, hiking, and rock climbing with his incredibly supportive wife, Suzanne.

Chris Ullman

Chris Ullman is a Computer Science graduate who came to Wrox five years ago, when 14.4 modems were the hottest Internet technology and Netscape Navigator 2.0 was a groundbreaking innovation. Since then he's applied his knowledge of HTML, server-side web technologies, Java, and Visual Basic to developing, editing, and authoring books. When not trying to reconstruct the guts of his own PC or trying to write extra chapters in a hurry, he can be found either playing keyboards in psychedelic band, The Beemen, tutoring his cats in the way of eating peacefully from their own food bowl and not the one next to theirs, or hoping against hope that this is the year his favorite soccer team, Birmingham City, can manage to end their exile from the Premier League.

NETINTRODUCING.

Table of Contents

Table of Contents

Table of Contents

Table of Contents

Table of Contents

Table of Contents

NETINTRODUCING.NETINTRODUCING.NETINTRODUCING.NETI
ODUCING.NETINTRODUCING.NETINTRODUCING.NETINTRODUCIN
ETINTRODUCING.NETINTRODUCING.NETINTRODUCING.NETINTR
CING.NETINTRODUCING.NETINTRODUCING.NETINTRODUCING.N
NTRODUCING.NETINTRODUCING.NETINTRODUCING.NETINTRODU
G.NETINTRODUCING.NETINTRODUCING.NETINTRODUCING.NETI
ODUCING.NETINTRODUCING.NETINTRODUCING.NETINTRODUCIN
ETINTRODUCING.NETINTRODUCING.NETINTRODUCING.NETINTR
CING.NETINTRODUCING.NETINTRODUCING.NETINTRODUCING.N
NTRODUCING.NETINTRODUCING.NETINTRODUCING.NETINTRODU
G.NETINTRODUCING.NETINTRODUCING.NETINTRODUCING.NETI
ODUCING.NETINTRODUCING.NETINTRODUCING.NETINTRODUCIN
ETINTRODUCING.NETINTRODUCING.NETINTRODUCING.NETINTR
CING.NETINTRODUCING.NETINTRODUCING.NETINTRODUCING.N
NTRODUCING.NETINTRODUCING.NETINTRODUCING.NETINTRODU
G.NETINTRODUCING.NETINTRODUCING.NETINTRODUCING.NETI
ODUCING.NETINTRODUCING.NETINTRODUCING.NETINTRODUCIN
ETINTRODUCING.NETINTRODUCING.NETINTRODUCING.NETINTR
CING.NETINTRODUCING.NETINTRODUCING.NETINTRODUCING.N
NTRODUCING.NETINTRODUCING.NETINTRODUCING.NETINTRODU
G.NETINTRODUCING.NETINTRODUCING.NETINTRODUCING.NETI
ODUCING.NETINTRODUCING.NETINTRODUCING.NETINTRODUCIN
ETINTRODUCING.NETINTRODUCING.NETINTRODUCING.NETINTR
CING.NETINTRODUCING.NETINTRODUCING.NETINTRODUCING.N
NTRODUCING.NETINTRODUCING.NETINTRODUCING.NETINTRODU
G.NETINTRODUCING.NETINTRODUCING.NETINTRODUCING.NETI
ODUCING.NETINTRODUCING.NETINTRODUCING.NETINTRODUCIN
ETINTRODUCING.NETINTRODUCING.NETINTRODUCING.NETINTR
CING.NETINTRODUCING.NETINTRODUCING.NETINTRODUCING.N
NTRODUCING.NETINTRODUCING.NETINTRODUCING.NETINTRODU
G.NETINTRODUCING.NETINTRODUCING.NETINTRODUCING.NETI
ODUCING.NETINTRODUCING.NETINTRODUCING.NETINTRODUCIN
ETINTRODUCING.NETINTRODUCING.NETINTRODUCING.NETINTR
CING.NETINTRODUCING.NETINTRODUCING.NETINTRODUCING.N
NTRODUCING.NETINTRODUCING.NETINTRODUCING.NETINTRODU
G.NETINTRODUCING.NETINTRODUCING.NETINTRODUCING.NETI
ODUCING.NETINTRODUCING.NETINTRODUCING.NETINTRODUCIN
ETINTRODUCING.NETINTRODUCING.NETINTRODUCING.NETINTR

Introduction

.NET – what is it? It is quite simply Microsoft's vision of "**software as a service**". The .NET vision can be split into several different areas:

- ❑ **.NET Framework**: the framework is an environment in which you can build, create, and deploy your applications and the next generation of components, termed Web Services. It includes three major building blocks, the common language runtime for the execution of applications in any language, a set of framework classes, and a new version of Microsoft's dynamic server-side web technology, ASP, in ASP.NET.

- ❑ **.NET Products**: all of Microsoft's major flagship products from Windows to Visual Studio and Office are being integrated into the vision and they will all offer services that will allow greater integration between products, relying on XML as a language to describe the data, and SOAP as a protocol for transmission of data between products.

- ❑ **.NET Services**: this is for third party developers to create corporate services on the .NET platform.

It is being marketed as the next big thing, comparable to the step forward from 16-bit to 32-bit programming. The .NET programming model intends to allow developers to focus on fewer resources and languages, via the introduction of a common language runtime, which means that objects, properties and methods are the same, no matter what language is used.

.NET also aims to bring what it terms "building block services" in the next versions of its products that will offer **identity** (a new level of security), **notification and messaging** (better, more integrated e-mail, voice mail and fax facilities), **personalization** (more powerful rules creation for notification and messages), **XML store** (universal and secure data transmission), **calendar** (more intelligent interruption and reminding the user of important events), **directory and search** (improved search engine services) and lastly **dynamic delivery**(to reduce configuration and proactively install or upgrade new services).

This book is designed to tell you exactly what you need to know, to cut through the fog and to bring you a clear picture of what .NET is, and what you can expect to be able to do using it.

Who Should Read this Book

This book is for experienced developers at the leading edge, or for businesses that have to already be developing solutions on the latest platform as soon as it comes out. The different sections of .NET are in varying stages of completion, and all are in beta programs. Therefore a high degree of technical competence and awareness of technologies such a COM, COM+, ASP, and VB is required on the part of the reader. Some experience of C, C++ or Java would be advantageous to anyone new to C#, although it's not essential. Each chapter will form a brief introduction and overview of a new topic and will not delve too deeply into any detail on any one subject.

This book is for the developers and programmers who want to know what .NET offers, and what changes it will effect for them. It's for VB, C++ and Java developers who wish to understand the next generation of programming and see what changes Microsoft has in store for its cornerstone Studio languages, Visual Basic, C++, and J++. It is for those wishing to know how this integrates with Microsoft's existing DNA architecture, and why DNA only forms part of the whole .NET vision.

What you will get in this book is an overview of the ways that each technology has changed, been updated or made obsolete. You will also get plenty of code examples that have been tested on the beta platform. This is intended to create a snapshot of the current stage of development of .NET. Not everything we describe will make it into the final products, nor will the names of the features remain the same, but we intend to demonstrate why certain features were created and how they might be likely to develop if they're still incomplete.

Minimum knowledge required would be a working understanding of VB, C++, and JScript languages, although an in-depth knowledge of any single one isn't required. You should have familiarity with COM and understand some of the general concepts in using COM to create and access components. You should also be happy with the workings of the web, databases, and components in general.

How to Get the Most from this Book

The software requirements for this book are as follows:

- ❑ Either Windows NT 4.0 (SP 4 or greater) with the Windows NT 4.0 Option Pack, or Windows 2000. You can use Windows 9x, but you may have difficulty running the web-based samples, since IIS does not run on Windows 9x.

  The Windows NT 4 Option Pack can be ordered (or downloaded free) from Microsoft's web site at: http://www.microsoft.com/ntserver/nts/downloads/recommended/NT4OptPk/default.asp.

- ❑ Microsoft SQL Server 2000 would be an advantage.

  A downloadable evaluation version of SQL Server is available at: http://www.microsoft.com/sql/productinfo/evaluate.htm.

- ❑ You will also need to download the .NET Framework from

  http://msdn.microsoft.com/downloads/default.asp?URL=/code/sample.asp?url=/msdn-files/027/000/976/msdncompositedoc.xml.

You can either download the entire 111MB `setup.exe` that installs the SDK, or you can download the SDK in pieces that are then stitched together by the supplied batch file. You can also check for the latest version available at the following location:

http://www.asp.net.

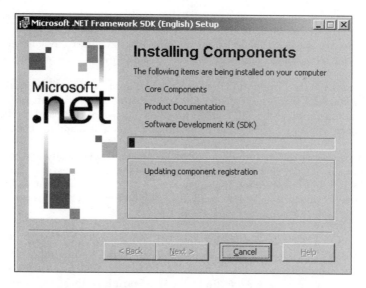

The Setup program will install the SDK core components, product documentation, and the SDK itself on your computer. It is recommended that you use a non-production test machine for installing and testing the SDK. It can be installed on Windows 2000 and Windows NT machines as well as on Windows 98 and Windows ME. You will also be required to install Internet Explorer 5.5 and Microsoft Data Access Components 2.6.

Installing the Framework SDK is relatively painless if your system has sufficient disk space and memory, but it takes a while to download and install, so be patient.

Installing Microsoft Visual Studio.NET Beta One

Microsoft has recently released the beta one of the next version of Visual Studio – Visual Studio.NET. It enables you to create Web Services with the ease and efficiency with which you can create a Visual Basic application. If you are an MSDN Universal subscriber you can download your copy of Visual Studio.NET beta one from:

http://msdn.microsoft.com/vstudio/nextgen/beta.asp.

If not, you can order your copy on CD from the same location.

What's Covered in this Book

This book consists of 13 chapters, the last of which is more like a case study, all combining to give you an introduction to .NET.

Chapter 1 introduces us to the whole area of .NET. We explain what it encompasses, and what functionality it has for us to manipulate. The chapter also goes into detail on where .NET originated, and the changes that are apparent due to its introduction. This includes a look at the user and program interfaces, and having a look at the languages we can use and how they have changed.

Chapter 2 introduces us to the Common Language Runtime, or the CLR, which enables the execution of code compiled for the .NET platform. It also looks at the Common Type System, or CTS, which provides every language running on top of the .NET platform with a base set of types and mechanisms for extending those types. We round off the chapter by looking at metadata and the concept of managed data.

Chapter 3 gives us an introduction to the new language designed specifically for .NET, called C# (C sharp). It compares the new language to a number of traditional languages, and shows us how it is different, and why it is an improvement. It also covers the datatypes found in C#, how we can manipulate the flow of code written in C#, and finishes by looking at C# classes, all giving us a good grounding in what is to be an important part of .NET.

Chapter 4 also looks at a .NET language, this time Visual Basic.NET (VB.NET). It covers the new capabilities that VB.NET has to offer over previous versions of VB, one important change being the introduction of inheritance. It shows how VB.NET fits into the .NET framework and then gives us a summary of the changes we can expect to find. We then learn how these changes will impact our current projects, before finishing with a couple of recommendations on how to get the best out of VB.NET.

Chapter 5 goes in depth into the Visual Studio.NET IDE. It looks at the features of the IDE and shows briefly how to use them. There are a few differences, which are examined in the chapter, but the main thing to note is that there is only one IDE, no matter what .NET language you may be using – giving a consistent feel to development, no matter which language you prefer.

Chapter 6 takes us into the .NET class framework. There are hundreds of classes and namespaces, of which the root namespace is the System namespace. The System namespace contains 25 second-level namespaces, and the chapter allows us to understand more about what they do and how they work by examining some of them in more depth. This chapter is key to understanding more about .NET and what it can do.

Chapter 7 looks at ASP.NET, the new version of ASP. We start with finding out exactly why we need a new version of ASP, before examining the differences between ASP and ASP.NET. The chapter then explores the features of ASP.NET, which include the new concept of code-behind, to give us a fuller picture of what we can do with the new technology.

Chapter 8 introduces us to the idea of Web Services within .NET. We take a concise look at how they work, before looking at how they are created and designed. This chapter also takes us through the process of designing our own, very simple, Web Service, to better illustrate the principles and ideas that we need to learn.

Chapter 9 looks at Windows Forms, better known as WinForms, which is the forms package that .NET uses to build Windows based applications. We look at the changes we can expect to find, and also describe some of the features already contained in this package.

Chapter 10 turns its attention to building components with .NET. Components in .NET are built upon the CLR. Components are also built to be re-used, and the way in which .NET allows re-use is through Assemblies. So, this chapter looks at assemblies, and what it must contain for us to be able re-use the code it contains. We also look at writing business objects and the concept of cross-language inheritance.

Chapter 11 concerns itself with ADO.NET, introducing the new and improved objects that are now available to us. We also look at ADO.NET's capabilities by using Visual Studio.NET to build our own small component. We can describe data very easily in ADO.NET by making use of XML, so we take a look at this as well in this chapter.

Chapter 12 gives us the information we want to know about the Enterprise Servers contained within .NET. We tell you what the common traits between all the enterprise servers are, and the availability, focus and new features of each product. This chapter mainly covers Application Center, BizTalk Server, Commerce Server, Exchange, and SQL Server, as well as looking at a few other enterprise servers in slightly less detail.

Chapter 13 takes a case study approach to building a .NET solution. We take a database, called BeautifulParts, give it the appropriate structure and data, and then create a web site, using the Web Services concept, that will allow us to place an order. The chapter then shows us how to create the files we will need to implement our site functionality, rounding off the book with a demonstration of what .NET can allow us to do.

Conventions Used

You are going to encounter different styles as you are reading through this book. This has been done to help you easily identify different types of information and to help you keep from missing any key points. These styles are:

> **Important information, key points, and additional explanations are displayed like this to make them stand out. Be sure to pay attention to these when you find them.**

General notes, background information, and brief asides look like this.

❑ Keys that you press on the keyboard, like *Ctrl* and *Delete*, are displayed in italics

❑ If you see something like, `BackupDB`, you'll know that it is a filename, object name or function name

❑ The first time you encounter an **important word**, it is displayed in bold text

❑ Words that appear on the screen, such as menu options, are in a similar font to the one used on screen, for example, the File menu

This is how code samples look the first time they are introduced:

```
Private Sub Command_Click
    MsgBox ("Don't touch me")
End Sub
```

Whereas code that you've already seen, or that doesn't relate directly to the point being made, looks like this:

```
Private Sub Command_Click
    MsgBox ("Don't touch me")
End Sub
```

Customer Support

We want to know what you think about this book: what you liked, what you didn't like, and what you think we can do better next time. You can send your comments, either by returning the reply card in the back of the book, or by e-mail (to feedback@wrox.com). Please be sure to mention the book title in your message.

Source Code

Full source code for the case study and the examples used in this book, can be downloaded from the Wrox web site at: http://www.wrox.com.

Errata

We've made every effort to make sure that there are no errors in the text or the code. However, to err is human, and as such we recognize the need to keep you informed of any mistakes as they're spotted and corrected. Errata sheets are available for all our books at www.wrox.com. If you find an error that hasn't already been reported, please let us know.

p2p.wrox.com

For author and peer support join the Visual Basic mailing lists. Our unique system provides **programmer to programmer™ support** on mailing lists, forums and newsgroups, all *in addition* to our one-to-one e-mail system. Be confident that your query is not just being examined by a support professional, but by the many Wrox authors and other industry experts present on our mailing lists. At p2p.wrox.com you'll find a list specifically aimed at SQL Server developers that will support you, not only while you read this book, but also as you start to develop your own applications.

To enroll for support just follow this four-step system:

1. Go to http://p2p.wrox.com.

2. Click on the .NET link on the left hand side of the page.

3. You will find a number of options relating to .NET – C_sharp, vb_dotnet, aspx and vs_dotnet – just click on the mailing list that is most appropriate to you in order to join.

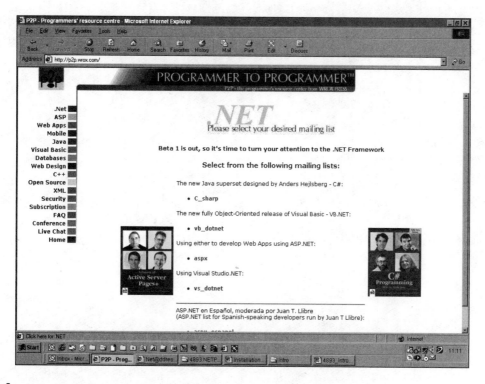

4. Fill in your e-mail address and password (of at least 4 digits) and e-mail it to us.

Why this System Offers the Best Support

You can choose to join the mailing lists or you can receive them as a weekly digest. If you don't have the time, or facility, to receive the mailing list, then you can search our online archives. Junk and spam mails are deleted, and your own e-mail address is protected by the unique Lyris system. Any queries about joining or leaving lists, or any other queries about the list, should be sent to: listsupport@p2p.wrox.com.

1

.NET Overview

In July 2000, Microsoft held the Professional Developers Conference (PDC) in Orlando, Florida, where they revealed many details to the public about their next generation platform for Windows and Internet software development – .NET.

Microsoft's .NET initiative is broad-based and very ambitious. It revolves around the .NET Framework, which encompasses the actual language and execution platform, plus extensive class libraries providing rich built-in functionality. At its core, the .NET framework embraces XML and SOAP to provide a new level of integration of software over the Internet. There is also a family of server-based products called .NET Enterprise Servers that are to be the next generation of Microsoft's BackOffice.

The .NET Framework introduces a completely new model for the programming and deployment of applications. In his PDC keynote speech, Bill Gates stated that a transition of this magnitude only comes along once every five to six years. The last comparable shifts were the switch from DOS to Windows in 1990 and the migration from 16-bit to 32-bit development (Windows 3.x to Windows 95/NT) in the mid-nineties.

Developers at PDC were excited by the prospect of a dramatically better architecture for software development within the .NET Framework, even though Microsoft made it clear that released products based on .NET are still well into the future. The first release will probably be Visual Studio.NET, the beta-one of which became available in November 2000. No firm dates are available for the full commercial release but general expectation is for fall 2001 at the earliest.

How important is this to Microsoft? Well, their executives have publicly stated that 80% of R&D resources in 2001 are being spent on .NET and the expectation is that most Microsoft products will be ported onto the .NET platform. Also C# (pronounced C-sharp), a new language specifically created for .NET, looks set to become the standard language for internal development within Microsoft.

A Broad and Deep Platform for the Future

Calling the Microsoft.NET Framework a "platform" doesn't begin to describe how broad and deep it is. It encompasses a virtual machine that abstracts away much of the Windows API from development. It includes a class library with more functionality than any other created to date, and a development environment that spans multiple languages. Further more, it exposes an architecture that makes multiple language integration simple and straightforward.

In short, .NET presents a radically new approach to software development. This is the first development platform designed from the ground up with the Internet in mind. Previously, Internet functionality has simply been bolted on to pre-Internet operating systems like Unix and Windows. This has required Internet software developers to understand a host of technologies and integration issues. .NET is designed and intended for highly distributed software, making Internet functionality and interoperability easier and more transparent to include in systems than ever before.

The vision of .NET is globally distributed systems, using XML as the universal glue to allow functions running on different computers across an organization or across the world to come together in a single application. In this vision, systems from servers to wireless palmtops, will share the same general platform, with versions of .NET available for all of them, and with each of them able to integrate transparently with the others. But this does not leave out classic applications, as we've always known them. .NET also aims to make traditional business applications easier to develop and deploy. Some of the technologies of .NET, such as WinForms, demonstrate that Microsoft has not forgotten the traditional business developer.

Your Introduction to .NET

This book will preview much of the technology and structure of .NET, concentrating on the .NET Framework. It should help the reader understand the magnitude of changes involved in the new technology; together with some of the benefits gained and costs endured. The aim is to enable intelligent decisions to be made about the short-term role of .NET, and establish a foundation from which further study can be conducted.

This first chapter will summarize many of the most important aspects of .NET. We'll start by looking at some of the serious drawbacks of current software development that prompted Microsoft to rethink their entire development structure. Then we'll progress to an overview of the overall vision and the major elements in the .NET Framework. Along the way, this chapter will refer to later chapters, which will fill in the details.

Please remember that this book discusses unreleased products. There will no doubt be many changes during the development cycle. In particular, many of the changes relating to language syntax and features are subject to revision. The bottom line is – don't bet the farm on the information presented here. Be prepared for changes as .NET moves closer to actual production.

Avoiding Confusion – the Role of the .NET Enterprise Servers

Microsoft has already released several products, which they describe as part of the .NET Enterprise Server family. More of these are coming, and most will be released by the time this book is published. Some of the marketing literature for these products emphasizes that they are part of Microsoft's .NET strategy.

However, it is important that you understand the difference between these products and the .NET Framework, which is the major focus of this book. The .NET Enterprise Servers **are not** built on the .NET Framework. Most of them are successors to previous server-based products, and they use the same COM/COM+ technologies their predecessors did.

Chapter 12 in this book summarizes these products and explains their purposes. These .NET Enterprise Servers still have a major role to play in future software development projects. When actual .NET Framework projects are developed, most will depend on the technologies in the .NET Enterprise Servers for functions like data storage and messaging.

When this book refers to .NET, it should be understood that this is generally intended to mean the technologies in the Microsoft.NET Framework.

What's Wrong With What We Have Now?

Starting in late 1995, Microsoft made a dramatic shift towards the Internet. The company was refocused on marrying their Windows platform to the Internet, and they have certainly succeeded in making Windows a serious Internet platform as well as a solid platform for all the business-oriented software developed with the Windows DNA programming model.

However, Microsoft had to make some serious compromises to quickly produce Internet-based tools and technologies. In particular, Active Server Pages (ASP) has always been viewed as a bit clumsy. After all, writing reams of interpreted script is a real step backwards from structured and object-oriented development. Designing, debugging and maintaining such unstructured code is also a headache.

Other languages such as Visual Basic have been used successfully in Internet applications on Microsoft platforms, but mostly as components that worked through Active Server Pages. Presently, Microsoft's tools lack the level of integration and ease-of-use for web development that would be ideal. A few attempts were made to place a web interface on traditional languages, such as `WebClasses` in VB, but none of these gained wide acceptance.

Microsoft has attempted to bring some order to the chaos with their concept of Windows DNA applications. DNA paints a broad picture of standard three-tier development based on COM, with Active Server Pages in the presentation layer, business objects in a middle layer, and a relational data store and engine in the bottom layer. The concept behind DNA is reasonably sound, but actually making it work has many challenges. Developing COM components requires a level of development expertise that takes a lot of time to reach, though some languages, such as Visual Basic, make it easier than others. Also, the deployment of DNA applications can be nightmarish, with many problems that can arise from the versioning and installation of components, and the components that they rely on.

Microsoft realized that, while it was possible to write good Internet applications with Windows-based technologies, it was highly desirable to find ways to develop applications faster and make it far easier to deploy them. Other platforms (such as Unix) and other development environments (such as ColdFusion) were continuing to raise the bar for developing Internet applications, making it essential that Microsoft address the limitations of the DNA programming model.

The Origins of .NET

In the beginning 1998, a team of developers at Microsoft had just finished work on a new version of Internet Information Server (version 4.0), including several new features in Active Server Pages. While developers were pleased to see new capabilities for Internet development on Windows NT, the development team at Microsoft had many ideas for its improvement. That team began to work on a new architecture implementing those ideas. This project eventually came to be known as Next Generation Windows Services (NGWS).

After Visual Studio 6 was released in late 1998, work on the next version of Visual Studio (then called Visual Studio 7) was folded into NGWS. The COM+/MTS team brought in their work on a universal runtime for all the languages in Visual Studio, which they intended to make available for third party languages as well.

The subsequent development was kept very much under wraps at Microsoft. Only key Microsoft partners realized the true importance of NGWS until it was re-christened as .NET and introduced to the public at the PDC. At that point, development had been underway for over two years, and most attendees were pleasantly surprised to see the enormous strides Microsoft had made.

The concepts in .NET draw inspiration from many sources. Previous architectures, from p-code in UCSD Pascal up through the Java Virtual Machine, have similar elements. Microsoft has taken many of the best ideas in the industry, combined with some ideas of their own, and brought them all into one coherent package.

The .NET Framework – an Overview

First and foremost, .NET is a framework that covers all the layers of software development from the operating system up. It provides the richest level of integration among presentation technologies, component technologies, and data technologies ever seen on a Microsoft platform. Secondly, the entire architecture has been created to make it as easy to develop Internet applications as it is to develop for the desktop environment.

.NET actually "wraps" the operating system, insulating software developed with .NET from most operating system specifics such as file handling and memory allocation. This prepares for a possible future in which the software developed for .NET is portable to a wide variety of hardware and operating system foundations. (Beta one of Visual Studio.NET supports all versions of Windows 2000 plus Windows NT4, Windows 9x, and Windows Millennium Edition.)

A Common Substrate for all Development

The major components of the .NET framework are shown in the following diagram:

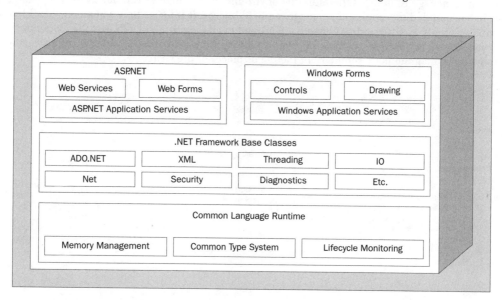

The framework starts all the way down at the memory management and component loading level, and goes all the way up to multiple ways of rendering user and program interfaces. In between, there are layers that provide just about any system-level capability that a developer would need.

At the base is the Common Language Runtime, often abbreviated to CLR. This is the heart of the .NET framework, the engine that drives key functionality. It includes, for example, a common system of data types. These common types, plus a standard interface convention, make cross-language inheritance possible. In addition to allocation and management of memory, the CLR also does reference counting for objects, and handles garbage collection.

The middle layer includes the next generation of standard system services such as ADO.NET and XML. These services are brought under the control of the framework, making them universally available and standardizing their usage across languages.

The top layer includes user and program interfaces. **Windows Forms** (often informally referred to as WinForms) are a new way to create standard Win32 desktop applications, based on the Windows Foundation Classes (WFC) produced for J++. **Web Forms** provide a powerful, forms-based UI for the web. **Web Services**, which are perhaps the most revolutionary, provide a mechanism for programs to communicate over the Internet using SOAP. Web Services provide an analog of COM and DCOM for object brokering and interfacing, but based on Internet technologies so that allowance is made for integration even with non-Microsoft platforms. Web Forms and Web Services, comprise the Internet interface portion of .NET, and are implemented through a section of the .NET Framework referred to as **ASP.NET**.

All of these are available to any language that is based on the .NET platform. For completeness, there is also a console interface that allows creation of character-based applications (not shown in the diagram).

The Common Language Runtime

Let's start with a definition. A runtime is an environment in which programs are executed. The Common Language Runtime is therefore the environment in which we run our .NET applications that have been compiled to a common language, namely **Microsoft Intermediate Language** (MSIL), often referred to simply as **IL**. Runtimes have been around even longer than DOS, but the Common Language Runtime (CLR) is as advanced over traditional runtimes as a light bulb is over a candle. Here's a quick diagrammatic summary of the major pieces of the CLR:

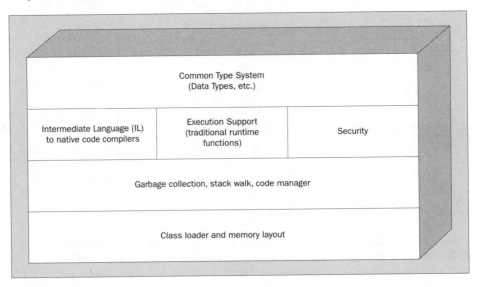

That small part in the middle, called Execution Support, contains most of the capabilities normally associated with a language runtime (such as the VBRUNxxx.DLL runtime used with Visual Basic). The rest is new, at least for Microsoft platforms.

Chapter 2 of this book will go into the Common Language Runtime in depth. However, since understanding the CLR is key to understanding the rest of .NET, here is a short introduction.

Key Design Goals

The design of the CLR is based on the following goals:

- ❏ Simpler, faster development
- ❏ Automatic handling of "plumbing" such as memory management and process communication
- ❏ Good tool support
- ❏ Scalability

Let's look at each of these in detail.

Simpler, Faster Development

A broad, consistent framework allows developers to write less, and reuse more. Less code is possible because the system provides a rich set of underlying functionality. Programs in .NET access this functionality in a standard, consistent way, requiring less "hardwiring" and customization logic to interface with these functions than is typically needed today.

Getting Rid of Plumbing

A lot of programming infrastructure is either handled automatically by the CLR or rendered completely unnecessary. That is, some of it is hidden, and some of it is just not there any more.

Memory management is an example of hidden infrastructure. Visual Basic developers stopped worrying too much about memory long ago. Today, C++ developers still have to, but not with the CLR, which has memory management functions built-in (though C++ developers have the option to do it themselves, and such *unmanaged* code is in fact the default for C++). If a C++ developer chooses to take full advantage of the CLR, it becomes unnecessary to use CoCreateInstance, for example, to instantiate a class, or malloc to set aside space for an array. A simple declaration statement will do it, and the CLR allocates the memory as necessary. Then it goes on to handle reference counting on instantiations and automatically do garbage collection when the reference count gets to zero.

Another example is proxies and stubs, which map interfaces on a remote object to the local system. The proxy handles communication with the remote object, and stands in its place locally, so that local processes can treat the remote object as if it were local, and the details of remote management are all handled behind the scenes. Contrast this with the work that is currently necessary to make DCOM work.

A lot of the missing plumbing is replaced by metadata – standardized information about components, interfaces, and processes that can be accessed in a consistent way. No more cycling through IUnknown to find out how to work with an interface – the CLR provides more flexible and much easier to use equivalents. A later section of this chapter covers metadata in more detail.

Tool Support

Though much of what the CLR does is similar to operating system functionality, it is designed first and foremost to support development languages. It furnishes a rich set of object models that are useful to tools like designers, wizards, debuggers, and profilers. And since the object models are at the runtime level, such tools can be designed to work across all languages that use the CLR. It is anticipated that third parties will produce a host of such tools.

It's also important to note that Microsoft is not restricting use of the CLR to Microsoft languages. Third party language vendors are encouraged to re-architect their languages to use the CLR, which offers a host of benefits. Besides taking advantage of all the CLR functionality (and thereby not having to write it or support it), using the CLR enables never before seen levels of cross-language integration. We'll discuss more of that later in the section on Multiple Language Support.

This capability of the CLR to work transparently with multiple languages has some huge benefits for developers. Debuggers offer the best example. The CLR makes it possible to write a source-level debugger that treats all languages equally, jumping from one language to another as necessary.

Simpler, Safer Deployment

It's hard for an experienced Windows component developer to see how anything can work without registration, GUIDs, and the like, but the CLR does. Applications produced in the .NET framework can be designed to install with a simple XCOPY. That's right – just copy the files onto the disk and run the application. We haven't seen this since the days of DOS (and some of us really miss it). This can work because compilers in the .NET framework embed identifiers (in the form of metadata, discussed below) into compiled modules, and the CLR manages those identifiers automatically. The identifiers provide all the information needed to load and run modules, and to locate related modules.

As a great by-product, the CLR can manage multiple versions of the same component (even a shared component), and have them run side-by-side. The identifiers tell the CLR which version is needed for a particular compiled module because such information is captured at compile time. The runtime policy can be set in a module to use the exact version of a component that was available at compile time, to use the latest compatible version, or to specify an exact version. The bottom line is that .NET is intended to eradicate "DLL Hell" once and for all.

This has implications that might not be apparent at first; for example, if a program needs to run directly from a CD (without first running an installation program). This was not feasible in Visual Basic after version 3, but the capability will reappear with Visual Basic.NET.

Another significant deployment benefit in .NET is that applications only need to install their own core logic. An application produced in .NET will not need to install a runtime, for example, or modules for ADO or XML. Such base functionality will be part of the .NET Framework, which will be installed separately and only once for each system. Those four-diskette installs for a VB "Hello, world" program will be a thing of the past!

Making all of this work automatically requires a sophisticated security infrastructure. The .NET Framework captures the origin of a piece of code, and the publisher of a module can be identified with a public encryption key. This allows a system to be set up so that it doesn't run untrusted software, which provides mechanisms to block viruses like the infamous ILOVEYOU. A method of a component, no matter how deep it is in the object model, can demand proof of authorization to run all the way back along the call chain that got to it.

Scalability

Since most of the system-level execution functions are concentrated in the CLR, they can be optimized and architected to allow a wide range of scalability for applications produced in the .NET Framework. As with most of the other advantages of the CLR, this one comes to all applications with little or no effort.

Memory and process management is one area where scalability can be built in. The memory management in the CLR is self-configuring and tunes itself automatically. Garbage Collection (reclaiming memory that is no longer being actively used) is highly optimized, and the CLR supports many of the component management capabilities of MTS/COM+ (such as object pooling). The result is that components can run faster, and thus support more users.

This has some interesting side effects. For example, the performance and scalability differences among languages become smaller. All languages compile to a standard byte code (IL – the Microsoft Intermediate Language), and there is discussion below on how the CLR executes IL. With all languages compiling down to similar byte code, it becomes unnecessary in most cases to look to other languages when performance is an issue. The difference in performance among .NET languages is minor – Visual Basic, for example, gives about the same performance as any of the other .NET languages.

There are early-stage plans for the CLR to be available on a wide range of devices. Eventually the vision is for .NET to be running at all levels, from smart palm-tops all the way up to web farms. That means the same development tools should work across the entire range – news that will be appreciated by those who have tried to use Windows CE development kits. Of course, this is an ambitious plan and may be subject to changes and retractions.

Metadata

Metadata is defined as "data about data", and in this case you can think of it as a deeper level of data about system level attributes. Metadata is the key to the simpler programming model that the CLR supports.

The metadata is generated by a compiler and stored automatically in an EXE or DLL. It's in binary, but the framework offers an API to export metadata to and from an XML schema or a COM type library. An XML schema export might be useful, for example, in extracting version and compile information for a repository on components. Here are some of the items in the metadata defined for the .NET framework:

- ❑ Description of a deployment unit (called an assembly)
    - ❑ Name, version, culture (which could determine, for example, the default user language)
    - ❑ A public key for verification
    - ❑ Types exported by the assembly
    - ❑ Dependencies – other assemblies which this assembly depends upon
    - ❑ Security permissions needed to run
- ❑ Base classes and interfaces used by the assembly
- ❑ Custom attributes
    - ❑ User defined (inserted by the developer)
    - ❑ Compiler defined (inserted by the compiler to indicate something special about the language)

Some of these, such as the custom attributes, are optional – the required ones are all managed automatically by the tools.

The metadata is one of the ways the CLR can support a wide variety of tools. Here are some of the possible consumers of .NET metadata:

- ❑ Designers
- ❑ Debuggers
- ❑ Profilers
- ❑ Proxy Generators
- ❑ Other compilers (to find out how to use a component in their language)
- ❑ Type / Object browsers
- ❑ Schema generators

Compilers are some of the most extensive users of metadata. For example, a compiler can examine a module produced by a different compiler and use the metadata for cross-language type import. It can also produce metadata about its own compiled modules, including such elements as flags that a module has compiled for debugging, or a language-specific marker.

Even information that might appear in a tool tip can be embedded in metadata. This extendable data store about a compiled module greatly facilitates the simpler deployment available under the .NET Framework. An API, called the Reflection API, is available for scanning and manipulation of metadata elements.

Multiple Language Integration and Support

The most ambitious aspect of the CLR is that it is designed to support multiple languages and allow unprecedented levels of integration among those languages. By enforcing a common type system, and by having complete control over interface calls, the CLR allows languages to work together more transparently than ever before.

Previously, one language could instantiate and use components written in another language by using COM. Sometimes calling conventions were difficult to manage, especially when Visual Basic was involved, but it could generally be made to work. However, subclassing a component written in a different language required a sophisticated wrapper, and only advanced developers did such work.

It is straightforward in the .NET Framework to use one language to subclass a class implemented in another language. A class written in Visual Basic can inherit from a base class written in C++, or in COBOL for that matter (at least one major vendor is at work on a COBOL implementation for .NET). The VB program doesn't even need to know the language used for the base class, and we're talking full implementation inheritance with no problems requiring recompilation when the base class changes.

How can this work? The information furnished by metadata makes it possible. There is no Interface Definition Language (IDL) in .NET because none is needed. A class interface looks the same, regardless of the language that generated it. The CLR uses metadata to manage all the interfaces and calling conventions between languages.

This has major implications; mixed language programming teams become far more feasible than before. And it becomes less necessary to force developers who are perfectly comfortable in one language to adopt another just to fit into a development effort. Cross-language inheritance promises to open up architectural options than never existed before.

One Microsoft person summed this up by saying that, as far as they are concerned, with .NET, the language used becomes a "lifestyle choice". While there will always be benefits to programming teams using a common language, .NET raises the practicality of mixed-language projects.

A Common Type System

A key piece of functionality that enables Multiple Language Support is a Common Type System, in which all commonly used data types, even base types such as Longs and Booleans, are actually implemented as objects. Coercion among types can now be done at a lower level for more consistency between languages. And, since all languages are using the same library of types, calling one language from another doesn't require type conversion or weird calling conventions.

This results in the need for some readjustment, particularly for Visual Basic developers. For example, what we called an `Integer` in VB6 and earlier, is now known as a `Short` in Visual Basic.NET. The adjustment is well worth the effort in order to bring VB in line with everything else – and, as a by-product, other languages get the same support for strings that VB has always had. (There are many details on adjustments for Visual Basic developers in Chapter 4).

Namespaces

One of the most important concepts in .NET is namespaces. They help organize object libraries and hierarchies, simplify object references, prevent ambiguity when referring to objects, and control the scope of object identifiers.

Namespaces are discussed in more detail in Chapter 6. For now, it is useful to know that class libraries are normally referenced in each language before they are used. The reference allows the types to be used in the code with abbreviations instead of detailed library references. In VB, this is done with an `Imports` statement, and that this can be thought of as similar in concept to checking a box in the `References` dialog in Visual Basic 6. For example, a typical VB form module in .NET might have the following lines at the beginning:

```
Imports System.WinForms
Imports MyDebug = System.Diagnostics.Debug
```

The first line simply makes all of the standard form properties and methods available to the code in the form module. This second line illustrates use of an alias. A branch of the object hierarchy can thus receive its own identifier, which is only valid in that code module. Instead of referring to the `System.Diagnostics.Debug` class object, the code in this module would refer to the `MyDebug` object.

Deployment and Execution

With all the intelligence in the .NET framework, there is a lot more going on at execution time with the CLR than we are accustomed to. Programs or components can't just load and go – there are several things that must happen for the whole structure to work.

Start with an Assembly, Build to an Application

The unit of deployment, as previously mentioned, is an assembly. It can consist of one or more files and is self-describing. It contains a "manifest" which holds the metadata describing everything exported from the assembly, and what's needed to deploy and run the assembly.

An assembly has its own version. Assemblies are combined to become applications. An application has one or more assemblies, and also may contain application specific files or data. Applications may have their own private versions of assemblies, and may be configured to prefer their private version to any shared versions.

Execution

Source code modules for an assembly are compiled (at development time) into the CLR's Intermediate Language (IL). Then IL is compiled into native code before execution. That compilation can take place in several ways, and at various times. Normally, however, compilation into native code is done only once and the results are cached for future use.

The CLR contains a couple of just-in-time (JIT) compilers, which convert IL to native code (binary code targeted at a specific machine processor). One is called "Econo-JIT" and it has very fast compilation, but produces un-optimized code. It is useful when the code, such as script in a batch file, will likely be thrown away and regenerated. The other is the standard JIT compiler, which operates a bit more slowly but performs a high level of optimization. It is used for most systems.

The JIT compilers produce code that is targeted at the specific processor on the machine. This is one of the reasons applications in .NET would normally be distributed in compiled IL, allowing processor-specific optimizations in native code to be done by the .NET compilers on a particular machine. An installation of a package can be set to pre-compile the IL code into native code during the installation if required.

Scripting also fits into this model, actually being compiled before it is used. In current systems interpreted script (in Active Server Pages or the Windows Scripting Host, for example) is never compiled. But in .NET, such script is sent through a language compiler the first time it is accessed, and transformed into IL. Then the IL is immediately transformed into native code, and cached for future use. Scripts are created in .NET the way they are now, with any editor you like, and require no explicit compilation step. The compilation is handled in the background, and is managed automatically so that a change to the script results in appropriate recompilation. VBScript developers are now encouraged to migrate to Visual Basic for web development, which is now the default language for producing ASP.NET pages.

With software compiled into a processor-independent intermediate language, .NET makes it possible to achieve future platform independence. It is architecturally possible for a CLR to be produced for platforms based on other processors or other operating systems, which would enable applications produced on Windows 2000 to run on them. Microsoft has not emphasized this in their announcements, but the capabilities of the CLR parallel in some respects those of the Java virtual machine, which is designed for platform independence.

The Next Layer – .NET Framework Base Classes

The next layer down in the framework provides the services and object models for data, input/output, security, and so forth. The next generation of ADO, called ADO.NET, resides here (though there will also be an updated version of regular ADO in .NET to provide compatibility for older code). Also included is the core functionality that lets you work with XML, including the parsers and XSL transformer.

Much of the functionality that a programmer might think of as being part of a language has been moved to the framework classes. For example, the Visual Basic keyword `Sqr` for extracting a square root is no longer available in .NET. It has been replaced by the `System.Math.Sqrt` method in the framework classes.

It's important to emphasize that all languages based on the .NET framework have these framework classes available. That means that COBOL, for example, can use the same function mentioned above for getting a square root. This makes such base functionality widely available and highly consistent across languages. All calls to `Sqrt` look essentially the same (allowing for syntactical differences among languages) and access the same underlying code.

> *As a side note, a programming shop can create their own classes for core functionality, such as globally available, pre-compiled functions. This custom functionality can then be referenced in code in the same way as built-in .NET functionality.*

Much of the functionality in the base framework classes resides in a vast namespace called System. The System.Math.Sqrt method was mentioned above. Here are just a few other examples of the subsections of the System namespace, which actually contains dozens of such subcategories:

Namespace	What it contains	Example Classes
System.Data	Classes and types related to basic database management	DataSet, DataTable, DataColumn, SQLConnection, ADOConnection
System.Diagnostics	Classes to debug an application and to trace the execution of code	Debug, Trace
System.IO	Types which allow reading and writing to files and other data streams	File, FileStream, Path, StreamReader, StreamWriter
System.Math	Members to calculate common mathematical quantities, such as trigonometric and logarithmic functions	Sqrt (square root), Cos (cosine), Log (logarithm), Min (minimum)
System.Reflection	Capability to inspect metadata	Assembly, Module
System.Security	Types which enable security capabilities	Cryptography, Permissions, Policy

The list above merely begins to hint at the capabilities in the System namespace. Chapter 6 will examine the System namespace and other framework classes in more detail, and you can find a full list of .NET namespaces in Appendix A.

User and Program Interfaces

At the top layer, .NET provides three ways to render and manage user interfaces (Windows Forms, Web Forms, and Console Applications), and one way to handle interfaces with remote components (Web Services).

User Interfaces

Windows Forms

Windows Forms (which, as previously mentioned, are often just called WinForms) are a more advanced and integrated way to create standard Win32 desktop applications. WinForms are descended from the Windows Foundation Classes (WFC) originally created for J++, so this technology has been under development for a while.

All languages that work on the .NET Framework, including new versions of Visual Studio languages, will use the WinForms engine instead of whatever they are using now (MFC or direct Win32API calls in the case of C++, the VB Forms Engine in the case of Visual Basic). This provides a rich, unified set of controls and drawing functions for all languages, as well as a standard API for underlying Windows services for graphics and drawing. It effectively replaces the Windows graphical API, wrapping it in such a way that the developer normally has no need to go directly to the Windows API for any graphical or screen functions.

WinForms are actually part of the framework classes in the System.Winforms namespace, which makes them available to all languages that are based on the .NET framework. Since WinForms duplicate the functionality of the VB forms engine, they give every single .NET language the capability of doing forms just like Visual Basic. The drag-and-drop designer for WinForms (which is in Visual Studio.NET) can be used to create forms visually for use with any .NET language.

Chapter 9 will look at WinForms in more detail and note significant changes in WinForms versus older Visual Basic forms.

Changing the Tradeoffs for Client Applications Versus Browser-based Applications

In the Windows DNA world, many internal corporate applications are made browser-based simply because of the cost of installing and maintaining a client application on hundreds or thousands of workstations. WinForms and the .NET framework have the potential to change the economics of these decisions. A WinForms-based application will be much easier to install and update than an equivalent Visual Basic client application today. With a simple XCOPY deployment and no registration issues, installation and updating become much easier.

This means that applications that need a rich user interface for a large number of users are more practical under .NET than under Windows DNA. It may not be necessary to resort to browser-based applications just to save installation and deployment costs, thus extending the life of desktop-based applications.

Web Forms

A part of ASP.NET, Web Forms are a forms engine. They provide a web browser-based user interface. A user interface can also be rendered with the updated version of Active Server Pages, but Web Forms represents the next generation of web interface development, including drag-and-drop development.

Divorcing layout from logic, Web Forms consist of two parts – a template, which contains HTML-based layout information for all user interface elements, and a component, which contains all logic to be hooked to the UI. It's as if a standard Visual Basic form were split into two parts: one containing information on controls and their properties and layout, and the other containing the code. Just as in Visual Basic, the code operated "behind" the controls, with events in the controls activating event routines in the code.

To make this new UI concept work, Web Forms have lots of built-in intelligence. Controls on Web Forms run on the server but make their presence known on the client. This takes lots of coordination and behind-the-scenes activity. However, the end result is web interfaces that can look and behave very much like Win32 interfaces today, and the ability to produce such interfaces with a drag-and-drop design tool. These web interfaces can also have the intelligence to deal with different browsers, optimizing their output for each particular browser. Supported browsers cover a broad range. At the top end are advanced modern versions like Internet Explorer 5.5, which support DHTML. At the other end are simpler, less capable browsers on hardware such as wireless palmtop devices. Web Forms will render themselves appropriately on all of these.

As with WinForms, Web Forms will be available to all languages. The component handling logic for a form can be coded in any language that supports .NET. This brings complete and flexible web interface capability to a wide variety of languages.

Server controls

Visual Basic developers are familiar with the idea of controls. They are the reusable user interface elements used to construct a form. The equivalent in a Web Form is called server-side controls.

Server-side controls essentially create a proxy on the server for a user interface element that is on a Web Form or Active Server Page. The server-side control communicates with local logic as necessary, and then intelligently renders its own UI as HTML as necessary in any pages that are sent out containing the control. It also handles its own HTML responses, and incorporates the returned data.

Server-side controls need significant intelligence to render HTML for different levels of browsers, and to coordinate events with the client on which the page is running. A wide variety of controls are expected to ship with Visual Studio.NET, bringing web-based interfaces much closer to Win32 interfaces. Third parties are expected to add even more options for server-side controls.

One of the most important and amazing features of server-side controls is that they manage their own state. In ASP.NET, it is no longer necessary to write a lot of tedious code to reload state information into HTML controls every time a page is refreshed. Web Forms handle state by sending a tokenised (compressed) version of the state information to the client browser each time a page is sent. The page then posts that state information back to the server when changing the page. The server controls grab this information, use or process it as necessary, and then send it out again with the next rendering of the page.

Console Applications

Though Microsoft doesn't emphasize the ability to write character-based applications, the .NET Framework does include an interface for such console apps. Batch processes, for example, can now have components integrated into them that are written to a console interface. *(The part of the .NET Framework which implements the console interface is not shown in the .NET Framework diagram earlier in the chapter.)*

As with WinForms and Web Forms, this console interface is available for applications written in any .NET language. Writing character based applications in previous versions of Visual Basic, for example, has always been a struggle because it was completely oriented around a GUI interface. Visual Basic.NET can be used for true console applications.

Program Interfaces

Web Services

Application development is moving into the next stage of decentralization. The oldest idea of an application is a piece of software that accesses basic operating system services, such as the file system and graphics system. Then we moved to applications, which used lots of base functionality from other, system-level applications, such as a database – this type of application added value by applying generic functionality to specific problems. The developer's job was to focus on adding business value, not on building the foundation.

Web Services represents the next step in this direction. In Web Services, software functionality becomes exposed as a service that doesn't care what the consumer of the service is (unless there are security considerations). Web Services allow developers to build applications by combining local and remote resources for an overall integrated and distributed solution.

In .NET, Web Services are implemented as part of ASP.NET, (diagrammed at the top level of the .NET Framework), which handles all web interfaces. It allows programs to talk to each other directly over the web, using SOAP. This capability requires very little work on the part of the developer. All that is needed is to indicate that a member should be included in the Web Services interface, and the .NET Framework takes care of the rest. This has the capacity to dramatically change the architecture of web applications, allowing services running all over the web to be integrated into one application.

It is hard to over-emphasize the potential importance of Web Services. Consider, for example, the potential for Web Services to replace packaged software. A commercial software company could produce a Web Service that, for instance, calculates sales tax for every jurisdiction in the nation. A subscription to that web service could be sold to any company needing to calculate sales tax. The customer company then has no need to deploy the sales tax calculator because is it just called on the web. The company producing the sales tax calculator can dynamically update it to include new rates and rules for various jurisdictions, and their customers using the Web Service don't have to do anything to get these updates.

There are endless other possibilities. Stock tickers, weather information, current financial rates, shipping status, and a host of other types of information could be exposed as a Web Service, ready for integration into any application that needs it.

Chapter 8 contains a detailed discussion of Web Services.

XML as the .NET "Meta-language"

Much of the underlying integration of .NET is accomplished with XML. For example, Web Services depend completely on XML for interfacing with remote objects. Looking at metadata usually means looking at an XML version of it.

ADO.NET, the successor to ADO for better remote manipulation of data, is heavily dependent on XML for remote representation of data. Essentially, when ADO.NET creates what it calls a dataset (a more complex successor to a recordset), the data is converted to XML for manipulation by ADO.NET. Then the changes to that XML are posted back to the data store by ADO.NET when remote manipulation is finished.

With XML as an "entry point" into so many areas of .NET, future integration opportunities are multiplied. Using XML to expose interfaces to .NET functions allows developers to tie components and functions together in new, unexpected ways. XML can be the glue that ties pieces together in ways that were never anticipated, both to Microsoft and non-Microsoft platforms.

How COM/COM+ Fits In

The internals of the .NET Framework do not depend on COM to tie themselves together. Components that are written purely for .NET use the interface conventions of .NET, which are executed and enforced by the CLR.

This has been misinterpreted in some quarters as the immediate death of COM and COM+. It reminds me of a great historical quote. When Mark Twain's obituary was accidentally published, he talked to journalists on his porch, and said "The rumors of my death are greatly exaggerated." So it is with COM/COM+.

The .NET Framework makes it transparent to deal with a COM/COM+ component as if it were a .NET component. Interface translation is automatic. And any .NET Framework component can also be treated as a COM component by traditional COM-based software.

Microsoft knew that the .NET Framework must integrate with existing software. Most organizations have a tremendous investment in COM/COM+. There is no need whatsoever to replace that investment. In fact, a lot of the existing software that needs to be used in conjunction with .NET is, in fact, in Microsoft packages such as SQL Server and Exchange. As discussed at the beginning of the chapter, the .NET Enterprise Servers are COM-based, and will be an important part of .NET development projects for quite a while to come.

Will COM and COM+ eventually die off as .NET comes to dominate? Perhaps. But it's not an issue any of us need be concerned with at present.

Additional Benefits

The major benefits of .NET discussed thus far can be summarized as:

- ❑ Faster development (less to do, the system handles more)
- ❑ Lots of built-in functionality through a rich object model
- ❑ A variety of ways to interface and integrate with the outside world
- ❑ More reuse
- ❑ Easy to integrate different languages into one system
- ❑ Easier deployment
- ❑ Scalability
- ❑ Easy to build sophisticated development tools
- ❑ Interfaces well to existing software

There are a couple of additional benefits that are worth mentioning.

Fewer Bugs – Whole Classes of Bugs Will Disappear

The architecture and capabilities of the CLR wipe out whole classes of bugs. Memory leaks, failure to clean up at the end of execution, and other memory management related problems become non-existent (assuming the developers of the CLR take care of their part). Instancing of classes is handled automatically (no more CoCreateInstance), and they are managed throughout their lifecycle.

Potentially Better Performance

The built-in capabilities of the CLR are to be used almost universally. Microsoft knows that, for .NET to succeed, these capabilities must be reliable and efficient, and they have invested the efforts of their very best architects and developers to make that happen.

This heavy investment in system level code should have the result of speeding up performance for all but the most optimized of applications. Critical and frequently used functions, no matter how ordinary, will usually be optimized to the hilt in the CLR.

Some Potential Downsides

Nothing comes completely for free. Here are a couple of ways in which there is a price to be paid to get the advantages of .NET

Language Incompatibilities

Making languages work in this new framework usually means adjustment to the language syntax. This introduces compatibility problems in moving existing code into .NET. Visual Basic is a particular problem, as we shall see in Chapter 4.

Transparency of "Source Code"

The bytecodes in the Intermediate Language are much higher level than the processor instructions that programs are compiled into today. While we can disassemble a program in current environments, the assembler-based result is of limited use. .NET programs disassembled from IL, on the other hand, will more closely resemble actual source code. They will also contain the information needed to understand data structures. Such disassembled programs make algorithms and code processes more transparent than with current environments, making it more difficult to protect intellectual property. Microsoft may eventually build in some kind of encryption to remedy this problem, or perhaps third parties can introduce tools that obfuscate the code, but there are no known plans at this point.

The First Step – Visual Studio.NET

The first technology to be released in the .NET framework will be the next generation of Visual Studio, which has been tagged Visual Studio.NET. It will include Visual Basic, Visual C++, and C# (the new language from Microsoft discussed below). Visual FoxPro is included in beta one of Visual Studio.NET, but the final status of this as a .NET language is not known at the time of writing.

Microsoft has been hinting for several months about what's going to be new in Visual Studio. Here are some of the confirmed changes and new features, as of beta one – keeping in mind that things can change before release.

Common IDE for All Languages

Microsoft has gradually been melding the Integrated Development Environment (IDE) for all their languages into one code base. In Visual Studio 6, Visual Basic was the last major holdout. That process is now complete, and the exact same IDE is to be used for all languages in the Visual Studio.NET suite.

However, a potentially bigger change is that Microsoft has completely opened up the IDE for other languages. Any third party language vendor can license the technology to have the language work within the .NET framework and place their language in the Visual Studio IDE. At least twenty languages are under consideration for such integration, including everything from Eiffel to COBOL.

Fully supporting a third party language in the .NET Framework, and thus Visual Studio, will require a lot of work. The vendor must create a compiler for the language that produces Intermediate Language bytecode instead of native machine code. The language's data types must be rationalized with the ones supported by the CLR. But the language vendor gets a lot in exchange, including an advanced development environment, plus debugging tools and complete cross-language integration.

Chapter 5 will look at the new Visual Studio IDE, and cover other new features of Visual Studio in more depth and detail.

The Common Language Specification

Languages that fit into .NET must satisfy the Common Language Specification (CLS), which sets the constraints the languages must meet. If a language adheres to this spec, it gets an appropriate level of language interoperability.

All .NET Languages Are Not Created Equal

There are actually three categories of compliance to the CLS that .NET languages can subscribe to. Briefly they are:

- ❑ **Compliant producer** – The components in the language can be used by any other language.

- ❑ **Consumer** – The language can reuse classes produced in any other language. This basically means the ability to instantiate classes in the way that, for example, scripting languages can instantiate COM objects today.

- ❑ **Extender** – Languages in this category can do more than just instantiate classes – they can also extend those classes using the inheritance features of .NET.

All the confirmed languages in the Visual Studio suite (VB, VC++, C#) are expected to satisfy all three categories of the CLS. Third party languages can select the levels of compliance that make sense for them.

Management of Multiple Language Projects

Since any number of languages can now be used in a project, the Visual Studio IDE will now look at projects in terms of all the modules being used, no matter what language they are in. The project explorer (actually called the Solution Explorer) is the same no matter what combination of languages is used.

Absence of Visual Interdev and J++

Visual Studio.NET does not have a separate piece identified as Visual Interdev. In effect, the functions of Visual Interdev have migrated into the IDE as a whole. There is an HTML editor, for example, which works across the whole IDE, and the new Solution Explorer bears a strong resemblance to the Resource Window in Interdev.

Also, Web Forms have basically taken the place of the drag-and-drop visual designer in Interdev, and have the advantage of working with any language.

J++ is gone for a different reason. Microsoft's continuing legal troubles with Sun have frozen Java-related efforts at Microsoft. The current J++ will be supported, but it cannot be enhanced and placed in the new Visual Studio at this point. In a sense, C# takes its place (more on that below), but it's possible that a real Java implementation from a third party will be available at or near Visual Studio.NET's release.

Chapter 5 covers more details on the changes and new features in Visual Studio.NET. It analyses the new IDE, and includes example screens to illustrate the changes.

Summary of Language Changes

Each of the major languages in Visual Studio is also in for changes. Here is a quick overview.

Visual Basic

VB gets the most extensive changes of any existing language in the Visual Studio suite. These changes pull VB in line with other languages in terms of data types, calling conventions, error handling and, most importantly, object orientation.

We don't yet know for certain what the new Visual Basic will be called, but the current favorite is Visual Basic.NET. This label will be used in the discussion below.

Most new features in VB, especially the object-oriented ones such as inheritance, are courtesy of the CLR. Visual Basic.NET basically piggybacks on the stuff that was going to be implemented anyway for C++, C# and third party .NET languages.

Chapter 4 covers the changes to Visual Basic, especially the syntax changes, in detail. It also includes recommendations for coding practices that will make eventual migration to .NET easier. Here are a couple of highlights:

Lots of Possible Incompatibilities

These are the biggest changes ever in VB – bigger even than the jump from VB3 to VB4. This introduces significant potential for incompatibilities.

Here's one example. In the current implementation of .NET, all arrays are zero-based. There is no provision for explicit array bounds, so any code that uses them could require manual changes. There are quite a few other examples covered in Chapter 4.

Microsoft intends to supply a conversion tool, which will assist in porting VB6 projects to .NET, but it will not do everything required. There will be some areas where the conversion tool merely places a note that indicates something needs to be done. And there are likely to be areas where it fails to realize a change is needed at all.

Object Features

Many of us have been clamoring for Visual Basic to support full object-oriented development since classes were introduced in version 4. With Visual Studio.NET our wish comes true. VB now includes full inheritance, parameterized constructors, and control over property and method overriding.

C++

The most significant changes in C++ revolve around the concept of "managed code". A C++ developer has the option of marking a section of the code to be managed by the CLR. The language then provides:

❑   Metadata describing the modules into which the code is compiled

❑   Location of object references (no CoCreateInstance needed – just use New to declare an object)

❑   Exception handling tables

Managed code then allows the runtime to handle the following:

❑   Exception handling

❑   Security

❑   Lifetime management

❑   Debugging

❑   Profiling

❑   Memory management, including garbage collection

C++ developers have the option do everything the old way ("unmanaged code"), and this is, in fact, the default allowing extensive backward compatibility.

This book does not include a specific chapter on C++, but the concept of managed code is discussed in more detail in Chapter 2 on the Common Language Runtime.

The New C# Language

Currently, developers in the Microsoft world have two major choices – use Visual Basic to get fast development or use C++ to get more control.

C++ has traditionally been a tough choice to make for anything except system-level development and large-scale commercial products such as word processors. Even developers expert at C++ had to learn a ton of Microsoft macros and arbitrary constants in order to produce results. Microsoft attempted to shorten the development time required for VC++ user interfaces and COM objects by offering MFC and ATL, but VC++ development remained the province of an elite group of developers.

With Visual Studio.NET, Microsoft introduces C#, a new language that combines the power of C++ with the simplicity of VB. Despite its name, C# code looks a lot like Java code – gone is the C++ convention of separating class declarations and definitions into separate header (.h) and implementation (.cpp) files: in C#, as in Java, classes are declared and defined in the same code blocks. Also in C#, as in Java, even the primitive data types (integers, floats, etc.) are objects with methods that you can call for type conversions and output formatting. Furthermore, C#, like Java, is consistently object-oriented in that programs begin not at some global function external to all classes as in VB, but with a call to an object method defined as "public static void Main()". Last but not least, C# discourages you from using pointers.

All C# code is managed by the CLR. That makes C# leaner and safer than C++. C# also dispenses with bug-prone idioms such as multiple inheritance and pre-processor macros. To guard against the kinds of memory errors that are difficult to debug, the C# compiler issues warnings for variables that are referenced before being initialized. Recent, valuable C++ additions such as namespaces, the intrinsic string type, and structured error handling have been included in C#. Tricky C++ "gotchas" like fall-through `switch...case` have been eliminated.

Using the built-in capabilities of the CLR, C# makes implementing components easy. Doing COM objects in C++ meant generating interface GUIDS, implementing `IUnknown` and `IClassFactory`, and providing self-registration code. C# component development is like Visual Basic component development in that you simply implement a class and compile it, letting the C# compiler and the CLR provide the messy plumbing invisibly.

C++ has been described as a language that gives the programmer "enough rope to shoot himself in the foot." With C#, the developer has just as much rope, but he has to explicitly ask for it. For example, a programmer can short-circuit the CLR's automatic garbage collection, but only by explicitly prefixing object references with the `fixed` keyword.

C# is particularly well suited to .NET development. In many respects, it is just a version of the .NET object model that can be read by people. There is a large degree of correspondence between C# constructs and Microsoft Intermediate Language.

With its unique combination of power and simplicity, C# may well become the tool-of-choice for developing business objects, data access objects, and controls, thus pushing Visual Basic upward to Web Form-based user interfaces and C++ downward to hardcore middleware and other system level functions. On the other hand, since Visual Basic receives almost all of the functionality of C# in .NET, it may continue to be the dominant application development language by inertia. After all, there are literally millions of developers who know Visual Basic. Only time will tell what the acceptance level of C# will be.

However, there is one place that's jumping into C# with both feet – Microsoft itself. C# is the dominant language being used to develop the .NET framework, and it is quickly growing to be the most-used language at Microsoft. An introduction to C# is included in Chapter 3, and is also covered in the Wrox book, *C# Programming with the Public Beta*, ISBN 1-861004-87-7.

Language Changes Affecting ASP.NET

The successor to ASP is called ASP.NET. There are many changes and improvements. We have previously discussed Web Services and Web Forms, which are part of ASP.NET. Now we will look at some changes in writing traditional ASP pages.

For starters, VBScript is gone, though existing VBScript can still be run with the real Visual Basic compiler. That means VB code in Active Server Pages can now use real data typing (goodbye variants!) and such constructs as classes. JavaScript is still available, and is also compiled and then run through the CLR.

Also, the choice of languages is much enlarged. A COBOL vendor at PDC showed an Active Server Page in .NET with COBOL used for the code. Most languages that work with the CLR should be available for use in the .NET version of Active Server Pages.

As mentioned in the section above on the Common Language Runtime, code in Active Server Pages for .NET is actually compiled on the fly before it is run. This may help to cure some cases where interpreted script causes performance problems.

Chapter 7 gives a more detailed look at ASP.NET, and is written to be helpful also for developers who don't currently work with Active Server Pages.

"How Does .NET Affect Me?"

You're probably reading this book because you want to know how you will be affected by .NET. Here are some of most important implications for developers, other technical roles, and end users.

Developers

The biggest impact of .NET is on software developers. They get new architectural options, simplified development, and hopefully more robust software. They also get a wider range of programming models to use.

A Spectrum of Programming Models

In existing Microsoft-based development tools, there are a couple of quantum leaps required to move from simple to complex. And sometimes the complex programming models are required to get more power. A developer can start simply with Active Server Pages, but when those become cumbersome, it's a big leap to learn component-based, three-tier development in Visual Basic. And it's another quantum leap to become proficient in C++, ATL, and related technologies for system-level work.

A key benefit of .NET is that there exists a more gradual transition in programming models from simple to powerful. ASP.NET Pages are more structured than traditional ASP pages, and provide on-the-fly compilation to get better performance. Visual Basic becomes a tool with wider applicability, as it becomes easy to build a web interface with Web Forms, and it also becomes possible to use advanced object – oriented designs. System level capabilities become more approachable with C#, and even C++ becomes more practical with managed code taking away a lot of the tedium.

This increases the odds that a developer will be able to settle in at the right balance of power vs. simplicity. When a developer's current programming model starts coming up short, there will be an option to get more power that doesn't require a radical readjustment.

Libraries of Pre-written Functionality

The evolution of Windows development languages has been in the direction of providing more and more built-in functionality so that developers can ignore the foundations and concentrate on solving business problems. .NET continues this trend.

One particularly important implication is that .NET extends the trend of developers spending less time writing code and more time discovering how to do something with pre-written functionality. Mainframe COBOL programmers could learn everything they ever needed to know about COBOL in a year or two, and very seldom need to consult reference materials after that. In contrast, today's developers spend a significant portion of their time digging through reference material to figure out how to do something that they may never do again. The sheer expanse of functionality available, plus the rapidly changing pace, make it a requirement that an effective developer also be a researcher. .NET accelerates this trend, and will probably increase the ratio of research time to coding time for a typical developer.

Infrastructure Engineers

A major design goal in .NET is to simplify the lives of folks who install and care for computing infrastructure. By alleviating "DLL Hell" and many other deployment problems, infrastructure workers should find themselves relieved of many of the most frustrating and tedious aspects of Microsoft platform deployment.

On the other hand, with applications becoming more distributed through web services, the need for reliable connections both within organizations and through out the Internet will increase. The responsibility for that will certainly fall on the infrastructure technicians.

End Users

Any new computing platform must ultimately benefit the end users, or else it's not of much value. .NET clearly does that, since once the .NET framework is on an end-user's system, adding new applications should be easier than ever before. Meaning that they should run into fewer technical glitches that require expert assistance.

More importantly, they will have access to new Web-enabled applications that have the potential to reach ever-higher levels of functionality and productivity. They will have applications that draw together information and processing services from all over the globe, and integrate them into an easy-to-use, customized form.

Cautions

No one knows for sure if .NET will live up to its billing. Many of us were surprised at PDC to see how far Microsoft had progressed with this very ambitious effort, but there remains a lot to be done. We are even more optimistic after seeing the stability and completeness of beta one for Visual Studio.NET. But it's important to recognize that building-in the intelligence that will be required for .NET to work is a huge undertaking, and there are risks that some pieces of it might take another generation or two to be truly ready for prime time.

There is also lots of uncertainty as to the time frames that will be required before the first .NET technology rolls into production status. In the meantime, it's important to understand enough about .NET to know when it makes sense to look seriously at using it, and to orient our current development practices in ways that will make eventual migration to .NET simpler and faster.

Now on to the details about .NET!

2

Intro to the CLR

At the core of the .NET platform is the Common Language Runtime (CLR). The CLR is responsible for managing the execution of code compiled for the .NET platform.

Code requiring the CLR at runtime in order to execute is referred to as "managed code". Compilers that target the .NET platform generate managed code that relies on a core set of services provided by the CLR. Some of the key benefits of the services provided by the CLR include:

- ❑ **Cross-language integration** – the CLR enables managed code written in one language to seamlessly integrate with code written in another language. This includes cross-language inheritance, exception handling, and marshaling.

- ❑ **Enhanced security** – the CLR enables managed code to declare the security they require and the gathering of evidence used to evaluate whether or not permission is granted.

- ❑ **Versioning and deployment support** – the CLR supports side-by-side execution of multiple versions of the same component, even within the same process.

- ❑ **Debugging and profiling services** – the CLR provides the necessary hooks to enable developers to debug and profile managed code. For example, developer tools have the ability to walk the stack of a managed code application, regardless of what language or languages the application was written in.

- ❑ **Memory management** – the GC (Garbage Collector) is responsible for collecting objects no longer referenced by the application.

It is equally important is to take a look at what the CLR is not:

❑ Despite the fact that managed code is compiled to an intermediate language (discussed in a later section), .NET programs are not interpreted by a "virtual machine". The CLR is responsible for compiling .NET applications to native machine code. The CLR then steps aside and the program executes as native compiled code.

❑ The CLR is not limited to the Microsoft platform. It is technically possible to port the CLR to a variety of hardware platforms, even other operating systems. .NET applications are not limited to the lowest common denominator features exposed by operating systems – they have the ability to take full advantage of the features of the underlying hardware and operating system.

❑ The CLR does not force the developer to rewrite an application in order to take advantage of the .NET Framework.

In this chapter, we will discuss the CLR core enabling technologies. We will discuss the CTS (Common Type System) shared by all languages targeted for the .NET platform. The CTS enables cross-language integration between all languages that target the .NET platform. We will then discuss the pervasiveness of metadata, how it is used by the CLR, and how to extend metadata with custom attributes. Finally we will discuss managed data and the role the CLR plays.

Why Do We Need a Common Runtime and Type System?

The primary goal of the .NET platform is to make it easier for the developer to write applications. Let's face it; COM developers are exposed to way too much detail. Why should you have to be concerned about GUIDs, HRESULTs, early versus late binding, managing reference counts, the type of threading model your component will run in, and proxy and stub layers if your component is located in a different apartment to the client? Every COM component has to implement COM plumbing code to implement the IUnknown interface and if the component is going to be accessible via automation, the IDispatch interface.

Luckily programming environments and frameworks such as VB and ATL come to the rescue and hide much of this complexity. For example, VB automatically generates the appropriate GUIDs for you and also manages reference counts for COM objects used within the application. ATL provides much of the COM plumbing for C++ developers and provide "smart pointers" to automatically manage reference counts. However, wouldn't it be nice if compiler manufacturers didn't have to rewrite all of this plumbing for every language? The CLR provides a common runtime for all languages that target the .NET platform and abstracts the developer from many of these details.

Many developers will argue that Visual Basic's implementation of COM leaves a lot to be desired. For example, VB decorates its classes with an underscore, and all of its parameters must be variant compliant. That means that C++ developers interoperating with code written in VB must convert all of their strings to the variant BSTR structure and their arrays to the SAFEARRAY structure. Since the variant structures are so cumbersome, C++ developers find themselves converting all inbound and outbound parameters from variant types to more friendly data types. As you can imagine, the application takes a performance hit every time this conversion process takes place. Wouldn't it be nice if there were a friendly set of data types that all languages used? As we will see, this is exactly what the Common Type System provides.

Traditional VB also has many limitations: multithreading, lack of implementation inheritance, lack of support for operator overloading, and so on. It takes a lot of effort to build these advanced features into a language. Wouldn't it be nice to be able to leverage a common set of features that is available to all languages? Well, since VB.NET is built on top of the .NET framework, many of VB's shortcomings have been eliminated. Any language built on top of the CLR can take advantage of all of the features provided by the .NET framework.

The Anatomy of .NET Applications

.NET applications are composed of three primary entities.

❑   An **assembly** is the primary unit of deployment of a .NET application

❑   **Modules** are the individual files that make up an assembly

❑   **Types** are the basic unit of encapsulating data with a set of behaviors

This is represented in the following diagram:

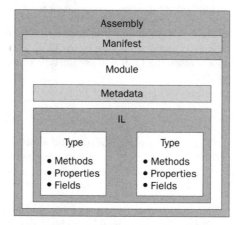

Let's briefly talk about each of the entities represented in the diagram.

Assembly

An assembly is the primary unit of deployment for managed code. An assembly is composed of a manifest and one or more modules. The manifest can be stored in a separate file or in one of the modules. The manifest contains information about the identity of the assembly, a declarative security request, a list of other assemblies it depends on, and a list of all exposed types and resources.

The identity information stored in the manifest includes its textual name and version number. If the assembly is public, the manifest will also contain the assembly's public key. The public key is used to guarantee uniqueness and may also be used to identify the source of the assembly.

The assembly is responsible for declaring the security it requires. Requests for permissions fall into one of three categories: required, optional, and denied. The identity information may be used as evidence for determining whether or not to approve the security requests.

The manifest contains a list of other assemblies it depends on and all types and resources exposed by the assembly. If any of the resources exposed by the assembly are localized, the manifest will also contain the default culture. The CLR uses this information to locate specific resources and types within the assembly.

The manifest also contains a list of other assemblies that the assembly depends on. The CLR uses this information to locate an appropriate version of the required assemblies at runtime. The list of dependencies also includes the exact version number of each assembly at the time the assembly was created. If the application fails, the CLR can use this information to revert back to the "known good" configuration.

Module

A module is either a DLL or an EXE Windows PE (Portable Executable). It contains Intermediate Language (IL), associated metadata, and may optionally contain the assembly's manifest.

IL is a platform independent way of representing managed code within a module. Before managed code can be executed, the CLR is responsible for compiling the associated IL into native machine code. The CLR provides multiple compilers for this purpose. The install-time compiler will compile all IL associated with an assembly when it is installed on the system. The JIT (just-in-time) compiler will compile the IL on a method-by-method basis the first time the method is called by the application.

The metadata associated with the IL provides additional information related to the types declared in IL. The metadata contained within the module is used extensively by the CLR. For example if the client and the object reside within two different processes, the CLR will use the type's metadata to marshal data between the client and the object.

Type

A type is a template used to describe the encapsulation of data and an associated set of behaviors. Unlike COM, which is scoped at the machine level, types are scoped at the assembly level. In the Common Type System section, we will learn about the two kinds of types: reference and value types. Reference types can be loosely thought of as classes whereas value types can be loosely thought of as structures.

A type has properties, methods, and fields. Fields constitute member data within the type. Members define particular behaviors exhibited by the type. Properties look like fields to the client but can have code behind them that usually performs some sort of data validation. For example, a Dog data type can expose a property to define its sex. Code could be placed behind the property to only allow it to be set to either "male" or "female".

Common Type System

Can't we all just get along? Each programming language seems to bring its own island of data types with it. For example, VB represent strings using the BSTR `struct` (the internal representation of the String data type), C++ offers `char` and `wchar` data types, and MFC offers the `CString` class. The C++ `int` data type is a 32-bit value where the VB `Integer` data type, prior to VB.NET, is a 16-bit value. Obviously passing parameters between applications written using different languages can be challenging.

To help resolve this problem, C has become the lowest common denominator for interfacing between programs written in multiple languages. An exported function written in C that exposes simple C data types can be consumed by VB, JAVA, Delphi, and a variety of other programming languages. In fact, the Windows API is exposed as a set of C functions.

Unfortunately in order to access a C interface, you must explicitly map C data types to the language's native data types.

Take, for example, the following GetUserName function exported from the advapi32.dll, written in C:

```
BOOL GetUserName(
    LPTSTR lpBuffer,    // name buffer
    LPDWORD nSize       // size of name buffer
);
```

A VB programmer would use the following statement to map to the GetUserNameA Win32 function (Note that GetUserNameA is the ANSI version of the GetUserName function):

```
Public Declare Function GetUserName Lib "advapi32.dll" Alias "GetUserNameA"_
                        (ByVal strBuffer As String, nSize As Long) As Long
```

Notice that the VB developer explicitly mapped the lpBuffer C character array data type to the strBuffer VB String parameter. Not only is this very cumbersome, but it's also very error prone. If the developer accidentally mapped a variable declared as Long to the lpBuffer the application would not generate any compilation errors. However, calling the function at runtime would more than likely result in an access violation. Wouldn't it be nice if there were a set of common data types that were used across all programming languages? That's exactly what the CTS provides for us.

The CTS provides every language running on top of the .NET platform with a base set of types and mechanisms for extending those types. Every type supported by the Common Type System is derived from System.Object. Therefore, every type supports the following methods:

Boolean Equals(Object)	Used to test equality with another object. Reference types should return true if the Object parameter references the same object. Value types should return true if the Object parameter has the same value. (Reference and value types will be discussed later in this section.)
Int32 GetHashCode()	Generates a number corresponding to the value of an object. If two objects of the same type are equal, then they must return the same hash code. This value is used extensively by the sorting algorithms implemented in System.Collections.
Type GetType()	Gets a Type object that can be used to access metadata associated with the type and as a starting point for navigating the object hierarchy exposed by the Reflection API. (The Reflection API will be discussed later in this section.)
String ToString()	The default implementation returns the fully qualified name of the class of the object. This method is often overridden to output data that is more meaningful to the type. For example, all base types return their value.

The core value types supported by the .NET platform reside within the root of the System namespace. These types are often referred to as "primitive types". They include:

Boolean	Represents a Boolean value of either true or false.
Byte	Represents an unsigned byte value and can be used to represent a positive integer between 0 and 255.
Char	Represents a Unicode character value.
DateTime	Represents a date and time value.
Decimal	Represents positive and negative values with 28 significant digits, ranging from 79,228,162,514,264,337,593,543,950,335 to negative 79,228,162,514,264,337,593,543,950,335.
Double	Represents a 64-bit, double precision, floating point number ranging from negative 1.79769313486231570E308 to positive 1.79769313486231570E308.
GUID	Represents a globally unique identifier (GUID). A GUID is a 128 bit integer that is considered unique.
Int16	Represents a 16 bit signed integer value that can range from negative 32768 to positive 32767.
Int32	Represents a 32 bit signed integer value that can range from negative 2,147,483,648 to positive 2,147,483,647.
Int64	Represents a 64 bit signed integer value that can range from 9,223,372,036,854,775,808 to positive 9,223,372,036,854,775,807.
Sbyte	Represents an 8 bit signed integer value that can range from negative 128 to positive 127.
Single	Represents a 4 byte, single precision, floating point number that can range from negative 3.402823E38 to positive 3.402823E38.
TimeSpan	Represents a period of time, either positive or negative.

Note that there are types that represent unsigned integers – UInt16, UInt32, UInt64 – but they are not CLS compliant. Many compilers will allow the developer to use keywords that serve as aliases to the types defined above. Use of the keywords allows the developer to use a more natural syntax when declaring variables for holding primitive types. For example, the following declarations are equivalent:

```
// C#:
long y;
// ... may seem more natural than ...
System.Int32 x = new System.Int32();
```

```
' VB:
Dim y as Long
' ... may seem more natural than ...
Dim x as New System.Int32
```

The .NET Framework exposes many types for many different purposes. For example, the System.XML namespace contains types used for creating, consuming, manipulating, and validating XML documents. Have a look at Chapter 6 for an overview of the .NET Framework.

Recall that types fall into two categories: value types and reference types. Which category a type falls into will depend on how instances of that type are treated by the CLR. Instances of reference types will always be created on the managed heap whereas instances of value types can be created on the stack. We will look at code that demonstrates this when we talk about creating custom types. For now, lets take a look at a high level picture of how the CLR allocates memory for an instance of a reference type.

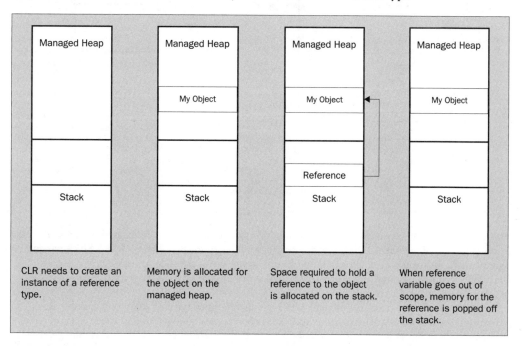

The previous diagram shows that first an instance of a reference type is created on the managed heap. Next, a reference to the object is created on the stack. When the variable containing the reference goes out of scope, the memory that was allocated on the stack will be popped off the stack. However, the memory allocated by the object will exist until the Garbage Collector executes. The Garbage Collector (GC) is discussed in detail in a later section.

Now let's take a look at how memory is allocated for an instance of a value type. In the example below, a variable is declared within the scope of a member function.

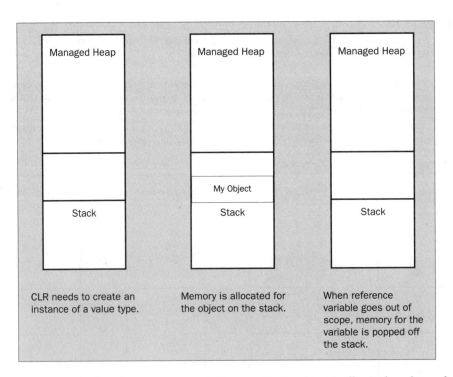

In this case, an instance of a value type is created. Memory for the object is allocated on the stack. Therefore, as soon as the variable goes out of scope, the memory allocated for the object is freed. Since we don't have to rely on the GC to free memory allocated for objects on the stack, instances of value types created on the stack are typically freed sooner and at a lower cost than their reference type counterparts.

Another difference in the behavior of value types versus reference types is when one variable is set equal to another, or passed as a parameter to a method call. When a variable of a *reference* type (A) is set equal to another variable of the same type (B), variable A is assigned a reference to B. Both variables reference the same object. When a variable of a *value* type (A) is set equal to another variable of the same type (B), variable A receives a copy of the contents of B. Each variable will have its own independent copy of the data. We will look at code that demonstrates this behavior in the next section, *Custom Types*.

Yet another difference between the behaviors of value types versus reference types is how equality is determined. Two variables of a given reference type are determined to be equal if both variables refer to the same object. Two variables of a given value type are determined to be equal if the state of the two variables are equal. Let's take a look at an example:

```
// C#:
// Declare and initialize two instances of the String
// value type.
string s1 = "test";
string s2 = "test";

// Expression evaluates to true.
if(s1 == s2)
    Console.WriteLine("s1 and s2 are equal.");
else
    Console.WriteLine("s1 and s2 are not equal.");
```

```
// Declare and initialize two instances of the File
// reference type.
System.IO.Directory d1 = new System.IO.Directory("c:\\winnt\\system32");
System.IO.Directory d2 = new System.IO.Directory("c:\\winnt\\system32");

// Expression evaluates to false.
if(d1 == d2)
    Console.WriteLine("d1 and d2 are equal.");
else
    Console.WriteLine("d1 and d2 are not equal.");
```

The final difference between value types and reference types is how instances of a type are initialized. When a variable is declared as a reference type, the variable is initialized with a default value of null. The variable will not reference an object until explicitly done so by the application. In contrast, a variable declared as containing an unboxed value type will always reference a valid object. All fields within the variable will be initialized as well.

Custom Types

The Common Type System wouldn't be very flexible if it didn't support the creation of custom types. A custom type is a set of data and related behavior that is defined by the developer. We will look at some examples of creating both value or reference types. In most .NET languages, reference types are defined by declaring classes. Let's look at the following C# code used to create and then test the behavior of a custom reference type:

```
public class Application
{
   class Test
   {
      public string    myString;
      public int       myInt;
   }
```

We define a custom reference type called `Test`. For the sake of simplicity, we define two public fields for `Test`, one of type string and one of type int. In general, it is better to expose properties as opposed to fields.

```
public static int Main(string[] args)
{
      // Notice that the declarations are NOT equivalent.
      // - x references an object of type Test.
      // - y is a reference to an object of type Test,
      //    but y does not reference an object yet.
      Test x = new Test();
      Test y;
```

In `Main`, we first declare two reference variables of type `Test`. Notice that the since `y` is not initialized with the new operator, it does not reference an object and has an initial value of null. We'll see later how this behavior is different for value types.

```
      x.myInt = 4;
      x.myString = "Test";

      // Reference to x is assigned to y.
      y = x;
```

Next we initialize the `myInt` and `myString` fields of the object referenced by x. We then set y equal to the newly initialized object.

```
        y.myInt = 1;
        y.myString = "Changed";

        Console.WriteLine(String.Format(
            "x:   myInt = {0} and myString = {1}",
            x.myInt, x.myString));
        Console.WriteLine(String.Format(
            "y:   myInt = {0} and myString = {1}",
            y.myInt, y.myString));
    return(0);
    }
  }
```

Finally we modify the fields of the object referenced by y and then write the value of the fields of the object referenced by x and y. Let's take a look at the output of the program:

```
x:   myInt = 1 and myString = Changed
y:   myInt = 1 and myString = Changed
```

Since x *and* y reference the same object, the output of x reflect the changes made to y. Hopefully this demo did not reveal anything that was surprising. However, there are times where you do not want this behavior.

There is a need for value types. For example, it would be very inconvenient and error-prone if the Decimal class behaved like reference types. Say we are writing an e-commerce application and need to return the invoice, including the total amount purchased and a subtotal that does not include tax and shipping. We create two reference variables called subtotal and total. Say our application calculates the subtotal, sets the total equal to the subtotal, and then adds tax and shipping to the total. We could not do something like this:

```
// Use a decimal reference type.
DecimalRef total = new DecimalRef();
DecimalRef subtotal = new DecimalRef();

// Calculate subtotal.

// Set total equal to total and apply tax and shipping.
total = subtotal;
total = total + tax + shipping;
// Oops ...
// We just applied tax and shipping to subtotal as well.
```

If `total` and `subtotal` were reference variables, then `subtotal` would always have tax and shipping applied to it as well, since `total` and `subtotal` would reference the same object. Instead, we would have to do something like this:

```
total = subtotal.Clone();
total = tax + shipping;
```

The syntax above is not very natural. I think you would agree that we would like to use the previous syntax with one exception. We would like to set total equal to the *value* of subtotal as opposed to its *reference*. This is where `System.ValueType` comes in.

Value types are derived from System.ValueType. Instances of types that derive from System.ValueType are copied by value and not by reference. As we will see in a moment, programming languages such as C# provide a very natural syntax for working with value types.

Let's take a look at a modified version of the previous program. This time we will implement and use a value type:

```
public class Application
{
    struct test
    {
        public string    myString;
        public int       myInt;
    }
```

We declare a struct instead of a class this time. Declaring test as a struct signals the C# compiler to have test derive from System.ValueType.

```
    public static int Main(string[] args)
    {
        // Notice that both declarations are equivalent.
        // Both x and y are instances of type test.
        test x = new test();
        test y;

        x.myInt = 4;
        x.myString = "Test";

        // Value of x is assigned to y.
        y = x;
```

We initialize x and then set y equal to x. Since x and y are both instances of value types, y is set equal to the *value* of x.

```
        y.myInt = 1;
        y.myString = "Changed";

        Console.WriteLine(
            String.Format("x:  myInt = {0} and myString = {1}",
            x.myInt, x.myString));
        Console.WriteLine(
            String.Format("y:  myInt = {0} and myString = {1}",
            y.myInt, y.myString));

        return(0);
    }
}
```

We then change the fields in y and finally write the value of the fields in both x and y to the console. Let's take a look at the output of the program:

```
x:  myInt = 4 and myString = Test
y:  myInt = 1 and myString = Changed
```

Notice that when we changed the value of the fields in y it did not affect x. This is exactly the behavior we require for primitive types.

There is another aspect with respect to value types that developers should be aware of. Recall that all value types derive from System.ValueType. System.ValueType overrides Object.Equals and Object.GetHashCode. The implementation of both methods uses reflection; (in a later section we will fire up the IL Disassembler and see for ourselves). Since there is a cost involved with using reflection to navigate the internals of the object, consider overriding these methods with a more direct and efficient method of determining an appropriate hash code and whether or not the value of two types are equal.

The only way the data encapsulated by an instance of a value type can be modified or accessed is through the corresponding variable. Due to the tight coupling between a value type variable and its data, when the variable goes out of scope, the data it encapsulates goes out of scope as well. For this reason, the CLR can allocate memory for value data types on the stack as opposed to the managed heap. Since the instance data is placed on the stack, it will automatically be freed when the block it was allocated in goes out of scope. This is much less costly, and in most cases more timely, than having the GC free the memory after it is no longer referenced.

Boxing and Unboxing Value Types

There are some cases where it makes sense to treat an instance of a value type as if it were an instance of a reference type. This is where the concept of boxing comes in. Boxing occurs when an instance of a value type is converted to a reference type. An instance of a value type can be converted either to System.Object or to any other interface type implemented by the value type.

Unboxing involves the explicit conversion of an instance of a reference type back to its original value type. Let's take a look at the following sample code that demonstrates boxing and unboxing:

```
public class Application
{
    struct test
    {
        public string    myString;
        public int       myInt;
    }

public static int Main(string[] args)
{
        test      x;
        Object    o1;
        Object    o2;
        test      y;

        x.myInt = 4;
        x.myString = "Test";

        // Step 1: Implicit boxing.
        // 1. Value of x is copied on the managed heap.
        // 2. Reference to copied value of x is assigned to o1.
        o1 = x;
```

In step one we are performing an implicit conversion of x from *value* type test to *reference* type System.Object. Let's do a quick review of what needs to occur. Since o1 is an instance of a reference type, its data must be stored on the managed heap. Since x is an instance of a value type, its data is copied by value. Now that we've reviewed the basics, let's dive into the details.

When o1 is set equal to x, the following steps are performed:

❑ Memory is allocated on the managed heap to store the value of x.

❑ The value of x is then copied onto the managed heap, which includes the value of myInt and myString.

❑ The reference to the data copied on the managed heap is stored in the memory previously allocated on the stack for o1.

```
// Step 2:  Reference to o1 is assigned to o2.
o2 = o1;
```

Next, o2 is set equal to the reference to the boxed object. Now o1 and o2 refer to the same object.

```
// Step 3:  Explicit unboxing.
y = (test)o1;
```

Next we will explicitly unbox the data stored on the managed heap referenced by o1. Unboxing is when we convert the boxed variable (the instance of a reference type containing a boxed instance of a value type) back to the original value type. We do so by converting o1 back to an instance of test. Then y is set equal to the data referenced by o1. Specifically, the data referenced by o1 is copied into the memory previously reserved on the stack for y.

```
x.myInt = 1;
x.myString = "Changed";
y.myInt = 9;
y.myString = "I've changed too.";

Console.WriteLine("x:   myInt = {0} and myString = {1}",
    x.myInt, x.myString);
Console.WriteLine("o1:  myInt = {0} and myString = {1}",
    ((test)o1).myInt, ((test)o1).myString);
Console.WriteLine("o2:  myInt = {0} and myString = {1}",
    ((test)o2).myInt, ((test)o2).myString);
Console.WriteLine("y:   myInt = {0} and myString = {1}",
    y.myInt, y.myString);
Console.WriteLine("Hash of o1 = {0}, o2 = {1}",
    o1.GetHashCode(), o2.GetHashCode());

    return(0);
    }
}
```

Finally, we change the value of the fields for x and y and then output the results to the console. Note that we unboxed o1 and o2 in the Console.WriteLine statements in order to gain access to the fields. Let's take a look at the resulting output:

```
x:   myInt = 1 and myString = Changed
o1:  myInt = 4 and myString = Test
o2:  myInt = 4 and myString = Test
y:   myInt = 9 and myString = I've changed too.
Hash of o1 = 2089308947, o2 = 2089308947
```

Three copies of the data are evident in the output. Changes made to either x or y did not affect the data behind the other variables. The implementation of `Object.GetHashCode` will return the unique index the runtime uses to identify a particular object. Note that this may not be the case for instances of types that derive from `System.Object`, since `GetHashCode` can be overridden to return a number that does not meet this criteria. With the knowledge of the implementation of `Object.GetHashCode`, we can verify that o1 and o2 reference the same object by the fact that their hash codes are equal.

So when would the developer want to intentionally box an instance of a value type? If an instance of a value type is passed multiple times to methods that expect a reference type, such as `System.Object`, and its value is not changed, consider boxing it once and then passing the boxed variable to the methods that expect a reference type. Since boxing does have a cost associated with it, explicitly boxing a variable once will perform better than having the variable implicitly boxed multiple times, especially for complex types where a significant amount of state must be copied.

```
test t;

// Four implicit boxing operations.
Console.WriteLine("{0}, {1}, {2}, {3}", t, t, t, t);

// One intentional implicit boxing operation.
Object o = t;
Console.WriteLine("{0}, {1}, {2}, {3}", o, o, o, o);
```

Since the most compatible overloaded method for `Console.WriteLine` accepts a string and four `System.Object` parameters, the first call to `Console.WriteLine` will implicitly box t four separate times. No boxing is performed on the second call to `Console.WriteLine` since we intentionally cast t to `System.Object` once and then passed the boxed version four times to `Console.WriteLine`.

Metadata

Metadata is information that enables components to be self-describing. Metadata is used to describe many aspects of a component, including classes, methods and fields, and the assembly itself. Metadata is used by the CLR to facilitate all sorts of things like validating an assembly before it is executed and performing garbage collection while managed code is being executed.

The use of metadata in the effort to describe components is not new to .NET: COM relies on metadata for its operation. For example, the component's type library contains metadata describing the classes exposed by the component and is used to facilitate OLE Automation. Additional metadata can be associated with your component by installing it within COM+. The developer can declare the support its component needs at runtime, such as transactional support, serialization, object pooling, and much more.

However, .NET refines the use of metadata within COM/COM+. A .NET component's metadata cannot get out of sync with the component itself. In addition, .NET makes a much clearer distinction between attributes that should only be set at compile time versus those that can be modified at runtime. Let's look at each of these points separately.

In COM and COM+, metadata is stored separately from the executable. The COM developer has an option to store the component's type library as a separate file. Furthermore, important COM metadata used at runtime, such as the component's GUID, supported threading model, etc. is stored in the registry. The problem only worsens in COM+ where all COM+ metadata is stored separately from the component.

As metadata is stored separately from the COM or COM+ component, installing and upgrading components can be problematic. The component must be registered before it can be used, and if the type library is stored in a separate file, it must be installed in the proper directory. Once the component is installed, upgrading it to a new version can be problematic. It is possible to install a new binary for the component without updating its corresponding metadata.

The process of installing and upgrading a .NET component is greatly simplified. Since all metadata associated with a .NET component must reside within the file that contains the component itself, no registration is required. Once a new component is copied onto the system, it can be immediately used. Upgrading the component becomes much less problematic since the component and its associated metadata cannot get out of sync.

Another problem with COM+ is that attributes that should only be set at compile time may be reconfigured at runtime. For example, COM+ can provide serialization support for "neutral" components. A component that does not require serialization must be designed to accommodate multiple requests from multiple clients simultaneously. Hopefully it is self evident that the developer knows at compile time whether or not a component requires support for serialization from the runtime. However under COM+, the attribute describing whether or not client requests should be serialized can be altered at runtime.

Metadata provided by the Assembly's manifest and describing the types is all the runtime needs to find and load types.

Attributes

Attributes are used to decorate entities such as assemblies, classes, methods, and properties with additional information. Attributes can be used for a variety of purposes. For example, the attribute can be informational only, used to request a certain behavior at runtime, or even invoke a particular behavior from another application. Let's take a look at an example in C#:

```
Using System;

[Serializable()]
public class Demo
{
    int x;

    [Obsolete("Use Method2 instead.")]
    public void Method1() {}

    public void Method2() {}

    public static int Main(string[] args)
    {
        Method1();   // Will generate a compiler warning.
    }
}
```

By decorating the Demo type with the Serializable attribute, the base class library will provide serialization support for instances of the Demo type. For example, you can use the ResourceWriter type to stream an instance of the Demo type to disk. An attribute was also associated with Method1 for the purpose of marking the method obsolete. Compilers that acknowledge the Obsolete attribute, such as VB.NET and C#, will display a warning at compile time if Method1 is referenced within the application. For example, the C# compiler will display the following warning when the above code is compiled:

```
'Demo.Method1()' is obsolete: 'Use Method2 instead.'
```

It is worthwhile noting that many .NET languages like C# and VB.NET allow the developer to use a shorthand notation for the name of the attribute. For example, the fully qualified name of the Serializable attribute is `System.SerializableAttribute`. C# allows developers to drop the Attribute from the end of the name. A less natural, yet equally valid way of declaring an attribute would be:

```
// C#:
[System.ObsoleteAttribute()]
public void Method1("Use Method2 instead.") {}

' VB.NET Equivalent:
Shared Sub <System.ObsoleteAttribute("Use Method2 instead.")> Test()
End Sub
```

Visual Studio uses attributes at design time. For example, the `DefaultValue`, `Browsable`, `Category`, and `Description` attributes drive the behavior of the property window.

There are many times where you would want to associate multiple attributes with an entity. The following are equivalent ways of declaring multiple attributes for a property in C#:

```
[Category("Appearance"), Description("Title displayed on top.")]
public string test
{
get {return test;}
set {m_test = value;}
}

[Category("Appearance")] [Description("Title displayed on top.")]
public string test
{
get {return test;}
set {m_test = value;}
}

[Category("Appearance")]
[Description("Title displayed on top.")]
public string test
{
get {return test;}
set {m_test = value;}
}
```

Custom Attributes

Unlike COM+, you have the ability to extend the metadata exposed by your components with custom attributes. Custom attributes are used extensively throughout the .NET Framework. The `Description`, `Category`, and `DefaultValue` attributes we reviewed in the previous section are custom attributes. Custom attributes are also used by design time controls to store their configuration information.

The developer may want to create their own custom attributes for informational purposes or to elicit the application hosting an object to invoke a certain behavior. For example, the following C# code creates a custom attribute that is used to record the author of a particular piece of code.

```
[AttributeUsage(AttributeTargets.Class | AttributeTargets.Method, AllowMultiple =
true)]
[Credit("John Smith", email="JohnB@xyzplant.com")]
public sealed class CreditAttribute : System.Attribute
{
    public string name;
    public string email;

    public CreditAttribute(string name)
    {
        this.name = name;
    }
}
```

We first use the predefined `AttributeUsage` attribute to describe how our custom attribute can be used in code. In this case, use a bit wise `or` to indicate that the attribute can be applied to methods and classes. Other possible options for where the attribute can be declared include:

Assembly	0x0001
Module	0x0002
Class	0x0004
Struct	0x0008
Enum	0x0010
Constructor	0x0020
Method	0x0040
Property	0x0080
Field	0x0100
Event	0x0200
Interface	0x0400
Parameter	0x0800
Delegate	0x1000
All	0x1FFF
ClassMembers	Class | Struct | Enum | Constructor | Method |Property | Field | Event | Interface | Delegate

Since multiple credits can be assigned, we allow the attribute to be declared multiple times. This is accomplished by setting the `AllowMultiple` property to true.

We then define the attribute class, which must derive from `System.Attribute`. We also use the optional `sealed` keyword to prevent our attribute class from being extended. We then create two public member variables to hold the name and e mail address of the developer who wrote the code.

Finally, every attribute class must have at least one constructor. In our case, we want to ensure that at least the name of the developer is defined.

Reflection API

All metadata associated with managed code can be accessed by the Reflection API. Developers can use the Reflection API to examine metadata associated with the currently executing assembly. Since every object derives from `System.Object`, every object supports the `GetType` method. The `GetType` method returns a `Type` object that can be used to access the metadata associated with the type.

You can navigate up the object hierarchy by calling `Type.Method`. You can access the metadata associated with individual fields, properties, and methods calling `Type.GetFields`, `Type.GetMethods`, or `Type.GetProperties` respectively.

Putting it All Together

Let's take a look at an example that utilizes what we have learned about attributes and the Reflection API. We will create a console application that, when executed with the /easteregg flag, displays the names and e-mail addresses of the programmers who wrote the different pieces of the executing assembly:

```
using System;
using System.Reflection;
```

We first import the `System` and `System.Reflection` namespaces to help improve the readability of our code.

```
[Credit("Bob Smith", email="bob@xyzcompany.com")]
[Credit("Jill Jones", email="jill@xyzcompany.com")]
public class Demo : Object
```

We use an extended version of the `CreditAttribute` attribute we defined previously to indicate who has worked on the `Demo` class.

```
{
    [Credit("Jill Jones", email="jill@xyzcompany.com")]
    public void Method1() {}

    [Credit("Bob Smith", email="bob@xyzcompany.com")]
    [Credit("Jill Jones", email="jill@xyzcompany.com")]
    public void Method2() {}
}
```

Next we will decorate the name of the developers who worked on the individual methods.

```
[Credit("John Doe", email="john@firmxyz.com")]
public class Application
{
    public static int Main(string[] args)
    {
        // Check to see if we were asked to display the credits.
        if(args.Length > 0 && args[0].ToLower() == "/easteregg")
        {
        CreditAttribute.DisplayCredits(Assembly.GetExecutingAssembly());
        }
```

```
            return 0;
        }
    }
```

Next we implement `Application.Main`. If the first command line argument is `/easteregg`, we call the
`CreditAttribute.DisplayCredits` static method to display the credits for all objects and methods
within the currently running assembly.

```
[AttributeUsage(AttributeTargets.Class | AttributeTargets.Method, AllowMultiple =
true)]
[Credit("John Smith", email="JohnB@xyzplant.com")]
public sealed class CreditAttribute : System.Attribute
{
    public string name;
    public string email;

    public CreditAttribute(string name)
    {
        this.name = name;
    }
```

Next we declare the `CreditAttribute` class. It is similar to the one we declared in the previous section,
except it has been extended to include four static methods used to display the credits for its classes and methods.

```
    public static void DisplayCredits(Assembly value)
    {
        // Display the credits for all exported types and methods
        // exposed by the assembly.
        Type[] ExportedTypes = value.GetExportedTypes();
        for(int i = ExportedTypes.GetLowerBound(0);
            i <= ExportedTypes.GetUpperBound(0); i++)
        {
            DisplayCredits(ExportedTypes[i]);

            // Display credits for all methods.
            MethodInfo[] Methods = ExportedTypes[i].GetMethods();
            for(int j = Methods.GetLowerBound(0);
                j <= Methods.GetUpperBound(0); j++)
            {
                DisplayCredits(Methods[j]);
            }
        }
    }
```

The `DisplayCredits` method accepts one parameter, a reference to an Assembly object. It then uses
reflection to iterate through all exported types and their methods. It then calls upon two overloaded versions
of the `DisplayCredits` method to write the credits to the console.

We first obtain the array of types (classes) exported by the assembly. Then we iterate through each type
calling an overloaded version of `DisplayCredits` responsible for displaying the credits for a particular
type. For each type, we obtain an array of methods exposed by the type and call an overloaded version of
`DisplayCredits` responsible for displaying the credits for a particular method.

```
public static void DisplayCredits(Type value)
{
    Object[]    custAttribs = value.GetCustomAttributes();
    string      credits = GetCredits(custAttribs);

    if(credits.Length > 0)
    {
        Console.WriteLine("\nCredits for type " + value.FullName + ":");
        Console.WriteLine(credits);
    }
}
```

This version of the DisplayCredits method is responsible for displaying the credits for a certain type. It does so by obtaining an array of custom attributes and passing that array to the GetCredits method. If there are credits associated with the type, we display a header and then the credits themselves.

```
public static void DisplayCredits(MethodInfo value)
{
    Object[]    custAttribs = value.GetCustomAttributes();
    string      credits = GetCredits(custAttribs);

    if(credits.Length > 0)
    {
        Console.WriteLine("\nCredits for method "
            + value.DeclaringType.FullName + "."
            + value.Name + ":");
        Console.WriteLine(credits);
    }
}
```

This version of the DisplayCredits method is responsible for displaying the credits for a certain method. It behaves similarly to the previous method with one exception: when the header is written to the console, we append the name of the method to the full name of the parent type. We call MethodInfo.DeclaringType to navigate to the Type object for the type that exposes the method and then we access its FullName property.

```
private static string GetCredits(Object[] value)
{
    string credits = "";

    for(int i = value.GetLowerBound(0);
        i <= value.GetUpperBound(0); i++)
    {
        if(value[i] is CreditAttribute)
        {
            CreditAttribute creditAttrib = (CreditAttribute)value[i];
            if(creditAttrib.email.Length > 0)
            {
                credits += creditAttrib.name
                    + " <" + creditAttrib.email + ">";
            }
            credits +="\n";
        }
    }
}
```

```
        return credits;
    }
}
```

GetCredits is a private method used by DisplayCredits. It accepts an array of objects and returns a formatted string containing the value of every CreditAttribute object in the array. It does so by iterating through the array until it encounters one of type CreditAttribute. It then casts the object to CreditAttribute and appends the name and email fields to the credit string. Once it has iterated through the entire array of objects, it returns the credits string to the caller.

When the above program is run with the /easteregg flag, the following output is produced:

```
Credits for type Demo:
Bob Smith <bob@xyzcompany.com>
Jill Jones <jill@xyzcompany.com>


Credits for method Demo.Method1:
Jill Jones <jill@xyzcompany.com>


Credits for method Demo.Method2:
Bob Smith <bob@xyzcompany.com>
Jill Jones <jill@xyzcompany.com>


Credits for type Application:
John Doe <john@firmxyz.com>


Credits for type CreditAttribute:
John Smith <JohnB@xyzplant.com>
```

As expected, the program displays the credits associated with each of the entities within the assembly.

Managed Data

Throughout this chapter we have talked about the behavior the CLR provides for managed code. One of the more important behaviors is the CLR's responsibility for managing the application's data. In this section we will dive into some of the important behaviors of the CLR as they relate to managed data. Specifically we look at how managed data is allocated on the managed heap and then we'll see how the Garbage Collector (GC) cleans up objects from the managed heap once they are no longer referenced by the application.

Managed Heap

The CLR introduces the concept of a managed heap. Recall that a heap is a region of one or more pages of reserved address space that can be subdivided and allocated into smaller chunks. The managed heap is a region of memory that is allocated and managed by the CLR. All managed objects (specifically, reference types) are allocated on the managed heap and the CLR is responsible for controlling access to these objects in a type safe manner. This is accomplished by only allowing managed code to directly access managed data.

One of the advantages of the managed heap is that memory allocations are very efficient. Typically when unmanaged code allocates memory on the heap, it scans through some sort of data structure looking for a free chunk of memory that is large enough to accommodate the allocation. The managed heap maintains a reference to the end of the most recent heap allocation. When a new object needs to be created on the heap, the CLR allocates memory on the top of memory that has previously been allocated and then increments the reference to the end of heap allocations accordingly. The following diagram represents this:

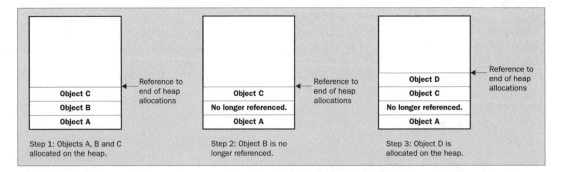

First, the CLR allocated memory for objects A, B, and C on the managed heap. Next the reference to object B was released by the application. Finally, memory for object D was allocated on top of the previously allocated memory (object C) and the reference to the end of the heap allocations was incremented accordingly.

You may be asking, "Sure allocations are fast, but what about memory fragmentation?" For example, the previous figure showed that object B is no longer referenced. However, memory for object D was allocated on top of the object C even if memory for object D could have instead been allocated between object A and C. Worse yet, after numerous allocations, there may not be sufficient memory on top of the managed heap to accommodate future requests. This is where the Garbage Collector comes in. If the CLR is unable to allocate memory on the managed heap, the Garbage Collector is invoked.

Garbage Collector

The Garbage Collector (GC) is responsible for removing objects from the heap that are no longer referenced, compacting the remaining allocations, and then finally resetting the reference to the end of the memory allocations on the heap. The GC may automatically be invoked by the CLR or the application may explicitly invoke the GC by calling `GC.Collect`.

The GC helps resolve many of the memory leak problems we are plagued with today. A memory leak occurs when memory is allocated by an application and is not freed after it is no longer needed by the application. As long as all references to the object are either implicitly or explicitly released by the application, the GC will take care of freeing the memory allocated to the object on the heap.

There are many scenarios that cause memory leaks in unmanaged code. For example, applications written using programming languages that allow the developer to explicitly allocate memory on the heap are vulnerable to memory leaks. A C++ application that allocates memory using the new operator must have a corresponding call to "free" or a memory leak would occur. However, memory allocated on the managed heap is always associated with an object. Since the GC collects the object after it is no longer referenced by the application, it is not possible for managed code to experience this type of memory leak.

Another scenario that causes memory leaks in unmanaged code is when two COM objects contain cyclical references. COM uses a reference counting mechanism to determine when an object should be released. Every time a reference to a COM object is obtained or released, the reference count is incremented or decremented accordingly. Once the reference count reaches zero, the COM object is responsible for releasing all resources and destroying itself.

One of the shortcomings of this mechanism is that cyclical references could cause objects to never be released. For example, say object A holds a reference to B and B holds a reference to A. Even if neither object is referenced by the application, the objects will not get destroyed because their reference count will never reach zero.

Since a managed object is not responsible for destroying itself, it does not need to maintain its own reference count. Instead the GC is responsible for cleaning up objects that are no longer referenced by the application. The GC determines which objects need to be cleaned up through a process of elimination.

The GC accomplishes this by leveraging the information the CLR maintains about the running application. The GC obtains a list of objects that are directly referenced by the application. Then for each of these "root" objects, it discovers all of the objects that are referenced by the "root" object. Once the GC has identified all objects directly and indirectly referenced by the application, the GC is free to clean up all remaining objects on the managed heap and compact the remaining objects. As the GC goes through a process of elimination when locating objects that are no longer referenced by the application, it is not possible for managed code to experience memory leaks caused by cyclical references.

Finalize

The GC calls the `Object.Finalize` method immediately before the object is collected. Reference types are able to override the `Finalize` method to perform any necessary cleanup. However, developers must be careful not to treat the `Finalize` method as if it were a destructor.

Destructors such as `Class_Terminate` in earlier versions of VB or `~MyClass` in VC++ do not have a functional equivalent in .NET. Since the GC has ultimate control over the lifetime of a managed object, there will more than likely be a delay between the time the object is no longer referenced by the application and when the GC collects it. Due to this, expensive resources that are released in the `Finalize` method may stay open longer than needed.

Another issue with relying on the `Finalize` method to perform necessary cleanup is that the GC will usually be triggered by low memory situations. Execution of the object's `Finalize` method will more than likely incur performance penalties due to page faults. Therefore the code path in the `Finalize` method should be as short and quick as possible.

All cleanup activities should be placed in the `Finalize` method. However, to ensure that resources are released in a timely fashion, objects that require timely cleanup should implement either a `Dispose` or a `Close` method. This method should be called by the client application just before setting the reference to null. So if you want to avoid having cleanup code execute during low memory situations, how can you get around this? You may also want to ensure that your cleanup code gets called. Your class can implement a `Dispose` method that can be called by the client when the object is no longer needed.

```
public class Demo : Object
{
    private bool m_disposed = false;

    public void Dispose()
```

```
    {
        if(! m_disposed)
        {
        // Call cleanup code in Finalize.
            Finalize();

            // Record that object has been disposed.
        m_disposed = true;

            // Finalize does not need to be called.
            GC.SuppressFinalize(this);
        }
    }

    protected override void Finalize()
    {
        // Perform cleanup here ...
    }
}
```

The Demo class overrides the Finalize method and implements code to perform any necessary cleanup. In this class, we are assuming that the cleanup code contained within the Finalize method should only be run once. We ensure that the Dispose method will only call Finalize once by checking the value of the private m_dispose property before calling Finalize and then setting it to True once Finalize has been called. We then call GC.SuppressFinalize to ensure that the GC does not call Finalize when the object is collected.

The primary advantage for centralizing all of the object's cleanup code in the Finalize method is to ensure that the object will be cleaned up properly before the GC collects it. The Finalize method serves as a safety net in case the Dispose or Close methods were not called before the GC collected the object. However, it is important to realize that if the GC has not collected the object before the application is terminated, the GC will not call the object's Finalize method. The following example demonstrates this behavior:

```
using System;
using System.Threading;

public class Demo : Object
{
    protected override void Finalize()
    {
        Console.WriteLine("Demo.Finalize was called.");
    }
}

public class Application
{
    public static int Main(string[] args)
    {
        // Demonstrate that the Finalize method is not called on App shutdown
        // by default.
        Demo myObject = new Demo();

        Console.WriteLine("Application is terminating.");
        return 0;
    }
}
```

The following output is displayed when the application is run:

```
Application is terminating.
```

Notice that since myObject was not collected prior to the application terminating, its Finalize method was not called. If code within your Finalize method must be called before the application terminates, you can call GC.RequestFinalizeOnShutdown. Calling this method at any time forces the GC to execute the Finalize method on every object before the application is terminated. We'll call GC.RequestFinalizeOnShutdown within the constructor:

```
public class Demo : Object
{
    public Demo()
    {
    GC.RequestFinalizeOnShutdown();
    }

    protected override void Finalize()
    {
        Console.WriteLine("Demo.Finalize was called.\n");
    }
}
```

Recompiling and executing our application produces the following output:

```
Application is terminating.
Demo.Finalize was called.
```

As you can see, Demo.Finalize was called before the application was terminated. However, think carefully before calling GC.RequestFinalizeOnShutdown within your applications: doing so can prolong the shutdown process of your application since the Finalize method must be called on every object within your application.

GC Optimizations

The .NET GC supports the concept of generations. The primary purpose of generations is to improve the performance of the GC. Garbage collection is an expensive operation. In general, it is more efficient to perform garbage collection over a portion of the managed heap as opposed to the entire managed heap.

Objects that have been recently created tend to have a higher probability of being garbage collected than objects that have been living on the system for quite some time. Generations provide an efficient mechanism for identifying recently-created objects versus long-lived objects. An object's generation is basically a counter indicating how many times it has successfully avoided garbage collection. In Visual Studio.NET Beta 1, an object's generation counter starts at zero and can have a maximum value of two. Let's take a look at an example that demonstrates this:

```
using System;

public class Application
{
    public static int Main(string[] args)
```

```
    {
        Object myObject = new Object();

        for(int i = 0; i < 4; i++)
        {
            Console.WriteLine(String.Format("Generation = {0}",
                GC.GetGeneration(myObject)));
            GC.Collect();
            GC.WaitForPendingFinalizers();
        }
    }
}
```

The code above creates an object and then iterates through a loop four times. For each loop, we display the current generation count for our object and then call the GC.

```
Generation = 0
Generation = 1
Generation = 2
Generation = 2
```

Each time the GC was run, the generation counter was incremented for myObject to a maximum of 2.

Recall that each time the GC is run, the managed heap is compacted and the reference to the end of the most recent memory allocation is updated. Afterwards, the objects of the same generation will be grouped together: generation two objects will be grouped at the bottom of the managed heap, followed by generation one objects. Since new, generation zero, objects are placed on top of the existing allocations, they will be grouped together as well.

So why is this significant? Recall that recently allocated objects have a higher probability of having shorter lives. Since objects on the managed heap are ordered according to generations, the GC can opt to collect newer objects. Obviously running the GC over a portion of the heap would be quicker than running it over the entire managed heap. You can ask the GC to execute with this behavior by passing a generation number to the GC.Collect method. The GC will then collect all objects no longer referenced by the application that belong to the specified generation or belong to a younger generation.

Another optimization is that a reference to an object may implicitly go out of scope and therefore be collected by the GC. Let's take a look at the following program:

```
public class Demo : Object
{
    public Demo()
    {
        Console.WriteLine("Demo.Demo was called on thread with hash code "
            + Thread.CurrentThread.GetHashCode());

        GC.RequestFinalizeOnShutdown();
    }

    protected override void Finalize()
    {
        Console.WriteLine("Demo.Finalize was called.");
    }
```

```
        }

public class Application
{
    public static int Main(string[] args)
    {
        // Create new object.
        Demo myObject = new Demo();

        // Force garbage collection.
        // Since myObject is no longer referenced,
        // it will be collected by the GC.
        GC.Collect();
        GC.WaitForPendingFinalizers();

        Console.WriteLine("Application terminating.");

        return 0;
    }
}
```

When the "release" version of the code is compiled and executed, the application produces the following output:

```
Demo.Finalize was called.
Application terminating.
```

myObject's Finalize method was called before the application terminated even though the reference to myObject was not explicitly released. Since myObject was never used by the application, it implicitly went out of scope as soon as it was created.

Pinning Objects

During compaction, objects will be moved to a lower place on the managed heap, filling the voids left by the collected objects. The GC is able to relocate these objects during runtime because the CLR maintains enough information about the code being executed to ensure that all references to the object are updated.

There are special circumstances where you may want to pass a pointer to an object on the managed heap to unmanaged code. However the pointer may become invalid if the GC relocates the object while compacting the heap. To prevent this from happening, you can ask the CLR to pin an object to a given place in memory before passing a pointer to it to unmanaged code. C++ developers do so explicitly using the __pin keyword and C# developers can use the fixed keyword. In C# it is impossible to obtain a "raw" pointer to an object on the managed heap without calling fixed.

IL Disassembler

One of the most handy tools that ships with the .NET SDK is the IL Disassembler (ildasm.exe). It is used to display the IL contained within a module. We will use the IL Disassembler to prove a previously made statement that the implementation of System.ValueType's Equals and GetHashCode methods use the Reflection API.

The IL Disassembler that shipped with the .NET PDC Tech Preview can be started by selecting Start | Programs | Microsoft .NET Framework SDK | IL Disassembler. Once the IL Disassembler has been launched, select File | Open and open mscorlib.dll. The PDC version can be found in the c:\winnt\compplus\v2000.14.1812 directory. Once mscorlib.dll has been loaded, expand the System folder, then the ValueType folder, and finally double click on the Equals method. A window similar to the one below should be displayed:

```
ValueType::Equals : bool(class System.Object)                          _ |□| x|
.method public hidebysig virtual instance bool
        Equals(class System.Object obj) il managed
{
  // Code size       136 (0x88)
  .maxstack  3
  .locals (class System.RuntimeType V_0,
           class System.RuntimeType V_1,
           class System.Object V_2,
           class System.Object V_3,
           class System.Object V_4,
           class System.Reflection.FieldInfo[] V_5,
           int32 V_6)
  IL_0000:  ldarg.1
  IL_0001:  brtrue.s   IL_000e
  IL_0003:  ldstr      "obj"
  IL_0008:  newobj     instance void System.ArgumentNullException::.ctor(clas
  IL_000d:  throw
  IL_000e:  ldarg.0
  IL_000f:  call       instance class System.Type System.Object::GetType()
  IL_0014:  castclass  System.RuntimeType
  IL_0019:  stloc.0
  IL_001a:  ldarg.1
  IL_001b:  call       instance class System.Type System.Object::GetType()
  IL_0020:  castclass  System.RuntimeType
  IL_0025:  stloc.1
  IL_0026:  ldloc.1
  IL_0027:  ldloc.0
```

The above window shows the IL for the Equal method. Notice that the Reflection API is used to navigate through the instance of the value type's fields to determine whether or not the values of the two objects being compared are equal.

As we have demonstrated, the IL Disassembler is a useful tool for learning about the implementation details of a particular module.

Summary

We've covered quite a bit of ground. We introduced the CLR and the services it provides to .NET applications. We also discussed why it is important to provide a common runtime and type system that can be targeted by multiple languages. We then discussed the three major entities of a .NET application:

❑   Assemblies

❑   Modules

❑   Types

We then dove into the CTS and discussed the two kinds of types supported by the CLR: reference types and value types. We learned about the differences between these two types and how each type is treated by the CLR, specifically:

❑ All types derive from `System.Object`.

❑ Releasing memory allocated on the stack for instances of unboxed value types when it goes out of scope is more efficient and – more than likely – more timely than releasing memory allocated on the stack for instances of reference types.

❑ A "boxed" value type behaves like a reference type and can be "unboxed" at any time.

❑ Explicitly "box" an instance of a value type before passing it multiple times to methods that accept `System.Object` parameters.

❑ Value types should override `Object.Equals` and `Object.GetHashCode` with a more efficient implementation than the one provided by `System.ValueType`.

Next we talked in depth about metadata. We discussed how metadata is used to make types "self describing". We looked at examples where metadata is used by the CLR and the .NET Class Library. Then we learned how to extend metadata by creating our own attributes. Finally, we briefly discussed the Reflection API.

Next we learned about the implementation details of managed data. We discussed how memory is efficiently allocated for objects on the managed heap. We then discussed how the GC locates and cleans up objects that are no longer referenced by the application. Next we discussed the `Finalize` method and why it should not be treated like a traditional object destructor, specifically:

❑ Perform all necessary cleanup in the `Finalize` method.

❑ Make the code path for the `Finalize` method as short and quick as possible.

❑ There is no way to accurately predict when an object no longer referenced by the application will be collected by the GC unless the GC is invoked explicitly.

❑ Whenever possible, do not implement the `Finalize` method in your class. `Finalize` is often called in low memory situations.

❑ If you implement the `Finalize` method, implement either a `Dispose` or a `Close` method that can be called by the client when the object is no longer needed.

❑ The order in which the GC collects objects on the managed heap is indeterminate. The `Finalize` method should not call methods on other objects referenced by the object being collected.

❑ There is no guarantee that the `Finalize` method will be called on an object unless `GC.RequestFinalizeOnShutdown` is called.

Finally, we reviewed the IL Disassembler utility (`ildasm.exe`). The IL Disassembler is used to display the IL contained within a module. We used the IL Disassembler to verify that the implementation of the `Equals` and `GetHashCode` methods overridden by `System.ValueType` does in fact use the Reflection API.

The next chapter will now move on to looking specifically at C#.

INTRODUCING.NETINTRODUCING.NETINTRODUCING.NETINTRODUCING.NE
ODUCING.NETINTRODUCING.NETINTRODUCING.NETINTRODUCI
ETINTRODUCING.NETINTRODUCING.NETINTRODUCING.NETINT
CING.NETINTRODUCING.NETINTRODUCING.NETINTRODUCING.N
NTRODUCING.NETINTRODUCING.NETINTRODUCING.NETINTROD
G.NETINTRODUCING.NETINTRODUCING.NETINTRODUCING.NET
ODUCING.NETINTRODUCING.NETINTRODUCING.NETINTRODUCI
ETINTRODUCING.NETINTRODUCING.NETINTRODUCING.NETINT
CING.NETINTRODUCING.NETINTRODUCING.NETINTRODUCING.
NTRODUCING.NETINTRODUCING.NETINTRODUCING.NETINTROD
G.NETINTRODUCING.NETINTRODUCING.NETINTRODUCING.NET
ODUCING.NETINTRODUCING.NETINTRODUCING.NETINTRODUCI
ETINTRODUCING.NETINTRODUCING.NETINTRODUCING.NETINT
CING.NETINTRODUCING.NETINTRODUCING.NETINTRODUCING.
NTRODUCING.NETINTRODUCING.NETINTRODUCING.NETINTROD
G.NETINTRODUCING.NETINTRODUCING.NETINTRODUCING.NET
ODUCING.NETINTRODUCING.NETINTRODUCING.NETINTRODUCI
ETINTRODUCING.NETINTRODUCING.NETINTRODUCING.NETINT
CING.NETINTRODUCING.NETINTRODUCING.NETINTRODUCING.
NTRODUCING.NETINTRODUCING.NETINTRODUCING.NETINTROD
G.NETINTRODUCING.NETINTRODUCING.NETINTRODUCING.NET
ODUCING.NETINTRODUCING.NETINTRODUCING.NETINTRODUCI
ETINTRODUCING.NETINTRODUCING.NETINTRODUCING.NETINT
CING.NETINTRODUCING.NETINTRODUCING.NETINTRODUCING.
NTRODUCING.NETINTRODUCING.NETINTRODUCING.NETINTROD
G.NETINTRODUCING.NETINTRODUCING.NETINTRODUCING.NET
ODUCING.NETINTRODUCING.NETINTRODUCING.NETINTRODUCI
ETINTRODUCING.NETINTRODUCING.NETINTRODUCING.NETINT
CING.NETINTRODUCING.NETINTRODUCING.NETINTRODUCING.
NTRODUCING.NETINTRODUCING.NETINTRODUCING.NETINTROD
G.NETINTRODUCING.NETINTRODUCING.NETINTRODUCING.NET
ODUCING.NETINTRODUCING.NETINTRODUCING.NETINTRODUCI
ETINTRODUCING.NETINTRODUCING.NETINTRODUCING.NETINT
CING.NETINTRODUCING.NETINTRODUCING.NETINTRODUCING.
NTRODUCING.NETINTRODUCING.NETINTRODUCING.NETINTROD
G.NETINTRODUCING.NETINTRODUCING.NETINTRODUCING.NET
ODUCING.NETINTRODUCING.NETINTRODUCING.NETINTRODUCI
ETINTRODUCING.NETINTRODUCING.NETINTRODUCING.NETINT

3

An Introduction to C#

In this chapter we will learn all about C#, and hopefully provide enough perspective so that you can understand C#'s role in enterprise development, and enough detailed information so that you can start coding your own C# applications and components immediately after reading it.

First, we'll discuss how C# relates to the .NET platform and the other .NET programming languages. Then we'll delve into the intricacies of C# syntax with a look at namespaces and datatypes. After exploring how flow is controlled in C# programs, we'll examine C#'s excellent object-oriented facilities. Finally, we'll conclude with a look ahead to C#'s bright future.

Trying out Code in this Chapter

The samples in this chapter are all relatively simplistic. If you want to try any of these out for yourself, then all you need is a text editor (Notepad is perfectly adequate), and a command prompt window. Simply type the code into Notepad, and save it with a `.cs` file extension in a folder somewhere on your system – for example, `c:\csharp`. Here's a basic `Hello World` example:

```
using System;
class test
{
    //This is a sample program.

    public static void Main()
    {
        string message = "hello";
        Console.WriteLine(message);
    }
}
```

Go to your command prompt, and go to the directory that you've just created, then type the following:

```
csc filename.cs
```

This will compile your code, and produce an executable of the same name in the same folder. All you then need to do to try out the code is type in the name of the executable, as shown below:

```
E:\WINNT\System32\cmd.exe

Microsoft Windows 2000 [Version 5.00.2195]
(C) Copyright 1985-2000 Microsoft Corp.

E:\>cd csharp

E:\csharp>csc test.cs
Microsoft (R) Visual C# Compiler Version 7.00.9030 [CLR version 1.00.2204.21]
Copyright (C) Microsoft Corp 2000. All rights reserved.


E:\csharp>test
hello

E:\csharp>_
```

The Sample Program – Life in C#

To illustrate the concepts presented in this chapter, many code samples have been taken from a C# implementation of John Conway's famous "Life" game. Life was chosen not only because it's fun and familiar, but also because an object-oriented implementation of it is a good opportunity to show off C#'s robust object-oriented facilities. In case you don't understand how Life works, a brief explanation of it will be provided later in this chapter.

You can download the code for this sample program from the Wrox website at http://www.wrox.com. Please remember that this code isn't meant to be the world's cleanest or cleverest implementation of Life, but a handy reference to as many C# features and idioms as could be put into one program.

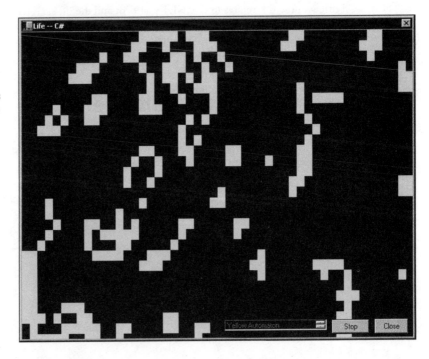

C# and Microsoft.NET

Now that we have the preliminaries out of the way, let's commence with our exploration of C#. We'll begin by investigating its relationships with the .NET framework and with three other programming languages.

A Concise, Elegant .NET Language

C# is a new programming language introduced with .NET. With C#, developers who prefer the elegance and conciseness of C-style syntax, or might already be familiar with Java or C++, can quickly implement applications and components that leverage the .NET Framework, are managed by the CLR (Common Language Runtime), and interoperate with components and application written in other .NET languages.

As C# integrates with the Visual Studio.NET IDE and supports its designers, you can use C# to code any of the types of .NET projects discussed elsewhere in this book, including:

- ❑ Console applications
- ❑ WinForm applications (Windows Applications)
- ❑ Web Form applications (Web Applications)
- ❑ ASP.NET applications (You can code ASP.NET pages in C#.)
- ❑ Web services
- ❑ Components (Class Libraries)
- ❑ Windows controls (These controls can be used on WinForms.
- ❑ Web controls (These controls can be used on Web Forms.
- ❑ Windows services

C# and C++

C# Compiles to Managed Code

C++ is C#'s closest relative. In fact, you can regard C# as a simpler, safer subset of Visual C++ for creating "managed" code.

By default, Visual C++ source code compiles to native machine code commands that are executed directly by a host computer's microprocessor. However, C# source code compiles to a higher-level Intermediate Language ("IL") that is compiled and monitored by the CLR at runtime. The CLR authenticates managed code and provides services that managed code can leverage.

C# is Simpler than C++

C# is simpler than C++, because C# makes it relatively easy to create graphical user interfaces and re-usable components. Like the other .NET languages that support WinForms, C# allows you to define windows simply by dragging controls from a toolbox onto forms and writing code to handle the controls' events. Similarly, when you create components, the C# compiler automatically outfits your components with the necessary hooks that clients need in order to plug into them, freeing you from the complexities of COM and ATL.

C# is Safer than C++

C# is safer, because it prohibits certain C++ idioms that tended to cause bugs. These prohibited idioms include (among others): preprocessor macros, fall-through `switch...case` statements, and pointers. That's right; in C#, there are no pointers, only references. As the CLR's garbage collector assumes the responsibility of periodically re-allocating the memory space once occupied by C# objects that are no longer referenced, your C# programs are safe from memory leaks. We will return to look at the garbage collector in a moment.

Embedding C++ in C#

If you want to use prohibited C++ idioms in your C# code because you need their power, and you're willing to assume the risk of bugs that using them entails, you can do so in blocks of C++ code prefaced with C#'s `unsafe` keyword. You can use `unsafe` to modify simple code blocks, methods in classes, or individual statements. Code in `unsafe` blocks still interacts with the CLR; `unsafe` only implies that the code uses idioms normally deemed dangerous by the C# compiler, and that the CLR is not able to verify such code.

The following code snippet demonstrates the use of the `unsafe` keyword. A function, `Summation`, uses pointers to calculate the sum of all integers from 1 to the value of the input argument. The line that invokes this function also uses the `unsafe` keyword to make the reference operator acceptable.

```
using System;
class UnsafeSample
{
    //This "unsafe" method uses pointers.
    unsafe static int Summation(int* number)
    {
        return (*number)*((*number)+1)/2;
    }

    public static void Main()
    {
        int i = 100;
        int j;

        //This "unsafe" statement uses
        //the address-of operator.
        unsafe j=Summation(&i);
        Console.WriteLine(j);
    }
}
```

As mentioned earlier, automatic garbage collection is one of the services provided by the CLR. For efficiency, the garbage collector periodically "compacts" memory, re-allocating active objects to contiguous blocks. If you use pointers in unsafe code blocks to refer to objects, you need a way to "pin" the objects to which they point so that the garbage collector won't re-allocate the objects out from under them. The `fixed` keyword allows you to do this. As an example, the following snippet of code creates an instance of `SomeClass`, a simple class with a single data member, and then manipulates the value of the instance's data member through a pointer modified with `fixed`.

```
using System;
```

```
class SomeClass
{
    public int DataMember;
}
class FixedSample
{
    public static void Main()
    {
        SomeClass obj=new SomeClass();
        obj.DataMember=5;
        Console.WriteLine(obj.DataMember);

        unsafe
        {
            fixed (int *   j=&(obj.DataMember))
            *j=10;
        }

        Console.WriteLine(obj.DataMember);
        Console.ReadLine();

    }
}
```

Managed C++

.NET extends Visual C++ with a set of keywords and header files for accessing elements of the CLR, such as the garbage collector from plain C++ code. These "extensions" allow you to reference .NET components from C++ applications, to quickly expose legacy COM components written in C++ as .NET components, and to create applications and components that combine passages of managed and unmanaged code.

C# Installs with Visual C++

This chapter was written using the beta one version of Visual Studio.NET. At least with that version, you have to install Visual C++ in order to invoke C# from the Visual Studio.NET IDE.

C# and Visual Basic

With .NET, VB's capabilities have expanded to include such advanced features as parameterized constructors, operator overloading, and attributes. Aside from its somewhat cleaner and more concise syntax, C# offers only one major technical advantage over Visual Basic.NET: the aforementioned support of unsafe blocks of pure C++. When deciding between C# and Visual Basic.NET, consider whether C#'s syntactical elegance and its support of unsafe code blocks are important to you.

C# and Java

Functionally equivalent passages of Java code and C# code resemble each other, probably because both languages are modernizations of C++. C#, however, retains some powerful C++ idioms that Java does not have, such as typesafe enumerations and operator overloading.

In addition to this, there are other factors that an organization choosing between Java and C# should consider. As C# leverages the .NET runtime, it can interoperate with code written in other .NET programming languages, such as Visual Basic.NET. Alternatively, a Java project necessitates that the entire development team start coding in the Java language, and this migration is typically an expensive process, involving re-training and/or new hires. However, because C# requires the .NET runtime and that runtime has not yet been implemented for non-Windows platforms, C# is not platform-independent – at least not at this time.

To put it briefly, you need to decide whether language interoperability or platform independence is more important to you, keeping in mind that platform independence may be in .NET's future.

Datatypes in C#

Now that we understand C#'s relationship with .NET and other programming languages, let's delve into the intricacies of C# coding. We'll begin our exploration with a look at C#'s datatypes, the structures that store the information that we want to manipulate.

Namespaces

Like other .NET languages, C# leverages the datatypes defined in the .NET base class library. These classes are grouped into "namespaces"; logical containers for classes that provide similar functionality. The `System.WinForms` namespace, for instance, defines controls and classes for creating WinForm applications.

A namespace is expressed as a series of words separated by periods. Often, the first word in a namespace is the name of the organization in which the classes were developed. By assigning classes to namespaces, we effectively give them long names, and thus are able to distinguish between two classes with the same name from different vendors when those classes are used within the same program. We'll wrap the classes in our Life application in a namespace.

```
namespace Harvey.Automata.AutomataClasses
{
    //Class definitions will go here.
}
```

The `using` keyword makes life easier for client programmers who use server classes that are stored in namespaces. Once a namespace is listed in a `using` statement, subsequent lines of code can refer to classes in that namespace via their short, relative names. Thus, the `using` keyword saves client programmers' keystrokes. Handily, it also provides a nice list at the top of a file to which later programmers can refer for a quick idea of the file's dependencies. Clients of our Life application might abbreviate our namespace in this way:

```
using Harvey.Automata.AutomataClasses;
```

Please note that, contrary to popular belief, the `using` keyword doesn't do any compile-time linking between modules. Such linking is the role of the references list as maintained in the References Dialog of the IDE. Again, the `using` keyword just saves keystrokes and provides a handy dependencies list.

Interestingly, the `using` keyword can also be used to alias types. The following sample code aliases the `System.Int32` type with a new name, `IntegerAlias`.

```
using IntegerAlias=System.Int32;

public class UsingExample
{
    public static IntegerAlias Main()
    {
        IntegerAlias i=1;
        IntegerAlias j=i+1;
        System.Console.WriteLine(j);

        return 0;
    }
}
```

The System Namespace

The Common Language Specification (CLS) describes a set of datatypes that a programming language must support in order to be considered .NET-compliant. This rich set of datatypes is very useful, and includes dedicated types for Boolean, string, integer, chronological, and financial values. These types are stored in the System namespace. C# supports these datatypes and aliases them with names that will feel familiar to C/C++ programmers.

Datatype	Description	Range
bool	Boolean type for True/False values.	True or False
byte	8-bit unsigned integer type.	0 to 255
char	Unicode (2-byte) character type.	Not applicable
decimal	Monetary type for financial calculations.	Approx. 1.0×10^{28} to 7.9×10^{28}
double	Floating point type.	Approx. $\pm 5.0 \times 10^{324}$ to $\pm 1.7 \times 10^{308}$
float	Floating point type.	Approx. $\pm 1.5 \times 10^{45}$ to $\pm 3.4 \times 10^{38}$
int	32-bit signed integer type.	-2,147,483,648 to 2,147,483,647
long	64-bit signed integer type.	-9,223,372,036,854,775,808 to 9,223,372,036,854,775,807
object	Type from which all others inherit.	Not applicable
sbyte	8-bit signed integer type.	-128 to 127
short	16-bit signed integer type.	-32,768 to 32,767
string	Type for strings of Unicode characters.	Not applicable
struct	A value type.	Not applicable
uint	32-bit unsigned integer type.	0 to 4,294,967,295
ulong	64-bit unsigned integer type.	0 to 18,446,744,073,709,551,615
ushort	16-bit unsigned integer type.	0 to 65,535

All of the types inherit from the object type. Thus, an object reference can be used to hold a reference to a variable of any specific type.

The size of the long type has been expanded to 64-bits to prepare for the introduction of the new 64-bit Windows operating system. There are signed and unsigned versions of each of the integer types.

All of the types define "objects" in the academic sense; the types have built-in methods that you can call for formatting and type conversions.

Value Types and Reference Types

Every class created with or used by a .NET language can be categorized as a **value type** or a **reference type**. Value types and reference types differ in two characteristics: where they are stored in memory, and how they behave in the context of assignment statements.

Value types are stored on the stack, and assignment statements between two value variables result in two separate, but identical, copies of the value in memory. Reference types are stored on the heap, and an assignment statement between two reference variables results in two references to a single value at one location in memory. We looked at this briefly in the previous chapter.

In the following code sample, an assignment of one value type to another creates two separate copies of the same value in memory.

```
using System;
public class SimpleClass
{
    public static int Main()
    {
        int i;
        int j;
        i=5;
        j=i;

        Console.WriteLine("i=" + i);
        Console.WriteLine("j=" + j);

        unsafe
        {
            if (&i==&j)
                Console.WriteLine
                    ("i and j have the same address.");
            else
                Console.WriteLine
                    ("i and j have different addresses.");
        }

        Console.ReadLine();
        return 0;
    }
}
```

In contrast, the next code sample shows an assignment between two reference values, the result of which is the creation of two references to a single copy of a value (the object) in memory.

```
using System;

public class ReferenceType
{
    public int DataMember;
}

public class SimpleClass
{


    public static int Main()
    {
        ReferenceType i;
        ReferenceType j;

        i=new ReferenceType();
        i.DataMember=5;
        j=i;

        Console.WriteLine
        ("i.DataMember=" + i.DataMember);
        Console.WriteLine
        ("j.DataMember=" + j.DataMember);
        unsafe
        {
            if (i==j)
                Console.WriteLine
                ("i and j have the same address.");
            else
                Console.WriteLine
                ("i and j have different addresses.");
        }

        Console.ReadLine();
        return 0;
    }
}
```

Most of the types that were "primitives" (simple, non-object types) in C++ are value types in C#: the integer types are value types, for instance. Classes that you create are reference types. Be aware that the `struct` type is a value type.

Now let's look at the syntax for instantiating value types and reference types in C#.

Instantiating Value Types

For value types, C# possesses the flexible syntax for declaration and initialization that C and C++ programmers know and love.

For clarity, you can create one variable per declaration statement. Alternatively, you can create several variables at the same time.

```
//A simple declaration
int i;
```

```
//A compound declaration
int x,y,z;
```

In compound declaration statements, you can initialize as many or as few of the variables as you want with a starting value.

```
//A simple declaration and initialization.
int i=5;
```

```
//A compound declaration and initialization.
int x=3,y,z=-2;
```

In fact, C# is so flexible that, like C and C++, it will allow you to create a variable, initialize it, and use it as the counter variable in a `for` loop all in a single line of code.

```
for (int j=0; j<5; j++)
```

To reduce bugs, the C# compiler will flag any variables in your code whose values are referenced before the variables have been initialized with starting values. This prevents any leftover values in memory that may not have been cleaned up by the operating system from interfering with the execution of your program. As an example, try compiling the following program.

```
using System;
public class ForcedInit
{
    public static int Main()
    {
        int k;
        Console.WriteLine(k);
    return 0;
    }
}
```

As variable k has not been provided with an initial value, the C# compiler will generate an error.

```
error CS0165: Use of unassigned local variable 'k'
```

To compile the program successfully, you'll have to initialize k with a starting value.

```
using System;
public class ForcedInit
{
    public static int Main()
    {
        int k=0;    //k is now initialized
        Console.WriteLine(k);
    return 0;
    }
}
```

Instantiating Reference Types

Creating an instance of a reference type requires the use of C#'s new keyword. When applied to a particular type, the new keyword creates an instance of the type on the heap and returns a reference to the instance so that you can store that reference in a variable. Then, throughout the program, you manipulate that object through that reference variable.

```
using System;

public class ReferenceType
{
    public int DataMember;
}

public class SimpleClass
{
    public static int Main()
    {
        ReferenceType objA;

        //The new keyword instantiates a ReferenceType
        objA=new ReferenceType();
        objA.DataMember=5;

        return 0;
    }
}
```

It's possible to create several different references to the same object.

```
public static int Main()
{
    ReferenceType objA;
    ReferenceType objB;
    ReferenceType objC;

    objA=new ReferenceType();
    objA.DataMember=5;
    //Here, we make objB and objC reference the
    //same instance of ReferenceType that objA does.
    objB=objA;
    objC=objA;

    return 0;
}
```

Once you have a reference to an object, you can destroy that reference by assigning it the value of null. Be aware that an object will persist in memory until all references to that object have been destroyed, and although inaccessible, will remain allocated until the next time the CLR's garbage collector does its work.

```
public static int Main()
{
    ReferenceType objA;
```

```
    //This instantiates a ReferenceType object and
    //assigns objA as a reference to it.
    objA=new ReferenceType();

    //This removes the only reference to the object,
    //preparing it for de-allocation by the garbage
    //collector.
    objA=null;

    return 0;
}
```

Periodically, the CLR's garbage collector de-allocates the space occupied by objects that are no longer referenced.

Type Conversions

To promote bug-free programs, C# is "strongly-typed". This means that conversions between variables of different types do not occur implicitly, but instead must be explicitly requested. The `bool` type, for instance, does not implicitly convert to an `int` type; you must request such a conversion in your code. This stringency forces you to consider the consequences of conversions between types, and avoids unintentional conversions that cause hard-to-find problems.

As an example, try to compile the following sample program.

```
using System;
public class Conversion1{
    public static int Main()
    {
        bool blnInstance;
        int i,j;

        blnInstance=true;
        i=blnInstance;
        blnInstance=false;
        j=blnInstance;

        Console.WriteLine(i);
        Console.WriteLine(j);

        return 0;
    }
}
```

You'll get this error:

```
error CS0029: Cannot implicitly convert type 'bool' to 'int'
```

In order for the program to work correctly, it will have to explicitly request type conversions between the `bool` variable and the two `int` variables. The `bool` type's `ToInt32` method allows us to do this.

```
using System;
public class Conversion1{
    public static int Main()
    {
        bool blnInstance;
        int i,j;

        blnInstance=true;
        i=blnInstance.ToInt32();
        blnInstance=false;
        j=blnInstance.ToInt32();
        Console.WriteLine(i);
        Console.WriteLine(j);
        return 0;
    }
}
```

Boxing and Unboxing

Conversions between value and reference types are possible. The conversion of a value type on the stack to a reference type on the heap is known as "boxing". Conversely, the conversion of a reference type on the heap to a value type on the stack is known as "unboxing".

In the following example, an int variable on the stack is boxed as an object variable on the heap, and then unboxed as another int variable on the stack. As this example shows, you accomplish boxing and unboxing by using a C-style cast, in which the parenthesized name of the target type precedes the variable that is being converted.

```
using System;
public class BoxingExample {
    public static int Main()
    {
        object objA;
        int j;

        //"i" is a value variable on the stack.
        int i=10;

        //This boxes "i" as a reference value on the heap.
        objA=(object)i;

        //This unboxes the reference value on the heap as
        //as an int value variable on the stack.
        j=(int)objA;

        Console.WriteLine(j);
        return 0;
    }
}
```

When unboxing a value, you have to make sure that the type on the stack is capable of containing the value on the heap. In the following program, for instance, the attempt to unbox an int value to a byte value will generate a runtime error. You need to exercise the same care in boxing and unboxing that you exercise in ordinary casting between value types.

```
using System;
public class BoxingExample {
   public static int Main()
   {
       int i=10;

       object objA;
       byte j;

       objA=(object)i;
       j=(byte)objA;

       Console.WriteLine(j);
       Console.ReadLine();

       return 0;
   }
}
```

Arrays

C# introduces a new syntax for handling arrays.

In one approach to array creation, you initialize the array with values at the same time that you declare it, using curly braces and an initialization list.

```
using System;

public class ArrayExample
{
   public static int Main()
   {
       //This declares AND initializes the array.
       int[] aryInt={1,2,3};
       return 0;
   }
}
```

This approach can be applied to the creation of multidimensional arrays as well.

```
using System;

public class ArrayExample
{
   public static int Main()
   {
       //This creates and initializes a 2-D array.
       int[,] aryInt=
       {
           {1,2,3},
           {4,5,6},
           {7,8,9}
       };

       return 0;
   }
}
```

Alternatively, you can declare an array to be of an indeterminate size and set its dimensions later using the new keyword. In our Life program, for example, one of our classes, the Automaton class, will possess a two-dimensional array of values ("cells") as a data member. In our class definition, we'll declare this array without specifying its size.

```
abstract public class Automaton
{
    protected bool[,] m_blnCell;
```

Later, in the class's constructor function, we can dynamically allocate the array with specific dimensions:

```
protected Automaton(int rows, int cols)
{
    m_intAge=0;
    m_intPopulation=0;
    m_intRows=rows;
    m_intColumns=cols;

    //Here, the array is dynamically dimensioned and
    //allocated.
    m_blnCell=new bool[m_intRows,m_intColumns];
}
```

Just in case you're wondering, C# permits "orthogonal" or "jagged" arrays: multidimensional arrays in which the number of columns varies from row to row. Creating an orthogonal array in C# is really a matter of creating an array *of* arrays. The following program, for instance, creates a "diagonal matrix" in which the first row has 1 column, the second has two columns, and the third has three.

```
using System;
public class ArrayExample
{
    public static int Main()
    {
        int[][] aryInt=new int[3][];
        aryInt[0]=new int[1];    //1 column in row 1
        aryInt[1]=new int[2];    //2 columns in row 2
        aryInt[2]=new int[3];    //3 columns in row 3
        return 0;
    }
}
```

All C# arrays inherit from the System.Array type, which provides some useful functionality in the form of class methods. In the following program, class methods on the System.Array type are used to reverse the elements in an array of integers and then re-sort them in ascending order.

```
using System;

public class ArrayExample
{
    public static int Main()
    {
        //Print out the elements in ascending order.
```

```
        int[] aryInt={1,2,3};
        foreach(int j in aryInt)
           Console.Write(j);

        //Reverse the elements and print them out.
        Array.Reverse(aryInt);
        Console.WriteLine();
        foreach(int j in aryInt)
           Console.Write(j);

        //Sort the elements and print them out.
        Array.Sort(aryInt);
        Console.WriteLine();
        foreach(int j in aryInt)
           Console.Write(j);

        Console.ReadLine();

        return 0;
    }
}
```

Enumerations

An enumeration is a custom integer type. When you declare an enumeration, you specify a set of values that an instance of that type can contain. In our Life program, for example, we define an enumeration, FormStateEnum, to represent the acceptable states that the user interface can be in.

```
    private enum FormStateEnum { StoppedState=0, StartedState=1, FrozenState=2 }
```

Once this enumeration is defined, we can use it to declare a data member that represents the state of the user interface (we'll talk more about this technique later).

```
    public class WinFormDisplay : System.WinForms.Form
    {
        private FormStateEnum m_enumFormState;
```

Enumerations make your code more correct by leveraging the compiler's power to flag attempted assignments of illegal values to enumeration variables. Enumerations make it easier to write code because IntelliSense can pop-up lists of acceptable enumerated values when you write assignment statements. Enumerations make your code more understandable because enumerated values can be referred to by intuitive names.

Constants

Sometimes it's necessary to provide a class with variables whose values are unchanging, or "constant." In our Life program, for instance, we want to provide client programmers with a couple of variables representing the maximum numbers of rows and columns that a matrix of cells can contain. As we don't want client programmers to change these variables' values, we can specify these variables as constants by prefacing their declarations with the const keyword.

```
abstract public class Automaton
{
    public const int MAX_ROWS=50;
    public const int MAX_COLS=100;
```

Containers

The `System.Collections` namespace provides ready-made container classes in the form of collections, queues, hash tables, and dictionaries. A single instance of one of these classes can contain objects of many different types. Furthermore, C# provides a set of interfaces for creating your own "type-specific" container classes that use early binding to maintain lists of objects of particular types.

You can iterate through objects in container classes using the `foreach` loop, which we'll discuss shortly.

Control Flow in C#

Now that we understand C# datatypes, let's look at the mechanisms for controlling how the thread-of-execution moves through C# programs.

Functions

Functions are one idiom that affect how control flows through a program. There are three principal reasons for creating a function:

❑ To package functionality that is likely to be re-used

❑ to centralize functionality that is likely to change

❑ To group confusing code under a friendly, intuitive name that helps to explain what the code does

Defining Functions

C# function definitions are just what you'd expect from a C-style language. Briefly, a C# function definition consists of a signature specifying the function's return type, name, and input parameters, followed by a block of code containing the function's implementation. Inside the body of the function, the `return` keyword denotes points at which the thread-of-execution can exit.

In C#, every function that you create is associated with a class. However, it is possible to create a static method, a function that can be called on the class itself rather than on an instance of the class. This allows you to call the function without creating an object. The .NET base class library delivers much of its functionality through static methods, such as those on the `System.Array` class, which we looked at previously.

The following code snippet defines a function, `Max`, that accepts two integer values and returns the greater of the two. The static keyword makes `Max` a "class method".

```
public static int Max(int Value1, int Value2) {
    int ReturnValue;
    if (Value2>Value1)
        ReturnValue=Value2;
```

```
    else
        ReturnValue=Value1;
    return ReturnValue;
}
```

Activating Functions

Like C# function definitions, C# function activations ("calls") are just what you'd expect from a C-style language. A C# function call consists of the name of the function that is being called followed by a set of parentheses containing input parameters that match those specified in the function's definition.

The following short program shows how the Max function introduced above could be activated.

```
using System;
public class FunctionSample
{
    public static int Max(int Value1, int Value2) {

        int ReturnValue;
        if (Value2>Value1)
            ReturnValue=Value2;
        else
            ReturnValue=Value1;
        return ReturnValue;
    }


    public static int Main(string[] args)
    {
        int k;
        k=Max(1,2);        //This line activates Max()
        Console.WriteLine(k);
        return 0;
    }
}
```

Function Parameters

In C# functions, value type parameters are passed by value, while reference type parameters are passed by reference. In practical terms, this means that, by default, changes that a function makes to a value type input parameter are only changes to a *copy* of the value that was passed in, and do not affect the value of the variable that was used as parameter in the function activation.

Perhaps a code sample expresses this concept more eloquently. In the following short program, the value of variable x remains as 10, even after the activation of the ChangeValue function, because ChangeValue's input parameter is passed by value – ChangeValue works on a *copy* of x's data.

```
using System;
public class ByValSample
{

    public static void ChangeValue(int y)
    {
        y=20;
```

```
        return;
    }

    public static int Main()
    {
        int x=10;

        Console.WriteLine("Before call,x="+x);
        ChangeValue(x);
        Console.WriteLine("After call,x="+x);
        Console.ReadLine();

        return 0;
    }
}
```

If you want to override C#'s default behavior and pass value type objects by reference, you can use C#'s ref keyword. Prefacing a formal argument in a function definition with the ref keyword specifies that the input argument will be passed by reference, so changes to the input parameter inside the function will change the value of the variable that was passed in.

In the following code sample, ChangeValue is able to change x's value from 10 to 20, because x is passed to ChangeValue by reference. ChangeValue's formal input argument refers to the same memory address that x does. A note on syntax: the ref keyword is required not only in the function declaration, but in the activation statement as well.

```
using System;
public class ByRefSample
{

    public static void ChangeValue(ref int  y)
    {
        y=20;
        return;
    }

    public static int Main()
    {
        int x=10;

        Console.WriteLine("Before call,x="+x);
        ChangeValue(ref x);
        Console.WriteLine("After call,x="+x);
        Console.ReadLine();

        return 0;
    }
}
```

Earlier, I said that the C# compiler will prevent you from referencing a variable's value before you have initialized that variable with a starting value. In most circumstances this is an excellent safety feature, but it would be very inconvenient to initialize a variable that is going to be passed as a by reference argument to a function. Prefacing an input argument in a function with C#'s out keyword allows that argument to be passed by reference, and prevents the C# compiler from complaining that it has not yet been initialized. Here's another version of the "ChangeValue" program, demonstrating how the out keyword can be implemented.

```
using System;
public class OutSample
{

    public static void ChangeValue(out int  y)
    {
       y=20;
       return;
    }

    public static int Main()
    {
       int x;

       ChangeValue(out x);
       Console.WriteLine("After call,x="+x);
       Console.ReadLine();

       return 0;
    }
}
```

A third keyword, params, allows you to create functions that can be called with a variable number of input arguments. To use the params feature, you simply define your function as receiving an array as an input argument and modify that input argument with the params keyword. Values passed to the function will be passed as elements in the array.

You might, for instance, create a function called Min() that receives several values and returns the smallest of them. In some cases, you could pass Min() two arguments, in other cases, you might pass it twelve.

```
public class MinClass
{
    //This method accepts a variable number of arguments
    public static int Min(params int[] values)
    {
       int intMin=-1;
       if (values.Length>0)
          intMin=values[0];

       for (int i=1;i<values.Length;i++)
       {
          if (values[i]<intMin)
             intMin=values[i];
       }

       return intMin;

    }

    public static int Main(string[] args)
    {
       int j,k;

       //Here, Min() is called with 2 input args
```

```
        j=Min(5,4);

        //Here Min() is called with 12 input args
        k=Min(5,4,3,2,1,3,5,6,7,5,100,-3);

        Console.WriteLine(j);
        Console.WriteLine(k);
        Console.ReadLine();

        return 0;
    }
}
```

If you run this program, you should get the following result:

Program Entry Point

Every C# WinForm application and every C# Console application must have a single class containing a single function that matches the following signature:

```
public static void Main(string[] args){
    //...
}
```

When a C# application is invoked, the CLR starts the thread-of-execution at the function matching this signature, passing any command line options to the program as elements of the string[] args array. The string[] args array is optional.

Conditionals

Conditional statements are another way in which a thread-of-execution can move between a program's branches. When writing conditional statements and expressions in C#, there are a couple of things of which you should be aware.

❑   C# conditionals are "short-circuiting". If you come to a language without short-circuiting conditionals – such as VB6 (although not Visual Basic.NET) – this behavior might throw you. Basically, if a predicate that participates in a compound AND expression evaluates to False, C# doesn't waste any time evaluating any of the rest of the expression because it cannot possibly evaluate to True. If one of the latter predicates is a function call and the expression short-circuits on an earlier, False predicate, the function won't be activated.

85

❏   As mentioned earlier, C#'s integer and Boolean types do not implicitly convert. This implies that you shouldn't write functions that return integer values and then treat the return values of those statements as if they were Booleans. (Writing functions that return false if they fail is a dangerous practice anyway, because it's all too easy for client programmers to forget to check the return values and then wonder why their programs don't work. The proper procedure is to use .NET's built in exception mechanism, and throw an error if a function fails).

Operators

C# provides several operators that can be used in conditional expressions.

Operator	Meaning
==	Equality operator
!=	Inequality operator
&&	Logical AND operator
||	Logical OR operator

if statements

C# if statements work just like if statements in C and C++. If the expression in the parentheses to the right of an if keyword evaluates to True, the statement or block of statements immediately following the if statement is executed.

```
if (ExpressionA)
{
    //The code in this block will execute if
// ExpressionA evaluates to "true."
}
```

C# also supports the else keyword so that you can link mutually exclusive if conditions together to express more complex logic.

```
if (ExpressionA)
{
    //This code executed if ExpressionA
    //evaluates to "true."
}
else if (ExpressionB)
{
    //This code executes if ExpressionA
    //evaluates to "false" and ExpressionB
    //evaluates to "true."
}
else
{
    //This code executes if both ExpressionA
    //and ExpressionB evaluate to "false."
}
```

Watch out for the classic error of following an `if` statement with a semicolon – this will disassociate the `if` statement from the code that it is intended to activate, causing that code to be executed regardless of whether the conditional expression is `True` or `False`. For example, in the following code, the misplaced semicolon in the `if` statement causes the block below the `if` statement to be executed, even though `ExpressionA` is `False`.

```csharp
public static int Main(string[] args)
{
    bool ExpressionA=false;
    if (ExpressionA); //The semicolon is misplaced here
    {
        Console.WriteLine("ExpressionA is true");
        Console.ReadLine();
    }

    return 0;
}
```

And yes, fans of concise C code, C# supports the ternary operator, a short-hand form of the `if...else` construction.

```csharp
//This is the longhand form of an if...else statement.
if (ExpressionA)
{
    j=FunctionA();
}
else
{
    j=FunctionB();
}

//This is the same if...else statement abbreviated with
//the ternary operator.
j=ExpressionA?FunctionA():FunctionB();
```

switch...case statements

`switch...case` statements work the same way in C# as they do in C and C++: they allow you to examine the value of a variable and take one of several possible courses of action based on that value. In this sample program, one of four messages is printed, based on the value of the `intValue` variable that is the subject of the `switch...case` statement.

```csharp
using System;
public class SwitchCaseDemo
{

public static int Main(string[] args)
{
    int intValue=1;

    switch (intValue)
    {
        case 1:
            Console.WriteLine(
```

```
              "The value of intValue is 1");
           break;
        case 2:
           Console.WriteLine(
           "The value of intValue is 2");
           break;
        case 3:
           Console.WriteLine(
           "The value of intValue is 3");
           break;
        default:
           Console.WriteLine(
           "The value is neither 1,2, nor 3");
           break;
     }

     Console.ReadLine();
     return 0;
   }
}
```

If you've spent much time programming in C or in C++, then you've probably committed the error of forgetting to equip a case statement (except for the last case statement) with a following break statement. When such a case statement is activated, program control "falls-through" the activated case statement to the one beneath it, executing the statements in that case block as well. Expert programmers can sometimes use this behavior profitably, but in most instances, "fall-through" case statements are unintentional errors, and they're *always* hard for maintenance programmers to interpret.

To help prevent such errors, the C# compiler requires that every case statement in every switch...case block be terminated with a break statement. case statements not equipped with break statements will be flagged as errors. As an example, remove the break statement from the case 1 statement in the sample program.

```
switch (intValue)
{
   case 1:
      Console.WriteLine(
      "The value of intValue is 1");
      //Note: the break statement has been removed.
   case 2:
...
```

When you try to compile this code, the C# compiler will respond with an error message.

```
error CS0163: Control cannot fall through from one case label ('case 1:') to
another
```

If you want to intentionally duplicate "fall-through" behavior, you can do so by using labels and goto statements cleverly, but such hacks are in bad style and generally suggest a need to rethink the code.

As demonstrated in the sample code, the default keyword allows you to equip a switch statement with a branch of code that will be activated if no case clause is activated.

```
default:
    Console.WriteLine(
    "The value is neither 1,2, nor 3");
    break;
```

Loops

In addition to sequencing and selection, iteration is another way of controlling how the thread-of-control moves through a computer program. Here, we'll discuss the types of loops that C# provides for implementing iteration.

while loops

C#'s while loops are just like while loops in C, C++, or VB.

A "pre-test" loop, a while's expression is evaluated and the statement (simple or compound) below it is executed if the value is determined to be True. At the end of the statement's execution, the expression is evaluated again. The statement is repeatedly executed until the while's conditional expression evaluates to false, or until a break statement is encountered, or until the program terminates.

```
while(ExpressionA)
{
    //Code here will be executed until ExpressionA
    //evaluates to false.
}
```

do...while loops

The do...while loop is much like the while loop except that it is a "post-test" loop. In practical terms, this means that the statement contained within the do...while loop is always executed at least once. After that initial execution, the statement continues to execute for as long as the specified condition evaluates to True, or until a break statement is encountered, or until the program terminates.

```
do
{
    //Code here will be executed at least once, and will
    //be repeated until ExpressionA evaluates to false.
} while(ExpressionA)
```

for loops

for loops are useful for repeating a simple or compound statement for a predetermined number of times.

```
for(i=0; i<5; i++)
{
    //Code here will be repeated for each increment of i until
    //i has the value of 5
}
```

On entering the loop, i is set to 0 and the conditional statement is tested. If it's true, the code within the loop is executed and the value of i is incremented. The next time the loop is executed, the condition is tested again. As soon as the value of i does not meet the condition, the loop is exited, and execution continues.

An interesting bit of minutiae: you can create an infinite loop with the following `for` statement.

```
for(;;);
```

foreach loops

The `foreach` loop allows you to iterate through the items in an array, in one of the container classes defined in `System.Collections`, or in a user-defined container class. We've already demonstrated the `foreach` statement in the previous section on *Arrays*.

```
foreach(int j in aryInt)
    Console.Write(j);
```

In order to be iterated through with a `foreach` loop, a container class must implement the `IEnumerable` interface. Later in this chapter, we'll demonstrate how to implement this interface to build a container class that can be iterated through by not only C#'s `foreach` statement, but by Visual Basic.NET's as well (see *C# Classes, Implementing Interfaces*).

Structured Error Handling

Although not normally considered a way of controlling program flow, C#'s structured error handling does indeed accomplish just that. It provides a formal method for determining how control will be routed through your code when different kinds of errors or anomalous conditions are encountered.

To implement structured error handling, C# provides three keywords for grouping code into blocks that are executed at different times.

❏   The `try` keyword prefaces blocks of code in which errors might be generated. When an error occurs in a `try` block, code in the `try` block creates a new `Exception` object and "throws" it outside the block. At that point, the thread of control leaves the `try` block.

❏   The `catch` keyword prefaces blocks of code that follow a `try` block and "catch" `Exception` objects that the `try` block might throw. Obviously, code inside a `catch` block is only executed if an error is encountered in the `try` block.

❏   The `finally` keyword prefaces blocks of code that must *always* be executed when a `try` block ends – whether that ending has come about through the successful completion of the `try` block's code, or through the throwing of an exception.

```
using System;
public class TryCatchFinallySample
{
    public static int Main()
    {
        //This code will throw an Exception.
        try
        {
            Console.WriteLine("try");
            int a=0;
            int b=10/a; //Division by 0 error.
        }

        //This code will catch the Exception.
```

```
        catch (Exception e)
        {
           Console.WriteLine("catch");
           Console.WriteLine(e.Message);
        }

        //This code always executes.
        finally
        {
           Console.WriteLine("finally");
        }
        return 0;
    }
}
```

Exception Classes

There are several child classes that inherit from the `Exception` base class. These include `IndexOutOfRangeException`, `NullReferenceException`, `InvalidCastException`, and others. The CLR can automatically throw an instance of one of these classes in response to a runtime error, or your code can do so deliberately if an unanticipated condition is encountered. The `Exception` class and its children have constructor functions that allow you to initialize them with strings containing detailed descriptions of the problems that have been encountered.

For an example, return again to the Life application. In it, a constructor function checks the values of its input arguments and raises an error if those values are illegal.

```
protected Automaton(int rows, int cols, byte percentageOfCellsInitiallyAlive)
    {
        //VALIDATE INPUT ARGUMENTS
        if ((rows<1)||(rows>MAX_ROWS))
        {
            throw new ArgumentException(
            "Illegal number of rows specified.");
        }
```

You can equip a single `try` block with multiple `catch` blocks, each of which catches a specific type of error. When one of these specialized `Exception` subclasses is thrown, the CLR activates the `catch` block most appropriate to the specific `Exception` subclass.

```
try
{
    //Code here may raise an exception.
}

catch (ArgumentException e)
{
//Code here will be activated if an
//ArgumentException is thrown.
}

catch (Exception e)
{
//Code here will be activated if an exception other
//than ArgumentException is thrown.
}
```

C# Classes

Object-oriented programming is where C# really shines. To plumb the depths of C#'s object-oriented features, we'll return to the Life sample program that was mentioned at the beginning of the chapter.

An Object-Oriented Life

I promised an explanation of the Life game for readers who aren't familiar with it. Here it is. If Life still doesn't make sense to you after you read this section, download the sample code from the Wrox site (http://www.wrox.com), compile it, and run it; a few pleasurable minutes spent toying with the application should clear up any confusion.

Briefly, Life consists of a two-dimensional matrix of cells that "evolves" from generation to generation through the application of a simple set of rules that determines cell birth, death, survival, and reproduction. These rules are as follows:

1. Dead cells with exactly three neighbors come to life.

2. Live cells with fewer than two neighbors die of loneliness.

3. Live cells with four or more neighbors die of overpopulation.

By repeatedly applying these rules to cells in the matrix and updating the matrix with the new population, a Life colony can evolve from ragged chaos into entrancing, pulsating patterns.

However, Life is only one kind of "cellular automaton". There are other cellular automata that are also played on two-dimensional matrices, but evolve differently through the application of different sets of rules. We'd like to develop a program that is flexible enough to display many different kinds of cellular automata. That's where object-oriented thinking comes in.

We'll develop a parent class, `Automaton`, which contains some default functionality and defines an interface that child classes can use. When future programmers want to plug a new kind of automaton into the user interface, they'll implement a new child class that inherits from `Automaton`. As we're conscientious software engineers, we'll try to implement the parent class, `Automaton`, in a way that maximizes the future programmers' chances of success.

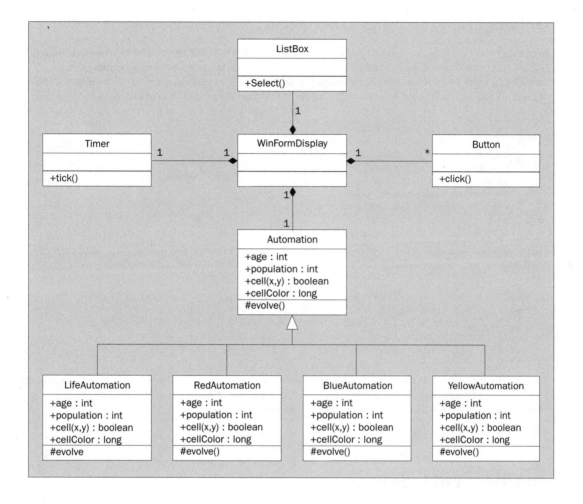

Access Modifiers

One of the ideals of object-oriented programming is "data hiding" – a class shields its callers from the "gory" details of how it performs the services that they request of it. In order to help you realize the benefits of data hiding, C# provides a set of "access modifiers". When placed before a class's data member, an access modifier controls who is able to see the data member.

- ❏ The `private` keyword modifies data members so that they are only visible to code within the class.

- ❏ The `protected` keyword modifies data members so that they are only visible to code within the class and to code in child classes that inherit from that class.

- ❏ The `internal` keyword modifies data members so that they are visible to code within the component that is being created but not to clients of that component.

- ❏ The `public` keyword exposes data members to all code: both code within the class, and code that uses the class.

The degrees of visibility provided by the access modifiers meet requirements stipulated by the CLS.

In our `Automaton` class, we want to mark certain variables as protected so that child classes that inherit from `Automaton` can access them but clients won't be able to. Child classes may need the values in these variables in order to do work, but clients might accidentally assign values to these variables if they could get to them. (Later on, we'll provide "read-only" access to these variables via C# properties.)

```
abstract public class Automaton
{

    protected int m_intPopulation;
    protected int m_intRows;
    protected int m_intColumns;
    protected bool[,] m_blnCell;
    protected int m_intAge;
```

There are a few constants that clients need to be aware of in order to use the `Automaton` class correctly. We'll expose these constants to clients by using the public keyword.

```
public   const int MAX_ROWS=50;
public   const int MAX_COLS=100;
public   const byte MAX_PERCENT_STARTING_ALIVE=75;
public   bool ALIVE=true;
public   bool DEAD=false;
```

Also, we want clients of `Automaton` classes to be able to tell these classes to `evolve()` from one generation to the next. So that clients can access the `evolve()` function, we'll modify `evolve()` with the `public` keyword, too. (We'll talk about what the abstract keyword means in just a bit.)

```
abstract public void Evolve();
```

Properties and Indexers

Simple Properties

A property is a controlled way of exposing a class's data members to client code. When a client sets a property's value, a class can use that value to take appropriate action, or can validate that value to make sure that it falls within an acceptable range. Similarly, a property can be used to make a data member "read-only" so that client classes can only interrogate it and not explicitly assign a value to it.

Like Visual Basic.NET, C# provides a dedicated syntax for defining properties. The read and write aspects of a property are defined as separate "get" and "set" clauses within a single block of code. A property without a `get` clause is write-only, and a property without a `set` clause is read-only.

In our Life application, the value of an `Automaton`'s `m_intAge` datamember will increment every time the `Automaton` object is told to `evolve()`. We want the client code to be able to determine the value of the `m_intAge` data member, but we don't want them to be able to set it. For this reason, we'll create a read-only `Age` property that provides the value of the `m_intAge` member through a `get` clause.

```csharp
public int Age
{
   get { return m_intAge; }
}
```

We'll also provide a read-only property that exposes an Automaton object's `PopulationSize`.

```csharp
public int PopulationSize
{
   get { return m_intPopulation; }
}
```

And another that exposes an `Automaton`'s `CellColor`.

```csharp
public virtual System.Drawing.Color CellColor {
   get { return System.Drawing.Color.White; }
}
```

An Advanced Property Example

Now let's look at a more advanced way of using properties.

You may remember that we defined an enumeration, `FormStateEnum`, that contains values representing the states that our application's user interface can be in: `FrozenState`, `StoppedState`, and `StartedState`. As the user interface cycles through these states, the various controls on the user interface (the Start/Stop button, the Close button, and the list box for selecting different automata) must be enabled and disabled.

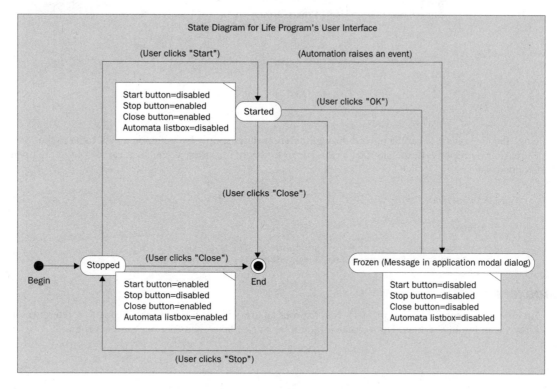

State Diagram for Life Program's User Interface

(User clicks "Start")

(Automation raises an event)

Start button=disabled
Stop button=enabled
Close button=enabled
Automata listbox=disabled

Started

(User clicks "OK")

(User clicks "Close")

(User clicks "Close")

Begin

Stopped

End

Frozen (Message in application modal dialog)

Start button=enabled
Stop button=disabled
Close button=enabled
Automata listbox=enabled

Start button=disabled
Stop button=disabled
Close button=disabled
Automata listbox=disabled

(User clicks "Stop")

To keep the controls on the user interface consistent with the interface's state, we'll create a property, FormState, that, when set, enables and disables the necessary user interface controls based on the property's new value.

```
private FormStateEnum FormState{
    set {

        m_enumFormState=value;
        switch (m_enumFormState)
        {
            case FormStateEnum.StoppedState:
                timer1.Enabled=false;
                this.btnEvolve.Text="Start";
                this.btnClose.Enabled=true;
                this.btnEvolve.Enabled=true;
                this.lstAutomata.Enabled=true;
                break;
            case FormStateEnum.StartedState:
                timer1.Enabled=true;
                this.btnEvolve.Text="Stop";
                this.btnClose.Enabled=true;
                this.btnEvolve.Enabled=true;
                this.lstAutomata.Enabled=false;
                break;
            case FormStateEnum.FrozenState:
                timer1.Enabled=false;
                this.btnClose.Enabled=false;
                this.btnEvolve.Enabled=false;
                this.lstAutomata.Enabled=false;
                break;
            default:
                throw new Exception("Form is in an" +
                                    "unanticipated state.");
        }
    }
    get {
        return m_enumFormState;
    }
}
```

Now, the user interface can be moved through different states simply by assigning a new value to the FormState property. In the interface's constructor function, for instance, the form can be put in the opening (stopped) state.

```
public WinFormDisplay()
{
    InitializeComponent();

    //Put the user interface in the opening state.
    this.FormState=FormStateEnum.StoppedState;
```

Indexers

An indexer is a special kind of property that exposes an array inside a class so that clients can reference that array via an intuitive syntax. For a practical example of an indexer, consider our sample program.

Each `Automaton` class contains a two-dimensional matrix of cells. After creating an `Automaton` object, a client will repeatedly tell that object to `evolve()` and then check the status of the cells in the `Automaton`'s two dimensional matrix. Certainly, we could provide a property called `Matrix()` that would expose the matrix to clients:

```
LifeAutomaton objLife=new LifeAutomaton(20,30);

//A Matrix property  would allow us to access the cells
//inside the object.
objLife.Matrix(0,0)=ALIVE;
```

However, that syntax seems a bit convoluted. As `Automaton` classes hide the details of how the `evolve()` function updates them, clients will tend to think of `Automaton` classes as glorified matrices – and this is a perception that our syntax should encourage, because it shields clients from complexity. An indexer would allow clients to apply array-style syntax to `Automaton` instances, and reference the array inside class more intuitively – *as if the Automaton instances themselves are two-dimensional matrices.*

```
LifeAutomaton objLife=new LifeAutomaton(20,30);

//The indexer allows the array inside the object to
//be addressed directly and intuitively.
objLife[0,0]=ALIVE;
```

Indexers are implemented using C#'s `this` keyword. Like properties, indexers can contain `get` and `set` clauses.

```
public virtual bool this[int row,int col]{
    get {
        return m_blnCell[row,col];
    }

    set {
        if (value!=m_blnCell[row,col])
            m_intPopulation+=(value?1:-1);
            m_blnCell[row,col]=value;
    }
}
```

Constructor Functions

An object's constructor function is invoked when that object is first instantiated. A constructor function configures its object to serve clients. A constructor function bears the name of the class in which it is defined and has no return type.

Like C++ classes, C# classes can have one or many constructor functions. Often, you'll create different constructor functions that accept different input arguments, whose values determine how the objects are configured.

For the `Automaton` class in our Life application, we'll define a constructor function that accepts three arguments:

1. The number of rows in the matrix of cells

2. The number of columns in the matrix of cells

3. The percentage of cells that should be alive in the first, randomly generated cell population

When invoked, the `Automaton` constructor will create a new matrix of cells and randomly populate it.

```
protected Automaton(int rows, int cols, byte percentageOfCellsInitiallyAlive)
{

    //Initialize the object's data members.
    m_intRows=rows;
    m_intColumns=cols;
    m_intPopulation=0;
    m_blnCell=new bool[m_intRows,m_intColumns];

    //Create a initial, pseudo-random population.
    for(i=0; i<m_intRows; i++)
    {
        for(j=0; j<m_intColumns; j++)
        {
            if (objRandomSequence.Next(100)<
                               percentageOfCellsInitiallyAlive)
            {
                m_blnCell[i,j]=ALIVE;
                m_intPopulation++;
            }
            else
            {
                m_blnCell[i,j]=DEAD;
            }
        }
    }
}
```

finalize() Functions

Traditional object-oriented languages like C++ allow classes to have "destructor" functions. The analog of constructor functions, destructor functions, are activated when the objects that contain them go out of scope, and they do any work that is necessary to clean up after their containing objects. In C++, destructor functions are indicated by the class name prefaced with a tilde (~).

Unlike more traditional programming languages, C# does not support destructor functions that are invoked when objects go out of scope. Instead, C# supports `finalize` functions. An object's `finalize` function is not automatically invoked when the object goes out of scope and is de-referenced, but at some point thereafter when the garbage collector encounters it in the list of objects that are to be finalized. As there may be a delay between an object's de-referencing and its finalization by the garbage collector, you shouldn't rely on `finalize` functions to handle resource contention between object instances.

```
public class FinalizeSample
{
    public FinalizeSample()
    {
```

```
        //Code here, in this constructor,
        //will be activated when a FinalizeSample
        //object is instantiated.
    }

    protected override void Finalize()
    {
        //Code here, in the finalize function,
        //will be activated when the CLR's
        //garbage collector deallocates the object.
    }
}
```

`finalize` functions have another, more serious problem: the CLR executes `finalize` functions on separate threads, and the creation of, and switching between, these threads can seriously drain system resources. In documentation, Microsoft encourages the intelligent and cautious use of `finalize` functions. To avoid any problems, and to set a good example, our Life application won't use any `finalize` functions.

Inheritance

Like data hiding, "code re-use" is another object-oriented ideal. Implementation inheritance allows child classes to re-use functions implemented in parent classes from which they inherit. In keeping with best practices suggested by leading object-oriented theorists, C# allows a child class to inherit interfaces from multiple parent classes, but implementation from only one parent class.

Abstract Classes

It's sometimes useful to define a class that provides an interface and some functionality for child classes but should never itself be instantiated. Such a class is said to be abstract, and is indicated in C# by use of the `abstract` keyword.

We want our `Automaton` class to be abstract. It defines an interface that child classes must match and provides default functionality that child classes can re-use, but it would be a mistake to allow clients to create an instance of `Automaton`.

```
abstract public class Automaton
{
```

As the `Automaton` class is marked as abstract, the C# compiler will throw an error if it encounters code in which a client tries to instantiate an `Automaton` object.

```
error CS0144: Cannot create an instance of the abstract class or interface
'Harvey.Automata.AutomataClasses.Automaton'
```

However, clients are free to implement creatable classes that inherit `Automaton`'s default functionality, such as its constructor function. The `LifeAutomaton` class, for example, inherits from the abstract class, `Automaton`.

```
sealed public class LifeAutomaton:Automaton
{
```

Virtual Methods

By default, a child class cannot re-implement a public method that is already implemented in its parent class. Attempts by a child class to do so will be flagged by the C# compiler.

A "virtual" method is one that can be re-implemented by child classes if they choose to do so. You make a method virtual by prefacing its implementation in the parent class with the `virtual` keyword. Child classes that choose to use their parent class's implementation do so silently. Child classes that choose to re-implement the virtual method provide their own implementations prefaced with the `override` keyword.

Our Life application makes good use of virtual functions and properties. Consider, for example, the virtual `CellColor` property that the `Automaton` class implements. In its default implementation, it returns the color "white".

```
abstract public class Automaton
{
    public virtual System.Drawing.Color CellColor {
        get { return System.Drawing.Color.White; }
    }
```

Classes that inherit from `Automaton` can choose to accept `Automaton`'s implementation (returning white) or to provide their own implementations that return different color values.

```
public class BlueAutomaton:Automaton
{
    public override System.Drawing.Color CellColor {
        get { return System.Drawing.Color.Blue; }
    }
```

Abstract Methods

An "abstract" method is one for which no implementation is provided. A child class that inherits an abstract method will be forced by the compiler to implement it using the `override` keyword.

In our Life application, the `Automaton` class includes an abstract method, `evolve()`.

```
abstract public class Automaton
{
    //The following "abstract" method has no default
    //implementation.
    abstract public void evolve();
```

When a child class inherits from `Automaton`, the C# compiler will force that class to provide an implementation for `evolve()`. The `evolve()` method should encapsulate the rules determining how the matrix of cells within that class evolve from generation to generation. In `LifeAutomaton`, for instance, the `evolve()` method counts the number of neighbors that each cell has and uses this number to determine the cell's birth, survival, or death.

```
sealed public class LifeAutomaton:Automaton
{
    public override void Evolve(){
```

```csharp
int i,j;
byte[,] byteNeighbors=new byte[m_intRows,m_intColumns];
int intOldPopulation=m_intPopulation;

//COUNT EACH CELL'S LIVING NEIGHBORS
for(i=0; i<m_intRows; i++)
{
    for(j=0; j<m_intColumns; j++)
    {
        if (m_blnCell[i,j]==ALIVE)
        {
            //INCREMENT NEIGHBOR COUNT OF
            //CELLS IN PREVIOUS ROW
            if (i>0)
            {
                if (j>0)
                    byteNeighbors[i-1,j-1]++;

                byteNeighbors[i-1,j]++;

                if (j<m_intColumns-1)
                    byteNeighbors[i-1,j+1]++;
            }

            //INCREMENT NEIGHBOR COUNT OF CELLS
            //IN THIS ROW
            if (j>0)
                byteNeighbors[i,j-1]++;
            if (j<m_intColumns-1)
                byteNeighbors[i,j+1]++;

                //INCREMENT NEIGHBOR COUNT OF CELLS
                //IN NEXT ROW
                if (i<m_intRows-1)
                {
                    if (j>0)
                        byteNeighbors[i+1,j-1]++;
                    byteNeighbors[i+1,j]++;

                    if (j<m_intColumns-1)
                        byteNeighbors[i+1,j+1]++;
                }

        }

    }

}
```

Note: the inclusion of a single abstract method within a class effectively makes that class abstract; that is, a class that contains an abstract method cannot be instantiated.

Sealed Classes

Prefacing a class with the `sealed` keyword prevents that class from ever serving as the parent to another class. In other words, such a sealed class cannot be subclassed, inherited from, or specialized. A client's attempt to use a sealed class as a parent class will elicit an error message from the C# compiler.

A component vendor might seal classes in his components to discourage customers from stealing his handiwork. Or an enterprise application developer might seal powerful business objects so that they cannot be subclassed to behave in inappropriate, non-secure ways. In our Life application, the `LifeAutomaton` class implements John Conway's Life cellular automaton, so, in tribute to Conway, I sealed that class so that it cannot be modified.

```
sealed public class LifeAutomaton:Automaton
{
```

C#'s `sealed` keyword is the equivalent of Java's `final` keyword.

Operator Overloading

Operator overloading allows you to determine how instances of the classes that you create behave in the context of C#'s operators: +, -, /, *, ==, etc.

Operator Overloading Code Samples

For this topic, and for the subsequent one, we'll take code samples from a `Matrix` class that implements a two-dimensional matrix of `ints`. This class contains a parameterized constructor for setting a `Matrix` object's size, properties for obtaining a `Matrix` object's dimensions, an indexer for getting and setting the values of the elements within a `Matrix` object, and a method for quickly filling a `Matrix` with values.

```
public class Matrix
{
    private int[,] m_lngElement;
    private int m_lngRowCount;
    private int m_lngColumnCount;

    //CONSTRUCTOR
    public Matrix(int rows,int columns)
    {

        m_lngRowCount=rows;
        m_lngColumnCount=columns;
        m_lngElement=new int[m_lngRowCount,m_lngColumnCount];

    }

    //PROPERTIES
    public int RowCount
    {
        get { return m_lngRowCount; }
    }

    public int ColumnCount
    {
        get { return m_lngColumnCount; }
    }
    //INDEXER
    public int this[int row, int column]
    {
        get {
```

```
            return m_lngElement[row,column];
    }

    set {
        m_lngElement[row,column]=value;
    }

}

public void AssignToEveryElement(int valueToAssign)
{
    int i,j;
    for (i=0; i<m_lngRowCount; i++)
        for (j=0; j<m_lngColumnCount; j++)
            this[i,j]=valueToAssign;
}
}
```

The following code snippet shows how a client could instantiate a `Matrix` object, set the value of its elements, and read those values back.

```
using System;
using Harvey.WroxDemo.Matrix;

public class MatrixClient
{
    public static int Main(string[] args)
    {
        Matrix objA=new Matrix(3,3);
        objA.AssignToEveryElement(1);
```

For your convenience, code for the `Matrix` and related classes is available at http://www.wrox.com.

Overloading Arithmetic Operators

As fans of discrete mathematics are aware, various mathematical operations can be applied to matrices. Matrices can, for example, be added together, subtracted from each other, and multiplied by each other. In order to be useful, our `Matrix` class must support such operations.

Certainly, we could provide special `Add()`, `Subtract()`, and `Multiply()` methods that clients could call, but wouldn't the `Matrix` class be more intuitive if the +, -, and * operators could be applied directly to Matrix instances? By overloading the arithmetic operators, we can make such easy syntax a reality.

```
Matrix objA=new Matrix(3,3);
Matrix objB=new Matrix(3,3);
Matrix objC;
Matrix objD;
Matrix objE;

objA.AssignToEveryElement(1);
objB.AssignToEveryElement(2);
objC=objA+objB;     //The addition operator is overloaded
objD=objA-objB;     //The subtraction operator is overloaded
objE=objA*objB;     //The multiplication operator is //overloaded.
```

The following code snippet shows how to overload the + operator for the `Matrix` class.

```
public static Matrix operator +(Matrix lhs, Matrix rhs)
{
    if ((lhs.ColumnCount!=rhs.ColumnCount)||(lhs.RowCount!=rhs.RowCount))
    {
        throw new Exception("Addition is impossible;"+
                            "matrices of incompatible dimensions");
    }

    int i,j;
    Matrix objSum=new Matrix(lhs.RowCount,lhs.ColumnCount);

    for (i=0; i<lhs.RowCount; i++)
        for (j=0; j<rhs.ColumnCount; j++)
            objSum[i,j]=lhs[i,j]+rhs[i,j];

    return objSum;
}
```

Now the CLR knows how to treat `Matrix` objects when arithmetic operations are applied to them. Note that the overload functions return references to a `Matrix` class. This is so that the reference can be stored in a reference variable, as the target of an arithmetic expression.

Overloading the Equality Operator (==) and the Inequality Operator (!=)

Two matrices are considered to be equal if they have exactly the same elements in exactly the same positions. To overload the equality operator (==) so that `Matrix` objects can be tested for equality, a `for` loop was implemented that iterates through the two `Matrix` objects, comparing their contents element-wise. Note that the overload function for this operator returns a Boolean value.

```
public static bool operator ==(Matrix lhs,Matrix rhs)
{
    boolblnIsEqual=((lhs.RowCount==rhs.RowCount)&&
                    (lhs.ColumnCount==rhs.ColumnCount));
    for (int i=0; i<lhs.RowCount && blnIsEqual; i++)
        for (int j=0; j<lhs.ColumnCount && blnIsEqual; j++)
            blnIsEqual=(lhs[i,j]==rhs[i,j]);

    return blnIsEqual;
}
```

To overload the inequality operator, a shortcut was used; the inequality operator simply invokes the equality operator and then negates its result.

```
public static bool operator !=(Matrix lhs,Matrix rhs)
{
    return !(lhs==rhs);
}
```

Overloading the Conversion Operators

Although we won't go into the matter at great length here, you should be aware that it is possible to overload C#'s conversion operators. Doing so allows you:

1. To dictate the way that one of your classes is converted to an instance of another type

2. To determine the way that objects of other types are converted into instances of your class

Overloading the Assignment Operator is not Permitted

C# does not allow you to overload the assignment operator (=).

Implementing Interfaces

Earlier, I mentioned that a C# class can inherit functionality from only one parent class, but can inherit *interfaces* from several. A C# class would inherit and implement an interface so that it could be used by clients that understand that interface. C#'s foreach statement, for instance, understands the IEnumerable interface, and can use this interface to iterate through collection classes that implement it.

For an example, we'll return to the Matrix class that we introduced in the previous section. It might be useful to equip the Matrix class with the IEnumerable interface so that a client could iterate through all of the elements in a Matrix instance using a foreach loop.

```
//Fill the matrix up with information
EnumerableMatrix objMatrix=new EnumerableMatrix(ROWS,COLUMNS);
for (i=0; i<ROWS; i++)
    for (j=0; j<COLUMNS; j++)
        objMatrix[i,j]=k++;

//Enumerate through items in the class using the //foreach construction
foreach(int intItem in objMatrix)
{
    Console.WriteLine(intItem);
}
```

Implementing the IEnumerable interface means providing implementations for several methods. In the following code sample, we create EnumerableMatrix, a class that inherits functionality from Matrix and implements the methods in the IEnumerable interface.

```
public class EnumerableMatrix:Matrix, IEnumerable {

    //Constructor
    public EnumerableMatrix(int rows,int columns):base(rows,columns){}

    //CODE FOR ENUMERATING THIS MATRIX AS IF IT WERE A
    //COLLECTION (foreach) FROM C# *or* VB CLIENTS...
    public MatrixEnumerator GetEnumerator() {
    return new MatrixEnumerator(this);
    }

        IEnumerator IEnumerable.GetEnumerator() {
        return GetEnumerator();
    }

    public class MatrixEnumerator: IEnumerator {
        int m_intIndex;
```

```
        EnumerableMatrix m_objMatrix;

        public MatrixEnumerator(EnumerableMatrix
        objMatrix)
        {
            m_objMatrix=objMatrix;
            m_intIndex = -1;
        }

        public void Reset() {
            m_intIndex = -1;
        }

        public bool MoveNext() {
            m_intIndex++;
            return(m_intIndex <
                    (m_objMatrix.RowCount *
                     m_objMatrix.ColumnCount));
        }
        public int Current {
            get   {
                int intRow=m_intIndex / m_objMatrix.ColumnCount;
                int intColumn=m_intIndex % m_objMatrix.ColumnCount;
                return (m_objMatrix[intRow,intColumn]);
            }
        }

    // The current property on the IEnumerator
    //interface:
    object IEnumerator.Current {
        get   {
            return(Current);
        }
    }
}
}
```

Advanced C# Features

Events

An event is a way for a server class to notify the clients that reference it about unusual occurrences. When an unusual occurrence transpires, the server class is said to "raise" the event to the clients, who "handle" the event as they are each in turn notified of it, taking some sort of appropriate action.

The entire Windows operating system is said to be "event-driven". A button control, for instance, raises a click event to the window that contains it when the user points at it and clicks a mouse key. In the window's handler function, it can take some appropriate action, such as save a file to disk or close itself.

C# allows you to outfit the classes that you create with events that they can raise to their clients. In the Life application, for example, `Automaton` objects can raise a message event back to the user interface when something significant happens, such as dramatic increases or decreases in the population.

How C# Events Work

The following is a succinct description of how events work in C#. It's intended for advanced programmers. If it doesn't quite make sense to you, just skip ahead to the next section, which provides a practical, hands-on approach to implementing events in your C# classes.

To implement events, C# uses a glorified form of function pointers.

An empty "delegate" function is listed at the top of the server class. This `delegate` function defines the signature that event-handling functions in client classes must match.

A client object that wishes to receive events from the server object must register with the server object, by effectively adding a pointer to its event handler function to a list internally maintained by the server object. When the server object wants to raise the event, it iterates through this list of function pointers, activating the handler functions in the client objects.

Implementing Events

Here, I'll present you with a list of steps that you can follow to outfit your C# classes for events. Between the steps, I'll drop in code samples from the Life application, which creates a `MessageToClients` event that `Automaton` objects can use to send messages to the user interface.

In the module containing the server class, forward-declare an external function with the delegate keyword.

```
public delegate void AutomatonEventHandler(string Message);
abstract public class Automaton
{
```

Within the server class, declare an instance of the delegate function modified with the `event` keyword. We'll call this the "connection point".

```
abstract public class Automaton
{
public event AutomatonEventHandler EventHandlerConnectionPoint;
```

Also in the server class, put in the code that "raises" the event by calling the connection point at appropriate times.

```
protected void MessageToClients(string Message)
{
    if (EventHandlerConnectionPoint!=null)
    {
        EventHandlerConnectionPoint(Message);
    }
}
```

In the client class, define event handler functions that match the signature of the `delegate` function declared in the server module. In the Life user interface, the event handler displays messages from `Automaton` objects in a message box.

```
public class WinFormDisplay : System.WinForms.Form
{
    public void MessageFromClient(string Message)
    {
        this.FormState=FormStateEnum.FrozenState;

        //This is an overloaded Win32 API call.
        MessageBoxA(0,Message, "Message from Automaton",0);

        this.FormState=FormStateEnum.StartedState;
    }
}
```

In the constructor function of the client class, cast references to your handler functions to the connection point type defined in the server module, and add those references to the server object's connection point.

```
public class WinFormDisplay : System.WinForms.Form
{
    public WinFormDisplay()
    {

        InitializeComponent();
        this.FormState=FormStateEnum.StoppedState;

        m_objAutomaton=new LifeAutomaton(ROWS,COLS, PERCENT_INITIALLY_ALIVE);

    //This registers the client to receive events
    //from the server object.
    m_objAutomaton.EventHandlerConnectionPoint+=new
                AutomatonEventHandler(MessageFromClient);

    }
}
```

Platform Invoke Services (PInvoke)

PInvoke Described

Platform Invocation Services (`PInvoke`) allows C# programs to invoke functions stored in C DLLs, including those C DLLs that supply the Win32 API: `gdi32.dll`, `user32.dll`, and `kernel32.dll`.

To use `PInvoke`, you simply define a C# wrapper function whose signature matches that of the C function that you want to invoke and modify the wrapper function's definition with the `sysimport` attribute. A value inside this attribute, "dll", references the DLL file in which the wrapper function can be found.

To invoke the external function from your C# code, you simply call the wrapper function. The CLR loads the DLL into memory, locates the desired function in that DLL, marshals the function call's parameters, and passes the thread-of-execution into the function.

A PInvoke Example

For an example of how `PInvoke` is implemented, refer again to the Life application. In it, we wrap up the Win32 API's `MessageBoxA` function so that it can be invoked from C# code.

```
public class WinFormDisplay : System.WinForms.Form
{
    [sysimport(dll="user32.dll")]
    private static extern int MessageBoxA(int hWnd,
            string Message, string Caption, int Type);
```

When the user interface receives an event notification from an `Automaton` object, it invokes the Win32 API function through the C# wrapper to display the text of the notification to the user in a message box.

```
MessageBoxA(0,Message,"Message from Automaton",0);
```

Be aware that the `System.WinForm` namespace provides a method for displaying message boxes. This API function was chosen because it is simple and consequently makes a nice demonstration.

Dangers of PInvoke

There are a couple of things that you need to keep in mind before using `PInvoke` in your C# programs.

❑   First, if you use `PInvoke` to make your C# programs directly reference the Win32 API, then those programs are tied to the Windows operating system. This dependency will make it harder to port your programs to other platforms if .NET CLRs are developed for those platforms in the future. If you can, try to use classes in the .NET class library instead of API calls. If you simply *must* use Win32 API calls, wrap those calls in classes that you can re-implement for future platforms.

❑   Second, the CLR cannot apply security checks to code in external DLLs. When `PInvoke` passes the thread-of-execution into external DLL functions, those functions can basically do whatever they want. To make sure that you recognize the security holes that `PInvoke` can open up, the .NET platform requires that any code using `PInvoke` be granted a full trust. Before using `PInvoke`, please consider whether it's worth the risks that it can introduce.

The Future of C#

With technical advances and ratified standards on the horizon, the future of C# looks bright.

Technical Advances

Microsoft has stated that future releases of C# will support generic programming, the ability to create classes that can be quickly modified to work with different data types. Generic programming saves developers time by allowing them to re-use code.

Generic programming as implemented in C++ involves the creation of class "templates" that can be compiled into actual classes tailored to specific types. The Standard Template Library provides the List template, for example, which you can compile into one list class that works with `ints`, another that works with `floats`, or another that works with objects of your own device.

Unlike C++'s approach to generic code, C#'s approach won't use templates, and the genericism will be handled *after* compile time, at the level of the CLR. This last characteristic implies that type generic classes created with C# could be used as a type-generic classes from any other .NET language.

C# Standardization

Microsoft will submit a C# standard for ratification by ECMA (the European Computer Manufacturer's Association), the same organization responsible for the JavaScript/ECMAscript standard. The approval of this standard would mean that vendors would be free to develop their own versions of C# and the CLR that target their particular platforms. In the future, perhaps, C# code that you write on PCs could be executed on cell phones or palmtop devices when Microsoft bring out a .NET Framework release targeted at mobile devices.

Summary

This chapter serves as an introduction to C#, the language of .NET (because Microsoft used C# to implement much of the CLR and the base class library). The chapter uses the Life application to show how C# works.

Firstly, it is important to find out how C# fits in with Microsoft.NET, and also how it compares and improves upon previous popular languages, such as Visual Basic and Java. In this section, we also went into greater depth on the differences between C# and C++ .

The next section for us to look at covered the datatypes to be found in C#, and looked at the differences between value types and reference types. We also looked at the helpfulness of arrays and enumerations. We then moved our attention to control flow and how C# achieves this by the use of functions, conditionals, loops and structured error handling.

The largest section of the chapter was given to the description and use of C# classes. In this section, we covered many of the important things we will need to know to use C#, such as properties and indexers, inheritance and operator overloading. We then briefly looked at some of the advanced features that we can expect to find.

If you enjoyed this chapter and want to learn more about C#, you might want to read "*C# Programming*", also from Wrox Press, ISBN 1-861004-87-7. This book addresses the issues discussed here in greater detail. However, for now, we will turn our attention to what's new in Visual Basic.NET, which just happens to be covered in the next chapter.

What's New in Visual Basic.NET

While the technical details of Microsoft.NET may be fascinating, it's just as important to know what it means to the people who write the code. More often than not, that means Visual Basic programmers. This chapter summarizes the substantial changes in store for those who develop software using Visual Basic.

Visual Basic.NET (sometimes referred to as VB.NET) is getting massive injections of new functionality: new object capabilities and new web capabilities head the list. Also, the general improvements of the .NET architecture, such as XCOPY deployment, become available in Visual Basic, because it is built on the Common Language Runtime (CLR).

However, migrating to VB.NET will require a steep learning curve. In previous updates, Microsoft have always tried to ensure backwards compatibility, but the transition to VB.NET is such a large step forward that this isn't the case this time, and any existing VB code will have to be modified if you want it to run on the .NET framework. Putting in new functionality and making VB work within Microsoft.NET has required many significant, but worthwhile syntax changes, and this has the potential to create more compatibility issues than have ever been faced before in a new version.

The changes can be roughly grouped into five areas:

- ❏ Adding complete object-oriented capabilities
- ❏ Adding better web interface capabilities
- ❏ Adding modern language capabilities such as structured error handling and free-threading
- ❏ Fitting Visual Basic into the Common Language Specification and the Common Type System
- ❏ Removing obsolete syntax from legacy versions of BASIC such as QuickBASIC

This chapter looks at each of these areas and summarizes major changes. Attention will also be focused on what you can do today to prepare for these future capabilities. For example, tips will be included on making current code easy to convert by avoiding syntax that will no longer be supported.

New Object Capabilities in Visual Basic

Many of us have been clamoring for VB to support full object-oriented development since classes were introduced in Version 4. With Visual Basic.NET, our wishes have been granted.

In fact, the base syntax of Visual Basic has changed, and it now becomes a true object-oriented language. For example, there is no syntactical difference between a `form` module and a class module in Visual Basic.NET – they both use the same object-based syntax, and inheriting a `form` class from the library of base classes only differentiates the `form`. We'll see an example of this in the section on inheritance.

The new object capabilities that are most important are:

- **Full inheritance** – The ability for individual subclasses to derive (**inherit**) properties, methods, and other capabilities from a base class.

- **Parameterized constructors** – The ability to pass information to a class at instantiation, to set its properties or affect its behavior

- **Overriding of members** – Allowing properties and methods in the base class to be altered in a sub class

- **Overloading of functions** – The capability for a member to have different implementations which process different argument lists

- **Shared members** – Properties or methods which are shared by all instantiations of a given class

Let's look at each of these in turn:

Full Inheritance

What is Inheritance?

Consider the following typical programming scenario. You have a payroll application, and there are several types of employee – full-time, part-time, hourly, salaried, etc. You would like to create a set of objects to handle all of these types in the payroll application.

Using Visual Basic 6 or earlier, the solution would probably be to create a single `Employee` class, and then set up a property for that class which indicated the sub-type (full time or hourly, for example). The logic in the `Employee` class would then need lots of `Select Case` logic to change its behavior depending on the subtype of employee. The `Calculate` method, for example, would have a `Select Case` that selected the algorithm for calculating pay, based on the employee type.

This is a classic case where the concept of inheritance is useful. Using inheritance, you could create a base class called Employee, which contained all the generic employee functionality. You could then add subclasses for each sub-type of Employee. Each sub-class would inherit from the base class, thereby gaining all of its functionality. Then, functionality that is specific to the subtype could be added to the sub-class, which would encapsulate the special logic for the subtype in one class.

This type of design has many advantages. For example, it is now much easier to add new sub-types of Employee.

Putting Inheritance in Visual Basic

Finally, VB gets full inheritance in Visual Basic.NET. The syntax is simple. A class indicates the base class using the Inherits keyword.

The base class is referred to inside the subclass' code with a reference to MyBase. This is a new keyword in Visual Basic, and simply provides a convenient way to refer to the base class.

There is some example code in the section on overriding later in this chapter, which illustrates the use of MyBase.

The replacement for standard VB forms, currently called WinForms (though the name is expected to change in beta two), provides an example. A form in WinForms is really a class module, but it inherits the capability to be a form from the .NET framework classes. Here is an example of the code at the top of a WinForms class:

```
Imports System.ComponentModel
Imports System.Drawing
Imports System.WinForms

Public Class Form1
    Inherits System.WinForms.Form
```

By inheriting from System.WinForms.Form, the class representing the form automatically gets all the properties, methods, and events that a form based on WinForms is supposed to have. This is similar to the way that a form in VB6 or earlier automatically gets standard form properties and methods, but in Visual Basic.NET, the inheritance of those members comes specifically because the class has inherited from System.WinForms.Form.

It gets better. A class can also become a form by inheriting from another form. Here's an example: suppose we create a form, Form1, which looks like this in the visual designer:

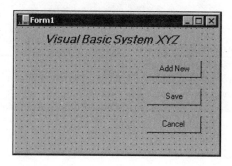

Now let's create a new form, `Form2`, which will have a visual layout like this:

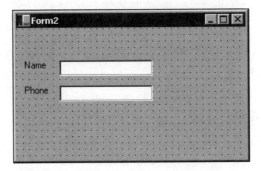

When `Form2` was created, it had the following code close to the top:

```
Imports System.ComponentModel
Imports System.Drawing
Imports System.WinForms

Public Class Form2
    Inherits System.WinForms.Form
```

Suppose we change the last line of that code to look like this:

```
Imports System.ComponentModel
Imports System.Drawing
Imports System.WinForms

Public Class Form2
    Inherits Form1
```

Now, if we instantiate `Form2` visually it looks like this:

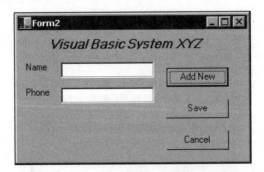

Notice that `Form2` now has two sets of controls. The first set is those controls that were placed on `Form2` by the Visual Designer. The second set of controls was originally placed on `Form1` in the Visual Designer, and was then inherited onto `Form2`. There are options to make inherited controls fixed in size and position, or to make them configurable by `Form2`.

And it's not just the visual appearance of the controls that is inherited. Any code that is behind the controls in `Form1` is inherited by `Form2`. If the **Add New** button, for example, had some processing logic in `Form1`, then when that button is pressed the `Form2`, the logic in `Form1` is executed.

Using inheritance this way has major implications for the architecture of VB forms-based projects. It is possible to create a base form with logic and visual elements needed by all forms, and then have other forms inherit to get that functionality. The logic and visual elements are encapsulated into one location, so that changing the base form causes all the forms inheriting from it to change automatically.

Of course, inheritance works for any class, not just for forms as in the example above. In fact, it doesn't matter if the base class is even in Visual Basic. The `System.WinForms.Form` class is actually written in C#. As long as the class is from a .NET language, Visual Basic.NET will inherit from it as if it were written in Visual Basic.NET.

As a final note, while Visual Basic.NET and the .NET framework supports full inheritance capabilities those capabilities do not include the **multiple inheritance** features that are present in C++ and some other object languages.

Parameterized Constructors

Another useful object-oriented capability found in most true object languages is parameterized constructors. That means that when an object is instantiated, parameters can be passed in to affect the object's behavior immediately. This ensures that an instantiation will immediately be in a valid state, rather than waiting for some important properties to be set before the object can be used. If an employee class requires an ID, for example, before it can function, a parameterized constructor can require that the ID be passed in at instantiation time.

Visual Basic did not contain constructors in previous versions. Instead it had events that occurred at instantiation; these were `Class Initialize` for classes and `Form Load` for forms. No parameters could be passed to these events. So code to handle the situation above would look like this in VB6 or earlier:

```
Dim objNewEmployee As New Employee
objNewEmployee.EmployeeID = ("123-45-6789")
```

Whereas, the code that does this in Visual Basic.NET might look like the following:

```
Dim objNewEmployee As New Employee("123-45-6789")
```

A constructor is not an event; it is a subroutine, and can thus have an argument list. However, as a constructor, it is designated to run automatically at instantiation. In Visual Basic.NET, the constructor is called `Sub New` and it is `Public` in scope. This routine can have parameters specified just as any other `Sub` would allow. To illustrate, when this line is run to create an instance of the `Employee` class:

```
Dim objNewEmployee As New Employee("123-45-6789")
```

The constructor in the code for the `Employee` class would start like this:

```
Sub New(sEmployeeID As String)
    ' Code to set up employee ID goes here
```

Including this argument in the declaration for Sub New means the argument will be required when every instantiation of the class is done. If the argument is left out of the code that is trying to instantiate the class, a syntax error will occur. Sub New can also be written to take optional arguments.

Here is another example, using a constructor to initialize a caption for a form named Form2.

Create a new Windows Forms project in Visual Basic.NET. The project will automatically include a form, named Form1 by default. Place a single command button on this form, and change the button's Text property to "Launch Form2". This will make the form look similar to the following when it is run:

Now insert another form, using the menu option Project | Add Windows Form. When this form is created, it will be named Form2 by default. The code designer will automatically create a constructor named Sub New in the form's Class module. It looks like this:

```
Public Sub New()
    MyBase.New

    Form2 = Me

    'This call is required by the Win Form Designer.
    InitializeComponent

    'TODO: Add any initialization after the InitializeComponent() call
End Sub
```

Change the Sub New constructor in Form2 to look like this:

```
Public Sub New(ByVal sTitleBarCaption As String)
    MyBase.New

    Form2 = Me

    'This call is required by the Win Form Designer.
    InitializeComponent

    'TODO: Add any initialization after the InitializeComponent() call

    'Note that the Caption property in VB6 is changed to the Text property
    Me.Text = sTitleBarCaption
End Sub
```

Now go back to `Form1`. Double-click the command button to bring up the button's click event (`Button1_Click`) in the code editor. In the click event, include the following logic. Note that the logic needs to include the parameter expected by the `Sub New`.

```
Dim frmNewForm As New "Form2("This Caption set at instantiation!")
frmNewForm.Show()
```

Now, when the program is run and the button on `Form1` is pressed, `Form2` will be instantiated. It should look like this (*note the text in the title bar*):

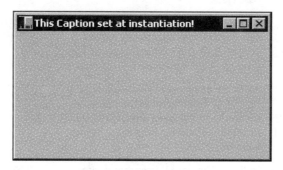

Overriding

When a subclass inherits from a base class, it has access to all the members (properties and methods) of the base class. In some cases, the subclass uses these members "as is", that is, just as they are implemented in the base class. However, sometimes a subclass needs to change or override a property or method of the base class to apply some special logic.

For example, suppose we are writing a game simulation, and we have a Player class. It has properties like the player's score. It also has a method called SelectMove to allow a player to select a move in the game. We might want to write a subclass of Player (perhaps called AdvancedPlayer) to implement a special strategy in the game. In that case, the AdvancedPlayer class would need to override the SelectMove method, which means replacing the SelectMove method in the base Player class with a special version in the AdvancedPlayer class.

Full overriding of properties and methods is supported in Visual Basic.NET, so that the subclass can substitute logic for a given property or method of the base class. The overriding logic can be completely separate from the base class, and the base method can be called from within the overriding class but doesn't exist as far as the outside world is concerned.

Members of the base class can only be overridden in subclasses if they are declared with the keyword Overridable. However, the base class has additional control. It can determine that a member (property or method) cannot be overridden in an inherited class, or do the opposite and require it to be overridden, by using the MustOverride keyword. There are several keywords that control this; here is a summary of them:

Keyword	Purpose	Code example
`Overridable`	Indicates that a member in the base class can be overridden in classes derived (inherited) from this class,	`Overridable Sub Clear()`
`Overrides`	Used in a member in a subclass to indicate that the member is overriding the member of the same name in the base class.	`Overrides Public Sub Dispose()`
`NotOverridable`	Indicates that a member in a base class cannot be overridden in any classes derived (inherited) from this class. This is the default for members.	`NotOverridable Function Name (nID as Long) As String`
`MustInherit`	An attribute of a class declaration for a base class. Indicates that the class cannot be instantiated directly – it must be inherited and then the subclass can be instantiated.	`MustInherit Class MyClass`
`MustOverride`	Indicates that any classes that derive (inherit) from this class must supply an override for this member. Only available for classes declared as `MustInherit`. A member that is marked as `MustOverride` only supplies an interface for the member. No logic, not even an End Sub or End Function line, is allowed.	`MustOverride Function Name (nID as Long) As String`

Here's an example of overriding. Suppose my base class looks like this:

```
Public Class Customer

    ' Public properties.
    Public Name As String
    Public Active As Boolean

    ' Use a constructor to initialize our public
    ' properties
    Public Sub New(ByVal sName as String, ByVal bActive as Boolean)
        Name = sName
        Active = bActive
    End Sub

    ' Use the Overridable keyword
    ' to let subclasses implement
    ' their own version.
    Public Overridable Sub CheckStatus()
        Debug.WriteLine ("Name: " & Name)
        Debug.WriteLine ("Active: " & Active)
    End Sub

End Class
```

Now, suppose I create a class that has the following code:

```
Public Class TargetCustomer
    Inherits Customer

    ' Declare another public property for this subclass
    Public DateToContact As Date

    ' Create a constructor for the subclass
    Public Sub New(ByVal sName As String, _
                    ByVal bActive As Boolean, _
                    ByVal datDateToContact as Date)

        ' Call the base class's constructor
        MyBase.New(sName, bActive)

        ' Initialize variables in this subclass.
        DateToContact = datDateToContact
    End Sub

    ' Override the base class's method
    Public Overrides Sub CheckStatus()
        'Call the base methods version
        MyBase.CheckStatus()

        ' Print out properties specific to subclass
        Debug.WriteLine ("Call them on: " & DateToContact)
    End Sub

End Class
```

Next I create an instance of the `TargetCustomer` class, which requires passing parameters to initialize its properties. I then call the `CheckStatus` method. The code would look like this:

```
Dim objNewTargetCustomer As New TargetCustomer_
                    ("ABC Company", True, #1/9/2001#)

objNewTargetCustomer.CheckStatus
```

The result in the immediate window would look like this:

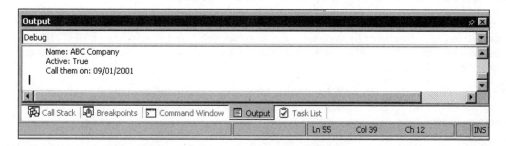

The first two lines are generated by the `CheckStatus` method in the base class (`Customer`), which is called within the `CheckStatus` method of the subclass (`TargetCustomer`). Then the third line is generated by code within that same `CheckStatus` method of `TargetCustomer`.

Overloading

Overloading is used when a member needs to behave differently depending on the types of the arguments that are passed to it. For example, a method named `Display` might need to accept integers or strings, and to behave differently for each. The `Overloads` keyword is used to do that, as in the following example. Both of these routines would be included in the same class:

```
Overloads Sub Display(ByVal number as Integer)
    ' display routine that handles number goes here
End Sub

Overloads Sub Display(ByVal sString as String)
    ' display routine that handles string goes here
End Sub
```

Without overloading, it would have been necessary to use one of two more complex techniques. Two separate display routines could be constructed with different names, one for a number and one for a string, or optional parameters could be used, but it would be necessary for the programmer using the routine to keep order and type of parameters straight.

Shared Members

Proper object designs usually completely isolate object instances from one another. However, it is occasionally helpful to have information shared by all active instances in a class. In VB.NET, shared members (properties or methods) can be constructed to do this. The concept is identical to what are called **static members** in C++.

The `Shared` keyword is used to create shared members. For example, to share a string data member called `CommonName`, this line of code would be used in the declarations section of the class:

```
Public Shared CommonName As String
```

A routine or variable declared this way is then available to all instantiations of a given class. If the `CommonName` property declared above were changed in one instantiation, it would change for all of them.

Web Interfaces in Visual Basic.NET

In today's web development projects, Visual Basic is mostly used for component development. That's because it has been hampered by minimal ability to create web-based user interfaces. DHTML pages and WebClasses never really caught on, with most developers sticking to Active Server Pages for actual user interface manipulation.

By moving Visual Basic to the .NET framework, Microsoft opens up huge options for web development. Visual Basic.NET is expected to make web development almost as drag-and-drop easy as VB1 made Windows development.

The .NET framework includes Web Forms, which are the avenue to drag-and-drop web interfaces. Web Forms work in Visual Basic as they do in any .NET language. A design surface receives web controls, which resemble form controls. There's an HTML page, which contains positioning and formatting information for the page, and a code module, which contains routines that can be attached to the page. Many of the routines are event routines, which are connected to events fired by the web controls.

Chapter 7 discusses Web Forms and the Server Controls that make them work, so we will not be discussing them in more detail here.

Web Services

Web Services provides a mechanism for programs to communicate over the Internet using the SOAP. Conceptually, this is similar to DCOM in that it enables distributed environments, but Web Services works in a much broader context; that is, SOAP (and the client) no longer care what technology is at the target of the call.

Chapter 8 covers Web Services in detail. In this chapter, we look at creating a new component that is Web Service enabled.

Web Service components are created by selecting the appropriate option when starting a new project. The dialog for starting a new project looks like this:

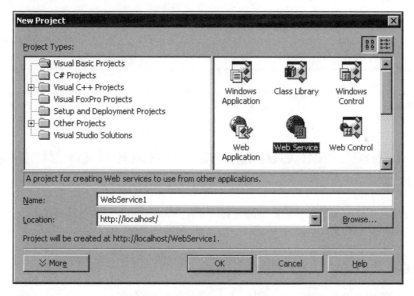

On the right-hand side are the types of projects that may be created, and on the bottom row of options is one for **Web Service**. Once selected, it sets up the project parameters for a class library that will be Web Service enabled.

A Web Service component will have some methods that need to be exposed as part of the Web Service, and others that are just for internal use and should not be exposed. Those that are to be a visible part of the Web Service interface are indicated with the `WebMethod` keyword. Otherwise they look just like other methods. Here is an example of a Web Service enabled `method`:

```
Public Function <WebMethod> Color(iIndex as Integer) As String
    Select Case iIndex
        Case 1
            Color = "Red"
        Case 2
            Color = "Blue"
```

```
        Case Else
            Color = "No Color"
    End Select
End Function
```

Note that the only way this differs from a standard function is the `<WebMethod>` in the declaration line.

If this method is accessed over the web, and the index (`iIndex`) is passed in as 2, then an XML packet will be returned. The simplest possible version of this packet would look like this:

Depending on the XML Protocol options that are chosen, there may be additional information in the XML packet returned.

Modern Language Capabilities Added to Visual Basic.NET

The history of the BASIC language goes back a long way. Newer languages have introduced much-improved features for common programming tasks. Now some of those features are being added to Visual Basic.NET.

Structured Exception Handling

Java and C++ developers have grown used to far better error handling capability than exists in VB. The `On Error` constructs used in VB have not improved significantly since QuickBASIC (the DOS ancestor of VB). Catching an error in a specific block of code was particularly clumsy, with the need to turn various kinds of error handling on and off at specific places. One of the side effects was that `On Error Resume Next` was often over-used and abused.

That is going to change. Now in VB, the following syntax can be used to handle errors and exceptions:

```
Try

    ' Some typical processing logic
    rsRecordset.Update

Catch

    ' This code runs when an error occurs in the code above
```

```
        LogError ("Unable to update the recordset")

    Finally

        ' This code always runs, either after the Try code if there
        ' was no error, or after the Catch code if there was
        rsRecordset.MoveNext

    End Try
```

If need be, the logic in the `Try` portion can use a statement named `Throw` to force an error. Then the logic in the `Catch` portion will be executed immediately. `Throw` is much like `Err.Raise` in earlier versions of VB. `On Error` syntax is still going to be supported, and the `Err` object will still be available.

Threading

Due to the nature of the Visual Basic runtime, Visual Basic has never taken advantage of the full range of threading options bound to COM. The threading model used in Visual Basic up to now is called **apartment threading**. It leads to some drawbacks for components written in VB, and it also does not give any control over the spawning of additional threads of execution for a program.

Courtesy of the common language runtime, Visual Basic now supports **free threading**. To launch a new thread, an object is declared of type `Thread`, and the address of the module to start running in the thread is passed at instantiation. The `Thread` class then has various methods to stop, suspend, resume, delete, and otherwise manage the thread.

Giving such threading capability expands the range of Visual Basic to include programs such as NT services. It helps put VB on a par with other languages.

Chapter 6 on the .NET Framework class libraries discusses more on the `Thread` object.

Fitting Visual Basic into the .NET Framework

The .NET framework is very flexible, but it was not practical to make it be all things to all people (or to all languages). To make different languages work together, the .NET framework requires consistency on data types and on some syntax elements.

A Recap of .NET Advantages for Visual Basic

As discussed in Chapter 1, the design of the .NET framework and the Common Language Runtime is based on a number of important goals. The ones that have the most impact on Visual Basic .NET include:

- ❑ Simpler, safer deployment of applications
- ❑ Scalability
- ❑ Multiple language integration

These advantages are huge. Dispensing with registration, GUIDs (Globally Unique Identifiers) and the like for middle tier components, bring n-tier development to a whole new sector of Visual Basic developers, rather than being restricted to those advanced developers who knew the intricacies of COM.

Putting Visual Basic on a par with other languages is also a big help. Visual Basic.NET has no significant restrictions on scalability when compared to C# or the other .NET languages. In fact, once Visual Basic code is compiled into Intermediate Language (MSIL), it is hard to distinguish a VB program from MSIL compiled from other .NET languages.

Of course, making Visual Basic easy to integrate with other languages is a big step. Developers, who have had to work extensively with the Windows API, or create DLLs in C++ that could be called by Visual Basic, understand how important this is. In .NET, calling conventions and class interfaces are the same no matter what the source language, making VB a first class citizen of the .NET world. The full inheritance capabilities discussed above are based on this transparent multiple-language integration in the .NET Framework.

Replacing Standard Visual Basic Forms with WinForms

Chapter 9 discusses the WinForms functionality of Microsoft.NET, which is available to all .NET languages. For Visual Basic developers, this means replacement of standard Visual Basic forms with WinForms. There are many similarities, but also some key differences.

The controls in WinForms are similar, but not identical, to the controls for Visual Basic forms. Some of the properties are changed, especially to get more consistency. For example, command buttons and labels no longer have a Caption property. Putting text in a control is done with the Text property, even for non-editable controls such as buttons, labels, and form captions.

There is also some new functionality for form layout. For example, it is possible in WinForms to anchor controls to form edges, allowing much form resize logic to be eliminated. Controls with their anchor property set are automatically resized as the form size changes.

A Common Type System

Chapter 1 mentioned that the Common Type System is a key foundation for multiple language support. It implements all commonly used data types as objects, and forces all languages to work with the same basic set of data types.

Of course, the designers of Microsoft.NET mostly had a C++ background, and their decisions on what data types to support reflects this. The types are not identical to the traditional data types in VB, and this results in the need for some readjustment. But the adjustment is worth it to get the advantages of .NET, and some of the changes are real improvements.

The most visible changes concern integer-type data types which support signed whole numbers. Here is a comparison table showing the changes:

Old type	New type	Size	Range
Integer	Short	16 bits	-32,768 to 32,767
Long	Integer	32 bits	-2,147,483,648 to 2,147,483,647
(N/A)	Long	64 bits	-9,223,372,036,854,775,808 to 9,223,372,036,854,775,807

This has a lot of potential to cause confusion but, again, is being done to bring VB in line with other languages. The biggest issue is that this can break calls to routines in DLLs or the Windows API that are expecting certain lengths. It can also affect code that does bit-wise arithmetic. While the migration tool supplied with Visual Basic.NET will automatically convert the old data types to the new, code that is cut-and-pasted would need to be manually fixed to convert these types, or the code will likely be broken.

The Currency data type will no longer be supported, and should be replaced in most circumstances by the Decimal data type (which is 96 bits – enough for financial calculations). The new 64-bit Long may also be useful in some logic doing currency manipulations because it is not subject to the size limitations of the old 32-bit Long.

The Decimal data type is a base data type in Microsoft.NET and is directly supported in declaration statements by the Visual Basic.NET compiler. In Visual Basic 6, Decimal was actually a subtype of Variant; that is, you couldn't declare a type to be Decimal. Instead, it was necessary to declare it as Variant, and then set the subtype within Variant to Decimal. However, in Visual Basic.NET, a variable can be declared as Decimal.

There's another new data type for single characters called Char. Note, however, that it is two bytes long because it holds Unicode character values. The most common expected use of the Char type is for character arrays, which those C guys wouldn't know how to live without.

The Variant type will no longer be available in Visual Basic .NET. The object type can be used in its place, since even intrinsic data types such as integer and string are considered objects in the .NET framework. The situations where a Variant was necessary in Visual Basic 6, such as declaring a variable that might have to hold different types, is now handled by the Object type.

Another data type not supported in .NET is fixed-length strings. However, there is a compatibility class that provides this functionality. So a declaration of:

```
Dim sFixedLengthString As String*16
```

should be declared as:

```
Dim sFixedLengthString As New VB6.FixedLengthString (16)
```

Finally, the Date type is handled differently in Visual Basic.NET. It is no longer stored in a Double type, but instead uses an eight-bit integer type internally. There are functions (ToDouble and FromADate) to convert back and forth.

Summary of Visual Basic Language Changes

Now let's get down to the detailed syntax changes. Many of the changes listed below are to bring Visual Basic into the Common Language Specification for .NET; others are to modernize the language, and a few simply remove obsolete syntax.

Lots of Possible Incompatibilities

As we've discussed, these are the biggest changes ever in VB – this introduces significant potential for incompatibilities. Some are known and are summarized below. Others will probably crop up soon.

Microsoft intends to supply a conversion tool that will assist in porting VB6 projects to .NET, but it will not do everything required. There will be some areas where the conversion tool merely places a note that indicates something needs to be done. And there are sure to be areas where it fails to realize that a change is needed. The migration tool is discussed in more detail towards the end of the chapter.

No More Default Methods or Properties

Let's examine an example of typical code in VB6 or earlier. In this example, assume `strName` is a string variable, and `txtName` is a text box.

```
strName = txtName      ' works in VB6 and earlier
```

This code works because the text box control has a default property, namely the text it holds. The above line is actually compiled as:

```
strName = txtName.Text
```

The first form will no longer work in the next version of VB because default properties and methods are no longer supported. The second form will be required.

Good coding practices have recommended against the first syntax example for years – it is not easy to read and can be misinterpreted. However, one related syntax form has been used rather commonly when working with data; it's not at all unusual to see lines like this:

```
strName = rsRecordSet("Name")     ' works in VB6 and earlier
```

This works because `Fields` is the default property of the `Recordset` object. This code actually means:

```
strName = rsRecordSet.Fields("Name").Value    ' will work everywhere
                                               ' including VB.NET
```

While it is necessary to add the `.Value` property, the `.Fields` inclusion is optional. This type of default member (in which parameters tip off the compiler that the default member is intended rather than the object reference) is available in beta one of Visual Basic .NET, but I'd recommend that this not be assumed until later beta versions are available.

SET and LET No Longer Supported

So, why take away default properties and methods? Well, let's look at a brief example. To set an object reference to a `Recordset`, current and previous versions of VB require syntax like this:

```
Set txtCity = txtNewCity    ' VB6 and earlier style
```

Without the `Set`, the code is not assigning object references – it is trying to assign a value to a default property, which for the textbox is `Text`. So, to keep things straight for the compiler, `Set` was used for objects, and `Let` statements (where the `Let` has long since been optional) were used for assigning values.

Now that default properties no longer exist, there is no longer any need for `Let`. The previous operation above will merely be coded as:

```
txtCity = txtNewCity          ' new VB.NET style
```

Different Syntax for Class Properties

In VB4, VB5, and VB6, up to three separate property procedures (`Let`, `Get`, and `Set`) are used for each property, although it was only required to use one. In Visual Basic.NET, `Let` property procedures are eliminated because there's no need to differentiate between object references and common variables. `Set` and `Get` procedures are then tied together with some new syntax, which resembles equivalent syntax in C#. Here's an example for the `IntegerProperty` property:

```
Private mintIntegerProperty as Integer

Public Property IntegerProperty As Integer

    Get
        IntegerProperty = mintIntegerProperty
    End Get

    Set
        mintIntegerProperty = Value
    End Set

End Property
```

This is a good deal cleaner than the equivalent VB6 (and earlier) syntax. It also removes a lot of pitfalls, such as changing the data type for a `Get`, but forgetting to do so for the equivalent `Let`.

With this syntax, you can't make a property read-only by merely leaving out the `Set` procedure. You must explicitly declare it with the `ReadOnly` keyword at the beginning of the property declaration. Then the `Set` block can be left out. There is also a `WriteOnly` keyword to make a property write-only, in which case the `Get` block is left out. Here is an example of the above property in the read-only form:

```
Public ReadOnly Property IntegerProperty As Integer

    Get
        IntegerProperty = mintIntegerProperty
    End Get

End Property
```

and in the write-only form:

```
Public WriteOnly Property IntegerProperty As Integer

    Set
        mintIntegerProperty = Value
    End Set

End Property
```

129

Required Parentheses on Methods, Functions, and Subroutines

Many of us have become sloppy about many calling conventions in VB. For example, here's some commonly used code:

```
MsgBox "Hello, World"
```

and here's another common construct:

```
Dim sDate As String
sDate = Date
```

Neither of these will work in the new VB because the compiler now requires the developer to always include parentheses, even for null argument lists. The equivalent working versions of the above examples in Visual Basic.NET are:

```
MsgBox ("Hello, World")
```

and:

```
Dim sDate As String
sDate = Date()
```

Note that you can't even insert the second example into VB6 code, but the `MsgBox` example here will work in VB6. The development editor will remove the parentheses as soon as you leave the line, but they are required for Visual Basic.NET.

Parameters are ByVal by Default

In VB6 and before, parameters in an argument list that were not declared `ByRef` or `ByVal` were assigned a default based on what type of parameter was involved. Intrinsic data types, such as integer, string, Boolean, etc., were defaulted to `ByRef`. Object references and other non-intrinsic types were defaulted to `ByVal`.

If a `ByRef` parameter is changed in the called routine, the changes are reflected in the calling code. Sometimes this is desirable, especially when the parameters become `ByRef` by default, but it can lead to subtle and hard to find bugs. Visual Basic.NET removes the problem. All parameters are `ByVal` unless explicitly declared otherwise.

New Declaration Capabilities

Visual Basic's syntax for declaring variables has always been a bit quirky, and most of the quirks are being removed in the .NET version. For starters, it is possible in Visual Basic.NET to declare a new variable and assign an initial value at the same time. Here's a sample:

```
Dim intHoursAvailable As Integer = 10
Dim intMinutesAvailable As Integer = intHoursAvailable * 60
```

Another VB quirk is allowing mixed declarations on a single line. This line is perfectly legal in VB6:

```
Dim strName as String, intAge As Integer
```

It will not work in Visual Basic.NET, however. The only way multiple variables can be declared on one line is if they are all the same type, and the declaration is made like this:

```
Dim strFirstName, strLastName As String
```

Notice that this line is syntactically valid in VB6, but has a different effect. In VB6, `strFirstName` would actually be declared a variant. But in Visual Basic.NET, both `strFirstName` and `strSecondName` are declared as strings.

The bottom line is that it is always good coding practice to declare every variable on its own line. If you've been doing this for a long time, you'll have less trouble changing over to Visual Basic.NET.

Changes in Declaring Arrays

VB developers will need to be especially on guard for a change in the way arrays are declared. Again, as per other language conventions, all arrays are zero-based, and the declared size is the actual number of elements.

This leads to differences with earlier versions. This line in VB6:

```
Dim strNames(10) as String
```

actually creates **eleven** elements (assuming that arrays are left at the default, which is zero-based), starting at index 0 and ending at index 10.

That line doesn't work the same way in Visual Basic.NET. The exact same line declares an array of exactly ten elements, starting at index 0 and ending at index 9. A reference to `strNames(10)` would cause an out-of-bounds error. VB developers will be familiar with this convention, because it's the way that elements in list and combo boxes work.

Assuming this change holds in the release version, it may introduce more problems in converting old code than any other single change. Many VB developers have long grown accustomed to using 1-based arrays, and seldom using the zero elements. Much of this code can probably not be automatically converted, making significant manual changes necessary.

The syntax to initialize values during declaration has an equivalent for arrays. In Visual Basic.NET, a whole array can be initialized like this:

```
Dim strNames(3) as String = ("Moe", "Larry", " Curly")
```

and referenced by `strNames(0)`, `strNames(1)`, `strNames(2)`. (Note that this will not work in VB6.)

Finally, arrays must be declared with `Dim`, and can no longer be declared with `Redim` and an empty index. `Redim` can only be used to resize arrays in Visual Basic.NET, and in that capacity works the same way as in VB6.

No Implicit Loading of Forms

VB forms have always been loaded whenever the first reference was made to them. This was not necessarily good coding practice, but it was supported. Implicit loading is not supported in beta one of Visual Basic.NET, so forms will have to be explicitly declared and loaded just like other objects. As we've previously discussed, a form is just a class module that inherits the ability to act like a form. Typical code would look like this, assuming that the project contains a form class named Form2:

```
Dim frmNewForm As New Form2()
frmNewForm.Show()
```

This is very similar to VB6 except for the required parentheses at the end of both lines.

Many Keywords Move to Shared Class Members

Many traditional VB keywords are being removed from the base language. In most cases, the equivalent capabilities are being replaced with members in shared classes in the .NET Framework. Here are some of the keywords being replaced, with their new name and location:

Keyword	Location in Visual Basic.NET (namespace)	Method / Property
Circle	System.Drawing.Graphics	DrawEllipse
Line	System.Drawing.Graphics	DrawLine
Atn	System.Math	Atan
Sgn	System.Math	Sign
Sqr	System.Math	Sqrt
Rnd	Microsoft.VisualBasic.Compatibility.VB6	Rnd
Round	Microsoft.VisualBasic.Compatibility.VB6	Round
Lset	System.String	PadRight
Rset	System.String	PadLeft
DoEvents	System.Winforms.Application	DoEvents
VarType	System.Object	GetType (returns an object of class Type, which has properties to get information)

This list should not be considered exhaustive – it just highlights some of the major changes.

Bitwise Operations

In Visual Basic 6.0, the operators And, Or, Xor, and Not are used for both Boolean operations (as in an If statement) and bit-wise operations (which do bit-wise arithmetic on variables). For example, here are two valid uses of the And keyword in VB6. The first is a Boolean operation for an If statement:

```
If (Len(sFirstName) = 0) And (Len(sLastName) = 0) Then
    MsgBox "No name supplied!"
End If
```

And the second is a doing some bit-wise arithmetic:

```
Dim iAttributes As Integer
Dim iMoreAttributes As Integer
iAttributes = &H101        ' this is hex for 257
iMoreAttributes = &H100   ' this is hex for 256
MsgBox(iAttributes And iMoreAttributes)
```

In the second case, the MsgBox would display 256, which is the bit-wise result of (257 And 256).

In Visual Basic.NET, And, Or, Xor, and Not are strictly for Boolean operations, like the first example above. The equivalent corresponding keywords for bit-wise arithmetic are BitAnd, BitOr, BitXor, and BitNo. So in Visual Basic.NET, the second example above must be changed to:

```
Dim iAttributes As Integer
Dim iMoreAttributes As Integer
iAttributes = &H101        ' this is hex for 257
iMoreAttributes = &H100   ' this is hex for 256
MsgBox(iAttributes BitAnd iMoreAttributes)
```

User Defined Types Replaced by Structures

In Visual Basic 6.0, a user-defined type is declared using the Type ... End Type construct. Such a type is publicly available, including all of its constituent elements (members). Here's an example:

```
Type Customer
    CustID As Integer
    CustPhone As String
    CustStatus As Boolean
End Type
```

In Visual Basic.NET, the Type statement is no longer available. In its place, a structure can be declared using the Structure ... End Structure syntax. Furthermore, every member of a structure must be declared as one of the following: Dim, Public, Protected, Friend, Protected Friend, or Private. Dim and Public both indicate public access, and the others give various restrictions on access. A similar structure in Visual Basic.NET for the user defined type in the preceding example, taking advantage of some of the declaration modifiers, might look like this:

```
Structure Customer
    Public CustID As Integer       ' Must declare access, even if Public.
    Dim CustPhone As String        ' Still defaults to Public access.
    Private CustStatus As Boolean  ' Can be made Private inside Structure.
End Structure
```

The syntax for accessing a structure is object syntax, and very similar to the syntax for accessing user defined types in VB6 and earlier.

Scope Changes for Variables

In Visual Basic 6.0, a variable can be declared anywhere inside a procedure, and regardless of the location of the declaration, the variable has full procedure scope, so it can be accessed anywhere else within the same procedure. If the variable is declared inside a block such a `For` loop, a `Do` loop, or an `If` block, the variable is still accessible outside the block. Here's an example in VB6:

```
Do
   Dim iAccumulator As Integer
   iAccumulator = iAccumulator + 1
Loop Until iAccumulator > 100
MsgBox iAccumulator
```

This will work just fine. The `MsgBox` will display 101 when the loop is finished, because the variable `iAccumulator` is available outside the `Do` loop, even though it was declared inside the loop.

Visual Basic.NET changes the rules. For any variable declared in a block – that is, a set of statements terminated by an `End`, `Loop`, or `Next` statement – the variable is only available inside the block. That is, it has **block scope**. The preceding example would have to change to something like this:

```
Dim iAccumulator As Integer
Do
   iAccumulator = iAccumulator + 1
Loop Until iAccumulator > 100
MsgBox iAccumulator
```

Block scope works a bit differently from procedure scope. If a variable is declared inside a block, it does not lose its value when the block is exited. The value is still there in case the block is re-entered. Even though the value is not lost, though, the variable cannot be referenced from outside the block.

Miscellaneous Changes

Optional parameters are still supported in Visual Basic.NET, but they now require a default value. The `Is Missing` construct is not supported.

Evaluation of conditionals is being brought into line with other languages. In particular, if a conditional has two parts, but evaluation of the first part makes it unnecessary to look at the second part, then no evaluation of the second part is made. Consider this line:

```
If (Len(strFirstName) <> 0) And (Len(strLastName) <> 0) Then
```

If the length of `strFirstName` turns out to be zero, then the conditional is false and it is unnecessary to evaluate the second part. This speeds up execution, which is why other languages do it this way.

Sloppy coders have been known to put function calls into conditionals, which carry out some action that changes values. They might write code such as:

```
If (Len(strFirstName) <> 0) And (InitializeRecord(intID)) Then
```

Such code could be affected by the change. In VB6, the `InitializeRecord` function would always be executed when the `If` is tested. In Visual Basic.NET, it will not be executed if the first part of the conditional is false. Bugs introduced by this change could be really difficult to track down.

Note that this code is poor programming practice anyway. Actions should not appear in conditionals. Good programming practice would change the above code to something like this:

```
Dim bRecordInitialized As Boolean
bRecordInitialized = InitializeRecord(intID)
If (Len(strFirstName) <> 0) And (bRecordInitialized) Then
```

The `Debug` object gets some changes in Visual Basic .NET. It is at `System.Diagnostics.Debug`, and its commonly used `Print` method has four replacements – `Write`, `WriteIf`, `WriteLine`, and `WriteLineIf`. The closest replacement for the old `Print` method is `Write`.

Other new capabilities include new options for formatting strings and parsing numbers, and new shorthand syntax for incrementing and decrementing a variable.

The list of changes in this section is not exhaustive. There are a host of minor changes, which are not listed. The Visual Basic.NET documentation continues to add documentation of these changes with each version, and it would be a good idea to check it out before doing serious development with Visual Basic.NET.

Retired Keywords

The following keywords are being retired, and will no longer be supported in Visual Basic.NET. Some are from pre-VB days, and were originally included in VB for compatibility with languages such as QuickBASIC.

- ❑ `Gosub`
- ❑ `On x GoTo` … (computed `GoTo`'s)
- ❑ `Let`
- ❑ `Option Base 0 | 1`
- ❑ `VarPtr, ObjPtr, StrPtr`
- ❑ `DefBool, DefByte, DefInt, DefLng, DefCur, DefSng, DefDbl, DefDec, DefDate, DefStr, DefObj, DefVar`

Almost all of these will need to be fixed manually in old projects that are upgraded to Visual Basic. NET.

Additional Impact on Current Projects

Designing for Web Forms

Many current VB projects will be candidates for converting to Web Forms to gain web functionality. This will not be a transparent conversion, but there are some things that can make it easier. Many of them are simply good design principles, but they are worth reiterating.

Any tiered design will transfer more easily to Visual Studio.NET. Fat VB clients, where all the business logic is mixed up with the UI code, will probably not be practical candidates for migration. This gives even more reasons for current projects to be undertaken with good multi-tiered design.

VB designs that depend heavily on code in control events may have problems in migration. The difficulty is that many events in the Web Forms world will require a server roundtrip. In a traditional VB form, events can be fired constantly and handled without noticing a performance hit, but that will not be true for Web Forms.

Calling Controls Directly

Another commonly used VB technique is to call a control on a form directly to get a value out of it. Controls are always considered `Public` in all existing versions of VB, so code like this works fine:

```
' code executed from a .BAS module in VB6 or earlier
strNewEmployee = frmEmployee.txtEmployeeID.Text
```

> *This syntax does not work in the PDC Technical Preview Pre-Beta version of Visual Basic.NET. The error message indicates that the control is now considered* `Private`.

There are good alternatives to this technique. In VB4 and later, custom properties are typically the best choice. That is, to fix the example above, `frmEmployee` would have a property procedure that looked like this:

```
Public Property EmployeeID As String

    Get
        EmployeeID = txtEmployeeID.Text
    End Get

    Set
        txtEmployeeID.Text = EmployeeID
    End Set

End Property
```

The code in the .BAS module would then become:

```
' code executed from a .BAS module
frmEmployee.EmployeeID = strNewEmployee
```

This technique has other advantages, which include the capability to change controls on the form without affecting the calling logic in other routines. That is, if the employee ID in the form were moved to a label instead of a text box, the code in the .BAS module would not need to change. Only the code in the form's property procedure would need to change to work with the label instead of the text box.

The Visual Basic Migration Tool

Microsoft has stated that a migration tool will be available to help move Visual Basic 6 projects into Visual Basic.NET. It will convert code modules, making syntax changes as necessary, and will insert TODO: items if it thinks manual changes are needed. VB Forms are also converted to WinForms, fixing the most common changes of control properties, and producing a class module for the form.

The MSDN Library contains an article called *Preparing Your Visual Basic 6.0 Applications for the Upgrade to Visual Basic.NET*. The article can be found at:

http://msdn.microsoft.com/library/techart/vb6tovbdotnet.htm

Here are some of the most important notes and recommendations from that article.

Dealing with DHTML Pages and WebClasses

Both DHTML pages and WebClasses have been replaced in Visual Basic.NET with Web Forms. The migration tool will not upgrade DHTML pages, and Microsoft recommends that WebClasses be left in Visual Basic 6. WebClasses can be upgraded to Visual Basic.NET, but will need some manual modifications before they will work.

Dealing with Data

Visual Basic.NET will still support use of DAO, RDO, and older ADO object models for accessing data. (The release version of the .NET framework is expected to include version 3.0 of ADO, as well as ADO.NET.) However, data binding to controls with DAO or RDO will not be supported. Such data binding will need to be changed to ADO to work in Visual Basic.NET.

Problems Converting Late-bound Objects

The migration tool will have the intelligence to take care of many changes with object models. For example, when upgrading a form with a label, any references to a `Caption` property will be changed to a `Text` property.

However, for this to work, the migration tool must know that it is dealing with a label. If a label object reference is late bound, it is not able to tell this. For example:

```
Dim objLabel as Object
Set objLabel = Me.Label1
objLabel.Caption = "Text to appear in the label"
```

If the above code from a VB6 program is encountered, then the migration tool will be unable to identify `objLabel` as a label control, since it was declared as type `Object`. That means it won't know to change the `Caption` property in the third line to a `Text` property.

The recommendation to avoid this problem is to use early binding whenever possible.

Use Intrinsic Named Constants Instead of Values

It is good programming practice to use Visual Basic's intrinsic constants for many settings. For example, this is good coding practice:

```
Me.WindowState = vbMaximized
```

This line could be coded with the actual value of the constant `vbMaximized`, which is 2. In that case, the line would be:

```
Me.WindowState = 2
```

The migration tool is not going to change either of these lines. However, in some cases the values of the intrinsic constants are changing in .NET. If the second form is used, the value being used may no longer match the intent. If the intrinsic constant form is used, there will be no trouble in migration.

Another example is using `True` and `False` instead of –1 and 0. In Visual Basic.NET, `True` becomes 1 instead of –1, but `False` stays the same. The code migration tool will not fix logic that uses –1 explicitly for `True`.

Problems with Fixed Length Strings in Structures

We previously discussed the fact that fixed length strings are not a native type in Microsoft.NET, but that a compatibility fix is available. The migration tool will apply this fix for types declared as fixed length strings.

However, the migration tool does not work for fixed length strings used in user-defined `types` (which are replaced by `Structures`). It is not possible to put a fixed length string in a structure. That means such cases will require manual adjustment. For example, this user defined type:

```
Type Customer
    CustID As Integer
    CustPhone As String*20
    CustStatus As Boolean
End Type
```

would need to be converted to:

```
Structure Customer
    Public CustID As Integer
    Public CustPhone As String
    Public CustStatus As Boolean
End Structure
```

Then, at some point in the logic when an instance of this structure is created, the `CustPhone` member would need to explicitly have exactly 20 characters placed in it, like this:

```
Dim stcCustomer as Customer
stcCustomer.CustPhone = String$(20, " ")
```

It would be important to check the length of `stcCustomer.CustPhone` every time it is changed to keep it at twenty characters.

This is not going to be worth the trouble in most cases, so if it is at all possible to switch to a variable length string in the structure, by all means do so. Of course, one of the typical uses of a user-defined type is to mimic a record layout that has fixed length fields in it, and this will be difficult to do with structures in Visual Basic.NET.

Upgrade Report and Comments

The migration tool will create an upgrade report as part of the migration process. This report will list changes that need to be made manually to the upgraded code. Comments are also placed in the code indicating the places changes are needed, and the comments are constructed in such a way that they show up in the new Task List, which is part of the new development environment. (Changes to the Visual Studio IDE are discussed in Chapter 5).

Recommendations

What else can you do to prepare for Visual Basic.NET? Here are some suggestions.

Syntax Conventions in Visual Basic Projects

There are several areas where coding conventions for present VB projects can relieve some of the problems likely with later migration to Visual Studio.NET. Here is a quick summary:

- ❑ Don't use default properties or methods
- ❑ Use parentheses even when they are optional
- ❑ Avoid API calls, or wrap them in a component for ease of conversion
- ❑ Only one variable on each declaration line
- ❑ Make arrays zero-based and do not use the nth element in an array declared to be size n
- ❑ Make all parameters explicitly `ByRef` or `ByVal`
- ❑ Place default values on all optional parameters
- ❑ Consider controls private to the form they are on – do not refer to them from outside the form (use property procedures instead)
- ❑ Use ADO instead of DAO or RDO for data access, especially data binding
- ❑ Use intrinsic constants whenever possible
- ❑ Don't use obsolete keywords such as `Gosub` and `DefInt`
- ❑ Use the `Date` type to store dates rather that putting a date in a `Double`

And, of course, keep logic encapsulated into components as much as possible.

Get the Latest Beta of Visual Studio .NET

The beta program for Visual Studio .NET will be very different from the beta cycle for previous versions. Some later beta versions will be available to anyone who requests them. As of writing, beta one of Visual Studio.NET is available, and is available to anyone with an MSDN Universal Subscription or anyone accepted into the beta program.

Start Using the SOAP Toolkit for Visual Studio 6

As previously mentioned, SOAP is a foundation technology of Microsoft.NET, and Web Services uses it as a protocol. Anyone expecting to remain current with leading-edge Internet-based systems should be very familiar with SOAP and systems based on it. Fortunately, that familiarity can be gained right now using Visual Basic 6 plus the SOAP toolkit, which is available for download at:

http://msdn.microsoft.com/xml/general/toolkit_intro.asp.

Visual Studio.NET will use SOAP extensively, and will hide a lot of the implementation details. The Visual Studio 6 SOAP toolkit requires a lot more manual work to get a distributed component working than will be needed in the .NET framework. However, it's worth the effort to become knowledgeable about the capabilities and limitations of SOAP. Understanding the details of SOAP is also very important if SOAP-compliant components will be implemented on a non-Microsoft platform.

Summary

Visual Basic is enormously popular, but it certainly has room for considerable improvement. Visual Basic.NET takes some giant steps towards putting Visual Basic on a par with any language available.

The price to be paid for this is considerable lack of upward compatibility for old projects. In particular, sloppy code will be difficult to migrate, and many older, poorly written systems will not be worth the effort.

However, well-written code will be feasible to migrate. And Visual Basic.NET systems, whether new, or migrated from older code, will run on a modern, streamlined development platform that offers smooth integration with the web and with other languages, and additional advantages well into the future.

NETINTRODUCING.NETINTRODUCING.NETINTRODUCING.NETINTRODUCING.NETINTR
DUCING.NETINTRODUCING.NETINTRODUCING.NETINTRODUCING.NETINTRODUCIN
ETINTRODUCING.NETINTRODUCING.NETINTRODUCING.NETINTRODUCING.NETINTR
CING.NETINTRODUCING.NETINTRODUCING.NETINTRODUCING.NETINTRODUCING.N
NTRODUCING.NETINTRODUCING.NETINTRODUCING.NETINTRODUCING.NETINTRODU
G.NETINTRODUCING.NETINTRODUCING.NETINTRODUCING.NETINTRODUCING.NETI
ODUCING.NETINTRODUCING.NETINTRODUCING.NETINTRODUCING.NETINTRODUCIN
ETINTRODUCING.NETINTRODUCING.NETINTRODUCING.NETINTRODUCING.NETINTR
CING.NETINTRODUCING.NETINTRODUCING.NETINTRODUCING.NETINTRODUCING.N
NTRODUCING.NETINTRODUCING.NETINTRODUCING.NETINTRODUCING.NETINTRODU
G.NETINTRODUCING.NETINTRODUCING.NETINTRODUCING.NETINTRODUCING.NETI
ODUCING.NETINTRODUCING.NETINTRODUCING.NETINTRODUCING.NETINTRODUCIN
ETINTRODUCING.NETINTRODUCING.NETINTRODUCING.NETINTRODUCING.NETINTR
CING.NETINTRODUCING.NETINTRODUCING.NETINTRODUCING.NETINTRODUCING.N
NTRODUCING.NETINTRODUCING.NETINTRODUCING.NETINTRODUCING.NETINTRODU
G.NETINTRODUCING.NETINTRODUCING.NETINTRODUCING.NETINTRODUCING.NETI
ODUCING.NETINTRODUCING.NETINTRODUCING.NETINTRODUCING.NETINTRODUCIN
ETINTRODUCING.NETINTRODUCING.NETINTRODUCING.NETINTRODUCING.NETINTR
CING.NETINTRODUCING.NETINTRODUCING.NETINTRODUCING.NETINTRODUCING.N
NTRODUCING.NETINTRODUCING.NETINTRODUCING.NETINTRODUCING.NETINTRODU
G.NETINTRODUCING.NETINTRODUCING.NETINTRODUCING.NETINTRODUCING.NETI
ODUCING.NETINTRODUCING.NETINTRODUCING.NETINTRODUCING.NETINTRODUCIN
ETINTRODUCING.NETINTRODUCING.NETINTRODUCING.NETINTRODUCING.NETINTI
CING.NETINTRODUCING.NETINTRODUCING.NETINTRODUCING.NETINTRODUCING.N
NTRODUCING.NETINTRODUCING.NETINTRODUCING.NETINTRODUCING.NETINTRODU
G.NETINTRODUCING.NETINTRODUCING.NETINTRODUCING.NETINTRODUCING.NET
ODUCING.NETINTRODUCING.NETINTRODUCING.NETINTRODUCING.NETINTRODUCI
ETINTRODUCING.NETINTRODUCING.NETINTRODUCING.NETINTRODUCING.NETINT
CING.NETINTRODUCING.NETINTRODUCING.NETINTRODUCING.NETINTRODUCING.
NTRODUCING.NETINTRODUCING.NETINTRODUCING.NETINTRODUCING.NETINTROD
G.NETINTRODUCING.NETINTRODUCING.NETINTRODUCING.NETINTRODUCING.NET
ODUCING.NETINTRODUCING.NETINTRODUCING.NETINTRODUCING.NETINTRODUCI
ETINTRODUCING.NETINTRODUCING.NETINTRODUCING.NETINTRODUCING.NETINT
CING.NETINTRODUCING.NETINTRODUCING.NETINTRODUCING.NETINTRODUCING.
NTRODUCING.NETINTRODUCING.NETINTRODUCING.NETINTRODUCING.NETINTROD
G.NETINTRODUCING.NETINTRODUCING.NETINTRODUCING.NETINTRODUCING.NET
ODUCING.NETINTRODUCING.NETINTRODUCING.NETINTRODUCING.NETINTRODUCI
ETINTRODUCING.NETINTRODUCING.NETINTRODUCING.NETINTRODUCING.NETINT
CING.NETINTRODUCING.NETINTRODUCING.NETINTRODUCING.NETINTRODUCING.

New Features in Visual Studio.NET

Other chapters in this book look at the technology behind Microsoft.NET. This chapter looks more closely at what a developer sees when he or she sits down to actually write Microsoft.NET systems – the Visual Studio Integrated Development Environment (IDE) and other new features of Visual Studio.NET.

The first chapter of the book discussed some of the major changes in Visual Studio.NET. Two of the major ones concern Visual Interdev and Visual J++. To review, Visual Interdev is no longer a separate product, but has had its functionality folded into the Visual Studio environment as a whole. Several items in this chapter will refer to features of the Visual Studio environment that are descended from Visual Interdev. Visual J++ is missing entirely because of the continuing legal complications between Microsoft and Sun. In a sense, its replacement is the new language C#, which is discussed in Chapter 3. Visual FoxPro is included with the Visual Studio beta one installation, but is not implemented in beta one as a .NET language (one based on the .NET Framework), so it is not discussed in this book.

The first chapter also mentioned WinForms and Web Forms, which are new to Visual Studio and available to all languages. Other chapters contain in-depth information on the structure and capabilities of WinForms and Web Forms, but we will include some brief discussion below on creating WinForms and Web Forms in the Visual Studio IDE.

The Visual Studio IDE

Microsoft's roots are in the developer community, and Visual Studio.NET demonstrates that Microsoft is still trying to find ways to make developers more productive. Microsoft didn't create the first IDE, but they have been on the forefront in recent years in adding features like IntelliSense that can boost developer productivity.

Visual Studio.NET's IDE is not revolutionary, but it does add several new functions and features that I think developers will be very happy to have. Overall, Visual Studio.NET will look familiar to users of previous Visual Studio versions. In many respects, it combines the best of the various IDEs that were previously used. It has a general look and feel similar to the Visual Basic 6 IDE, but takes, for example, the Solution Explorer window from the Project Explorer in Visual Interdev.

Unlike previous versions, in Visual Studio.NET, exactly the same IDE is used for all Visual Studio languages. In fact, the IDE is designed specifically to manage projects using more than one language at a time. The languages used in, and managed by, the Visual Studio.NET IDE can be extended beyond Microsoft languages to a long list of third party languages that are being brought into the .NET framework.

To satisfy such a wide variety of developers, who may be coming from a host of previous languages, there are a lot of options and configurable features that can allow the IDE to be customized to the needs of a particular developer.

A Tour of the Visual Studio.NET IDE

When Visual Studio.NET is first installed and run, a window similar to the following is displayed.

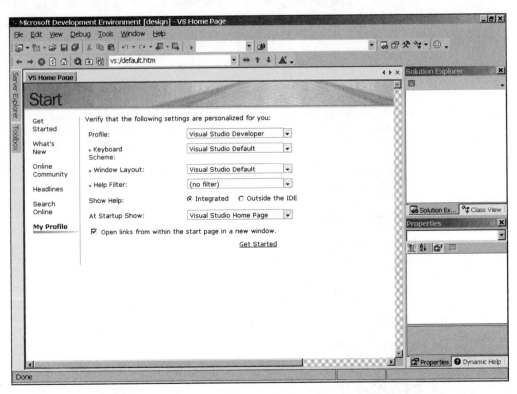

This is the Visual Studio Home Page, a new concept that wraps up many customization options and other capabilities into an easy-to-use and extendable package. At first startup, the selected option on the left of the Home Page is My Profile to allow the new user to select an appropriate profile to adapt the environment to their needs.

Profiles

Visual Studio.NET will be used by developers with different backgrounds, so there are several options a developer may choose to make the environment simulate an expected layout from earlier versions. By choosing an overall "profile", several aspects of the IDE are customized at once, such as the position of the code window and properties windows, and what windows take precedence in the environment. For example, if the Visual Basic profile is selected, the toolbox, by default, is always on the screen. For other profiles, such as Visual Studio default, the toolbox becomes a tab on the left side of the screen, in a similar way to the Server Explorer tab, and must be selected by hovering the mouse pointer over it, which causes the toolbox to "slide out".

The examples in this section mostly use the layout from the Visual Studio Developer profile. When other profiles are used, this will be mentioned. In particular, some of the examples use the Visual Basic Developer profile instead.

Selecting Help Options

Answering a long-standing gripe about Visual Studio 6, the help system can be filtered to offer language help for just one language. As seen in the sample screen, the Help Filter is set to Visual Basic Documentation, but other languages are available in the drop down. (The help is also installed by default to not require insertion of the MSDN disks, which were the main source of help in Visual Studio 6.) The user also has the choice of showing the help inside the IDE (as a tabbed window in the same area that code is shown), or completely outside the IDE as a separate window that can be positioned and manipulated.

The Home Page

Once a profile is selected, the startup screen for Visual Studio.NET looks like the following figure (assuming the Visual Studio Developer profile is selected).

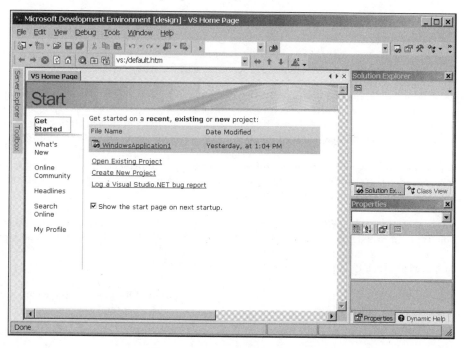

This Home Page lists the projects worked on most recently, together with options to open an existing project or create a new project. The Log a Visual Studio.NET bug report option will hopefully not be necessary in the release version.

A Place for News and Information

Notice that there are several categories to the left of the Home Page window, such as Headlines. Some of this content comes from the web, and some comes from XML files in one of the Visual Studio directories or the Visual Studio help files. The What's New section is a particularly good source of valuable information on changes in Visual Studio.NET, taken from the help files. Headlines is from the MSDN web site and gives Microsoft a place to communicate new information about Visual Studio to users, such as availability of service packs.

Creating a New Project

If the Create New Project option is selected from the Home Page (or if File | New | Project is selected from the pull down menus) then the dialog depicted below appears.

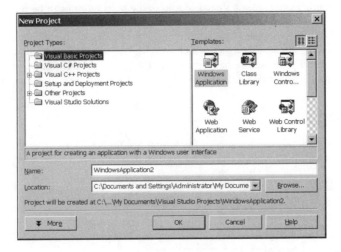

This style of option dialog is becoming popular with Microsoft. Rather than use tabbed dialogs, a tree structure is displayed in the left windows, and the contents of the right windows vary to reflect the currently selected option in the tree. Note the types of projects that can be selected. Several of them are new, such as the web-based ones (Web Application, Web Service, and Web Control Library).

Some projects are language-dependent. Many of the same types of project are present in both the Visual Basic Projects folder and the Visual C# Projects folder; for example, including Windows Application for WinForms, and Web Application for Web Forms.

The set of projects available for C++ varies form that available to Visual Basic and C#. It includes some of the same types of projects as Visual Basic and C#, but named differently – for example, a project for a Web Service in C++ is called a "Managed C++ Web Service". However, most of the C++ projects are specific to C++, including projects based on ATL and MFC.

Other folders contain projects that span multiple languages. Some of these are in the Setup and Deployment Projects folder, which is discussed briefly later in this chapter.

To show some more sample screens, we will select the Windows Application option under Visual Basic Projects. The following screens will basically be the new version of the equivalent screens for developing a forms-based project in Visual Basic 6.

Working on a WinForm

The first screen for a new Visual Basic WinForms project looks like the figure below:

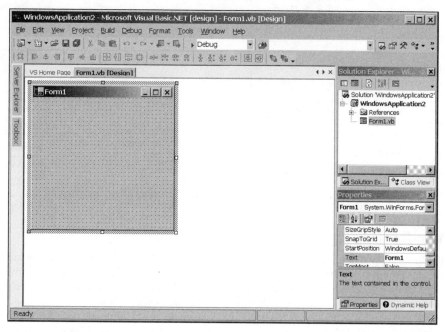

This looks generally familiar to a VB6 developer, except that the toolbox is not shown, but is instead a pullout tab on the left hand side. It also works in the same way as VB6, using drag-and-drop from the toolbox onto the form surface to lay out the form. (As previously mentioned, the toolbox can be set to be on the screen all the time. One quick way to do that is to click on the pushpin in the upper right corner of the toolbox when it is pulled out. This will cause it to stay on the screen.)

The toolbox is a little different to VB6: instead of the icon-only grid of available controls, a linear list is presented, with each control having both an icon and a description. This is another example of a Visual Interdev-influenced feature in Visual Studio.NET.

With the toolbox pulled out, the WinForms design screen looks like the figure below. Some developers may find this arrangement a bit awkward, because the toolbox covers up part of the design surface so that it's not possible to drag and drop to all locations on the surface. I'd recommend using the pushpin to keep the toolbox in place during any serious form design.

The list of controls in the toolbox is similar to that available in Visual Basic. Some of the differences are covered in Chapter 9, *Windows Forms*, later in the book. One of the most notable is that there is a control that places a standard Windows drop-down menu on the form, called a `MainMenu` control. Another control, called a `ContextMenu` control, provides pop-up windows. These controls give the developer a far superior way to manipulate menus in WinForms than was available in VB6.

The user can customize the toolbox in Visual Studio. Selecting the **Tools | Customize Toolbox** option displays a tabbed dialog with various options for controlling the toolbox. Some of the capability that was formerly in the **Project | Components** dialog in Visual Basic 6 has been moved to this new dialog in Visual Studio.NET

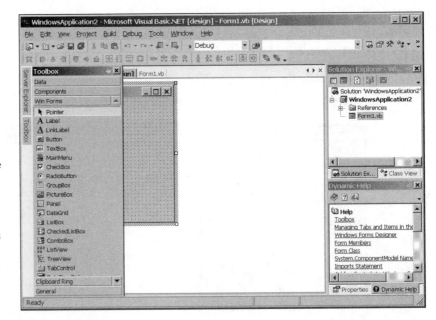

Tabbed Windows

One of the first things you notice about the interface is the prevalence of tabs at various locations to change the content of windows. Just below the toolbars is one set of tabs currently containing **VS Home Page** and **Form1.vb [Design]**. This set of tabs is above the window VB6 developers expect to contain form layouts and code. This window now handles additional displays. It allows selection of the Home Page, for example, and it is no longer MDI-child based by default. It now only shows one item, namely the one whose tab is selected. In the screen above, only two tabs are present, but more tabs appear here as code windows and additional forms are created. (The old MDI child arrangement can still be set by going to **Tools | Options** dialog and checking **MDI Environment**).

The Solution Explorer

The Solution Explorer will be familiar to Visual Interdev users. It is a replacement for the Project Explorer in Visual Basic 6, and looks generally similar. However, it holds many project elements besides code and forms. We'll see an example from a Web Forms project later in this chapter.

Just below the Solution Explorer is another set of tabs. The **Class View** tab will be familiar to C++ users; it allows an alternate way to look at the class structure of the elements in a project. If it is selected for the project above, it looks like the following figure:

The Class View allows exploration of the base class for a given class, as well as the class members (properties and methods). The icons next to the members give information such as whether the member is private (in that case it has a padlock icon). The Class View is useful in some instances that the Object Browser would have been used for in VB6. (The Object Browser is still available in Visual Studio.NET, and is accessed through View | Other Windows | Object Browser).

The Properties Window and Dynamic Help

Another tab is present below the Properties Window. The Properties Window itself is not much changed from Visual Studio 6, but the other option on the tab, Dynamic Help, is new.

Dynamic Help guesses what you might be interested in looking at from what you have done recently. The figure below shows a sample screen from using Dynamic Help.

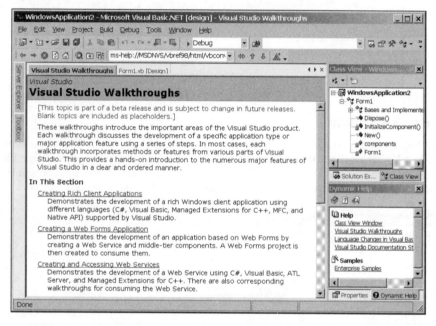

Notice that the Dynamic Help window (on the lower right) has an entry for Class View Window. That entry appears because the Class View Window (above the Dynamic Help window, and discussed previously) had just been displayed. Another option in the Dynamic Help is Visual Studio Walkthroughs, and this option has been selected. Note the walkthroughs that are available; these are great getting started options to learn how to do the basics for the different types of projects which can be created in Visual Studio.NET.

As an example, selecting the Creating and Accessing Web Services walkthrough gives the screen shown below, which shows step-by-step instructions for building a web service. This is merely the first set of steps in the walkthrough. There are additional steps for Implementing the Web Service and for Testing and Deploying the Web Service, which can be seen by scrolling the Help window further down.

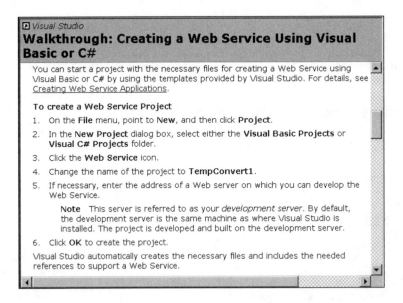

The New Code Window

One of the biggest and most useful enhancements in the Visual Studio.NET IDE is the new code window. As in Visual Studio 6, the code window is accessed by either selecting a source file in Solution Explorer, or by right-clicking a form and selecting **View Code**. Below is a sample screen showing the code from the form (Form1) that was inserted automatically when the WinForms project was created.

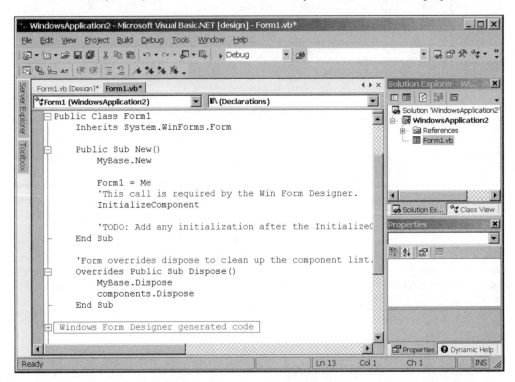

This code editor window looks mostly familiar, except for the gray line on the left with the plus and minus signs. This line is the visual indication that the code inside routines in Visual Studio.NET can either be visible or hidden. This feature is called **Outlining**.

Notice that there is a minus sign next to every routine (sub or function). This makes is easy to hide or show code on a routine-by-routine basis. If code for a routine is hidden, the routine declaration is still shown, and has a plus sign next to it to indicate that the body code is hidden.

This outlining feature should be very useful when a developer is working on two or three key routines in a module, and wishes to avoid scrolling through many screens of code that are not important to the current task.

There is, however, another option to show or hide larger regions of code. In Visual Basic and C#, the #Region directive is used for this. Regions have a description that appears next to the plus sign used to show the code. For example, in the previous figure there is a code section labeled Windows Form Designer generated code at the bottom of the figure. It is hidden because normally there is no need for the developer to see or manipulate this code. However, if the plus sign is clicked it comes into view. The next figure shows what the code window looks like after the plus sign is clicked.

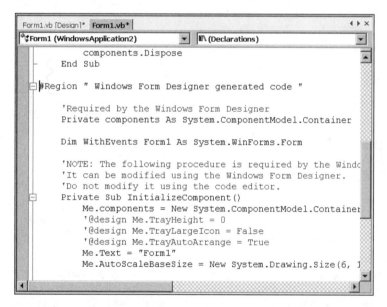

The outlining enhancement to show and hide sections of code was probably inspired by the fact that the Visual Studio.NET designers generate a lot of code when a project is first begun. Items that were hidden in Visual Studio 6 (such as the logic which sets initial form properties) are actually in the generated code in Visual Studio.NET.

In most respects, doing all of these functions in code is an improvement because it is easier for the developer to see what is going on, and possibly to manipulate the process in limited, special cases. However, that designer-generated code normally does not need to be seen or changed by the developer, so leaving it in the code window would cause it to be in the way most of the time. Instead, it is hidden and out of the way. As a nice side benefit, developers can hide their own code when it is not relevant to the task at hand. Outlining can be turned off by selecting Edit | Outlining | Stop Outlining from the Visual Studio menu.

The Task List

There are a number of optional windows that can be used in Visual Studio.NET. One that is sure to be popular is the Task List. First seen in Visual Interdev, the Task List is a great productivity tool to track pending changes and additions in code. It's also a good way for the Visual Studio.NET environment to communicate information the developer needs to know, such as errors in the current code. Visual Basic developers will be happy to know that the Task List can show all current syntax errors in the code, so it's not necessary to do a "Run With Full Compile" and then look at errors one at a time. When the task list is displayed, it normally appears just below the window that holds code and forms.

The task list is displayed with the Show Tasks option on the View menu. There are several options available. Following is a screen with this menu selected, showing the various options for showing tasks:

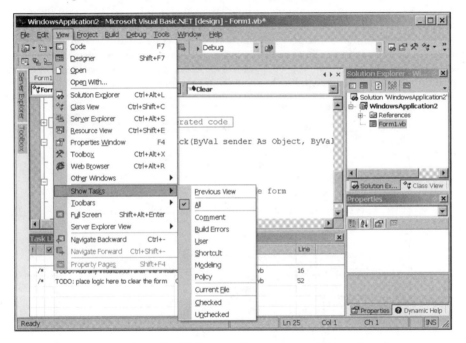

The Comment option is for tasks embedded into code comments. This is done by creating a comment with the apostrophe, and then starting the comment with TODO:. This can be followed with any text desired. Such a comment will show up in the task list if the Comment option or the All option is selected. The new code window screenshot shown previously has such a comment approximately in the middle of the code window. In addition to using the TODO: token, a user can create their own comment tokens in the options for Visual Studio (Tools | Options | Environment | Task List).

The figure below shows a task list with a couple of TODO: items displayed.

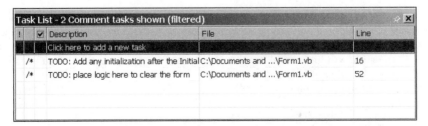

In the screen above, the first task (which can be seen in the code in the new code window screenshot previously) was actually placed in comments by the form designer. The second task was inserted manually inside a new method for the form named Clear.

As well as helping developers track these tasks, embedding the tasks in code brings another benefit: clicking on a task in the task list causes the code editor to make the location of the task comment the current location for editing. This means that a developer can jump right to the location for a task without hunting through code for it.

Another view of the task list that is useful is Build Errors. This view summarizes all the things that prevent a clean build of the code, and, as with tasks embedded in comments, clicking on a build error task takes the code editor to the location of the error. It's not necessary to explicitly choose Build for these errors to display – the environment automatically checks code continuously and inserts build errors into the list. As with other tasks, build errors are also included when the Task List is set to view all tasks.

The user also has the option of simply typing tasks into the list. These are shown when the User option for filtering the task list is selected, or when all tasks are displayed.

The Server Explorer

As development has become more server-centric, developers have a greater need to discover and manipulate services on the network. The Server Explorer is a new feature in Visual Studio.NET that makes this easier.

Visual Interdev made a start in this direction with a Server Object section in the Interdev toolbox. The Server Explorer is more sophisticated. It allows, for example, exploration and alteration of SQL Server database structures that would have previously been done with the SQL Enterprise Manager.

The Server Explorer is a pullout tab on the left side of the IDE. When it is extended, the window looks like that below:

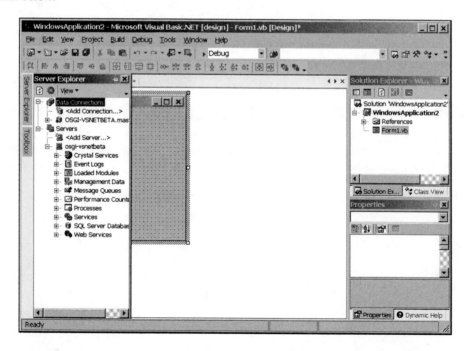

Notice the wide variety of server resources that are available for inspection, or for use in the project. The Server Explorer makes it unnecessary for a developer to go to an outside resource to find, for example, what message queues are available. The <Add Server> option allows a new server to be selected and inspected. The Server Explorer even provides the ability to stop and restart services on the server.

The Server Explorer subsumes must of the functionality in the Data View in Visual Studio 6. However, it is far more powerful, and easier to use.

As an example of the Server Explorer's capabilities, the figure below shows the screen that appears when the Add Connection option is chosen. This screen brings together all the information needed to establish a connection to a server database in a tabbed dialog. Some elements of this dialog are similar to other screens that have been used in the past, such as the ODBC Connection dialog in the Control Panel. However, this screen is more accessible to the developer.

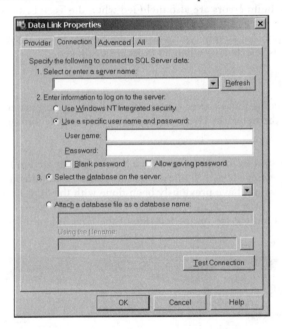

Some Differences when Developing Web Forms

The above examples have all used sample screens from a WinForms project. There are a few differences when developing a Web Forms project that are worth noting. The biggest difference is that the design surface for a Web Form is actually a web page editor.

The next figure shows a typical start screen for a Web Forms project.

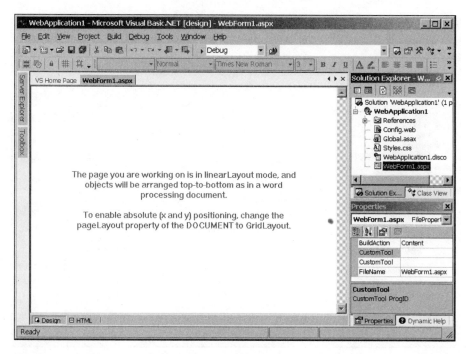

One obvious change is that the Solution Explorer contains a lot more elements. The design surface also ensures that the user knows how controls are positioned differently in Web Forms. As mentioned above, this design surface is actually a web page editor, which allows insertion of text and other elements as well as web controls that will be discussed below.

The Web Page Editor

Note the tab in the lower left portion of the screen. Two tabs, labeled **Design** and **HTML**, give different views of the web page being designed. The Design view is a WYSIWYG display that is almost a cross between the typical form layout view in Win Forms and a web page editor such as FrontPage. The HTML view shows the actual HTML that is used behind the page to create and position the controls that are being placed on the design surface. Either view can be used to modify the web page layout.

This design surface is inspired by a similar construct in Visual Interdev. However, the design mode for Web Forms is far more powerful than the visual designer included in Interdev. The advent of server-side web controls makes Web Forms much closer to the drag-and-drop design experience of VB forms.

The toolbox for Web Forms contains different controls to the toolbox used for Win Forms because it contains the server-side web controls specifically designed for Web Forms. The following figure shows the Web Forms design screen with the toolbox pulled out so that a partial listing of the web controls is visible.

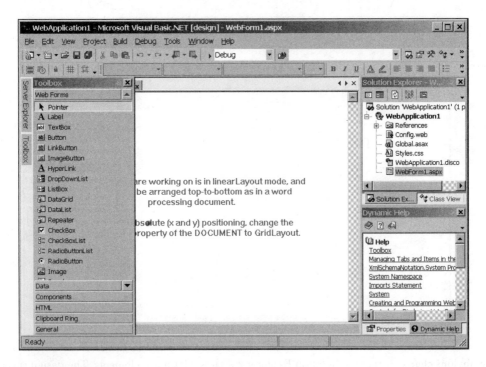

Layout of Web Forms

There are two quite different ways of laying out Web Forms. Both involve selecting controls in the toolbox and placing them on the design surface. Where they differ is where the controls end up on the design surface and the way controls are positioned in the underlying HTML. They are called Linear Layout and Grid Layout: Linear Layout is the default. Which of these is applied to a given Web Form is determined by the PageLayout property of the form.

In Linear Layout, the design surface is similar to a word processing document. The user can insert text and paragraph marks, and the result is translated into HTML. When a control is dropped onto the design surface, it is placed in the middle of the text that was previously entered, at the point where the cursor is currently positioned.

In Grid Layout, the controls are actually placed on a grid on the design surface. They are not interspersed with the underlying text. This allows for a WYSIWYG style display similar to FrontPage and is a big improvement over the original layout editor included with Interdev.

The differences between these layout techniques show up most dramatically in the underlying HTML template. In Web Forms, any control that is placed on the design surface has code generated for it in the underlying HTML template. For example, placing a button on the Web Form in Linear Layout mode will cause the following code to be inserted into the HTML template:

```
< asp:Button id=Button1 runat="server" Text="Button"></asp:Button >
```

This declaration for the control includes no positioning information at all. The control is merely rendered in the Web Form at whatever point it is encountered when running the form.

If a button is dropped in Grid Layout form, however, the inserted code is more complex. It looks something like this:

```
<tr valign=top>
    <td width=0 height=44></td>
    <td></td>
    <td colspan=2>
<asp:Button id=Button3 runat="server" Text="Button"></asp:Button></td></tr>
```

Moreover, this code will be in the middle of an HTML table declaration. The table positioning, plus the positioning information in the HTML above, arrange the control in the position in which it was dropped on the form.

Toolbars in Visual Studio.NET

There is a long list of available toolbars in Visual Studio.NET, and each developer should spend some time exploring them to find the most useful combination. The figure shows the screen that allows the user to select the toolbars that will be displayed in the environment:

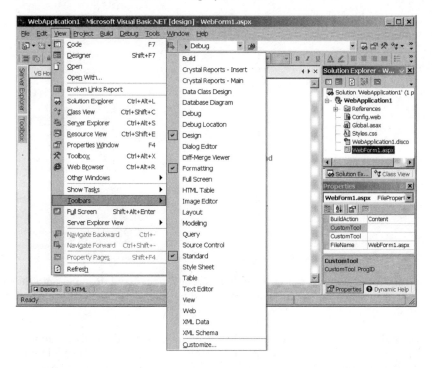

This is a lot of toolbars! In addition to choosing which toolbars to be displayed, the user can, as in Visual Studio 6, manipulate the buttons that are included on each toolbar, create their own toolbars, and dock or float each one as desired.

As in previous versions of Visual Studio, the toolbars are dynamic and can change position and buttons based on the current project type; for example, the toolbars change slightly for a Web Forms project. A different toolbar for positioning and layout of controls is used, shown at the far left of the bottom toolbar at the top of the screen in the two figures previous to the one on the preceeding page. Compare this toolbar to the one in an equivalent position in the figure found in the *Working on a WinForm* section.

The Component Designer

Visual modules are not the only ones with designers in Visual Studio.NET; components have a designer also. The figure below shows the design surface and the toolbox for the Component Designer. The Component Designer is accessed by selecting Project | Add Component and then selecting the Component Class template.

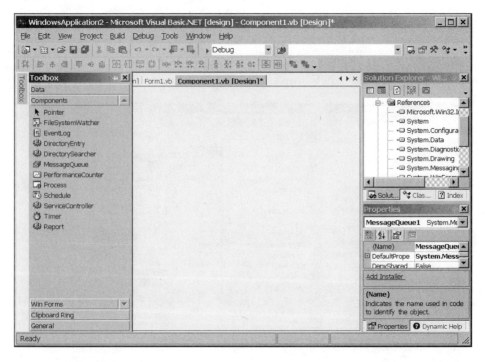

As with the visual designers, elements from the toolbox can be dragged and dropped onto the design surface. Once that happens, they receive a default name and have logic automatically generated to integrate them into the component.

The toolbox shown in the previous figure suggests that many areas of pre-defined functionality are available to components in Visual Basic.NET. Once these functional pieces are dragged onto the design surface, their properties become available in the Property Window, and their events become available in the code window. This makes it much easier to integrate, for example, a message queue. Very little explicit coding is required in Visual Studio.NET to integrate a message queue with a process because the designer takes care of setting the message queue to typical defaults and writing the instantiation code for the queue. Below is the property box for a message queue that was dragged onto the design surface.

The designer also adds the code to instantiate the message queue. It looks like this:

```
Private components As Container
Private WithEvents MessageQueue1 As System.Messaging.MessageQueue

'NOTE: The following procedure is required by the Component Designer
'It can be modified using the Component Designer.
'Do not modify it using the code editor.
Private Sub InitializeComponent()
    Me.components = New System.ComponentModel.Container()
    Me.MessageQueue1 = New System.Messaging.MessageQueue()

    '@design Me.TrayLargeIcon = False
    '@design Me.TrayAutoArrange = True
    '@design MessageQueue1.SetLocation(New System.Drawing.Point(7, 7))
End Sub
```

Visual Modeler Placed in the Visual Studio.NET IDE

Also integrated with the Visual Studio.NET IDE is a visual modeler that provides construction for various kinds of development diagrams. It is descended from the Visual Modeler included with Visual Studio 6, but handles more types of diagrams.

The Visual Modeler allows diagramming in UML of classes, relationships, and use cases. It also provides more traditional flowcharting and diagramming of COM interfaces. The following is a sample screen in the Visual Modeler. In the sample, a class diagram for a `Person` class has been created in UML, with several attributes (properties) of the class.

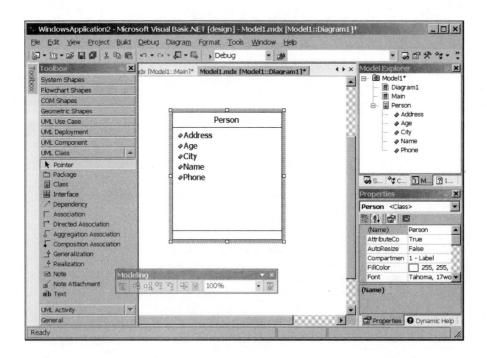

The Menu Structure of Visual Studio.NET

The menus in Visual Studio.NET during normal development are similar in general to those in Visual Studio 6. There are fewer top-level items, and more layered menus. (The menus change with other modes; for example, the menus are different when Visual Modeler is active, as shown in the previous figure.)

The View menu is now particularly rich. The previous figure relating to toolbars showed this menu opened up. There are many, many options for windows and dialogs that can be displayed. This menu should be one of the first areas of deeper investigation for a developer just getting started with the Visual Studio.NET environment.

The File, Edit, and Project menus are similar to Visual Basic 6, with a few changes: for example, the File menu has new submenus for Recent Files and Recent Projects, and the Edit menu in Visual Studio.NET has new submenus at the bottom for Advanced, Outlining, and IntelliSense.

The Build menu will be familiar to C++ users, but is a change from Visual Basic 6. It takes on the Make xxxx.exe option on the Visual Basic 6 File menu, but also has some additional options, including batch building and deploying.

The old Run menu in Visual Basic 6 has been folded into the Debug menu in Visual Studio.NET. The ability to run a program in the same way as in VB6 is on the Debug menu under the option Start without Debugging.

The Tools menu in Visual Studio.NET has some new options added compared to the Visual Basic 6 equivalent, and one significant option has been taken away, namely Add Procedure.

The Query and Diagram menus from Visual Basic 6 are missing from the top level. Their functions are folded into the View menu. Note that these options are only available on the menu while connected to a datasource – otherwise they are grayed out.

Macros in Visual Studio.NET

C++ developers have long had one feature that many Visual Basic developers craved – macros. In Visual Studio.NET, macros become part of the environment and are available to any language. However, as in the Microsoft Office suite, macros can only be written with Visual Basic syntax.

Macro options are accessible from the Tools menu. Here is a figure showing a screen with the Macro menu open.

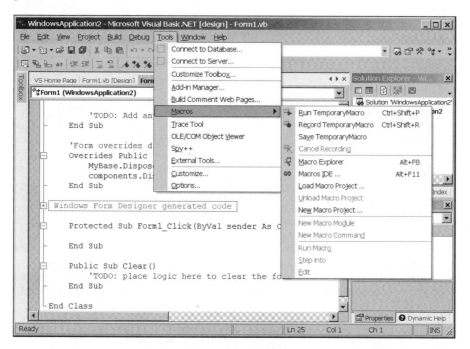

The idea of macros will be familiar to advanced word processing users. The idea is to record a series of keystrokes and/or menu actions, and then play them back by pressing a certain keystroke combination.

For example, suppose one particular function call with a complex set of arguments is constantly being called on in code, and the function call usually looks about the same except for minor variations in the arguments. The keystrokes to code the function call could be recorded and played back whenever needed, which would insert code to call the function that could then be modified as necessary.

Macros can be far more complex than this, containing logic as well as keystrokes. Microsoft Word users are familiar with the idea of recording macros into Visual Basic code, to allow for editing and customization of macros. Going even further, Visual Studio.NET has the most complete functionality for recording, altering, and playing macros that I have ever seen in any product. The macro capabilities of Visual Studio.NET are so comprehensive that macros have their own Integrated Development Environment! The figure below shows this macro IDE.

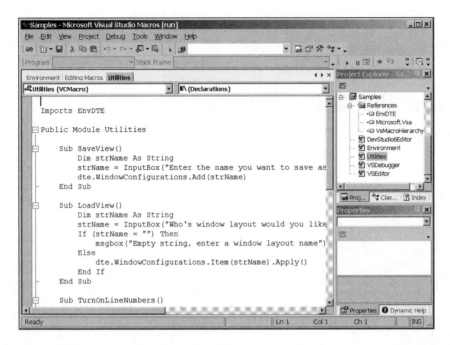

No doubt there will be much exchanging of useful macros over the Internet once Visual Studio.NET developers start creating them. Of course, ILOVEYOU taught us that script viruses can be dangerous, so we'll need to be careful, for example, that a macro is not e-mailing our source code to someone!

The New Deployment Tools

The Package and Deployment Wizard in Visual Basic 6 has been replaced with a much more comprehensive set of tools in Visual Studio.NET, which of course works with all of the Visual Studio.NET languages. To access the new tools, select the File | Add Project | New Project option. On the New Project dialog, select the Setup and Deployment Projects option on the left hand side, and the dialog shown below comes up:

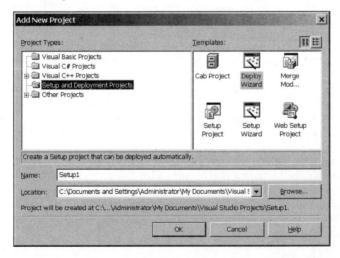

The Setup Wizard option is closest to the VB6 Package and Deployment Wizard, and the Setup Project option is a bare-bones alternative for creating a setup program. The other options offer new capabilities, including the ability to setup a web-based project (Web Setup Project). The Deploy Wizard arranges a setup for a remote machine, and the Cab Project assists with creation and management of Windows cabinet (Cab) files.

The option that starts with Merge Mod... on the screen is the Merge Module Project. These projects are used to package files or components that will be shared between multiple applications. They create a merge module (.msm) file that includes all files, resources, registry entries, and setup logic for a component. This .msm file can then be merged into other deployment projects.

Visual Editors for XML, XSD Schemas, and XSLT files

Visual Studio.NET uses XML and related technologies throughout – as a data store, as a formatting mechanism, and as glue to tie together functional areas. So it's no surprise that Visual Studio.NET includes editors for web-related files, such as XML, XSLT, and, of course, HTML files.

These editors are all accessed through the Project | Add New Item option, which displays the dialog box shown below:

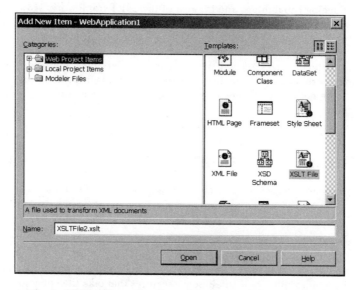

These editors are similar to XML editors that have been around for a while: they do auto-generation of closing XML tags, for example. While there are commercial editors that probably have more features, the advantage of these editors is their complete integration into the Visual Studio.NET environment.

Debugging across Projects and Processes

A major innovation in Visual Studio.NET is the most comprehensive debugger ever seen in a Microsoft environment. Using the technologies inherent in the .NET framework, the debugger can:

❑　Move transparently from language to language in a single project

❑　Debug into and through components that are imported into a project

❑　Track execution from one process to another

❑　Carry debugging into stored procedures

The debugging screens look a lot like those Visual Studio developers are accustomed to. The difference is mostly the increased reach of the debugger into areas where it could not go before.

C++ in Visual Studio.NET

While most of the attention in Visual Studio.NET is being placed on Visual Basic.NET and the new C# language, C++ is very much a part of Visual Studio.NET. The flexibility of the .NET framework makes C++ less necessary than before – for example, it is now possible to write an NT service in Visual Basic.NET. However, there are circumstances in which C++ will continue to be important. There are even new versions of the Microsoft Foundation Classes and the Active Template Library installed with Visual Studio.NET, though these technologies can be replaced for some situations by .NET Framework technologies.

The good news for C++ partisans is that they can use Web Forms, WinForms, the new IDE, the new multi-language debugging capabilities, and the rest of the .NET framework. However, to do much of that, C++ will need to be set to use managed code, which takes away the memory management and other low-level functions that are normally done in C++ (the default in C++ is to use unmanaged code).

The jury is still out on how much C++ will give way to C#. Certainly Microsoft is getting into C# in a big way, so that may portend a much smaller role for C++. While using C++ for areas system level code is still likely to be necessary in some cases, using C++ for more application-oriented projects may become less common.

Other Features and Comments

Here is a brief section on a couple of other changes between versions of Visual Studio that are worth mentioning.

Extended IntelliSense

IntelliSense has been a popular feature of Microsoft tools and applications since it was first introduced. Visual Studio.NET includes some new IntelliSense features that take the concept even further.

For example, if you type `Exit` and a space, IntelliSense will display a list of keywords that could follow `Exit` in a dropdown list. Other keywords that have dropdowns to present available options include `Goto`, `Implements`, `Option`, and `Declare`. IntelliSense also displays more tooltip information in the environment than before, and it also includes a feature to help the developer match up pairs of parentheses, braces, and brackets.

Source Control

Beta one of Visual Studio.NET does not include a new version of SourceSafe. To use SourceSafe with beta one, it must be installed from an older version of Visual Studio.

However, the ReadMe.htm file that comes with beta one indicates that a new version is being planned, and is expected in later beta versions

Source control is referred to in the File menu, and integration of SourceSafe with Visual Studio.NET is expected to be comparable to that in Visual Studio 6, with enhancements to better handle specific .NET capabilities such as multiple language projects.

Summary

In this chapter, you have been introduced to the Visual Studio.NET IDE – if you are familiar with earlier versions of Visual Studio, you will find that the layout is not much different, but, on the whole, Visual Studio.NET is a much more sophisticated beast to work with!

We covered items such as the differences between developing WinForms as opposed to Web Forms, and some of the differences in the visual representation of some of the functionality of the IDE.

In the next chapter, we'll dive into details and look at the .NET Framework itself.

NETINTRODUCING.NETINTRODUCING.NETINTRODUCING.NETINTRODUCIN
DUCING.NETINTRODUCING.NETINTRODUCING.NETINTRODUCIN
ETINTRODUCING.NETINTRODUCING.NETINTRODUCING.NETINTR
ING.NETINTRODUCING.NETINTRODUCING.NETINTRODUCING.N
NTRODUCING.NETINTRODUCING.NETINTRODUCING.NETINTRODU
G.NETINTRODUCING.NETINTRODUCING.NETINTRODUCING.NETI
ODUCING.NETINTRODUCING.NETINTRODUCING.NETINTRODUCIN
ETINTRODUCING.NETINTRODUCING.NETINTRODUCING.NETINTR
CING.NETINTRODUCING.NETINTRODUCING.NETINTRODUCING.N
NTRODUCING.NETINTRODUCING.NETINTRODUCING.NETINTRODU
G.NETINTRODUCING.NETINTRODUCING.NETINTRODUCING.NETI
ODUCING.NETINTRODUCING.NETINTRODUCING.NETINTRODUCIN
ETINTRODUCING.NETINTRODUCING.NETINTRODUCING.NETINTR
CING.NETINTRODUCING.NETINTRODUCING.NETINTRODUCING.N
NTRODUCING.NETINTRODUCING.NETINTRODUCING.NETINTRODU
G.NETINTRODUCING.NETINTRODUCING.NETINTRODUCING.NETI
ODUCING.NETINTRODUCING.NETINTRODUCING.NETINTRODUCIN
ETINTRODUCING.NETINTRODUCING.NETINTRODUCING.NETINTR
CING.NETINTRODUCING.NETINTRODUCING.NETINTRODUCING.N
NTRODUCING.NETINTRODUCING.NETINTRODUCING.NETINTRODU
G.NETINTRODUCING.NETINTRODUCING.NETINTRODUCING.NETI
ODUCING.NETINTRODUCING.NETINTRODUCING.NETINTRODUCIN
ETINTRODUCING.NETINTRODUCING.NETINTRODUCING.NETINTR
CING.NETINTRODUCING.NETINTRODUCING.NETINTRODUCING.N
NTRODUCING.NETINTRODUCING.NETINTRODUCING.NETINTRODU
G.NETINTRODUCING.NETINTRODUCING.NETINTRODUCING.NETI
ODUCING.NETINTRODUCING.NETINTRODUCING.NETINTRODUCIN
ETINTRODUCING.NETINTRODUCING.NETINTRODUCING.NETINTR
CING.NETINTRODUCING.NETINTRODUCING.NETINTRODUCING.N
NTRODUCING.NETINTRODUCING.NETINTRODUCING.NETINTRODU
G.NETINTRODUCING.NETINTRODUCING.NETINTRODUCING.NETI
ODUCING.NETINTRODUCING.NETINTRODUCING.NETINTRODUCIN
ETINTRODUCING.NETINTRODUCING.NETINTRODUCING.NETINTR
CING.NETINTRODUCING.NETINTRODUCING.NETINTRODUCING.N
NTRODUCING.NETINTRODUCING.NETINTRODUCING.NETINTRODU
G.NETINTRODUCING.NETINTRODUCING.NETINTRODUCING.NETI
ODUCING.NETINTRODUCING.NETINTRODUCING.NETINTRODUCIN
ETINTRODUCING.NETINTRODUCING.NETINTRODUCING.NETINTR
CING.NETINTRODUCING.NETINTRODUCING.NETINTRODUCING.N
NTRODUCING.NETINTRODUCING.NETINTRODUCING.NETINTRODU
G.NETINTRODUCING.NETINTRODUCING.NETINTRODUCING.NETI
ODUCING.NETINTRODUCING.NETINTRODUCING.NETINTRODUCIN
ETINTRODUCING.NETINTRODUCING.NETINTRODUCING.NETINTR
CING.NETINTRODUCING.NETINTRODUCING.NETINTRODUCING.N
NTRODUCING.NETINTRODUCING.NETINTRODUCING.NETINTRODU
G.NETINTRODUCING.NETINTRODUCING.NETINTRODUCING.NETI
ETINTRODUCING.NETINTRODUCING.NETINTRODUCING.NETINT

6

.NET Class Framework

In the previous chapters we've learned how the .NET Framework provides many advantages over the traditional COM environment, with features such as automatic garbage collection, side-by-side execution and cross-language inheritance, exception handling, and debugging. Most of these features are implemented by the .NET Framework's Common Language Runtime (CLR); however, the .NET Framework also provides another important component, called the .NET Class Framework. The .NET Class Framework is a hierarchical class library that, among other things, can be utilized across multiple languages and platforms. The .NET Class Framework not only enables programmatic access to the features of the new .NET runtime environment, but also integrates the functionality found in several existing COM libraries within a single API. For example, the .NET Class Framework provides classes, interfaces and structures for installing and configuring applications and services, manipulating data found in databases, XML documents, and text files, and accessing Message Queues, the Event Log, and the file system.

In this chapter we'll discuss the .NET Class Framework in detail. Specifically, we will:

- ❑ Analyze the benefits of the .NET Class Framework over the traditional COM model
- ❑ Understand the purpose and use of Namespaces in the .NET Class Framework
- ❑ Discuss the Common Type System (CTS) and its role in multi-language development
- ❑ Build sample applications that utilize various classes in the .NET Class Framework

This chapter is not intended to be a complete reference to the .NET Class Framework. Instead, the goal for this chapter is to introduce the key concepts surrounding the .NET Class Framework and analyze some practical code examples of the most commonly used classes. Hopefully after reading this chapter you will have a solid understanding of the .NET Class Framework and be able to begin writing applications that take advantage of the new runtime environment.

When writing code for the .NET platform, one of the hardest questions to answer is "What language should I use?" For this chapter, the code examples are in VB.NET because of the large number of developers familiar with Visual Basic. However, one of the major benefits of the .NET Class Framework is that it can be utilized from any language that supports the Common Language Specification (CLS) and the .NET Framework's Common Language Runtime (CLR). This includes C#, VB, JScript, VC++ with managed extensions, and any of the 22 or more languages being released by third parties.

Now that you have an idea of what to expect from this chapter, let's get started. Before we jump into code samples and begin using the .NET Class Framework, let's discuss some of the problems with the current platform and learn more about the benefits of the .NET Class Framework.

Problems with Unmanaged Applications

After reading the introduction to this chapter I'm sure you're probably thinking, "Why do we need a new Class Library?" Before I answer that question, take a look at some of your code from an existing, unmanaged application. What do you see? If your Windows application is like most, then there is probably a scattered mix of method calls to COM components, the Win32 API and the language-specific class library such as the Visual Basic Runtime (VBRun), Microsoft Foundation Classes (MFC), or Windows Foundation Classes (WFC).

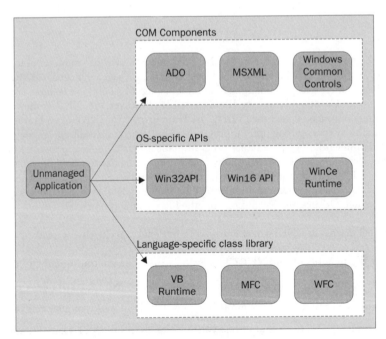

This hybrid programming model is the source of several problems and limitations with unmanaged applications and components. Some of these problems include:

❑ **Multi-language development was difficult**
COM provided us with the ability to develop and instantiate objects in virtually any language. However, the lack of shared system defined data types made cross-language communication between clients and COM objects difficult. Some languages, such as Visual Basic and JScript, didn't support many of the more sophisticated data types that could be utilized in C++.

Additionally, because every language provided its own language-specific runtime and class library, developers were required to learn an entirely new object model in order to write code in another language. Even common tasks such as creating and writing to a text file were drastically different in different unmanaged languages. What COM really needed was a common type system and a common object model that could be shared by multiple languages.

❑ **COM(+) libraries were unorganized**
With COM there was no way to organize a set of related components other than building the components within the same library. This limitation made it difficult to create a sophisticated library containing a large number of classes without also creating a maintenance nightmare. Sometimes object models could become so unorganized that they became difficult to code against without a steep learning curve. These problems were further escalated when working with the Win32 API, which gave the impression of being an unorganized mix of thousands of unrelated functions. What COM needed was a way of organizing components, interfaces and enumerations within a compiled library.

❑ **Extending existing classes was difficult**
The typical development approach in the traditional COM environment was to encapsulate logic and processing within COM components. In fact, component developers frequently provided component-based wrappers around complex Win32 API functions by encapsulating function calls in COM components. While this development methodology of utilizing components for encapsulation was (and still is) extremely beneficial, encapsulation was one of the only object-oriented programming concepts provided by COM. With COM it was difficult to extend the functionality provided by a component unless you owned the source code. Granted, you could always extend existing components by encapsulating method calls to them within new components, but this approach often results in performance degradation, complex designs and maintenance problems. A much better solution would be to simply inherit the behavior and functionality of the existing component and override the methods you want to extend. Although C++ and Java provided this functionality as part of their languages, COM was unaware of advanced object-oriented programming concepts such as Inheritance.

These problems have frequently been a source of criticism by developers targeting other platforms using technologies such as Cold Fusion, Java Server Pages (JSP) and Enterprise Java Beans (EJB). Most of these developers have the impression that developing applications for the Windows platform is difficult and that the Windows platform is not suitable to developing enterprise-level applications.

It was apparent to Microsoft that these issues (and the developers' concerns) couldn't be addressed with simply a new COM-based class library. What we needed first was a new version of COM. The .NET Framework is just that – a new version of COM that provides both an intelligent run-time environment, called the Common Language Runtime (CLR), and a single, comprehensive class library called the .NET Class Framework. In earlier chapters we've discussed the features provided by the Common Language Runtime. Now let's turn our attention to the .NET Class Framework and learn how it resolves the problems with the unmanaged programming model.

Introducing the .NET Class Framework

The .NET Class Framework is not just another class library as you might think of one in the traditional COM environment. Instead, the .NET Class Framework it is an entirely new, object-oriented, hierarchical, and unified class library that can be used in a consistent manner across multiple languages and platforms. The .NET Class Framework provides hundreds of Classes, Interfaces, and Structures and that can be used to perform tasks such as:

- ❑ Accessing and manipulating data stores

- ❑ Developing components and web services

- ❑ Managing and changing application configuration

- ❑ Working with Directory services, Event Logs, Processes, Message Queues and Timers

- ❑ Managing resources such as images and strings

- ❑ Sending and receiving data across a variety of network protocols

- ❑ Creating and managing threads

- ❑ Accessing metadata information stored in assemblies

- ❑ Developing WinForm applications

- ❑ Developing ASP.NET Web Form applications

- ❑ Managing the .NET Common Language Runtime

- ❑ Interoperating with unmanaged code

- ❑ Defining, managing and enforcing application security

The .NET Class Framework provides a number of benefits that overcome the problems and limitations of unmanaged applications. Some of these benefits include:

- ❑ **Cross-Language Interoperability**

  The .NET class framework eliminates the need for existing language-specific libraries such as VBRun, MFC and WFC by providing a single, unified class library that can be utilized from any language that supports the .NET Framework. While the .NET Common Language Runtime *enables* multiple-language development by providing a shared runtime environment, the .NET Class Framework *simplifies* multi-language development by effectively providing a common language API. Consequently, developers no longer have to learn multiple object models when developing applications with multiple languages. Instead, developers can utilize the language they feel the most comfortable with, and/or the language that best meets the needs for a given task. For example, the .NET Class Framework provides a universal Debug class that can be used from any .NET language to write text into the command window in Visual Studio.NET or the .NET SDK debugger. When necessary, developers can also quickly learn additional languages without facing a steep learning curve, because the most significant difference between the .NET languages is the syntax. The following diagram illustrates how the .NET Class Framework replaces all of the language-specific APIs and effectively provides a single API that can be used from any .NET language for the development of any type of application:

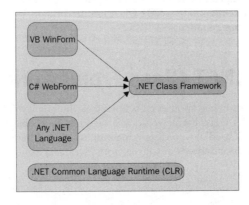

The .NET Class Framework also facilitates cross-language interoperability by supplying a standard set of classes, interfaces and structures that can be used in any language that targets the .NET Common Language Runtime. In the .NET Framework classes, interfaces and structures are sometimes generically referred to as types. The standard types and the rules that compilers and the Common Language Runtime must follow when declaring, using, and managing the types is called the Common Type System (CTS). The support and use of a standard type system is the key factor that enables the Common Language Runtime to provide features such as cross-language inheritance, exception handling and debugging.

We'll discuss more about the Common Type System and its relationship to the .NET Class Framework later in this chapter.

❑   **Consistent and Unified Programming Model**

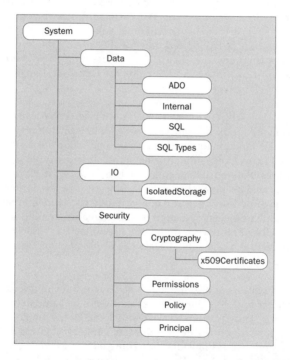

The .NET Class Framework removes the need for many existing COM libraries by defining hundreds of equivalent managed classes, structures, and interfaces within a single, unified programming model. In order to prevent naming conflicts and provide structure to the programming model, the .NET Class Framework organizes these types through the use of namespaces. A **namespace** is simply a *logical* grouping of related classes, interfaces, and structures. A namespace can also contain other namespaces, enabling class libraries to be organized hierarchically. For example, the System namespace, the root namespace within the .NET Class Framework, contains the core datatypes such as Object, Int32, and String, classes such as Console, Convert, and Math and 25 second-level namespaces. Some of these second-level namespaces include System.IO, which contains classes used to access files and streams, System.Data, which contains classes for accessing data stores using ADO.NET, and System.Security, which consists of types used to manage application security in the .NET environment. In fact, the classes, interfaces and structures used to develop WinForm and Web Form applications and controls are also part of the .NET Class Framework and can be located in the System.WinForms and System.WebForms namespaces. We'll discuss some of these namespaces in more detail later in this chapter.

To further increase uniformity, all classes, interfaces, structures and namespaces in the .NET Class Framework have consistent design patterns and naming conventions. For example, all interfaces are prefixed with a capital "I", enumerations typically have the suffix "Enum" and Exception classes typically have the suffix of "Exception". Microsoft defines some of these design patterns and naming conventions guidelines in the .NET Framework SDK so you can develop custom class libraries that are also consistent with the .NET Class Framework.

❑ **Object-Oriented and Extensible Class Library**

Finally, the .NET Class Framework is a fully extensible class library that takes advantage of advanced object-oriented concepts supported by the CLR, such as inheritance, polymorphism, and method overloading. The Class Framework provides both *abstract*, or *mustinherit*, base classes, and classes that inherit or *derive* from the base classes. For example, the `System.WinForms.Form` class, which is the foundation for developing WinForm applications, inherits from the `System.WinForms.ContainerControl` base class, which provides the ability to hosts or contain WinForm controls. Most of the time, these derived classes in the .NET Class Framework will meet your needs. However, you can easily customize or extend the behavior and functionality of any class by simply defining custom classes that inherit from any class in the .NET Class Framework and overriding the individual methods you want to customize. Additionally, the Common Language Runtime enables inheritance to cross language boundaries.

Polymorphism is the ability to create two or more classes that can be used interchangeably at runtime. Consequently, polymorphism allows you to easily change which class is used to provide a particular functionality without re-writing major portions of code. In order for classes to be used interchangeably, they have to define the same methods and properties with the same signatures. Polymorphism comes in two forms – interface-based and inheritance-based. Interface-based polymorphism allows objects to be used interchangeably by implementing the same interfaces and consequently the same methods. Inheritance-based polymorphism allows objects to be used interchangeably by inheriting from the same base class. The .NET Class Framework frequently uses interface-based polymorphism because it is generally more flexible, since a .NET class can implement any number of interfaces but can only inherit from one base class.

The .NET Class Framework also frequently leverages a technique called *Method Overloading*, which allows a class to define multiple methods with the same name but different signatures. For example, the `System.Console` class, which facilitates the development of console or command-line applications, defines 15 different versions of a `WriteLine` method. All of the `WriteLine` methods are responsible for writing a line of text to the command window. However, each method takes a different set of parameters and has slightly different behavior. One version of the `WriteLine` method accepts a single string parameter, another allows you to pass in a character array, and a third implementation allows you to pass in a string and any number of arguments. Method overloading greatly simplifies and provides uniformity to the .NET Class Framework's programming model by reducing the number of unique method names. It also facilitates extensibility by allowing additional variations of a method to be added in the future. For example, the `Console` class could be modified to provide an additional `WriteLine` method that accepts a filename as a parameter and displays the contents of the file in the command window.

Now that you have been introduced to the concepts surrounding the .NET Class Framework, let's begin exploring some of the most commonly used namespaces and learn how to utilize the .NET Class Framework to develop managed applications and components.

Inside the .NET Class Framework

As I mentioned earlier, the .NET Class Framework contains hundreds of namespaces, classes, interfaces, and structures. The root namespace in the hierarchical .NET Class Framework is the System namespace. The System namespace contains 25 second-level namespaces, and these second-level namespaces logically partition the functionality provided by the .NET Class Framework. In this section we will explore some of these namespaces and discuss the classes, interfaces and structures they contain.

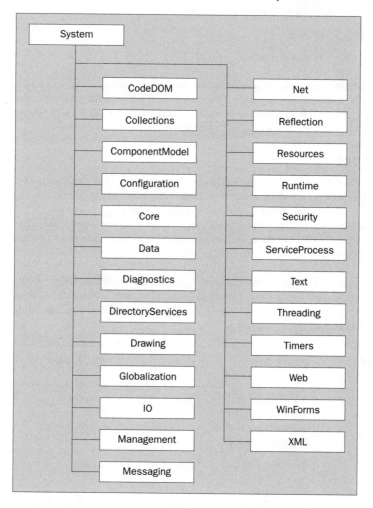

System Namespace

In addition to containing the second-level namespaces, the System namespace also contains many commonly used classes, interfaces, and structures. The types contained in the System namespace are used to:

❑ Develop console applications and Windows Services

❑ Define the base data types such as Object, Integer, and String

- ❏ Determine information about the operating system and environment
- ❏ Manage garbage collection
- ❏ Convert and format types
- ❏ Generate random numbers
- ❏ Perform math calculations
- ❏ Define standard system exceptions
- ❏ Raise and handle events
- ❏ Retrieve time zone information

Since some of these tasks are so fundamental to developing applications, services and components for the .NET Framework you will definitely want to familiarize yourself with the types contained in the System namespace. In fact, it would be impossible to write an application in .NET that does not use any of the classes, interfaces or structures in the System namespace.

The System Types

As I mentioned earlier, the System namespace contains the base types that compose the Common Type System. These System types are shared across all of the .NET languages. Many languages, including Visual Basic.NET and C#, provide language-specific aliases for the System types to simplify the programming model and provide backwards compatibility with existing code. For example, the System.Boolean type has an alias of Boolean in Visual Basic and an alias of bool in C#. However, you can write code using a type's alias or its fully qualified name interchangeably.

The following table lists the most commonly used types, briefly describes each type, and specifies each type's alias in Visual Basic.NET, C# and when compiled to the Microsoft Intermediate Language (MSIL). Notice that some of the types are not part of the Common Language Specification (CLS), and, consequently, are not necessarily supported by all .NET languages.

Fully-qualified Name	Description	CLS Type	MSIL alias	VB alias	C# alias
System.Byte	An 8-bit (1-byte) unsigned integer containing a value from 0-255.	Yes	unsigned int8	Byte	byte
System.Sbyte	An 8-bit (1-byte) signed integer containing a value from 0-255.	No	int8	*Not supported*	sbyte
System.Int16	A 16-bit (2-byte) signed integer containing a value from -32,678 to 32,767.	Yes	int16	Short	short

Fully-qualified Name	Description	CLS Type	MSIL alias	VB alias	C# alias
System.Int32	A 32-bit (4-byte) signed integer containing a value from -2,147,483,648 to 2,147,483,647.	Yes	int32	Integer	int
System.Int64	A 64-bit (8-byte) signed integer containing a value from -9,223,372,036,854,775,808 to 9,223,372,036,854,775,807.	Yes	int64	Long	long
System.UInt16	A 16-bit (2-byte) unsigned integer containing a value from -32,678 to 32,767.	No	unsigned int16	*Not supported*	ushort
System.UInt32	A 32-bit (4-byte) unsigned integer containing a value from -2,147,483,648 to 2,147,483,647.	No	unsigned int32	*Not supported*	uint
System.UInt64	A 64-bit (8-byte) unsigned integer containing a value from -9,223,372,036,854,775,808 to 9,223,372,036,854,775,807.	No	unsigned int64	*Not supported*	ulong

Table continued on following page

Fully-qualified Name	Description	CLS Type	MSIL alias	VB alias	C# alias
System.Single	A single-precision (32-bit or 4-byte) floating-point number containing a value from -3.402823E38 to -1.401298E-45 for negative values and from 1.401298E-45 to 3.402823E38 for positive values.	Yes	float32	Single	float
System.Double	A double-precision (64-bit or 8-byte) floating-point number containing a value from -1.79769313486231E308 to -4.94065645841247E-324 for negative values and from 4.94065645841247E-324 to 1.79769313486232E308 for positive values.	Yes	float64	Double	double
System.Object	A 32-bit (4-byte) address that references to an instance of a class.	Yes	class System.Object	Object	object
System.Char	A single 16-bit (2-byte) Unicode character.	Yes	wchar	Char	char
System.String	A string of up to approximately 2 billion Unicode characters.	Yes	class System.String	String	string

Fully-qualified Name	Description	CLS Type	MSIL alias	VB alias	C# alias
System.Decimal	A 96-bit (12-byte) signed integer that can contain up to 28 digits on either side of the decimal point.	Yes	decimal	Decimal	decimal
System.Boolean	A 32-bit (4-byte) number that contains either true (1) or false (0).	Yes	bool	Boolean	bool

System.Object Class

The Common Language Runtime and the rules of the Common Type System require that all managed classes ultimately inherit from the System.Object base class. This requirement ensures that every class supports a minimum set of methods and functionality. The following example defines a custom class in Visual Basic.NET that inherits directly from System.Object. Note that in some languages, such as VB and C#, the inheritance from System.Object is automatically provided by the compiler. However, it's good programming practice to explicitly inherit from System.Object even though it's not required in these languages.

> **The code for this chapter is available for download at www.wrox.com.**

```
Public Class Author
    Inherits System.Object

    'Define the Fields for this class
    Public FirstName As String
    Public LastName As String

End Class
```

The System.Object class replaces the Variant data type that was provided in COM because a variable of the type System.Object can hold a reference to any object. For example, the following creates an instance of our custom Author class and casts the reference to the type System.Object:

```
Dim objAuthor As System.Object

'Create a new instance of the Author class
Dim pAuthor As New Author()

'Set the First and Last names of the Author
pAuthor.FirstName = "James"
pAuthor.LastName = "Conard"
```

```
'Acquire a reference to the System.Object type for
'...the Author object
objAuthor = pAuthor
```

The `System.Object` class also enables you to make late-bound method calls on objects, just as you could through COM's `IDispatch` interface (using the `Object` datatype) in previous versions of Visual Basic. Late-bound method calls enable you to call a method on an object without knowing the signature of the method you will be calling at compile time. For example, the following code makes a late-bound call to the `FirstName` and `LastName` properties on our `Author` object even though these properties are not explicitly defined on the `System.Object` class:

```
'Make a latebound method call using the System.Object type
MessageBox.Show("Author's Name: " & _
                objAuthor.FirstName & " " & _
                objAuthor.LastName)
```

Note that in order for late-bound method calls to work as demonstrated in this example using Visual Basic.NET, you must turn off the Option Strict compiler option by using the following line of code at the top of your program:

```
Option Strict Off
```

The Option Strict compiler option provides strict type checking of your code at compile time. If you don't turn off the Option Strict compiler option, then late-bound method calls will cause compile errors. Turning off the Option Strict compiler option is generally not a good idea, because it introduces the risk of run-time exceptions when converting between types. However, as an alternative, you can utilize the `System.Type` class for making late-bound method calls without sacrificing strict type checking. For more information about the `System.Type` class, consult the .NET SDK.

In addition to the implicit behavior that's provided when working with the `System.Object` class, it also defines the following *public* methods (these methods are also illustrated in the following UML class diagram):

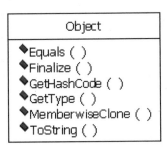

- ❏ **Equals** – The `Equals` method accepts an additional object as a parameter and returns a Boolean value indicating whether or not the two objects are equal.

- ❏ **GetHashCode** – The `GetHashCode` method returns an integer value called a Hash Code that represents the object's value. The Hash Code is used as the key when the object is added to a specific type of collection such as a `HashTable` class.

❑ **Finalize** – The Finalize method may be called by the Common Language Runtime to notify the object that it is about to be destroyed by the Garbage Collector (GC). By default, this method does nothing. However, the `Finalize` method can be overridden by derived classes in an attempt to free resources and perform other cleanup operations before the GC reclaims the object. The `Finalize` method is not guaranteed to be called by the CLR, so your objects should not depend on its execution.

❑ **MemberwiseClone** – Creates and returns a copy of the current (source) object. The `MemberwiseClone` method does not create copies of objects that the source object references through properties, fields, or private, member-level variables. Instead, the new object will refer to the same objects as the original source object. The type of object clone is called a **shallow copy**. A **deep copy** would create a copy of the source object and a copy of every object referenced by the source object. Deep copies can be performed through the use of the `ICloneable` interface.

❑ **GetType** – The `GetType` method returns an instance of the `System.Type` class, which can be used to acquire information about the object, through its metadata, and perform late-bound operations.

❑ **ToString** – The `ToString` method returns the object as represented as a String. This String value is *not* formatted or translated to match the culture of the operating system.

The `Equals`, `ToString`, and `GetHashCode` methods can be overridden by inheriting classes in order to provide more specific implementations of these methods.

System.Exception Class

One of the major problems with the COM environment and unmanaged code is the lack of a standard mechanism to handle and raise errors. In an unmanaged application there are three general techniques for managing errors:

❑ COM `HRESULT` values

❑ Language specific techniques such as Visual Basic's Err Object

❑ Evaluating Return Values

The .NET Framework provides an infrastructure for handling errors in a standard and consistent way through the use of **Exceptions**. An exception is any error condition or unexpected behavior that occurs during the execution of a managed application. Exceptions replace the need for the traditional error handling techniques we have become accustomed to in the unmanaged, COM-based environment. They can be raised or thrown across process and machine boundaries by the Common Language Runtime itself or any type of application. The Common Language Runtime also allows Exceptions to be handled or caught by code written in any language, regardless of the language that threw the exception. Additionally, when calling unmanaged COM objects, the CLR automatically maps failure `HRESULTS` into corresponding exceptions that can be caught just like any other exception. The opposite is also true. If unmanaged code calls into managed code and an exception is thrown, the CLR will automatically convert the exception into a `HRESULT` that indicates failure.

The .NET Framework implements exceptions through the use of the `System.Exception` class. The `System.Exception` class is the base class from which all exceptions (ultimately) derive. Exceptions cannot be thrown or caught unless they (eventually) inherit from the `Exception` class. The `System.Exception` class defines several properties and methods that are used to store and manage information about the exception. These properties and methods include:

❏ **Message** – The read-only `Message` property returns a String containing the text information about the exception.

❏ **HelpLink** – The read-only `HelpLink` property returns a String containing the URN or URL to a help file that provides more information about the exception.

❏ **Source** – The `Source` property returns and sets a String containing the name of the application or object that generated the error.

❏ **HRESULT** – The `HRESULT` field contains the hidden COM `HRESULT` value returned when calling methods on COM objects through .NET's COM Interoperability support.

❏ **StackTrace** – The read-only `StackTrace` property returns a single String containing all of the information about the call stack including the methods, source files and the line numbers where the Exception was thrown. The `StackTrace` property is particularly useful for determining where an error occurred.

❏ **InnerException** – The read-only `InnerException` property returns a reference to an inner exception that caused the current exception to be thrown. As we will see later in this chapter, the `InnerException` property can be used recursively to determine the hierarchy or chain of exceptions that occurred within an application.

❏ **TargetSite** – The read-only `TargetSite` property returns an instance of the `MethodBase` class contained in the `System.Reflection` namespace. This returned `MethodBase` object can be used to determine information about the method that threw the exception.

❏ **GetBaseException** – The `GetBaseException` method returns an instance of a `System.Exception` class that is the original or innermost exception in the exception chain. This method is a shorthand technique for recursively working through the Exception hierarchy by repeated calling the `InnerException` property on the object returned.

❏ **SetHelpLink** – The `SetHelpLink` method sets the value that should be returned from the `HelpLink` property.

Besides the base `System.Exception` class, the .NET Class Framework also defines several other standard exception classes. These standard exception classes are specifically designed to represent a particular type of error. For example, the `ArgumentNullException` class represents an error where a required argument was null. Some of these specific exception classes provide additional properties and methods that are used to capture information specific to the type of exception. However, since all exceptions must ultimately inherit from the `System.Exception` class, the properties and methods of the `System.Exception` class are implemented by all types of exceptions.

The following table lists some of the most common exception classes provided by the .NET Class Framework contained in the `System` namespace. Notice that this is only a partial listing – there are many other exception classes that are defined in other namespaces:

Exception Class	Base Class	Description
Exception	Object	Base class for all Exceptions.
SystemException	Exception	Base class for all runtime generated errors.

Exception Class	Base Class	Description
CoreException	SystemException	Base class for all fatal runtime errors.
IndexOutOfRangeException	CoreException	Thrown by the runtime when an array is accessed with an invalid index.
NullReferenceException	CoreException	Thrown by the runtime when a method or property is called on a null object reference.
InvalidOperationException	SystemException	Thrown by methods when in an invalid state.
ArgumentException	SystemException	Base class for all Argument Exceptions. Subclasses of this exception should be thrown whenever possible.
ArgumentNullException	ArgumentException	Thrown when a null value is specified for a required argument.
ArgumentOutOfRangeException	ArgumentException	Thrown when one of the arguments to a method is not in a given range.
OutOfMemoryException	SystemException	Thrown by the runtime when there is not enough memory to continue the execution of the program.
RankException	SystemException	Thrown when an array with the wrong number of dimensions is passed to a method.
NotSupportedException	SystemException	Thrown when an invoked method is not supported.

Table continued on following page

Exception Class	Base Class	Description
PlatformNotSupported Exception	NotSupportedException	Thrown when an invoked method is not supported on the current platform.
ExecutionEngineException	CoreException	Thrown by the runtime when an internal CLR error occurs.
FormatException	SystemException	Thrown when the format of an argument is invalid.

Now that we've discussed some of the basic concepts about the System.Exception class, let's learn how to use exceptions in our .NET applications. In the following sections we will learn how to:

❑   Catch and throw exceptions

❑   Use various properties and methods of a System.Exception class

❑   Access an exception's call stack

Throwing Exceptions

In Visual Basic.NET and C# exceptions can be raised or thrown using the throw statement. The throw statement accepts a reference to an object derived from the System.Exception class and immediately passes the object up the call stack where it can be handled by the caller.

There are two general situations where you might want to throw an exception:

❑   An application integrity, data integrity or business rule has been violated

❑   An unexpected exception occurred and you want to notify the caller

Exceptions should only be used in these exceptional cases to indicate that an error has occurred. Exceptions should not be used for normal or expected errors or for the normal flow of execution in an application.

The following example creates an instance of the System.Exception class and throws the new exception to the caller when the String parameter strParameter1 is empty:

```
Private Sub SomeMethod(ByVal strParameter1 As String)
    If strParameter1.Length = 0 Then
        'The Parameter strParameter1 is empty. Raise an Exception.
        Throw (New System.Exception())
    End If
    'Do processing here...
End Sub
```

As you can see from this example, throwing exceptions is relatively straightforward. However, in order to effectively use exceptions, there are a couple of general rules you should follow:

❑   Throw the most specific exception possible

❑   Set the appropriate properties on the Exception object before throwing it to the caller

Let's revise our example to apply these rules. First we'll create an instance of the
`System.ArgumentNullException` class instead of the generic `System.Exception` class. The
constructor for the `ArgumentNullException` class accepts the name of the parameter that was null or
empty as the first parameter and the exception message as the second parameter. Next, we'll set the `Source`
property of the new `ArgumentNullException` object equal to the name of our procedure:

```
Private Sub SomeMethod(ByVal strParameter1 As String)

    If strParameter1.Length = 0 Then
        'The Parameter strParameter1 is empty. Raise an Exception.
        Dim excpArgumentNull As New System.ArgumentNullException _
                        ("strParameter1","Parameter cannot be empty!")

        'set the Source property on the new ArgumentNullException class
        excpArgumentNull.Source = "SomeMethod"

        'Throw our ArgumentNullException
        Throw (excpArgumentNull)
    End If

    'Do processing here...

End Sub
```

Handling Exceptions

Visual Basic.NET and C# implement exception handling through the use of `Try`, `Catch`, and `Finally`
code blocks. The `Try` block contains the code that is susceptible to throwing an exception. It's good
programming practice to always encapsulate code within a `Try` block even if you don't expect an exception
to ever occur. For example, the following code calls the function `SomeMethod` that we defined in the last
code sample and passes it an empty string as a parameter:

```
Try
    'Call our sample method
    Somemethod("")
End Try
```

When an exception occurs in a `Try` code block, the exception is passed up the call stack until a qualifying
handler for the exception is found. If no handler can be found, the Common Language Runtime displays a
generic Message Box containing the exception name, message and the full stack trace from where the
exception was thrown. Exception handlers are blocks of code defined by the `Catch` statement. In the
definition, `Catch` blocks declare an object variable, which holds a reference to an exception object when the
code in the `Catch` block is executed.

For example, the following code defines a `Catch` block for the `Try` statement in the above example. When
the exception is caught, the code in this `Catch` block displays a Message Box to the user, containing the
`Message` and `Source` properties of the exception:

```
Try
    'Call our sample method
    Somemethod("")

Catch excp As System.Exception

    'An unexpected Exception occured. Display the information
```

```
'...about the Exception to the user.
MessageBox.Show("This exception was caught in the general handler: " _
               & ControlChars.CrLf & ControlChars.CrLf _
               & "Message:  " & excp.Message & ControlChars.CrLf _
               & "Source:  " & excp.Source, _
               Me.Text, MessageBox.IconError)
```

```
End Try
```

A single `Try` block can have multiple `Catch` blocks, and each `Catch` block can be designed for a specific type of exception. The above code catches all exceptions. The Common Language Runtime automatically throws any exceptions that occurred in the `Try` block to the first appropriate `Catch` block that it finds that handles that particular type of exception. For example, in the following code sample we have added an additional `Catch` block that handles exceptions of the specific type `ArgumentNullException`. When the `ArgumentNullException` is caught, its properties, including the `ParamName` property specific to this type of exception, are displayed in a Message Box:

```
Try
    'Call our sample method
    Somemethod("")
```

```
Catch excpArg As System.ArgumentNullException

    'An ArgumentNullException occured. Display the information
    '...about the Exception to the user.
    MessageBox.Show("This exception was caught in the specific handler: " _
                   & ControlChars.CrLf & ControlChars.CrLf _
                   & "Message:  " & excpArg.Message & ControlChars.CrLf _
                   & "Source:  " & excpArg.Source & ControlChars.CrLf _
                   & "ParamName:  " & excpArg.ParamName, _
                   Me.Text, MessageBox.IconError)

Catch excp As System.Exception

    'An unexpected Exception occured. Display the information
    '...about the Exception to the user.
    MessageBox.Show("This exception was caught in the general handler: " _
                   & ControlChars.CrLf & ControlChars.CrLf _
                   & "Message:  " & excp.Message & ControlChars.CrLf _
                   & "Source:  " & excp.Source, _
                   Me.Text, MessageBox.IconError)
```

```
End Try
```

Notice in the above example, our specific `Catch` block is defined before the general `Catch` block that we created earlier. This allows the `Catch` block for the exceptions of the type `System.Exception` to act as a default handler for all types of exceptions. The CLR requires you to always order `Catch` blocks from the most specific to the least specific type of exception they are handling. As a result, you will be able to handle the specific exception before it is caught by a general `Catch` block.

The `Finally` block is used to encapsulate code that should always be executed regardless of whether or not an exception occurred. The `finally` block is typically used to perform clean up operations within a procedure. The following example appends on a `Finally` block to the try to catch statements in our previous example.

After the code in the Try block and the appropriate `Catch` block(s) has been executed, the code in the `Finally` block will display a simple Message Box to the user:

```
Try
    'Call our sample method
    Somemethod("")

Catch excpArg As System.ArgumentNullException

    'An ArgumentNullException occured. Display the information
    '...about the Exception to the user.
    MessageBox.Show("This exception was caught in the specific handler: " _
                & ControlChars.CrLf & ControlChars.CrLf _
                & "Message:  " & excpArg.Message & ControlChars.CrLf _
                & "Source:   " & excpArg.Source & ControlChars.CrLf _
                & "ParamName:   " & excpArg.ParamName, _
                Me.Text, MessageBox.IconError)

Catch excp As System.Exception

    'An unexpected Exception occured. Display the information
    '...about the Exception to the user.
    MessageBox.Show("This exception was caught in the general handler: " _
                & ControlChars.CrLf & ControlChars.CrLf _
                & "Message:  " & excp.Message & ControlChars.CrLf _
                & "Source:   " & excp.Source, _
                Me.Text, MessageBox.IconError)

Finally

    'Display a message to the user indicating that
    '...we are in the Finally block.
    MessageBox.Show("Executing the Finally block...", _
                Me.Text, MessageBox.IconError)

End Try
```

Using StackTrace with an Exception

When an exception is created, but before it is thrown, the Common Language Runtime captures the information about the call stack and stores it with the exception object. The entire call stack can be retrieved as a formatted string through the `System.Exception`'s `StackTrace` property.

The following example demonstrates the use of the `StackTrace` property by creating a call stack four levels deep, throwing an exception, and finally writing the exception's `StackTrace` property value to the debugger:

```
Protected Sub btnStackTrace_Click(ByVal sender As Object, ByVal e As
System.EventArgs)
    Try
        'Call our first method
        StackTraceMethod1()

    Catch excp As System.Exception
        'Write the Exception's StackTrace string to the debugger
```

```
        Debug.WriteLine(excp.StackTrace)
    End Try
End Sub

Private Sub StackTraceMethod1()

    'Call the next method
    StackTraceMethod2()
End Sub

Private Sub StackTraceMethod2()

    'Call the next method
    StackTraceMethod3()
End Sub

Private Sub StackTraceMethod3()

    'Call the next method
    StackTraceMethod4()
End Sub

Private Sub StackTraceMethod4()
    'Throw a general System.Exception to the caller
    Throw (New System.Exception("This is an exception..."))
End Sub
```

When the above sample is executed, the following text is written to the debugger:

```
at System.Exception_Examples_VB.Form1.StackTraceMethod4() in C:\Net\.NET
Overview\Code\System.Exception Examples VB\frmSystem.Exception.vb:line 180

at System.Exception_Examples_VB.Form1.StackTraceMethod3() in C:\Net\.NET
Overview\Code\System.Exception Examples VB\frmSystem.Exception.vb:line 176

at System.Exception_Examples_VB.Form1.StackTraceMethod2() in C:\Net\.NET
Overview\Code\System.Exception Examples VB\frmSystem.Exception.vb:line 170

at System.Exception_Examples_VB.Form1.StackTraceMethod1() in C:\Net\.NET
Overview\Code\System.Exception Examples VB\frmSystem.Exception.vb:line 164

at System.Exception_Examples_VB.Form1.btnStackTrace_Click(Object sender, EventArgs
e) in C:\Net\.NET Overview\Code\System.Exception Examples
VB\frmSystem.Exception.vb:line 71
```

As you can see from the above example, the StackTrace property is invaluable in debugging because it can quickly tell you the fully-qualified method or property name, source file and line number where an exception occurred.

An exception object can also be used to create and populate the StackTrace class contained in the System.Diagnostics namespace. The StackTrace class provides programmatic access to the individual fields and properties that describe each call in the call stack.

System.Collections

The `System.Collections` namespace contains classes, interfaces and structures used to manage groups or *collections* of objects. This namespace is a perfect example of how the .NET Class Framework replaces many existing COM libraries and provides a single unified programming model. In the COM environment there were several different components that provided the ability to manage groups of objects. These components were scattered across several unrelated libraries. For example, the commonly used `VBA.Collection` component was defined in the Visual Basic for Applications library, while the `Scripting.Dictionary` component was included in the Microsoft Scripting Runtime library. Additionally, many developers have implemented their own custom collection classes in order to support specific object types or expose functionality that is not provided by either of these two components.

The `System.Collections` namespace provides several different classes, sometimes called collection classes, which can be used to manage a set of objects. Each of these classes is designed to provide a unique behavior and set of functionality. Some of these collection classes include:

- ❑ `ArrayList`
- ❑ `BitArray`
- ❑ `HashTable`
- ❑ `NameValueCollection`
- ❑ `Queue`
- ❑ `SortedList`
- ❑ `Stack`
- ❑ `StringCollection`

However, before we start using these classes, let's briefly discuss the interfaces defined by the `System.Collections` namespace and learn some of the concepts that are the same for all the collection classes.

System.Collections Interfaces

The classes contained in the `System.Collections` namespace are centered on five main interfaces: `IEnumerable`, `IEnumerator`, `ICollection`, `IList`, and `IDictionary`. Understanding these five core interfaces is the key to effectively using the `System.Collections` classes. The relationship between these interfaces is illustrated in the following UML class diagram. Notice that the `IEnumerator` interface is inherited by the `ICollection` interface and the `ICollection` interface is then inherited by the `IList` and `IDictionary` interfaces. Although the `IEnumerable` and `ICollection` interfaces are implemented by all collection classes in order to expose general collection functionality, the `IList` and `IDictionary` interfaces are used to expose functionality and behavior that is specific to certain types of collections. We'll discuss the relationship between the `IEnumerable` and the `IEnumerator` interfaces in the next section.

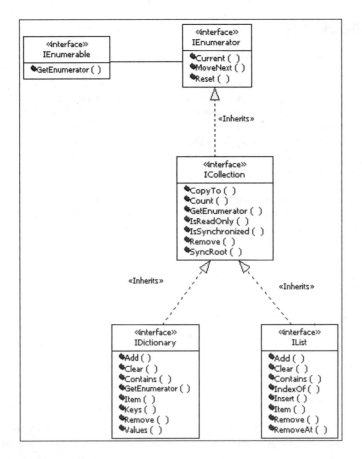

IEnumerable & IEnumerator Interfaces

A fundamental requirement of a collection class is the ability to enumerate or iterate through the group of objects the collection is managing. The `IEnumerable` and `IEnumerator` interfaces allow collection classes to expose simple enumeration functionality in a standard way. Consequently, all collection classes contained in the `System.Collections` namespace implement the `IEnumerable` interface.

The `IEnumerable` interface defines a single method called `GetEnumerator`. When invoked, `GetEnumerator` returns a separate object, called an enumerator, which implements the `IEnumerator` interface. After the client acquires a reference to the enumerator it can begin iterating through the individual objects in the collection by calling the properties and methods defined by the `IEnumerator` interface.

Let's take a look at a simple example that demonstrates the use of the `IEnumerable` and `IEnumerator` interfaces in conjunction with the `System.Collections.NameValueCollection` class. The `NameValueCollection` class is simply a dictionary that stores a list of name or keys and associated values. It is similar to the `Scripting.Dictionary` class available in COM. The following code enumerates through all of the objects contained in our pre-populated `NameValueCollection` object (`m_pNVCollection`) and displays a message box containing each object's key and value.

First, we need to declare some local variables and acquire a reference to the `IEnumerable` on our `NameValueCollection` object:

```
Dim pIEnumerable As System.Collections.IEnumerable
Dim pIEnumerator As System.Collections.IEnumerator
Dim strKey As String
Dim strValue As String


'Acquire a reference to the IEnumerable interface
'...on the NameValueCollection object
pIEnumerable = m_pNVCollection
```

Next, we need to call the GetEnumerator method on the IEnumerable interface reference and obtain a reference to the IEnumerator interface on the returned enumerator object:

```
'Acquire a reference to a new enumerator for our
'...NameValueCollection object
pIEnumerator = pIEnumerable.GetEnumerator()
```

Finally, we can iterate through the objects in the NameValueCollection by calling methods on the enumerator's IEnumerator interface. The MoveNext method returns True until it moves past the last object in the collection. The IEnumerator interface's Current property returns a reference to the current object. Notice in this situation, because we are working with a NameValueCollection object, the type of the object returned from the Current property is a String, which represents the key for the current item in our collection. Other implementations of the IEnumerator class return the actual object in the collection when the Current property is called. However, once we have the key, we can call the Item property of the NameValueCollection object to obtain the actual value:

```
While (pIEnumerator.MoveNext() = True)

    'Get the current item's key and value into variables
    strKey = pIEnumerator.Current().ToString()
    strValue = m_pNVCollection.Item(strKey)

    'Display the Item's info in a MessageBox
    MessageBox.Show("Key: '" & strKey & "'      " _
                            & "Value: '" & strValue & "'")
End While
```

After looking at the last code example I'm sure you're probably thinking that there has to be an easier way to iterate through objects in a collection. Thankfully, Visual Basic and C# both provide the ForEach statement, to hide us from the IEnumerable and IEnumerator interfaces.

The following example shows how the ForEach statement significantly reduces the amount of code we would normally have to write when enumerating a collection:

```
Dim objCurrentItem As System.Object
Dim strKey As String
Dim strValue As String


For Each objCurrentItem In m_pNVCollection

    'Get the current item's key and value into variables
    strKey = objCurrentItem.ToString()
```

```
        strValue = m_pNVCollection.Item(strKey)


        strValue = m_pNVCollection.Item(strKey)

        'Display the Item's info in a MessageBox
        MessageBox.Show("Key: '" & strKey & "'      " _
                              & "Value: '" & strValue & "'")
    Next
```

ICollection Interface

All of the collection classes contained in the System.Collections namespace implement the ICollection interface. Since the ICollection interface inherits the IEnumerable interface, all of these classes are also required to implement the methods defined by the IEnumerable interface. The ICollection interface defines methods and properties that expose general information about the collection, such as its size, read/write status and thread safety.

IList Interface

The IList interface defines properties and methods that can be used to add, remove and retrieve objects within a collection. This interface is implemented by specific types of collection classes that manage sequential lists of objects – some examples of these include System.Array, System.Collections.ArrayList, and System.Collections.StringCollection. Since the IList interface inherits ICollection, these classes also implement the ICollection and IEnumerable interfaces. We will use the ArrayList class and methods of the IList interface later in this chapter.

IDictionary Interface

The IDictionary interface also defines properties and methods that can be used to add, remove, and retrieve objects in a collection. However, unlike the IList interface, the IDictionary interface is designed for classes that want to manage groups of unordered objects as key-value pairs. Each element in the collection must have a unique, non-null key. Although this key can be any type of object, it is typically a String value. The classes that implement the IDictionary interface include System.Collections.Hashtable and System.Collections.SortedList. Since the IDictionary interface inherits ICollection, these classes also implement the ICollection and IEnumerable interfaces.

ArrayList Class

The ArrayList class is simply an intelligent array that dynamically increases and decreases in size as objects are added and removed. As the name suggests, the ArrayList class implements the IList interface as well as several additional methods that extend the basic functionality exposed by the IList interface. The ArrayList class combines the efficiency of an array with the simplicity of a list. It is particularly useful in situations where you would normally use an array, but you don't want to mess with logic to handle allocation and de-allocation, sorting and searching.

Instantiating the ArrayList Class

To demonstrate the features and functionality of the ArrayList class, I've constructed a simple example using a Windows Form. As you can see in the following screenshot, the Windows Form simply displays a System.WinForms.ListBox control populated with the same values that stored in the ArrayList.

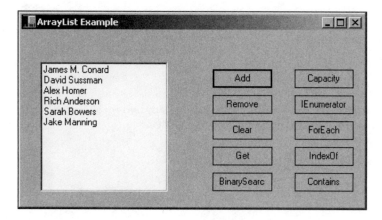

In the declarations section of the Windows Form class, declare and instantiate our ArrayList class:

```
Public Class frmArrayList
    Inherits System.WinForms.Form

    Private m_objArrayList As New System.Collections.ArrayList()
```

In this example we've used the default constructor, which doesn't accept any arguments. When using the default constructor, the ArrayList object will have the default property values and it will be completely empty. However, the ArrayList class also provides two other constructors. One constructor receives a reference to an IList interface from which it copies all of the objects into the ArrayList and the other constructor accepts an integer that specifies the initial Capacity of the ArrayList.

Adding and Removing Items

Since the ArrayList class implements the IList interface, elements can be added and removed using the Add and Remove / RemoveAt methods respectively:

This example adds an item to our ArrayList and to the ListBox control when the btnAdd button is clicked:

```
Protected Sub btnAdd_Click(ByVal sender As Object, _
                           ByVal e As System.EventArgs)

    Dim strValue As String

    'get a Value from the user
    strValue = InputBox("Enter the value for the new Item: ")

    'Add a new item to the ArrayList object
    m_objArrayList.Add(strValue)

    'Add a new Item to our List control
    lstData1.Items.Add(strValue)
End Sub
```

The following code removes the item selected in the ListBox control from our ArrayList when the btnRemove button is clicked:

```
Protected Sub btnRemove_Click(ByVal sender As Object, _
                              ByVal e As System.EventArgs)

    Dim intSelectedItemIndex As Integer

    'Exit this procedure if there aren't any selected items
    If lstData1.SelectedItems.Count = 0 Then
        Exit Sub
    End If

    'Get the Selected Item's index
    intSelectedItemIndex = lstData1.SelectedIndex

    'Remove the item selected from our ArrayList object
    m_objArrayList.RemoveAt(intSelectedItemIndex)

    'Now remove the selected ListItem from the ListView
    lstData1.Items.Remove(intSelectedItemIndex)
End Sub
```

The `ArrayList` class also provides the methods `AddRange`, `InsertRange` and `RemoveRange`. These methods allow you to add and insert groups of items by passing a collection (object implementing `ICollection`) of the items to add and remove groups of items by specifying a starting index and the number of items to remove from the `ArrayList`.

As we discussed earlier, the `ArrayList` object automatically allocates and de-allocates in its internal array as objects are added and removed. The `ArrayList` provides two properties that expose information about the size of the internal array: `Count` and `Capacity`. The read-only `Count` property, defined by the `ICollection` interface, returns the actual number of objects in the `ArrayList`. The `Capacity` property returns and sets the number of array locations that are allocated at a given time. If the `Count` exceeds the `Capacity` as items are added, then the `ArrayList` automatically allocates the additional number of locations as specified by the `Capacity`.

For example, the following code adds 64 Strings to our `ArrayList`. Since the default `Capacity` is 16, when the 17th String is added, the `ArrayList` allocates an additional 16 locations in the internal array and the `Capacity` property is changed to 32. When the 33rd String is added, the `ArrayList` allocates an additional 32 locations in the internal array and the `Capacity` property is changed to 64; and so on. Essentially, the `Capacity` doubles in size each time the actual number of objects in the `ArrayList` exceeds the `Capacity`.

```
Dim intIndex As Integer
Dim strValue As String

'Clear the objects out of the ArrayList
m_objArrayList.Clear()

For intIndex = 0 To 64 Step 1

    'Build the Item's value using the index
    strValue = "NewItem" & intIndex
```

```
'Add an item to the ArrayList
m_objArrayList.Add(strValue)

'Write the new item's index and the current capacity
'...of the ArrayList to the Debug window
Debug.WriteLine("Added Item #" & CStr(intIndex) _
            & " Current Capacity:  " & m_objArrayList.Capacity)

Next
```

In some situations where you are working with a relatively large group of objects, this automatic allocation behavior might be undesirable. For example, imagine a situation where you have 130 objects you want to manage in an `ArrayList`. Based on the default initial capacity of 16, the `ArrayList` will reallocate space four times and its internal array size will be 256. That means there are 126 locations allocated that are not being used! Instead of relying on the default capacity, improve performance and reduce the memory footprint when working with `ArrayLists` by setting the `Capacity` property to your desired size.

```
Dim intIndex As Integer
Dim strValue As String

'Clear the objects out of the ArrayList
m_objArrayList.Clear()

'Set the initial capacity of the ArrayList
m_objArrayList.Capacity = 64

For intIndex = 0 To 64 Step 1

    'Build the Item's value using the index
    strValue = "NewItem" & intIndex

    'Add an item to the ArrayList
    m_objArrayList.Add(strValue)
Next
```

The `Capacity` property can also be set when creating an instance of an `ArrayList` class by passing an integer value into the constructor:

```
Private m_objArrayList As New System.Collections.ArrayList(64)
```

Referencing Items

Objects in an `ArrayList` can be accessed by index using the standard Item property defined by the `IList` interface. The following example uses the Item property to get the value for the item that is selected in the `ListBox` control:

```
Dim intSelectedItemIndex As Integer
Dim strValue As String

'Exit this procedure if there aren't any selected items
If lstData1.SelectedItems.Count = 0 Then
    Exit Sub
End If
```

```
'Get the Selected Item's index
intSelectedItemIndex = lstData1.SelectedIndex

'Get the Value for the selected list item by its index
strValue = m_objArrayList.Item(intSelectedItemIndex).ToString()

'Display the Item's info in a MessageBox
MessageBox.Show("Index: '" & intSelectedItemIndex & "'      " _
                        & "Value: '" & strValue & "'")
```

The Item property is sufficient for acquiring a reference to an object when you know the object's index; however, what happens when you don't know the index of an object in the ArrayList? The ArrayList object provides two methods for this situation: IndexOf and LastIndexOf. IndexOf searches forward in the ArrayList for the first occurrence of a specified object, whereas LastIndexOf searches backward in the ArrayList for the last occurrence of a specified object. The Equals method of the System.Object class is used to determine the equality. When an occurrence is found, these methods return the index of the matching object. If a match is not found then −1 is returned. The following example searches our ArrayList for the first occurrence of a String:

```
Dim intIndex As Integer
Dim strValue As String

'Get the Value we are searching for
strValue = InputBox("Enter the value you want to find:")

'Get the Value for the selected list item by its index
intIndex = m_objArrayList.IndexOf(strValue)

If intIndex <> -1 Then
    'A match was found

    'Display the Item's info in a MessageBox
    MessageBox.Show("Index: '" & intIndex & "'      " _
                            & "Value: '" & strValue & "'")

Else
    'No matches were found
    MessageBox.Show("No matches were found in the ArrayList!")
End If
```

Both of these methods also provide overloaded implementations that accept a starting index as well as a stopping index.

If you only want to know whether or not an object is contained in an ArrayList than you can use the Contains method:

```
Dim strValue As String

'Get the Value we are searching for
strValue = InputBox("Enter the value you want to find:")

If m_objArrayList.Contains(strValue) = True Then
```

```
         'The object exists
         MessageBox.Show("Your value was found!")

      Else
         'No matches were found
         MessageBox.Show("No matches were found in the ArrayList!")
      End If
```

Summary

In this chapter we've just barely scratched the surface in our exploration of the .NET Class Framework – a complete reference to the .NET Class Framework could span several books. However, we have discussed the core concepts of the Class Framework, which apply to all namespaces and types within the Class Framework. If you're going to begin developing applications using the .NET Framework, you can't avoid working with the .NET Class Framework: it is an integral component of the entire .NET Framework that provides object models for developing custom class libraries, console applications, Web Form or WinForm controls or applications, and Web or Windows Services.

Specifically, in this chapter we:

❑   Discussed the benefits of the .NET Class Framework

❑   Learned about the role of Namespaces and the Common Type System (CTS)

❑   Utilized some of the classes in the System and System.Collections namespaces

In the next chapter, we will discuss and utilize the new version of Active Server Pages called ASP.NET, which primarily consists of classes, interfaces and structures defined in the System.Web.* namespaces.

ODUCING.NETINTRODUCING.NETINTRODUCING.NETINTRODUCI
ETINTRODUCING.NETINTRODUCING.NETINTRODUCING.NETINT
CING.NETINTRODUCING.NETINTRODUCING.NETINTRODUCING.
NTRODUCING.NETINTRODUCING.NETINTRODUCING.NETINTROD
G.NETINTRODUCING.NETINTRODUCING.NETINTRODUCING.NET
ODUCING.NETINTRODUCING.NETINTRODUCING.NETINTRODUCI
ETINTRODUCING.NETINTRODUCING.NETINTRODUCING.NETINT
CING.NETINTRODUCING.NETINTRODUCING.NETINTRODUCING.
NTRODUCING.NETINTRODUCING.NETINTRODUCING.NETINTROD
G.NETINTRODUCING.NETINTRODUCING.NETINTRODUCING.NET
ODUCING.NETINTRODUCING.NETINTRODUCING.NETINTRODUCI
ETINTRODUCING.NETINTRODUCING.NETINTRODUCING.NETINT
CING.NETINTRODUCING.NETINTRODUCING.NETINTRODUCING.
NTRODUCING.NETINTRODUCING.NETINTRODUCING.NETINTROD
G.NETINTRODUCING.NETINTRODUCING.NETINTRODUCING.NET
ODUCING.NETINTRODUCING.NETINTRODUCING.NETINTRODUCI
ETINTRODUCING.NETINTRODUCING.NETINTRODUCING.NETINT
CING.NETINTRODUCING.NETINTRODUCING.NETINTRODUCING.
NTRODUCING.NETINTRODUCING.NETINTRODUCING.NETINTROD
G.NETINTRODUCING.NETINTRODUCING.NETINTRODUCING.NET
ODUCING.NETINTRODUCING.NETINTRODUCING.NETINTRODUCI
ETINTRODUCING.NETINTRODUCING.NETINTRODUCING.NETINT
CING.NETINTRODUCING.NETINTRODUCING.NETINTRODUCING.
NTRODUCING.NETINTRODUCING.NETINTRODUCING.NETINTROD
G.NETINTRODUCING.NETINTRODUCING.NETINTRODUCING.NET
ODUCING.NETINTRODUCING.NETINTRODUCING.NETINTRODUCI
ETINTRODUCING.NETINTRODUCING.NETINTRODUCING.NETINT
CING.NETINTRODUCING.NETINTRODUCING.NETINTRODUCING.
NTRODUCING.NETINTRODUCING.NETINTRODUCING.NETINTROD
G.NETINTRODUCING.NETINTRODUCING.NETINTRODUCING.NET
ODUCING.NETINTRODUCING.NETINTRODUCI
RODUCING.NETINTRODUCING.NETINT
NETINTRODUCING.NETINTRODUCING.
NG.NETINTRODUCING.NETINTRODUCING.NETINTROD
G.NETINTRODUCING.NETINTRODUCING.NETINTRODUCING.NET
ODUCING.NETINTRODUCING.NETINTRODUCING.NETINTRODUCI
ETINTRODUCING.NETINTRODUCING.NETINTRODUCING.NETINT

7

ASP.NET

It seems such a short time ago when Microsoft released Active Server Pages, and yet, in the space of five years, it has gone from being an obscure geek's plaything to one of the most popular and prominent methods of displaying dynamic information on a web site, and for creating distributed Web applications. However, if you read Mark Ander's introduction to the Wrox Press book *A Preview of Active Server Pages+*, you'll see that within a year of its birth, some of the top developers in Microsoft had already decided that it was too complicated for their liking, and were working on a set of improvements! In web development one year is a long time, four years an eternity, and the emergence of technologies such as XML has demanded that ASP integrates and upgrades constantly to keep pace.

Windows 2000 has hardly finished installing on many businesses machines and already the .NET framework is waiting in readiness, featuring new tools and applications. Ultimately, it will form part of a future operating system. On top of this, ASP has been completely reinvented to provide a suitable means for helping to put the new principles of the framework into practice.

ASP.NET started life as Active Server Pages Plus (ASP+), but was recently renamed to fit into Microsoft's .NET strategy. In fact, at time of writing, ASP.NET is still in beta, and despite the changes in the naming of the product, the technology itself is robust. This is why Microsoft has included the beta version of the new ASP.NET technology as part of the .NET Framework SDK. In this chapter, we're going to have look at some of the most important new aspects of ASP.NET, all of which are featured in the beta.

ASP.NET's biggest benefit over ASP is that it brings a language-independent way of creating components and dynamic web applications that can produce output on any platform or device, which is specifically tailored to the target client. This is undoubtedly a big selling point behind the .NET framework; a common approach to programming. No matter which programming language you are using, everybody will be able to access the same objects, the same properties, and methods. However, it's also more than a matter of just calling a component written in another language (standard COM provided this) – you can also inherit from a class written in another language.

.NET also introduces the idea of Web Services, which might ultimately replace components in the future. (We'll look into Web Services in detail in the next chapter.) ADO is still supported in .NET, and Microsoft plan to have version 3.0 of the popular data access technology available in the final release of .NET. There's also a new way to access and work with your data in the form of ADO.NET, which introduces some new objects, and even a set of objects intended specifically for use with SQL Server, which connect directly – bypassing OLEDB completely. However, while these two areas play a significant role in ASP.NET development, they're not exclusive to ASP.NET – they also interact with the whole .NET Framework. So instead we're going to concentrate on the large scale changes made to ASP itself in this chapter; the new controls, the new objects, the changes made to existing objects and changes to the configuration of ASP and IIS.

In this tour we're going to look at:

❑ Reasons why we need a new version of ASP

❑ How different ASP.NET pages are from ASP pages

❑ The new features in ASP.NET

❑ ASP.NET controls

❑ Code behind

❑ Configuration

❑ Application and Session State

❑ Security

❑ Creating your own custom controls in ASP.NET

Why Do We Need a New Version of ASP?

If, like me, you were drawn to ASP by its simplicity and ease of use, then you might be wondering what could be added to make things easier. When Dynamic HTML was introduced, it was sold as a way of simplifying a lot of the aspects of HTML, but for the main part it introduced a lot of complexities, and forced web site developers who previously knew nothing but HTML to learn basic programming skills so that they could write script. It offered a lot of great advances, but it didn't make the learning process any easier. This is where ASP.NET is different. Many of the innovations are aimed directly at the web developer who doesn't know much beyond HTML. Let's look at some of the most compelling reasons very briefly now. We'll then demonstrate some of these advantages with actual code a little later in this chapter.

Less Code

One of the greatest benefits of ASP.NET is that it reduces the amount of coding you will need to write in an application. There are several features in ASP.NET that are all geared towards reducing the amount of code you need to write. Firstly, the introduction of server controls means you can use HTML-like tags to accomplish something that in ASP required both HTML and scripting. For example, you can bind the contents of a control to a data store, simply by adding a new attribute. If you wanted a control to keep state between web pages when someone refreshed a page, with ASP you'd also have to write some script code. Again, you don't have to do this any more, because ASP.NET can automatically keep track of state for you.

Secondly, it allows you to use structured programming. With ASP, the benefits of procedures and functions were usually thrown out of the window, and in some ways you were almost cast back to the days of micro-computers, the BASIC languages, and endless mazes of spaghetti code. This in turn made it very hard to re-use the code in any meaningful way. This was because when ASP was first released, Microsoft provided little education on how to write good ASP applications. You could use functions and procedures, but without calling these via events, you were still confined to a sequential execution order. To re-use commonly used parts of code you could also use include files, but these brought their own shortcomings. Now, with the addition of languages that contain a true event-driven programming model, code re-use becomes a much more practical proposition.

ASP.NET also introduces two concepts that help reduce the amount of code needed. One is **code behind** (short for code behind forms): once an ASP.NET page is compiled, this creates a base class from which the page can inherit. The second is that of **user controls**. These allow the user to re-use sections of their own code, and take the place of includes files. This is on top of the already existing ability to write your own components, which has also been overhauled and improved.

Compiled Code

ASP.NET uses compiled code. This is a big step forward from previous ASP. Whereas ASP pages were interpreted every time the page was run, in ASP.NET, the first time a page is run, it is compiled into a .NET class. The class is then stored in a cache, and the cached version of the class will be used on any future calls to the page. Any changes to the page are recognised automatically, the class is recompiled, and the cached version changed. This leads to a large increase in performance, as the page doesn't have to be interpreted every time it is accessed.

Strong Typing

One large problem with scripting languages is that they don't actually allow you to use data types as you would in VB or C++. Given that ASP had the facilities to parse, execute and cache a page, it was a little irritating that you couldn't assign a type to your variables. For the sake of simplicity, it was easier not to have to worry about the different typing of each variable, but, under the covers, the script code that seemed to create every variable as a variant type actually kept track of which subtype the variable was.

Since variants all have the same amount of memory allocated to them, no matter what the subtype, a variant containing an integer and a variant containing a string take up the same amount of resources, and this has an impact on performance in ASP pages. In a strongly-typed language, the memory allocations would vary according to the type of information the variable contained. Using variants also caused some problems when using certain COM components or interfaces. It also meant that you couldn't be completely ignorant about variable types anyway, since it's not possible to add a number to a date and expect ASP to do all the hard work for you. Secondly, strong typing is good programming practice and should be encouraged.

Easier Use of Components

Using a scripting language meant that the functionality of your applications was always going to be limited due to the sandboxing of programs. To circumvent this, you were forced to add outside components to your web pages, written in either VB, Java, or C++. Components have always been a big part of ASP, but to get them to function correctly has sometimes required some extra effort on the part of the developer.

First, they had to be registered, which was an extra step in the process. Secondly, if you wished to make improvements to the component, it was quite common to find that the previous version of the component had been locked – you'd have stop and restart some of the IIS services just to get it to relinquish it's hold on the component so you could update it. If you wanted to configure the component in any way, you could find yourself trawling through the registry or some such application to make these changes. Each ASP.NET page is now a COM compliant component, whereas ASP script languages could only call a COM components default interface; so many of these versioning and integration difficulties have now been resolved.

Better Tools Support

ASP has always been a bit of an oddity when using it with other tools. In fact, many developers still prefer to use Notepad when developing ASP pages, rather than tools such as Visual Interdev. This isn't only due to programmers' Luddite tendencies, but because in many ways the development process was actually complicated by using other tools. The new component-based, event-driven programming model of ASP.NET makes it much easier to integrate tools from Microsoft and third party developers.

Separation of HTML from ASP Code

The original authors of the first HTML standard must still despair over the way their simple, straightforward HTML code has been convoluted, first by the addition of presentation detail (see the <FONT> tag and its ilk) and then scripting code. What started as a simple way to represent the structure of a web document ended up as a file that handled everything from the design of the page, to the way it connects to the database. Style sheets have already gone some way to separating out presentational content from the document, (although it is XML and XSL that fully facilitate this separation), and now ASP.NET makes it possible to remove the ASP scripting from the page.

One of the few advantages that Java Server Pages enjoys over ASP is that JSP offers separation of code and markup. This makes JSP applications easier to maintain and update. However, with these improvements in ASP.NET, yet again the clear cut advantages boil down to being dependent on your choice of programming language and platform.

Works on any Client

In theory, ASP also worked on any client, and even came with a browser capabilities component, which allowed you to assess the different features that a user's browser either supported or didn't have installed. However, despite this, it was still often difficult to write an ASP page that you could guarantee would work on the variant versions of Netscape, Internet Explorer, Opera, and other lesser known HTML browsers. The problem was that ASP generates HTML code, and there are quite a few inconsistencies between the way the browsers handle and interpret HTML. In ASP.NET there are now several server side components, which generate output specifically for a target browser and the **Adaptive User Interface** (**AUI**) will support other devices, for example WAP devices. In fact, you'll find a different set of controls at your disposal depending on your client type.

Better Integration with XML

The creation of web services has led to the creation of services whose specific purpose is the generation and the utilization of XML files. Also, the upgrading of ADO to ADO.NET means that there is much greater support for XML. As XML is the data description language, web services actually send data back and forth in XML format.

And Other Advantages...

And it doesn't stop there: there's better scalability, ASP.NET is now more crash tolerant than ASP, there's a greater set of security management features, debugging has been vastly improved with the addition of a trace facility, and page caching is now much more flexible. We could go into detail about these features too, but to keep this as an overview instead of an entire book, we'll now look at what ASP.NET actually is, and start by comparing ASP.NET pages with its predecessor, ASP pages.

How Different are ASP.NET Pages from ASP Pages?

To put it bluntly, they're completely different. In fact, it's almost better to think of ASP.NET and ASP as two separate, although related, technologies. Whereas ASP relied on a scripting language (either VBScript or JScript) to access its object model, ASP.NET lets you use fully-fledged compiled programming languages such as Visual Basic, C#, even COBOL, or any other .NET-compliant language. The .NET framework offers one method for handling many common program tasks via a set of common APIs, accessible through any of its programming languages.

However, having said that, for the ASP developer, the way code is placed in the page and the way it is recognized by the server hasn't changed that much. ASP.NET pages still look pretty similar to ASP pages, and while there's a lot of new features on offer, the learning curve won't be that great for ASP developers. We'll take a look at the differences between ASP pages and ASP.NET, to give you a platform on which to get started.

.aspx instead of .asp

The first difference to notice is that ASP.NET pages are known as ASP Web Forms pages. They are identified by the `.aspx` suffix that is attached to the end of the filename instead of the `.asp` extension. When the ASP.NET DLL receives a request with a `.aspx` suffix, it parses and compiles the file into a .NET class, or uses an already compiled .NET class. Even pure HTML files with a `.aspx` suffix will be sent to the parser. In fact, ASP pages and ASP.NET pages are sent to two different places. The DLL that processes your ASP.NET pages is the `XSPISAPI.DLL`, and this is of course separate to the `ASP.DLL`. The `ASP.DLL` does still exist, and your standard ASP pages will still be sent to this DLL for processing. So, traditional ASP will still be supported for legacy applications. However, if you send your ASP pages to the ASP.NET parser (that is, put a `.aspx` suffix on them), you might have to do some brief amendments to get them to work as intended.

Placing ASP.NET Code in Your Pages

The way you delimit ASP.NET code from the HTML in your Web Form pages will be familiar to users of ASP, since it is done using the `<SCRIPT>` tags, with the RUNAT attribute set to `Server`. The default language for scripting is now Visual Basic, and VBScript is no longer supported. If you want to code in a different language, you need to specify which language you're using by including a `Language="xyz"` attribute. To define a page in VB.NET you could do the following:

```
<SCRIPT LANGUAGE="VB" RUNAT="SERVER">
... code here ...
</SCRIPT>
```

Since Visual Basic is the default language, the language tag in the above example isn't essential, and could be omitted. To define a page using C# language, you would do the following:

```
<SCRIPT LANGUAGE="C#" RUNAT="SERVER">
... code here ...
</SCRIPT>
```

Of course there's nothing to stop you using the <% %> delimiters as well. As long as your page is saved with a `.aspx` suffix, it will be sent to the ASP.NET compiler. The <% %> delimiters are used to add inline code. One thing to note, though, is that you can't add procedures inline, so the following code would cause an error:

```
<% Sub Page_Load()
      Response.Write("Hello")
   End Sub %>
```

Coding the Old Way

In ASP pages things were done on a strictly sequential basis. While ASP pages were dynamic, they didn't react to any outside events unless transactions or remote scripting were involved. The code was executed sequentially all the way down the page, even if the ASP code was broken into separate blocks interspersed throughout the HTML.

Coding in ASP.NET Pages

When executing an ASP.NET page, a strict set of events occurs. The first is the `Page_Init` event, which is followed by the `Page_Load` event. This `Page_Load` event is always fired, and will always be the first event once the page has finished loading. After that, the events initiated by the controls on the web page are dealt with. When the page is closed (that is, the user shuts the browser down or moves on a page), the `Page_Unload` event will be fired after all other events have been dealt with.

So, if you want code to execute before any events take place on our Web Form page, then you need to place the code in the `Page_Load` event:

```
<SCRIPT LANGUAGE="VB" RUNAT="SERVER">
Sub Page_Load()
... code here ...
End Sub
</SCRIPT>
```

Lastly, any code placed outside of these main events or subprocedures can be used for declaring global variables.

Server Controls

Server controls are a new addition in ASP.NET, and affect the structure and look of your ASP pages. They take the form of HTML-like tags, with an ASP prefix to identify them from other user created controls. They have a RUNAT attribute set to `Server`, which indicates that they are to be executed by the server:

```
<ASP:CheckBox id="CheckBox" Text="This is a CheckBox" RUNAT="Server" />
```

The RUNAT attribute must be part of the control to make the server-side event code work correctly

This is an example of the check box server-side control, which only requires one line of text. Generally, server controls are very similar to the client-side HTML elements that they generate, as we shall see later in the chapter.

Of course, there is plenty more going on behind the scenes, but this is just intended to give you an idea of what's new and unfamiliar when you look at an ASP.NET page. So, without further ado let's look at how you go about installing and running ASP.NET.

Getting Started with ASP.NET Beta

ASP.NET comes as part of the.NET framework SDK. One place where ASP 3.0 really fell down was that it was only available on Windows 2000. Many developers wanted the benefits that ASP 3.0 offered, but were unwilling to move to a new and as yet relatively untried operating system, and so have decided to stick with ASP 2.0. ASP.NET, on the other hand, will be supported on all Windows platforms from Windows 95 onwards (that is, Win 95/98/ ME/ NT 4 Workstation and Server, 2000 Pro, Server and Advanced). Having said that, it is only really targetted at Windows 2000 and NT4. The versions available for Windows 95 and Windows 98 will have much reduced functionality, since they can't run IIS as a web server. Thankfully, ASP.NET doesn't replace the existing installation of ASP – it's happy to co-exist with your existing configuration, so you can continue to use your existing ASP pages.

What Might Change in the ASP.NET Final Release?

Of course, as all we have to go on now is a beta, it's fair to say that there will be elements of ASP.NET that will change by the final release. While essentially much of it will be the same as you see now, we'll cast our eye very quickly over some areas that might change in the coming months.

XHTML Compliance

ASP.NET does not currently support XHTML. The output that ASP.NET produces is HTML 3.2 compliant, while the XHTML specification is basically the HTML 4.01 spec written as an XML document. This wouldn't be a problem except for the fact that a lot of the HTML 4.0 spec has been working to undo aspects of HTML 3.2 that compromised the separation of presentation logic and structure. So, the result is that the HTML code that ASP.NET generates isn't compliant with the HTML 4.0 and therefore neither is it compliant with the XHTML standard.

The main reason for this seems to be that just about all browsers can cope with HTML 3.2, but even the latest releases of Internet Explorer and Netscape fall down on their support of HTML 4.0 in areas, and can give unpredictable output. We've already mentioned that a lot of effort has been made to ensure that the output generated can be parsed by any browser. While Microsoft are endeavoring to make sure that the final version of ASP.NET is as XHTML compliant as possible, the two slightly conflicting aims, one of meeting standards, and the other of keeping code that is readable on any client, are going to be difficult to reconcile. The Adaptive User Interface should handle this and generate appropriate HTML for the target browser, enabling rich features for only those devices that can support them.

Client-Specific Output Formats

There are several new controls that are pitched at specific browsers, and take advantage of each browser's dynamic HTML capabilities. In particular, the validation controls which we will be looking at shortly are capable of detecting whether a browser is IE4 or later, and can display their output using relatively new (that is, later than IE3) features such as Cascading Style Sheets (CSS). In the current beta, available during the writing of this chapter, these were about the only controls that could do this, but it is hoped that many of the server controls will also make use of these "browser-sensitive" abilities.

Features of ASP.NET

As already mentioned, if we went into any depth on the new features, we'd take up a whole book, so this will be a necessarily short joyride through ASP.NET's most significant new features. Because of the vast amount of new features, we will be breaking them down into separate categories. Some of the features directly affect the pages, but others make improvements to the methods in which ASP persists sessions between web pages, and improve the debugging and tracing facilities. We'll break down each of these features into relevant categories.

ASP.NET Pages

Many of the advantages ASP.NET offers over ASP aren't actually related to the improvement in the way pages are coded, but deal with the behind the scenes work that features such as web services provide. As mentioned earlier, the advantages in coding are the additional typing and structural features that fully compiled languages like Visual Basic and Visual C++ offer. However there are still quite a few innovations that will enhance your basic web pages.

HTML Server Controls

One of the most dramatic improvements that ASP.NET brings is that of being able to run HTML server controls. These are controls that are generally HTML elements containing attributes that can be seen on the server; in other words, form controls. These are created using the tag-like structure of HTML and run via the ASP.NET DLL:

```
<ASP:ListBox ID="ListBox1" runat="server">
   <ASP:ListItem>Clever</ASP:ListItem>
   <ASP:ListItem>Not too bright</ASP:ListItem>
   <ASP:ListItem>Thick</ASP:ListItem>
</asp:ListBox>
```

The great thing about these controls is that they don't require any extra learning, as they map directly on to their HTML client-side equivalents. So the ASP list box produced by this code is actually just the same as the following HTML code:

```
<SELECT NAME=ListBox2 SIZE=3>
   <OPTION>Clever</OPTION>
   <OPTION>Not too bright</OPTION>
   <OPTION>Thick</OPTION>
</SELECT>
```

You'll find that there are new server controls for each of the common HTML form controls. These server-side controls make use of their HTML equivalents, and bestow them with the following advantages. The first is that they automatically keep a "memory" of which control item has been selected. So, without any further coding being needed, state is automatically maintained between pages. If you try running the following code and then try selecting an option from the list and clicking on the submit button:

```
<html>
<body>
<form RUNAT="Server">
IQ:
<ASP:ListBox ID="ListBox1" RUNAT="Server">
    <ASP:ListItem>Clever</ASP:ListItem>
    <ASP:ListItem>Not too bright</ASP:ListItem>
    <ASP:ListItem>Thick</ASP:ListItem>
</ASP:ListBox>
<p />
<input type="submit" value="Submit">
</form>
</body>
</html>
```

The browser's display won't change at all, but if you view the source code, you'll find that some interesting additions have been made:

```
<html>
<body>
<form METHOD="POST" action="aspplus.aspx" id="ctrl1" name="ctrl1" >
<input type="hidden" name="__VIEWSTATE" value="a0z-721127884__x">
IQ:
<select name="ListBox1" id="ListBox1" size="5">
    <option value="Clever">Clever</option>
    <option selected value="Not too bright">Not too bright</option>
    <option value="Thick">Thick</option>
</select>
<p />
<input type="submit" value="Submit">
</form>
</body>
</html>
```

First, you'll see that ASP.NET has added four attributes to the <form> tag and removed the RUNAT tag. The first attribute sets the METHOD attribute to POST, while the second adds the destination page (your current page) under the POST attribute. The last two attributes created are an id and a name for the form. This is done without any intervention from the user. The second thing to note is that a hidden <input> control has also been added to the form.

The first question people often ask about server controls is how they manage to "remember" their state? The hidden <input> control is the answer. When the form is submitted, the code is returned back to the client from the server, with the selection the user made reflected as HTML code. If you think back to how much code we would have had to have previously written to implement this state handling, you can see how much we save. ASP.NET does it for us with no extra coding!

You'll also see that the <ASP: > tags have now been changed into the corresponding HTML tags, so that the browser knows what to display.

Server-side Processing of Client-side Events

We've already said that ASP unfortunately led to spaghetti code, and a removal of some of the advantages introduced by object-based programming. One main advantage of languages such as Visual Basic is that you're freed from a strictly sequential execution order when coding (that is, where line 1 is followed by line 2, or function a calls function b) by the event driven programming model. Even in client-side JavaScript and VBScript it is possible to wait for the raising of a specific event, but ASP programmers up to this point couldn't react to client-side events on the server-side. ASP.NET now allows you to use already familiar events such as `onclick` and `pageload` on your server-side controls, and then write event handlers for them in a language such as VB or C#.

You can add these events to the new ASP.NET controls, just as you would add them in Dynamic HTML to client-side controls, with just two additions. In Dynamic HTML an onclick event for a button control might look like this:

```
<input type="button" id="button1" value="Click me" onclick="ClickEventHandler()">
```

To get the server to deal with the event, all you need to do is add an event to the server-side control, in the same way the event was added to client-side control:

```
<asp:button id="button1" value="Click me" onclick="ClickEventHandler()"
runat="server"/>
```

The difference is how they're dealt with. With the former, when the event is raised, the browser deals with it (although it would have to be a browser that recognized DHTML). With server-side controls, the event is still raised by the browser, but instead of being dealt with by the browser, the client raises a **postback event**, which is returned to the server. It doesn't matter what kind of event was raised, the client will always return a postback event to the server. Another advantage is that the browser type doesn't have to recognize DHTML, so it will work on all browsers and not just modern ones. However, certain events are impossible to deal with on the server-side, such as key presses or mouse clicks. These are not passed onto the server and have to be handled by the client.

The advantage of passing events to the server is that it adds better structure to your code, because you can separate out your event handling code in your ASP.NET applications entirely. There are some disadvantages too – wherever possible it's a good idea to do client processing, to offload work from central CPUs to improve performance. Let's look at brief example of server-side processing to demonstrate how it works.

Example of Server-Side Processing

This example contains three server controls. The first is a check box to register a user's choice, the second is a button which will raise the event and the third is a label control. As with ASP, you still can't render dialog boxes directly in ASP.NET, and to display information dynamically to the screen, you can use the label control. The label control is the equivalent of an HTML <span> tag.

We're just taking the event raised when a user clicks on the button and running a short VB event handler. This event handler monitors the check box in the example and displays a different message in the label control depending on whether or not the check box has been selected.

```
<html>
<head>
<script language="vb" runat="server">
Sub ClickHandler(Sender As Object, E As EventArgs)
   If Request("ExtraInfoBox") = "on" then
      Message.text = "You will hear from us shortly"
   else
      Message.text = "You will not receive any further information from us"
   end if
End Sub
</script>
</head>
  <body>
<Form RUNAT="Server">

  <ASP:CheckBox ID="ExtraInfoBox"
         Text="Do you want to receive extra information?" Runat="server" />
  <BR>
  <BR>
  <ASP:Button ID="Button1" Text="Click Here to Submit"
                         onclick="ClickHandler" runat="server"/>

  <ASP:Label ID="Message" runat="server"/>
</Form>
  </body>
</html>
```

This message would only be displayed once a click event has been raised:

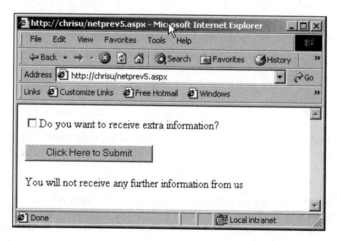

The click event handler code is placed in the <head> element on the page and it requires two parameters, the first of which has type `Object` and is named `Sender`, the second of which is type `EventArgs` and is named `E`. Both of these parameters are passed to any server-side event that can be raised by ASP.NET. These are standard parameters, which all event procedures are passed.

The `sender` parameter of type object represents the object that raised the event. The `E` parameter is an event class that captures the state associated with the event. It allows us to pass in the event arguments and use properties of the event object in the code.

One downside of event handling on the server side is the extra round trip needed to the server, which means the performance of the page can be adversely affected.

The ASP.NET Control Families

So far, we've only looked at one type of server-side control in ASP.NET: the intrinsic controls. There are in fact four different sets of server-side controls in ASP.NET, and we'll make some important distinctions between them.

Intrinsic Controls

The controls we've used in our examples so far are known as intrinsic controls. The intrinsic controls are the ones that map directly onto HTML elements. Within the intrinsic controls there are several groups of controls that correspond with the HTML FORM and TABLE elements. First we'll look at the controls that map directly onto the different types of the INPUT and SELECT elements in HTML forms. These controls are:

❑   ASP:RadioButton– maps to INPUT element, type RADIO

❑   ASP:CheckBox – maps to INPUT element, type CHECKBOX

❑   ASP:ListBox – maps to SELECT element

❑   ASP:DropDownList – maps to SELECT element

❑   ASP:TextBox – maps to TEXTAREA element

You could use a check box in the following way in ASP.NET:

```
<ASP:CheckBox ID="ExtraInfoBox" Text="Do you want to receive extra information?"
runat="server" />
```

This would be displayed in the following way, as in the previous example:

☐ Do you want to receive extra information?

The CheckBox item uses several attributes. For instance, ID gives the control a name that can be identified in code, and TEXT specifies the text you want displayed along side the control.

Rich Controls

Rich controls are similar to the built-in components that have come with ASP over the last few releases. While Microsoft promise a large set of advanced controls, so far there are just two, the Calendar control, and one that will be very familiar to ASP users, the Adrotator control. We'll look at the new control first.

Calendar

This is a pretty self-explanatory control, and is very easy to use. It provides a lot of attributes that can enable you to customize it to varying degrees, but at its simplest requires none at all.

```
<asp:Calendar runat="Server"/>
```

It is much simpler than the old way of creating ASP components by having to use the `CreateObject` method of the `Server` object, having to ensure that the ProgID of the object was correct, and so on. The above code is all that is needed to provide a straightforward calendar:

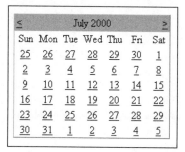

There are reams of self-explanatory attributes that can be used to customize the calendar accordingly.

- ❑ `BackColor`
- ❑ `BorderWidth`
- ❑ `BorderStyle`
- ❑ `BorderColor`
- ❑ `CellSpacing`
- ❑ `CellPadding`
- ❑ `ShowGridLines`
- ❑ `Width`
- ❑ `Height`

You can apply these attributes to the calendar control, just as you would set a normal group of HTML attributes

```
<asp:Calendar runat="Server"
  BackColor="Cyan" ForeColor="DarkBlue"
  BorderWidth="2" BorderStyle="Dotted"
  CellSpacing="3" CellPadding="3"
  ShowGridlines="true"
  Width="250" Height="250"
/>
```

In which case the display would look like this:

≤		July 2000				≥
Sun	Mon	Tue	Wed	Thu	Fri	Sat
25	26	27	28	29	30	1
2	3	4	5	6	7	8
9	10	11	12	13	14	15
16	17	18	19	20	21	22
23	24	25	26	27	28	29
30	31	1	2	3	4	5

These attributes can also be applied to localised areas of the calendar, so that, for instance, they only affect the days, or the weekend.

- ❏ `TitleStyle`
- ❏ `DayHeaderStyle`
- ❏ `DayStyle`
- ❏ `WeekendDayStyle`
- ❏ `SelectedDayStyle`

These are added to the previous attributes above and separated from them with a hyphen, for example:

```
<asp:Calendar runat="Server"
BackColor="Cyan" ForeColor="DarkBlue"
BorderWidth="2" BorderStyle="Dotted"
CellSpacing="3" CellPadding="3"
ShowGridlines=true
Width="250" Height="250"
TitleStyle-Height="50"
TitleStyle-BackColor="PaleBlue"
/>
```

These changes would only affect the title bar of the calendar.

There are also two events which you can hook up the calendar control to: one which is triggered when the day changes, and the other being triggered when the month changes. These events are the `OnSelectionChanged` and `OnVisibleMonthChanged` events respectively.

Ad Rotator

`Ad Rotator` is a huge improvement over its old ASP cousin. For starters, in place of the text file which contained the information about the ads, you now find that the file of ads is created as an XML file. The XML file contains an `AD` element that is composed of up to five elements:

- ❏ `ImageURL` – the URL of the image to be displayed
- ❏ `TargetURL` – the destination URL of the ad, when clicked on
- ❏ `AlternateText` – the text displayed when the cursor hovers over the ad
- ❏ `Keyword` – a non-obligatory attribute which lets you specify which category you'd want your ad in
- ❏ `Impressions` – a weighting for the ad, the larger the number, the more times your ad will be displayed

A typical Ad Rotator XML file might look like this:

```
<Advertisements>
   <Ad>
      <ImageUrl>http://p2p.wrox.com/progtoprog.jpg</ImageUrl>
      <TargetUrl>http://p2p.wrox.com</TargetUrl>
      <AlternateText>Programmer's Support and Resource Centre run by
      programmers for programmers</AlternateText>
      <Keyword>Support</Keyword>
```

```
        <Impressions>1000</Impressions>
    </Ad>
</Advertisements>
```

You can place as many ads as you want between the `<Advertisments>` tags, as long as they are delimited by a separate set of `<Ad>` tags. The XML file is then referenced via the Ad Rotator control's `AdvertisementFile` attribute in your `.aspx` page.

```
<asp:adrotator AdvertisementFile="advert.xml" BorderWidth=0 runat="server" />
```

The Ad Rotator control when placed in a `.aspx` page would then display the following when viewed in IE5:

You can go ahead and try this now. It might take a little while for the graphic to download, but as long as the `.aspx` file and the XML file are in the same directory, it will work correctly. All the code for this chapter is available for download from www.wrox.com.

Of course, the main strength of the Ad Rotator control is to display a number of ads, so you need to place a set of adverts in the file and then go back and refresh the page each time to see different ads.

List Controls

The List controls are used in conjunction with ADO.NET. They provide data binding facilities allowing you to use display data from a data store via a control. We also have the ability to bind to sources like arrays, not just DataSets in ADO.NET. We can also use templates to change the layout etc, and display a fully-featured list output with editing ability. ADO.NET is discussed in more detail in Chapter 11.

There are three types of control, which fall under the category of list control, the `DataGrid` control, the `Repeater` control, and the `DataList` Control.

DataGrid Control

For those of you who have spent ages fiddling around with databases, trying to get the correct information out of a database and then using `Response.Write` so that it comes out in an organized format in an HTML table, the `DataGrid` control is a revelation. It allows you to bind to a database and then display the output in an HTML table format with the minimum of fuss.

The `DataGrid` control takes the following format:

```
<asp:DataGrid id="AdataGrid" runat="server"/>
```

To get the information from the database, you still have to supply the relevant information, such as the connection string that supplies the user id, password, name of the server to connect to, and the name of the database on the server. This is exactly the same as it was in ASP using ADO. You also have to supply the SQL query to the database to get it to return the data.

Previously, when using ASP and ADO, when you returned the information, either in the form of a recordset or connection object, you still had to get the information back out of the object, and this usually involved stepping through each row for each field in the database.

This is where the DataGrid control deviates from the norm. We use a new object, the DataSet object to capture the information from the database using the FillDataSet method to populate it. This is a method of the "new" Command object. We just supply the name of the variable containing our DataSet object and the name of the table (the returned results in the DataSet object, not tables in the database) to the method. We can then reference the DataGrid control itself in the page with its id, and supply information automatically. We bind the object (that contains a reference to the control) to the table using the DataBind() method.

You can place it in an example like so:

```
<%@ Import Namespace="System.Data" %>
<%@ Import Namespace="System.Data.SQL" %>
<html>
<head>
    <script LANGUAGE="VB" RUNAT="SERVER">
   Sub Page_Load (Sender As Object, E As EventArgs)

      Dim objConnection As SQLConnection
         Dim objCommand      As SQLDataSetCommand
         Dim strConnect      As String
         Dim strCommand      As String
          Dim ds1        As New DataSet

      strConnect = "server=localhost;uid=sa;pwd=;database=pubs"
         strCommand = "select * from Authors"

      objConnection = New SQLConnection(strConnect)
         objCommand = New SQLDataSetCommand(strCommand, strConnect)

      objCommand.FillDataSet(ds1, "Authors")

      DataGrid1.DataSource=ds1.Tables("Authors").DefaultView
         DataGrid1.DataBind()
   End Sub
   </script>
</head>
<body>

  <ASP:DataGrid id="DataGrid1" runat="server" />
</body>
</html>
```

This returns the following output:

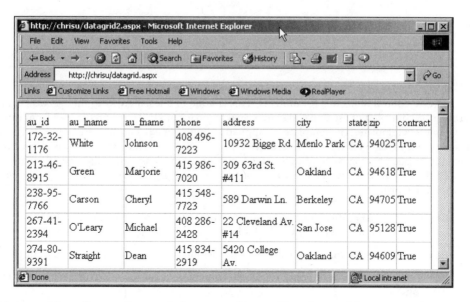

A quick scan of the code actually reveals three new objects, although two of them, SQLConnection and SQLDataSetCommand, are simply SQL Server-specific versions of the Connection and DataSetCommand objects. We'll discuss these in greater detail when we look at ADO.NET in Chapter 11, but for now it's only the DataSet object that is significantly different.

The code for the most part is strikingly familiar:

```
strConnect = "server=localhost;uid=sa;pwd=;database=pubs"
strCommand = "select * from Authors"

objConnection = New SQLConnection(strConnect)
objCommand = New SQLDataSetCommand(strCommand, strConnect)
```

We create a connection string, and a string that supplies the SQL for the query. We create an SQLConnection object and SQLDataSetCommand object using the connection and command strings.

It's the FillDataSet method that returns the results of a query into the DataSet and fills the DataSet Object ds1 with records.

```
objCommand.FillDataSet(ds1, "Authors")
```

We then set the DataSource property, telling our DataGrid where to get the data from. And lastly, we bound the DataGrid to our data source.

```
DataGrid1.DataSource=ds1.Tables("Authors").DefaultView
DataGrid1. DataBind()
```

The DataGrid control also provides features that allow you to customize the look of the control, with a large selection of properties that can be accessed as attributes. We could alter the gridlines and the style of each cell as follows:

```
<ASP:DataGrid id="DataGrid1" runat="server"
gridlines="None"
itemstyle-backcolor="beige" />
```

Repeater Control

The `Repeater` control binds to a list of items. This is done in the same way as the `DataGrid`, but unlike the `DataGrid` control, it doesn't provide any visual feedback at all. To get any output from this control, you have to use a template. The template is supplied within template tags that are placed within the bounds of the server-side control. There are five types of template, which can all be used concurrently. Running the `Repeater` control applies the style specified in the template to the correct elements in the control. To define any of the templates, you need to set the `NAME` attribute of the `Template` tag to one of the following five properties:

❑   `HeaderTemplate`: this template is used to surround the opening and header tags in HTML code. For example. we could set up the header and footer to give us a table.

❑   `FooterTemplate`: this template is used to surround the closing and footer tags in HTML code.

❑   `ItemTemplate`: this is the only required template and is used once for each row from the data source.

❑   `AlternatingItemTemplate`: like the `ItemTemplate`, but instead of rendering it once for each row, it is only used for every other row. We need to have both the `ItemTemplate` and `AlternatingItemTemplate`, the one being rendered after the other, with the `ItemTemplate` being rendered first.

❑   `SeparatorTemplate`: this template is used to surround HTML line breaks and the like which help space out an HTML page.

You may find that the templates in a `Repeater` control can at first be quite confusing, as one HTML element such as a table can have three or four different templates mixed up in it. Also, templates don't follow the normal nesting rules of HTML, in that you can open and close a header template while not containing any fully-defined tags within its body of the template (although the tags should still be closed correctly within the page).

The advantage of this control is that it offers flexibility when creating styles and layout for different sections of one HTML element. We'll create an example that uses the `Repeater` control to create a table and display alternating white and beige backgrounds. We'll also alter the table heading so that it appears with bold type:

```
<%@ Import Namespace="System.Data" %>
<%@ Import Namespace="System.Data.SQL" %>
<html>
<head>
   <SCRIPT LANGUAGE="VB" RUNAT="SERVER">
   Sub Page_Load (Sender As Object, E As EventArgs)

      Dim objConnection As SQLConnection
      Dim objCommand    As SQLDataSetCommand
      Dim strConnect    As String
      Dim strCommand    As String
      Dim ds1       As New DataSet
```

```
        strConnect = "server=localhost;uid=sa;pwd=;database=pubs"
            strCommand = "select * from Authors"

        objConnection = New SQLConnection(strConnect)
            objCommand = New SQLDataSetCommand(strCommand, strConnect)

        objCommand.FillDataSet(ds1, "Authors")

        Repeater1.DataSource=ds1.Tables("Authors").DefaultView
            Repeater1.DataBind()
    End Sub
    </script>
</HEAD>

<body>

<ASP:Repeater id="Repeater1" runat="server">
    <template name="HeaderTemplate">
        <table>
            <thead>
            <TR >
              <TD style="font-weight: Bold">Author Last Name</TD>
              <TD style="font-weight: Bold">Author First Name</TD>
            </TR>
            </thead>
        </template>
        <template name="ItemTemplate">
        <TR>
    <TD>
        <%# Container.DataItem("au_lname") %> <br />
          </TD>
    <TD>
    <%# Container.DataItem("au_fname") %> <br />
    </TD>
</TR>
    </template>
    <template name="AlternatingItemTemplate">
        <TR>
    <TD style="background-color:beige">
        <%# Container.DataItem("au_lname") %> <br />
          </TD>
    <TD style="background-color:beige">
    <%# Container.DataItem("au_fname") %> <br />
    </TD>
</TR>
    </template>
    <template name="FooterTemplate">
        </table>
        </template>
</ASP:Repeater>
  </body>
</html>
```

As you can see, the ASP.NET code needed to populate the control is identical to before. The only thing that has changed is the control itself. Inside the first template we create a header with the `<template>` element and inside this we have the following:

```
<thead>
    <TR >
        <TD style="font-weight: Bold">Author Last Name</TD>
        <TD style="font-weight: Bold">Author First Name</TD>
    </TR>
    </thead>
```

However, it's the ItemTemplate that displays the body of the table. There are two templates, one for the white background rows, and one for the beige background rows. However, in all these templates there are two, oft-repeated lines that do all the work:

```
<%# Container.DataItem("au_lname") %>
```

and:

```
<%# Container.DataItem("au_fname") %>
```

This line is simply a method which supplies a field from our data source. The `Container.DataItem` displays a single item from the corresponding column supplied in the parentheses. The final display looks something like this:

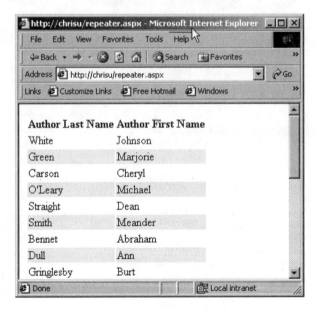

Data List Control

The `Data List` control allows for even greater customization. In fact it is a far more complex than the last two controls we looked at, in that it's a truly interactive control which allows selection and editing – whereas the last two are simple output only controls. It does this by adding more properties (such as `RepeatColumns`, which specifies the number of columns, and `RepeatDirection`, which describes how the items should flow across the page). These allow you to directionally render the table. It also adds a couple of templates which offer rendering options for particular situations:

- ❑ SelectedItemTemplate: indicates the elements to render when a selection has been made in the Data List control.

- ❑ EditItemTemplate: controls the layout of an item in edit mode. Typically these are textbox controls if the data is text or numeric.

These two template selections are slightly more complex to use, as they require linking event handlers and binding to a command column on the data list. In addition to the templates added by the Data List control, there are also a set of events which the control can react upon:

- ❑ OnCancelCommand

- ❑ OnDeleteCommand

- ❑ OnEditCommand

- ❑ OnItemCommand

- ❑ OnItemCreated

- ❑ OnUpdateCommand

The events are all self-explanatory, so we won't expand upon them any further. As the Data List control functions in a similar way to the Repeater control, but requires a fair amount of extra coding, we won't linger with it.

Validation Controls

In any area of programming, one of the most tedious but valuable tasks can be the coding for the "what if" circumstances to ensure that your application doesn't break if the user enters an unforeseen value or response. The code needed to protect your applications tends to be repetitive, and often seems to be little more than testing for the obvious. To make the task of validating data that has been entered much easier, ASP.NET introduces a set of six validation controls. They allow you to test for a common set of circumstances, customize your routines, and summarize the display. There is even an attribute to display the error message of your choice when a bad response is encountered. The six controls are:

- ❑ RequiredFieldValidator – ensures that a value of some sort has been entered on a field of your page.

- ❑ CompareValidator – looks to see if the value contained within a field is equal to a certain value, or checks to see that it is equal to a value held in another control.

- ❑ RangeValidator – checks to see whether a value lies within a particular range.

- ❑ RegularExpressionValidator – matches a value with a particular regular expression.

- ❑ CustomValidator – takes the value from a field and passes it to a function for a customized validation routine.

- ❑ ValidationSummary – a compilation of all of the results passed on by the ErrorMessage attribute of each validation control. We will look at this shortly.

To make sure your application performs the necessary validation, all you need to do is add these server controls into your page and set their properties correctly. Some other quick rules for using these controls are: first, that they must be placed in between the opening and closing <FORM> tags; and secondly, the RUNAT attribute of <FORM> has to be set to "Server", otherwise the controls won't function correctly.

Each of the different controls has slightly different attributes that it uses, depending on the kind of validation it performs. The `RangeValidator` takes `MinimumValue` and `MaximumValue` attributes, which delimits the range of values you wish to accept. We'll now run through a quick example here which takes a number between 1 and 10 and uses the `RangeValidator` control to make sure nobody enters a number smaller than 1 or greater than 10:

```
<HTML>
<HEAD></HEAD>
<BODY>

<FORM ACTION="validate.aspx" METHOD="POST" RUNAT="SERVER">
What is your name?
<INPUT ID="Login" TYPE="Text" RUNAT="SERVER"/>
<BR>
Pick a number between 1 and 10?
<INPUT ID="Number" TYPE="Text" RUNAT="SERVER"/>
<BR>
<INPUT TYPE="Submit" VALUE="Press button" RUNAT="SERVER"/>

<asp:RangeValidator ID="range_valid" RUNAT="SERVER"
ControltoValidate="Number"
TYPE="Integer"
MinimumValue="1"
MaximumValue="10"
display="dynamic">
<BR>
<BR>Error! You didn't enter a number between one and ten did you?

</asp:RangeValidator>

</FORM>
</BODY>
</HTML>
```

If you view this page on the browser and try and enter a number outside the specified range, the control will then display the following message in red:

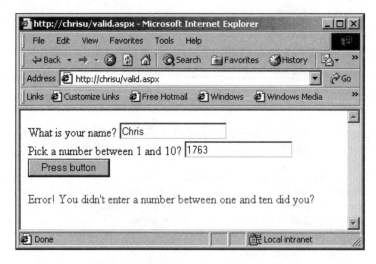

The control is the part of the page that does all of the work; it takes several compulsory attributes:

```
<asp:RangeValidator ID="range_valid" RUNAT="SERVER"
ControltoValidate="Number"
TYPE="Integer"
MinimumValue="1"
MaximumValue="10"
display="dynamic">
<BR>
<BR>Error! You didn't enter a number between one and ten did you?

</asp:RangeValidator>
```

The ControlToValidate attribute supplies the ID of the actual control you wish to perform validation on. Firstly, it takes it from the ID attribute specified in the HTML control. Secondly, it needs to know what kind of values you wish to accept; integers, decimals, or even text. We've already mentioned the self-explanatory MinimumValue and MaximumValue. This just leaves Display, which can be set to Dynamic, Static, or None, depending on whether you want the error message displayed dynamically, per page refresh, or not at all. You'll find that the error message you wish to display is placed after the attributes and before the closing tag, or, alternatively, it can be placed in the error message attribute, which each control has.

If you wish to provide several checks, then you can just add them one after the other within the <form> tags. We'll add a second validator control to our example, the RequiredField validator, to check whether the user has entered a name or not.

We'll also use the ValidationSummary control to provide a summary of the errors encountered. Each validation control has an error message attribute, and it is this that is gathered by the ValidationSummary control to provide a summary. We'll also need to make some amendments to the existing controls as well by moving them to before the control they are intended to validate:

```
<HTML>
<HEAD></HEAD>
<BODY>
<FORM ACTION="validate.aspx" METHOD="POST" RUNAT="SERVER">
What is your name?
<asp:RequiredFieldValidator ID="field_valid" RUNAT="SERVER"
               ControltoValidate="Login"
               TYPE="Text"
               ErrorMessage="Error! You didn't enter your name, did you?"
               display="dynamic">
               *
</asp:RequiredFieldValidator>
<INPUT ID="Login" TYPE="Text" RUNAT="SERVER"/>
<BR>
Pick a number between 1 and 10?
<asp:RangeValidator ID="range_valid" RUNAT="SERVER"
               ControltoValidate="Number"
               TYPE="Integer"
               MinimumValue="1"
               MaximumValue="10"
ErrorMessage="Error! You didn't enter a number between one and ten did you?"
```

```
                       display="dynamic">
                       *
</asp:RangeValidator>
<INPUT ID="Number" TYPE="Text" RUNAT="SERVER"/>
<BR>
<INPUT TYPE="Submit" VALUE="Press button" RUNAT="SERVER"/>
<asp:ValidationSummary id="validSummary" runat="Server"
               headerText="The following errors were found:"
               showSummary="True"
               displayMode="list" />
</FORM>
</BODY>
</HTML>
```

Now if you run the program, you will find that whichever box generates the error will be marked with an asterisk, together with a message displayed underneath the form:

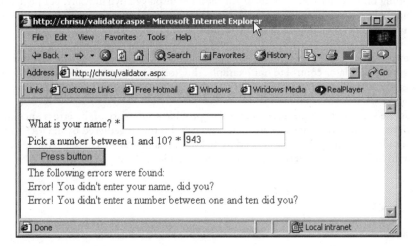

There are a total of three controls in the code. You might have noticed that inside the opening and closing tags for the first two controls we supplied asterisks. This is to override the default error messages from being displayed. This is also why we've moved the controls to before their corresponding input controls. Now instead of displaying the contents of the error message attribute, they just display an asterisk next to the control they are validating. The `ValidationSummary` control is placed at the bottom of the form. This will display a list of the errors generated underneath the text provided in the `HeaderText` attribute.

User Controls

The techniques we've discussed so far for adding controls to your web forms can also be applied when creating web form pages and then calling them in different pages as though they were separate controls. These are known as **user controls** (although were formerly known as pagelets in previous pre-beta versions of ASP.NET). User controls are re-usable sections of code or content that can be inserted into your web page at any place. The only differences between user controls and normal web form pages is that user controls don't contain the <HTML>, <BODY> or <FORM> elements in their code (although the page that is calling them should).

In ASP, it was common to use Include files to fulfill this purpose. However, there are several advantages to using user controls instead. Firstly, user controls are self-contained and provide a separate namespace, so there can be no variable naming conflicts without the main page. These controls must be saved with a `.ascx` extension to identify them (again, this has changed from `.aspc` in pre-beta versions). Secondly, they don't have to be in the same language as the web page that is hosting the control. Thirdly, they can have parameters which can be set via attributes in the page. And lastly, they can be used as many times as you wish within one page, as each time you use them, a separate instance is created which helps you get around the limit of one form per page.

To create a user control, you need to use the `@Register` directive, which allows you to include the `.ascx` file as a new HTML tag in a web page:

```
<%@ Register TagPrefix="Namllu" TagName="Usercontrol" Src="control.ascx" %>
```

In fact, when you use the new customized tag, it's very similar to using the tags in intrinsic controls that we looked at earlier in this chapter. In place of the ASP prefix that we saw, we insert our own namespace, which was defined previously in the `TagPrefix` attribute, and we also use the tag name as defined in the `TagName` attribute. In its simplest form, a web page that contains a user control might look like this:

```
<%@ Register TagPrefix="Namllu" TagName="Usercontrol" Src="control.ascx" %>
<html>
<body>
  <form runat="server">
   <Namllu:Usercontrol id="MyControl" runat="server"/>
  </form>
</body>
</html>
```

We'll have a quick look at an example of creating our own user control and inserting it into a `.aspx` page. This control will just provide a list of Western European countries in a drop-down list box (I could do every country, but it would take up a lot of space). This was a typical use for includes files in ASP, so it makes sense to see how easy it is to do this in ASP.NET.

First, we'll create the control:

```
<select size="1" name="country">
<option></option>
<option> Andorra</option>
<option>Austria</option>
<option>Belgium</option>
<option>Cyprus</option>
<option>Denmark</option>
<option>Finland</option>
<option>France</option>
<option>Germany</option>
<option>Greece</option>
<option>Iceland</option>
<option>Ireland</option>
<option>Italy</option>
<option>Liechtenstein</option>
<option>Luxembourg</option>
<option>Malta</option>
```

```
<option>Monaco</option>
<option>Netherlands</option>
<option>Norway</option>
<option>Portugal</option>
<option>San Marino</option>
<option>Spain</option>
<option>Sweden</option>
<option>Switzerland</option>
<option>Turkey</option>
<option>United Kingdom</option>
<option>Vatican City</option>
</select>
```

We save this as `country.ascx`. Then we create the page that we'll be inserting it into:

```
<%@ Register TagPrefix="namllu" TagName="Country" Src="Country.ascx" %>
<HTML>
<HEAD>
</HEAD>
<BODY>
<TR>
<td valign="TOP" align="CENTER">

<b>Application for European Clients</b>
<form runat="server">
<table>
<tr><td>First Name:</td>
<td><input type="text" size="30" name="firstname" ></td></tr>
<tr><td>Last Name:</td>
<td><input type="text" size="30" name="lastname" ></td></tr>
<tr><td>House:</td>
<td valign="top"><input type="text" size="50" name="house"></td>
<tr><td>Street:</td>
<td valign="top"><input type="text" size="50" name="street"></td>
<tr><td>Town:</td>
<td valign="top"><input type="text" size="50" name="town"></td>
<tr><td>Postal Code:</td>
<td valign="top"><input type="text" size="50" name="postcode"></td>
<tr><td>Country:</td>
<td valign="top">
<Namllu:Country id="Country1" runat="server"/> <!-- user control //-->
</td>
</tr>
</table>
<br>
<INPUT TYPE="SUBMIT" VALUE="Click here to submit application" RUNAt="SERVER">
</form>
</BODY>
</HTML>
```

We save this as `userctl.aspx`. Then when you run the `.aspx` page, it automatically includes the user control, in the same way as ASP would use an include file:

User controls can also be used to expose custom properties and functions which can be used in the parent page, as well as allowing you to create custom headers and footers for the page, or even view the ASP.NET source code.

Programming with Code-Behind

As we can now compile pages or sections of pages, this gives rise to new techniques for separating code from content. We've looked at user controls already, but, as we saw earlier, another alternative to using server-side includes is **code-behind forms**. This is where we can create a base class in ASP.NET for the .aspx page to inherit from. This is similar to the notion of web classes that were introduced in VB6. This is also very similar to the principles of user controls, but without some of the restrictions, such as not being able to use the <HTML>, <BODY> and <FORM> elements. In effect, the whole page becomes an object, and you can then use it and the inherited methods and properties in a separate page. However, it doesn't go as far as requiring you to compile the page and create a separate DLL. Let's have a look at adding a code-behind page now.

Adding a Code-Behind Page

As with user controls, you create a class file first and save this. This is a typical VB class file, called MyClass.vb:

```
Public Class MyClass
    Sub Render(writer as HtmlTextWriter)
        writer.Write("<B>The time is " & System.DateTime.Now & "
        in web server land</b>")
    End Sub
End Class
```

> Note that this class wouldn't work as displayed, because the **Render** method has to be overriden.

Next, you need to inherit from the ASP.NET `Page` class, otherwise your page won't be able to use it, so you need to add the `Inherits` clause to your class:

`Inherits` is a Visual Basic-specific keyword. In C#, you would use `Using`.

```
Public Class MyClass
    Inherits System.Web.UI.Page
    ...
    rest of code here
    ...
End Class
```

To be able to add a code-behind class to your page, you need to start your page with an `<%@Page` Directive in the `.aspx` file. You set the class name in the `Inherits` attribute of the `@Page` Directive. You also need to specify the location of the class file within the same directive. The location is set in the `Src` attribute. A typical page directive would look like this:

```
<%@Page Inherits="MyClass" Src="\classfiles\MyClass.vb" %>
```

If you omit a class file then ASP.NET will assume that the class file is in the bin directory. We'll look at how you would go about creating fully blown custom controls at the end of this chapter.

ASP.NET Web Services

One of the .NET framework's cornerstones is the provision of programming services on the client by the web server or web services. Web services are application logic that are programmatically accessible and are used to expose programming functionality on the Internet, while hiding from the programmer the intricacies of COM or HTTP. Web services don't generally render viewable output. Instead, they perform tasks, the results of which can be used by the client. This is an essential addition needed for cross-platform usage. We're not just talking about being able to browse a web page with a browser on a UNIX platform from a web server running on Windows 2000, but rather, large-scale component usage.

For example, Web services make it possible for a stock-ticker component written in C# and compiled on Windows 2000 to be run and used on Netscape Navigator on X-windows on Linux. To make this possible, XML is very heavily involved. Such a component would use XML schemas to store its information. And this information would be transmitted to the client using the SOAP (Simple Object Access Protocol) protocol. We will meet Web Services in the next chapter, where we'll also look at some examples.

ASP.NET Configuration

Quite often in ASP, you'd find that you'd have to run to the web server administration tool to adjust settings on the server, as anything from the script timeout to the buffering had to be changed manually via the IIS MMC. This changes in ASP.NET with the introduction of an XML configuration file, `Config.web`. While you can still use IIS to adjust the server settings, any changes made will be reflected in the `Config.web` file, and not the IIS metabase (the normal repository for IIS information). The advantage of this is that the file is easily human-readable, but can be updated automatically by ASP.NET without any need for user interaction.

Secondly, on a more local scale, the file that dealt with application configuration in ASP (global.asa) has been replaced by a more comprehensive variant global.asax. This now allows for extra events and for directives to be added to the file. In all though it hasn't changed too greatly. We'll look at both files briefly now.

Configuration Files – Config.web

Config.web shares some of its behaviour with the global.asa (and also global.asax) file, in that there can be several Config.web files on a server, and each Config.web file applies to the resources contained within the directory it is contained in, and to any children of that directory (although it is possible for child folders to set their own configuration settings). The Config.web file is optional, and if you don't have a Config.web file in your application, then ASP.NET will automatically default to using the installed version in WINNT\Microsoft.NET\Framework\v1.0.2204 (using beta one in Windows 2000).

Config.web contains details about the applications, and they can be set within the XML tag <configuration>. In fact, if you run a search on the machine you have loaded the .NET framework onto, you should be able to find an example of the Config.web file. Any changes made to Config.Web will affect any files below it in the application structure. The format of the Config.web file is as follows:

```
<configuration>
   <configsections>
      <!—config section subelements go here -->
   </configsections>

   <httpmodules>
       <!-- http module subelements go here -->
   </httpmodules>

   <httphandlers>
      <!-- http handlers subelements go here -->
   </httphandlers>

   <sessionstate>
      <!-- session state subelements go here -->
   </sessionstate>

</configuration>
```

Within the configsections of the file, there must be an entry (a configsection handler) for each of the subelements that follow it in the configuration file. So here you would expect entries for HTTP modules, HTTP handlers and session state.

Configuration Section Handlers and Settings

The previous example doesn't show every possible option for the file, so here's a list and short description of all the possible settings:

❑　<appsettings> : Defines application information, such as a Data Source Name

❑　<browsercaps> : Configures settings for the new browser capabilities component

❑　<compilation> : Holds all of the compilation settings for ASP.NET

❑　<configuration> : Configuration section for all configuration settings

- ❑ `<configsections>` : A list of all of handlers associated with each config section

- ❑ `<customerrors>` : Defines custom error messages

- ❑ `<globalization>` : Sets the globalization settings for the application

- ❑ `<httphandlers>` : Refers to a component that implements the `IHTTPHandler` interface and allows users to get at the raw IIS API

- ❑ `<httpmodules>` : Adds, removes or clears HTTP modules

- ❑ `<location>` : Sends settings to a particular location such as a file or folder

- ❑ `<processmodel>` : Holds the process model settings for IIS

- ❑ `<security>` : Defines all security settings

- ❑ `<sessionstate>` : Sets the behavior of the session state via five settings, such as the timeout, port number, or whether cookies are allowed or not

- ❑ `<trace>` : Sets the trace service on ASP.NET

- ❑ `<webcontrols>` : Identifies the locations of controls on the client

- ❑ `<webservices>` : Controls the settings of web services

`Config.web` is used just for application settings and is intended to be easily extensible by third parties. It shouldn't be confused with `global.asax` which is used just for events and state settings.

Application Configuration Files – Global.asax

I'd heard whisperings that `global.asa` was to disappear entirely as session management would get completely revamped in ASP.NET, but this never materialized. `Global.asax`, like its predecessor, is placed in the root folder of the application it contains configuration information about. It still takes the same format of having `OnStart()` and `OnEnd()` event handlers for the `Session` and `Application` objects, although within the context of the language that is being used. For example, a `global.asax` in VB would look like this:

```vb
<script language="vb" runat="server">

Sub Application_OnStart()
    'Initialization Code
End Sub
Sub Application_OnEnd()
    'Initialization Code
End Sub
Sub Session_OnStart()
    'Initialization Code
End Sub
Sub Session_OnStart()
    'Initialization Code
End Sub

</script>
```

In other words, pretty much identical to the `global.asa` file. However, there is a much larger list of possible events that you can use in `global.asax`.

The Available New Events in global.asax

Here's a list of all of them:

- ❑ `BeginRequest` – fired whenever a new request is received
- ❑ `AuthenticateRequest` – signals that the request is ready to be authenticated
- ❑ `AuthorizeRequest` – signals that the request is ready to be authorized
- ❑ `ResolveRequestCache` – stops the processing of requests that have been cached
- ❑ `AcquireRequestState` – indicates that the request state should be obtained
- ❑ `PreRequestHandlerExecute` – indicates that the Request Handler is just about to execute
- ❑ `PostPreRequestHandlerExecute` – indicates that the Request Handler has finished
- ❑ `ReleaseRequestState` – indicates the request state should be stored
- ❑ `UpdateRequestCache` – indicates that the code should be added to the cache
- ❑ `EndRequest` – called when the request has ended
- ❑ `PreRequestHeadersSent` – indicates that the Request Headers are just about to be sent
- ❑ `PostRequestHeadersSent` – indicates that the Request Headers have been sent

Directives

We also mentioned that you can use directives within the `Global.asax` file. There are three types of directive, `application`, `import`, and `assembly`. They can all take attributes as well. These directives allow you to use classes within `Global.asax` without having to use the full namespace (`import`), define attributes for a class (`application`) or specify references to other assemblies (`assembly`). They are placed at the head of the file using the following syntax:

```
<%@ directive {attribute=attribute_value}%>
```

We've already seen some of these in action earlier, such being used to register our user control in an ASP.NET page:

```
<%@ Register TagPrefix="Namllu" TagName="Usercontrol" Src="control.ascx" %>
```

Using Global.asax and Global.asa

One very important point is that `Global.asax` doesn't replace `Global.asa`, since you can use it alongside any old `Global.asa` files. The `Global.asax` file will only apply to the new ASP.NET applications, while `Global.asa` will only work with old ASP ones.

ASP.NET Application and Session State

One of the main features ASP boasted was the ability to track users and remember information from page to page, and also to create a cohesive application, rather than a disparate set of web pages which were only tenuously linked. The `Session` object relied on a cookie written to the user's machine to hold details between pages, while the `Application` object tied together a whole set of pages and allowed for global variables to be created and hold information for the entire duration of the application.

Both of these objects have been updated in ASP.NET, especially the `Session` object, which has been changed quite extensively. Let's take a look at both of them now.

Application State

The `Application` object remains quite similar to what went before. There's still only one application object created for each instance of a site running on a machine. Global variables and objects created with application scope persist for the duration of the application. The main difference is that when the `Global.asax` file, that we've just discussed, is altered, the current application object is destroyed and restarted. You still have the ability to lock and unlock the object to prevent corruption of values.

One new update is that the `Application` object is now thread-safe. Previously, there was a bug in ASP 3.0 that had marked the object as free threaded, when it was actually apartment threaded, and this meant that if you tried to store an item such as the `Dictionary` object in it, you could end up crashing the whole server by causing a memory leak. Apart from that, little else has changed.

Session State

The `Session` object now has a new object associated with it, the **Session State Store**. This is an external object that is managed by the **.NET State Server Process**, which runs as a separate Windows NT/2000 Service. This can even run on a separate machine to the web server – thus it could sit on a machine behind a web farm and state could be available irrespective of what machine routed the HTTP request. This is useful because if there is an application crash, you won't automatically lose all of the information you have stored. It also means that if you terminate or restart services on the server, it won't lose the information either. The process doesn't store live objects, but rather it stores information as binary data blobs, and as a result you can also store these in a SQL Server database.

There's a second large-scale change with the `Session` object: it no longer requires the use of HTTP cookies. A reasonable amount of users deem cookies invasive and turn them off in the browser. Previously, this would cause any ASP applications that used the `Session` object to not work as expected, although there was the cookie munger ISAPI filter that overcome this. Now, if a user isn't using cookies, ASP.NET provides an option to use a **munged URL** instead of a cookie. The session ID is then placed in the midst of the URL, and can be used to track sessions as well:

```
http://www.wrox.com/SESSIONID$0222299999ABCDEF/apage.aspx
```

This solves the cookie problem, as when the inbound munged URL is received. ASP.NET can then use the unique identifier to locate and restore session information for the ASP.NET application.

The `Session` object still supports the `Contents` and `StaticObjects` collections, but if you wish to change any of the configuration information relating to it, you do this via the `<sessionstate>` `config section` of `Config.web`, which we looked at briefly in the previous section.

ADO.NET

Any alterations made to ASP wouldn't be complete if they didn't affect the objects that ASP uses to connect and interact with its data stores: the ActiveX Data Objects, or ADO for short. In fact, ADO has undergone a similar metamorphosis to ASP, to become ADO.NET. There are a realm of changes in ADO.NET, such as a new object model, namespaces, and a set of server side controls for binding (which we touched upon earlier). The reason we need a new object model is to address the fact that the Web works in such a disconnected manner: ADO.NET was designed specifically to work in this type of environment.

While ADO.NET has a new object model, some of the objects in it map directly onto their old ASP namesakes. The largest difference in the ADO.NET object model is the removal of the `Recordset` object and its replacement by the `DataSetCommand` object. The `DataSetCommand` object reflects that we can now deal with more types of data than just recordsets. There are also now `DataSet` and `DataView` objects, and finally, a set of unique SQL Server objects (which connect to SQL Server by using the native SQL Server language rather than connecting via OLEDB). This managed provider for SQLServer will be built into ADO.NET, and it will be possible to write custom providers for other databases to communicate in a similar way.

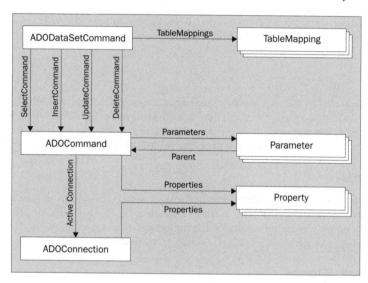

Secondly, the .NET framework introduces the concept of namespaces, which ADO.NET makes heavy use of. To programmers of C++ and Java, this will be all too familiar, but if you're coming from a VB or purely scripting background, then this might be new. Previously, to get things to work in ADO, ASP developers had to include the file adovbs.inc to get a full set of constants, or, in more recent times, the MSADO15.DLL. Now, though, just as in Java, you can import namespaces that would allow the objects and constants to be used. In fact, if you wish to use any of the ADO.NET objects, you first have to import any of the five relevant namespaces:

❑   System.Data

❑   System.Data.ADO

❑   System.Data.SQL

❑   System.Data.XML

❑   System.Data.SQLTypes

Third, there are a set of server-side HTML list controls that have attributes for linking to data sets. There are three main controls; the data grid control, the repeater control, and the data list control, all of which we've already considered earlier in the chapter.

Data in Web Applications

The changes that have been made in ADO.NET aren't just changes for change's sake, they reflect the constantly transforming nature of applications on the Web. More and more, once connections are made to the data server, the connection is terminated, and any work to be done to the data has to be done "offline". Data of this type is termed **disconnected**, and ADO made provision for the support of disconnected recordsets, but ADO.NET goes much further.

Using disconnected data stores isn't quite as straightforward as using normal data sources. There has to be a way to reconcile the data you have on the client with the data that is held in the data store. ADO.NET has a `DataSet` command object, which supports basic create, read, update and delete functionality. These operations need to be performed without a continuous connection to the server. ADO.NET can still work in several situations with a connected data store, but it's much more advantageous to be able to work in this disconnected way, as you don't have to continually maintain a link to the server, thereby saving on network resources, and it's also much faster to work with the data offline than via a connection.

Once again, the changes in ADO.NET are too detailed to outline fully in this chapter, and as they affect much more than just ASP.NET, we'll be looking at them in a separate chapter.

Caching

While caching is provided by the independent language compilers themselves, ASP.NET also provides two sets of caches to help improve performance. These are the **Output cache** and the **ASP.NET cache**. The former is used when calling the same dynamic page for different users, and the latter is used within pages to pass values from page to page, or to improve the efficiency of the code.

The Output Cache

Dynamic output caching involves caching the dynamically created ASP code and then using it if the same URL is called again. Fortunately, ASP.NET is clever enough to be able to check the URL for a querystring or form, and will only supply the cached version if the names and values match exactly. It is used to cache requests that otherwise wouldn't be cachable. It is enabled by default.

The OutputCache Page Directive

There is a directive which allows you to set the expiration time of the cache. The `OutputCache` directive takes a duration attribute which can set the number of seconds for which the cache will persist the information:

```
<%@OutputCache Duration="10"%>
```

With this directive, the dynamically created information is stored for 10 seconds, and the cached copy would be re-used when the URL and querystring matches.

The ASP.NET Cache

The second cache is used to store our own objects, and can be used to pass values between pages. This isn't to say it is a substitute for the `Session` object, as it doesn't store values for individual users. The cache class is utilized in much the same way as the `Application` and `Session` objects themselves, using a key and value setting as follows:

```
Cache("Key") = "A text value"
```

It has a `Remove` method, which allows you to delete the key and value as well.

```
Cache.Remove("Key")
```

You can set times for the expiration of this cache as well, and prioritize which items in a cache should be expired first. There's a lot more than we have space to go into here.

Error Handling and Debugging Techniques

Error handling was something that was pretty non-existent in the first versions of ASP, but has been improving ever since. Custom error pages were introduced in IIS5.0 / ASP 3.0, but have been further improved in ASP.NET. Tracing is also now much easier with the addition of a `Trace` object. Previously you were usually relegated to inserting `Response.Write` messages in the appropriate positions. Also the addition of an ASP.NET debugger is another useful extra to add to our toolbox.

Custom Error Pages

In ASP 3.0, via the Internet Services Manager, you were able to alter the pages that a user was directed to, depending on the HTTP error encountered. The alterations to this facilty in ASP.NET mean that you can use the `Config.web` file to redirect users to a custom page when an error is encountered.

Error Handling

It's also now possible for ASP.NET controls to throw exceptions to halt the process of execution. This is in effect like creating a custom error. Take for example the following code:

```
if (TestValue<50)
    throw new Exception ("You must enter a value greater than 50")
```

Here, instead of generating output within the program, a fully-fledged error would be caused, which would be handled by ASP. NET, looking to the developer like any syntactic error. You can use this to generate customized error information, or handle situations that might cause more awkward/dangerous errors (such as infinite loops).

The ASP.NET Debugger

For far too long, ASP has lacked the ability to step through your code and set arbitrary breakpoints so that you can jump in and out of your code and follow the thread of execution. ASP.NET adds a debugger to your set of tools, which is a much-needed boon for developers.

Ignoring the SDK documentation, which infers that you need Visual Studio.NET already installed to run the debugger (you don't), and going to the **FrameworkSDK** folder under **Microsoft.NET** in **Program Files**, you'll find a **GUIDebug** folder, which contains the debugger. The debugger (`Dbgurt.exe`) is effectively the Visual Studio debugger, and it will allow you to run `.aspx` files. There are a few little tips and tricks needed to get it up and running.

First, before you even run the `Dbgurt.exe`, you need to make sure that you've already run a .aspx file at some point on your browser – you'll see why shortly. When you run `Dbgurt.exe`, the IDE will appear, and you need to select the **Debug** menu and choose the **Processes** option. Click on the **Show system processes** box and choose the `xspwp.exe` process:

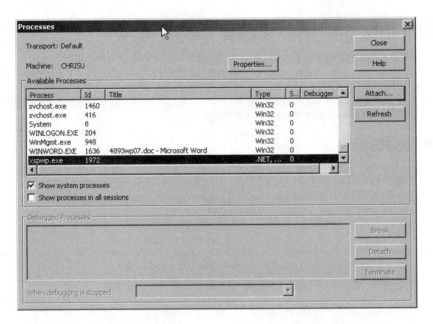

If you haven't run any .aspx files since start up, or you haven't clicked the **Show systems processes**, then this process won't appear in the list. Select the process, click on the **Attach** button, and click on the **OK** button on the dialog that appears. The **xspwp** process will now appear in the debugged processes.

Select **Close** on this dialog, and you are now free to open a .aspx file and set breakpoints and step through the code, just as you would do in Visual Studio.NET. In fact, the debugger from now on is functionally identical to the Visual Studio.NET one. The only downside is that you can't change any of the code at runtime.

Tracing in ASP.NET Pages

Another first for ASP.NET is the addition of a trace facility. This can be enabled by the TRACE attribute of the PAGE directive, which should be added to the top of your .aspx page:

```
<%@Page Language="VB" Trace="True" %>
```

This provides extra information which is appended to your web page display at the foot of the page when you run a .aspx file.

Writing to the Trace Object

You can supply extra annotations and information to your trace output, using the Write method of the Trace object as follows:

```
<%Trace.Write ("Our annotation", "Click event handled successfully")%>
```

If we go back to our first example at the beginning of the chapter, which asked tongue-in-cheek for a user's IQ, and add a click event handler in which we return our trace information, we can show just how much information is generated. The following code is just the same as earlier, with the exception of the trace page directive, the event handler, and the server-side button control:

```
<%@Page Language="VB" Trace="True" %>
<html>
<head>
<SCRIPT language="vb" runat="server">
Sub ClickEventHandler(Sender As Object, Args As EventArgs)
Trace.Write("Our annotation", "Click event handled successfully")
End Sub
</script>
</head>
<body>
<form RUNAT="Server">
IQ:
<ASP:ListBox ID="ListBox1" runat="server">
    <ASP:ListItem>Clever</ASP:ListItem>
    <ASP:ListItem>Not too bright</ASP:ListItem>
    <ASP:ListItem>Thick</ASP:ListItem>
</asp:ListBox>
<p />
<asp:Button id="button1" text="Submit" onclick="ClickEventHandler"
runat="server"/>
</form>
</body>
</html>
```

If we run this and click the button, you can see where in the execution of the page our event was handled:

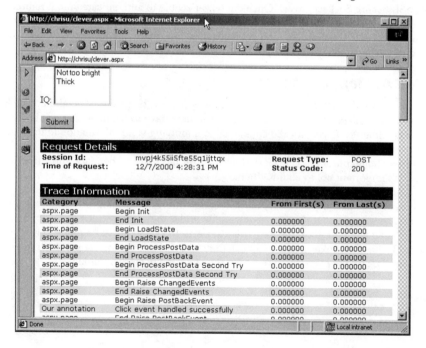

Using Trace Output

As you can see, there is a large amount of information generated, and it is broken up into separate sections that show a control tree which has a list of all controls instantiated as well as the Cookies, HTTP headers, and ServerVariables collections.

Application-level Tracing

You can also use tracing in complete applications by adding a trace directive to your `Config.web` file. Typically, you would amend `Config.web` to look something like this:

```
<configuration>
    ...
    <trace enabled="true" outputmode="true"/>

</configuration>
```

Then all pages in the application will display trace output.

Security

Large changes have been made to the security system in general, and you'll find that ASP.NET can use the Microsoft Passport service to check whether users can access a resource. Microsoft Passport is a service that uses cookies to check whether a user has valid credentials for using a service. This process is termed **authentication**. For example, imagine that you tried to access a protected resource for which you didn't have permission; the server would return an HTTP 302 error and would now redirect you to the Passport login service.

The Passport login service would provide you with a login form, which would be submitted back to the server using SSL(Secure Sockets Layer). Once the server is able to authenticate you, it redirects you back to the original URL, with the authentication information encrypted within the URL querystring. You would then be allowed access to the resource, and authentication information, known as a **ticket**, would be attached to the URL querystring at every step.

Forms Based Authentication

In ASP.NET, as we've already mentioned, this process is done with cookies. If a valid cookie is presented, then the user can go straight to the resource. If not, then they have to login. So you can be authenticated in one of two ways; either by having a valid cookie, or by supplying valid information in the login form. Only then will Microsoft Passport **authorize** you to use the form and allow access to the resource. These are two separate processes; authentication, checking to see if a user has valid credentials; and authorization, releasing the resources. It's important not to confuse them.

ASP.NET allows you to pass the necessary authentication information using HTML forms, and the information can be set up within the `config.web` file under the security `configsection`. Inside, the security section is an authentication section. The `authentication` tag has a mode attribute, which can be set to `Cookie`. Inside the cookie section, you can then specify both the format you wish somebody to supply their information in, and the page to redirect to, if they lack the necessary cookie:

```
<security>
    <authentication mode="cookie">
        <cookie cookie=".ASPXAUTH"
                loginurl="/confirmlogin.aspx"
                decryptionkey="?@@@~1$$%">
            <credentials passwordformat=clear>
                <user name="Chris" password="secret"/>
                <user name="Vervain" password="alsosecret"/>
            </credentials>
        </cookie>
    </authentication>
</security>
```

There are several attributes to consider here, the `Cookie` attribute is the name of the HTTP cookie to use for authentication. By default, this will be `.aspxauth`. `Loginurl` is the reference to the page that the user will be redirected to if they don't supply a valid cookie. If the information being supplied is sensitive, then help file suggests that it should be a secure `https:` link that you refer to. The last one is the `decryptionkey`, which provides the key needed to decrypt the authentication information or ticket.

Within the cookie tags there is also a set of credentials tags, which supply the user name and password. Although this might seem an insecure way of storing the information, it is possible to supply other values to the `passwordformat` attribute that also allows you to display the passwords in an encrypted form.

You can then use the `CookieAuthentication` class and the properties and methods it provides to generate and check form fields when supplied by the user.

Impersonation

ASP.NET also allows you to "impersonate" another user by running an application with the identity of the client on whose behalf they are running the code. This is usually done to avoid having to deal with authentication and authorization in ASP.NET. IIS is relied on to authenticate the user, and the authentication ticket is sent by IIS to the application that requires the access to the resource.

Security is a huge topic, and we could spend a lot of time on it, so we'll move on before we get too deeply into it.

Creating Your Own Custom Controls

We've now started moving beyond some of the ASP.NET features and towards features, which affect the .NET framework as a whole. There is one last feature to consider, which isn't strictly about using ASP.NET, but rather the ability to embed other reusable sections of other languages into your `.aspx` pages.

The idea of writing your own components has been a staple in ASP since the beginning. We've already seen a simplified version of this ability, which allows you to embed user controls in a web page. However it's long been possible to write controls in C++ and Visual Basic that can be inserted into a web page to add extra functionality. While ASP gave you this ability, the advantage in ASP.NET is that controls are even easier to write, and you're not restricted by the number of languages you can write the control in. Also, you no longer need worry about dealing with threading models when creating controls, as ASP automatically creates controls that are both-threaded. ASP.NET will make sure that your page is never accessed by more than one thread at a time.

This is a huge topic in its own right, so we'll just run very quickly through an example of creating your own control to demonstrate what new ASP.NET brings to the party.

When to Use Custom Controls?

We've already discussed user controls, which seem to offer one solution to our problem, but one downside is that they just make use of existing web form functionality. There are very often scenarios when you want to do something that just isn't possible with HTML forms controls or any number of them combined. In which case you'll have to develop your own in custom control. You can use custom controls written in different languages together on the same page, they are very self-contained and therefore easy to reuse. Also, they don't have any specific looks, and allow you to get away from having to use HTML form controls, and ultimately, you can use templates with them.

In this example we're going to develop a quick example control which just displays the time. Of course, this is something easily achievable via VB normally, but we're demonstrating how to add functionality that might or might not be available in the host language.

The Example Time Control

While you can choose to author a control in any language, we're going to create the control in VB, for simplicity's sake. But whatever language you choose to use, it's still really quite straightforward.

The code for the control goes in a separate class file first. If you use C#, then this file will have the .cs suffix, but as we're using VB it will have the .vb suffix.

Step 1 – Creating the .vb file

We create the following file in a normal text editor.

```
Imports System
Imports System.Web
Imports System.Web.UI

Namespace MyControl
    Public Class TimeControl
        Inherits Control
        protected Overrides Sub Render(writer as HtmlTextWriter)
            writer.Write("<B>The time is " & System.DateTime.Now & " in web
            server land</b>")
        End Sub
    End Class
End Namespace
```

This is saved as `TimeControl.vb`. There are a couple of things inside the control we just need to mention as we haven't come across them before. The first is the `Render` method of the `Control` class which we make use of to display our text. Basically, every control has a `Render` method, which is used to display content. If you wish to make use of this particular method to display your own content, then you had to declare a new method in place to **override** the inherited one. The process of overriding just means submitting the `overrides` keyword in front of your Visual Basic procedure. However, just to complicate things slightly, this method is protected, so you also need to declare the procedure protected beforehand.

Next, we pass in a reference to the `HtmlTextWriter` object and use the `Write` method to display our text and use the VB function.

Step 2 – Creating the Batch File

To compile the class, you can create a batch file (which contains the information needed to call the compiler), compile the control, and create the DLL. This file can be created in a text editor, and provides information on where to find the namespace for your control.

Firstly, the batch file needs to direct the output of the compilation to the web application's bin directory. This is so that ASP.NET knows where to locate the namespace specified in the @Register directive contained in the web form page that holds the control. Secondly, we need to reference System.Web.dll, so that ASP.NET knows where to find the classes we imported in the .vb file.

The batch file should look something like this:

```
set outdir=\bin\Time.dll
set assemblies=C:\WINNT\Microsoft.NET\Framework\v1.0.2204\System.Web.dll
vbc /t:library /out:%outdir% /r:%assemblies%  TimeControl.vb
```

This needs to be saved as make.bat. The last line that begins with vbc is a call to the Visual Basic compiler telling it to add the assemblies using the /r parameter. If you had created a control in a different language here, such as C#, then you would change the call to the appropriate compiler instead.

In fact, there's nothing to stop you calling the compiler directly in command prompt. But to save you having to supply the above information each time, it's easier to save it in a batch file.

Step 3 – Building the DLL

Next, start up the command prompt and run the batch file to create the DLL.

Now the control has been created, it is ready to be added to our ASP.NET page.

Step 4 – Testing the Control in an ASP.NET page

To add the control, you use the register directive, just as we did with the user controls, and use the TagPrefix and Namespace attributes to uniquely identify our custom control.

```
<%@ Register TagPrefix="Time" Namespace="MyControl" %>
<html>
<body>

<Time:TimeControl runat="server"/>

</body>
</html>
```

The control name is taken from the class name we created in the URL, combined with the namespace we specified. If you save the page and run the control, you will see the following:

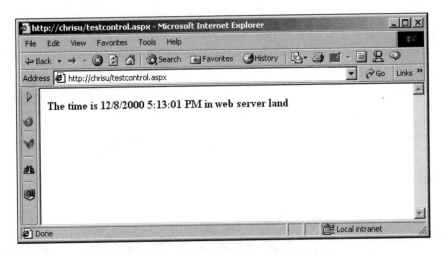

The functionality of the VB code is utilized within the custom control.

Adding Properties

One of the great things is that you can come back to your controls and carrying on adding new features and aspects. We've already seen that we can override existing properties and features inherited from the control base class, but it's also possible to add your own new properties, methods and events. We haven't got the space to cover all three aspects, and they're all quite similar, so we'll just briefly look at how we can add a new property to the control we've just created that changes the color of the time and date that we have displayed.

In Chapter 4, we saw that VB.NET introduces a new format for setting properties, within one `Public` property clause, rather than two separate ones, using the `set` and `get` accessor functions. We're going to use this new syntax in our time control and use the property to change the color of the text displayed by our custom control:

```
Imports System
Imports System.Web
Imports System.Web.UI

Namespace MyControl

    Public Class Style

        ' default constructor - sets the default color
        Public Sub New()
            _Color = "Red"
        End Sub

        ' Private member variable
        private _Color As String

        ' pubic property
        Public Property Color As String
            Get
                Color=_Color
            End Get
```

```
        Set
            _Color=value
        End Set
    End Property

End Class

Public Class TimeControl
    Inherits Control

    protected Overrides Sub Render(writer as HtmlTextWriter)

        writer.Write("<B>The time is <font color='" & _
        MyStyle.Color & "'>")
        writer.Write(System.DateTime.Now & "</font> in web _
        server land</b>")

    End Sub

    ' instantiate using 'New' keyword
    Private locValue2 As New Style()

' this property only needs to be readonly, since you never set the property '
directly
    Public ReadOnly Property MyStyle AS Style

        Get
            MyStyle=locValue2
        End Get

    End Property
End Class
End Namespace
```

All we've done is added a constructor in our control to set our default text color to red, created a color property inside a style class, and instantiated a version of this class as the read-only MyStyle property. We then used the timecontrol render method to set the property color to our new default, by setting the color attribute of the FONT property to our new property. Nothing could be simpler. If you run the control now, the text will be displayed as red.

If we wanted to change the property actually in the testcontrol.aspx page itself, then we could do this by changing the new property by setting it an attribute of the control:

```
<%@ Register TagPrefix="Time" Namespace="MyControl" %>
<html>
<body>

<Time:TimeControl id="timectl" mystyle-color="white" runat="server"/>

</body>
</html>
```

When we create the property, it becomes available as a control attribute. Or equally, we can set the property via our ASP.NET code, by directly accessing and changing the `mystyle.color` property for our time control.

```
<%@ Register TagPrefix="Time" Namespace="MyControl" %>
<html>
<body>

<Time:TimeControl id="timectl"  runat="server"/>

<SCRIPT LANGUAGE="VB" RUNAT="SERVER">
</SCRIPT>

</body>
</html>
```

Try either of these and run the the .aspx file. As we've set the font color to white, you can see the effect of our `style` property, although without seeing the inital output of some of our control. However, if you just highlight the code, so that it appears in reverse colors, you can see it as follows:

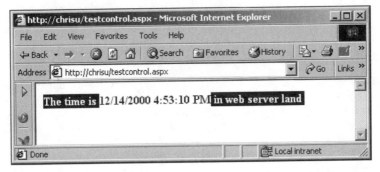

And, as you can see, our `time` control now has a color property, which can be altered in the control itself, or via our .aspx page.

Composite Controls

Composite controls are where you can add extra existing controls to your control code to provide extra functionality. Composite controls are actually equivalent to user controls, but rather than using the .ascx format to hold them, they are persisted in assemblies. Child controls provide their own rendering logic, so unlike the previous custom control, where we had to override the Render method, this isn't necessary with composite controls.

The advantages of using custom controls is that you can save yourself a lot of extra coding, the code can be easily extended at a later date, and you don't have to get involved with the underlying HTML that these controls can generate.

Control Builders

Lastly, you can add subelements to your control via the use of control builders. Control builders are responsible for dealing with element declarations that are made within a control. The control builder can specify a COM+ class for each element, and then this class will process it. Each custom control will have a default control builder. Depending on whether the control declaration is linked to a custom control or a literal control, the control builder will either create a new class and add the child control to the parent, or map the contents to a literal control.

Summary

In this lightning tour of ASP.NET, we've tried to take a brief look at all of the new features. The set of controls that come with ASP.NET are perhaps the most eye-catching aspect. The intrinsic controls offer us server-side versions of already popular HTML form controls. The data binding controls allow us a way of connecting to the database, without getting bogged down in the intricacies of ADO.NET. The supplied components that came with ASP are replaced by the rich controls, although one or two of them such as the Ad Rotator control will be familiar to ASP users. Lastly, the ability to create user controls offers the developer an alternative to server-side include files that is more secure and has its own namespace, so that variable clashes become a thing of the past.

We deferred discussion on two major features, namely, Web Services and ADO.NET, as they have an impact on .NET outside the scope of ASP.NET. Web Services are application logic that is made available to any language, and can be used on the Internet, while ADO.NET updates and enhances the set of objects that formed ADO. Instead, we took a brief journey through the changes made to the configuration, and the `Application` and `Session` objects. The changes here are all geared to making configuration more accessible to the user via code, and in the case of the `Session` object, to make ASP.NET applications more secure and more universal than previous ASP ones. We overviewed the new error-handling, debugging, and trace facilities, and talked about the the new form authentication processes which improve security. Lastly, we examined how new features of ASP.NET enable us to create components more easily, and use them within our web form pages.

8

Web Services

Web Services are programmable business logic components that serve as "black boxes" to provide functionality or features to your web or desktop application using standard Internet protocols (HTTP, SSL, etc.) for communication. This chapter explains what Web Services are and how you can use them within your ASP.NET applications. We begin by explaining the concept of Web Services and then show you how you can set up your development environment to use and develop them. You can either be a supplier of a Web Service, the consumer of one, or both. Whichever you are there will be sets of rules you need to follow or steps you need to perform. We shall see what development tools and wizards Microsoft has provided to ease these steps. Finally, we will take a look at the actual development, deployment and testing of a real-world Web Service application.

What are Web Services Anyway?

As a concept, Web Services are very simple to understand. Think of them as the ability for a programmer to execute a function or subroutine call from within a page, wherever the code may be, on a different page. This page can be on the web server, on a different machine next to the web server, or on a different machine zillions of miles away. Access to Web Services is not restricted to any one type of programmer alone. Any desktop application, or console application with the ability to access a Web Service Provider over the Internet can consume its services.

Let's take that one step at a time. Say you are writing a piece of code in ASP (yes, plain old ASP, not ASP.NET) where you wanted to convert a fraction into a percentage value. As you are smart, you know that VBScript has a built-in function called `FormatPercent` that will accept a number and return a neatly formatted percentage number. Your code would therefore look like this:

```
Dim strValue
StrValue = FormatPercent(16.0/64.0, 2)
Response.Write strValue
```

The above code would result in the following output:

```
25.00%
```

The fraction was converted into a percentage, and the percent symbol (%) was appended to its end. The second argument (`StrValue`) indicated how many decimal places we wanted in our result. Pretty simple, right? Now think about this…how did the ASP page know what to do when it was compiling the code and reached the statement on line 2 that had your function call `FormatPercent`? Well, in this case, the function was a **built-in function** and therefore it could be found within the run-time DLL for VBScript from where it could be invoked.

The path the ASP compiler took could be visualized like this:

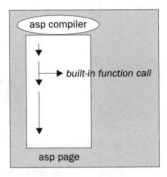

If, instead of using this built-in function, you decided to write your own to do the same thing, you could write the code as follows:

```
Dim strValue
StrValue = FormatAsPercent(16.0/64.0, 2)
Response.Write "FormatAsPercent = " & strValue

Function FormatAsPercent(byval iFraction, byval iDecimals)
    Dim iResult
    iResult = FormatNumber(iFraction * 100, iDecimals)
    FormatAsPercent = Trim(iResult) & "%"
End Function
```

You would get an identical result in this case (with different text, of course):

```
FormatAsPercent = 25.00%
```

This time, how did the ASP compiler know where to find the function called on line 2 (`FormatAsPercent`)? Well, it found it later on in the same page (`Function FormatAsPercent`) and executed the code within the function.

Again, we can visualize how the ASP compiler did its work using this diagram.

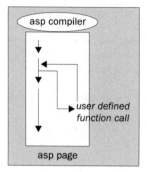

What if, the function FormatAsPercent was in a separate file on your Web Site (say, IncSharedCode.asp) and your main asp page (main.asp) needed to call this function. How would you do it? Well, you would need to #include the page containing the function within the main page as follows:

```
<!--#include file="IncSharedCode.asp" -->
<%
StrValue = FormatAsPercent(16.0/64.0, 2)
%>
```

The ASP compiler would, at run time, stitch the include file along with the main asp page and be able to find the function definition to use it within your code as visualized in this diagram.

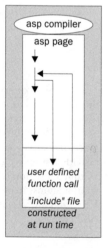

And you would get the same result. So, you can call a function that is built-in, or is within your page, or is within your Web Site. Now extend this thought further, what if the function FormatAsPercent was so complicated and proprietary that not all web developers could code it? What if the function was coded by Mr SuperbProgrammer in Timbuktu and available for sale? You could purchase the code and include it within your web page. However, each time Mr. SuperbProgrammer changes the code and enhances the function, you would need to purchase and include the new code within your application. What if there was a way by which your web page could make a call to Mr. SuperbProgrammer's function that was sitting on **his** web server in Timbuktu, across the Internet, in exactly the same way as the function was called from your own web page? Web Services allows you to do precisely that!

With Web Services, Mr. SuperbProgrammer would simply package the `FormatAsPercent` function as a Web Service. Any web page that he gives access to can then, at run time, knock on the door of his web server, access the function, execute the code within it and return with the results. Each time Mr. SuperbProgrammer changes his code and enhances it, you, the web developer, have nothing to do. The next time your page is executing, it will automatically execute the new code. In fact, assuming Mr. SuperbProgrammer did not change his mechanism to call the function (the interface), you will not even need to be aware that there is an enhanced new version executing.

A very simple visualization of this process is given in this diagram:

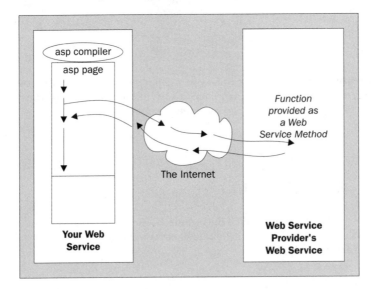

This has been a very simplistic explanation of what Web Services can do for you. However, by explaining it this way, it makes it very easy to understand the concept and see how Web Services are a natural evolution of what we, as web developers, have been doing anyway – but taking it to the next level. Remember, a Web Service will not be doing something as silly as converting a number into percent format. It can provide a piece of complex coding that you would not be able to do on your own. For example a Web Service could provide a simple piece of code execution or could perform the entire business logic for your application. Within a function call, the Web Service can access databases, update values, perform lookups and make computations. In effect, the functionality within a Web Service is only limited by your imagination. What VBXs did for Visual Basic versions 1 to 3 and what OCXs did for VB 4 onwards, Web Services will do for ASP.NET.

So, How Do Web Services Work?

Accessing functions and components from across different machines is not a new concept. After all that is what Microsoft's own Distributed Component Object Model (DCOM) was all about. Similarly, other technologies have tried to do the same thing – Sun's Remote Model Invocation (RMI), The Object Management Group's Common Object Request Broker Architecture (CORBA), or even Internet Inter-Object Request Broker Protocol (IIOP). However where Web Services deviates from these technologies is by not relying on any proprietary standards or platforms. Instead, it uses Internet Standards (HTTP and XML) to perform its functions. Until now, distributing application logic across a local network is the most that it has been feasible to expect. With Web Services it is possible to distribute application logic across the Internet.

Unlike DCOM, CORBA or RMI that rely on very tight integration between the server and the client (both need to know in advance how to talk to each other – the Interface methods and properties exposed by the server need to be known in advance), Web Services are modelled after a very **loose coupling** between the service provider and the service consumer (the client). This means that development on either the client or the server side can continue without breaking the other's applications and having to recompile them. What this means is that Web Services rely on asynchronous, message-based technologies that use established web protocols (HTTP, SMTP or XML) for communication.

In the case of a tightly coupled system, (COM or DCOM), when a client makes a request to a server for a particular method exposed by that server, the client needs to make many assumptions about the server; for example, about how the component will be activated and destroyed, what its interfaces are called, and so on. In the case of a loosely coupled system, (like a messaging system or Web Services), the client/server interaction is packaged into self-describing units (called messages) that are put on to the network wire. In this case the actual handshaking and interfacing occurs at the wire level; the only assumption made by the client is that the server will understand its message. The client does not make any assumptions about what will happen once the server receives the message. In essence the server becomes a black box whose internal workings are unknown. As long as the message is properly formatted, the server can receive and understand it, and as long as the reply is properly formatted, the client who receives it can understand the reply. The key, therefore, is a common **data description format** that will work across the disparate systems over the Internet allowing the client and the server to communicate with each other. That's where XML and the new SOAP (Simple Object Access Protocol) come in.

The Three Musketeers of Web Services

It is not sufficient for you to develop a Web Service and then set up shop on the Internet. This is not a case of "if you build it, they will come". Your consumers need to know that you exist and that you are open to provide a service. In addition, they need to know exactly what service you are providing and what arguments you are expecting when those services are invoked. Finally, you need to conform to an agreed standard with your consumers when it comes to accepting a service call, or returning a reply.

If you are a consumer of a Web Service, you face the same three issues. First, you need to know who is out there providing Web Services. Then, you need to know exactly how the service provider has defined his data types and formats and the arguments he is expecting for the service calls. Finally, you need to talk to him in a format he can understand so that you can invoke a service call and be able to understand his reply.

These three elements form the Infrastructure layer for Web Services. They are:

- ❏ **Web Service Wire Formats**: Web Services use open Internet communication protocols (HTTP, SSL, etc.) to enable universal communications between different providers and consumers, independent of platform and technology.

- ❏ **Web Service Description**: In order to be able to interact with a Web Service it is necessary to understand its service description. A Web Service Description defines all the supported interactions that a Web Service offers and enumerates the data types, number and order of arguments required to carry out the interaction as well as the data type of the returned result.

- ❏ **Web Service Discovery**: Web Services make their presence, capabilities and functionality known through the process of discovery. Literally, this is the web developer, or a message, knocking on the door and saying, "Hey, are you out there? Can you help me?"

These three infrastructure elements correspond to three technology elements that make Web Services work.

❑   Web Service Wire Format = SOAP

❑   Web Service Description = Service Description Language (WSDL)

❑   Web Service Discovery = SOAP Discovery, a.k.a. DISCO

Of course the success of the above elements depends on one key factor, their wide spread acceptance by industry.

SOAP: Web Services use XML as the standard method for (amongst other things), formatting a request to invoke a remote object's method call from a client as well as formatting the reply package back from the server. The basic wire format used by Web Services is the Simple Object Access Protocol (SOAP), a lightweight XML-based protocol that is currently under consideration by the World Wide Web Consortium (W3C) for incorporation into the XML standards. A consortium of technology companies including Ariba, Commerce One, Compaq, DevelopMentor, Hewlett-Packard, IBM, IONA Technologies, Lotus, Microsoft, SAP AG, and UserLand Software put forth the SOAP standard and submitted it to the W3C for consideration. According to the W3C's initial document on SOAP, available at http://www.w3.org/TR/SOAP/, "SOAP is a lightweight protocol for exchange of information in a decentralized, distributed environment. It is an XML based protocol that consists of three parts: an envelope that defines a framework for describing what is in a message and how to process it, a set of encoding rules for expressing instances of application-defined data types, and a convention for representing remote procedure calls and responses."

SOAP allows Web Services to be packaged and communicated across the Internet using HTTP or HTTPS protocols. This enables the client and the server to share a common understanding of the Web Service request and its subsequent reply. SOAP is a messaging protocol that is not limited to Remote Procedure Calls (RPC). It does not require synchronous execution or request/response interaction, and SOAP messages can have multiple parts addressed to different parties. SOAP defines an envelope formatting and processing mechanism for arbitrarily complex message structures. Furthermore, SOAP has an extension mechanism, allowing loose coupling between senders and receivers of messages, which allows for richer messaging facilities such as workflow routing and guaranteed delivery in systems such as the Microsoft BizTalk Framework.

SOAP Discovery: The SOAP Discovery specification, built on SOAP/XML allows a client (a developer or a development tool) to automatically discover what services and features a Web Service provides. SOAP Discovery can then report this information back to the client so that a dialogue can occur. The DISCO (short for Discovery of Web Services) specification defines a discovery document format (based on XML) and a protocol for retrieving the discovery document, enabling developers to discover services at a known Uniform Resource Locator (URL).

Services Description Language (SDL): It is not sufficient that a client and a Web Service providing server just communicate with each other using XML. Once the Web Service has defined how it will represent data types and what its arguments are for the different methods it exposes, there needs to be a way to describe the specific details of this to the client. For example, the client needs to know that in order for a particular method to be invoked, it needs to send two arguments, not one, and that they both need to be integers and not strings, etc. The client also needs to know what kind of result is going to be sent back in order to be able to process it. The Services Description Language (SDL) is an XML grammar that developers and development tools can use to represent the capabilities of a Web Service.

Once these three elements are in place, a web developer can easily find a Web Service that meets his or her requirements, instantiate it as an object, access it within their web applications and use its functionality.

I know what you are thinking. Do I have to learn three new specifications and grammar to use this new Web Services thing? No. That's why there are development tools. For example, Microsoft ships a number of tools that make life easier for ASP programmers. The SOAP toolkit for Visual Studio 6 enables you to develop a complete Web Service, package it within the SOAP framework and even call it, without having to write SOAP code. The next version of Visual Studio, Visual Studio.NET is currently in beta one and allows you to develop Web Services, taking care of all the housekeeping and plumbing work and allowing you to focus on the business logic. For COM-oriented developers, what this means is that many SOAP compatible Web Services can act just like COM components. You can instantiate an object and then call its methods. Behind the scenes, these tools convert your calls, package it into SOAP/XML specifications and invoke it across the wire.

Getting Started with Web Services

You can build and apply Web Services using one of two techniques. Either you can use any text editor together with the .NET Framework SDK installed on a web server, or you can use the new Microsoft Visual Studio.NET Beta–1 software. Web Services are a part of the .NET Framework and do not necessarily require any special development tools other than the .NET Framework SDK; though it must be remembered that Web Services will only run on a machine that has the .NET Framework SDK installed.

Consult the Introduction for information on installing the .NET Framework SDK.

Writing a Web Service

The time it takes to write a Web Service depends on the amount of functionality that needs to be available within that Web Service. A very simple Web Service can be written in a few minutes, but it will not, by its nature, be very useful. However, the steps involved in writing a simple or complex Web Service are the same. The difference is the business application logic within its methods, which you alone control. In this section, we shall see how to write a very simple Web Service and then go on to look at how to write one that would function usefully in the real-world web.

A Very Simple Web Service

Let us build a very simple Web Service. Assume that you are the provider of real time stock quotes. You own a proprietary database that tracks the stocks on Wall Street and would like to provide this information (for a fee, of course) to your consumers. You want your consumer to utilize your Web Service by providing you with the symbol for the company. Then you, in turn, will provide the real time stock price. Let us see how we can build a Web Service to do this.

Our focus will not be on obtaining real time stock prices – that will involve proprietary database access etc. For the sake of the example, we will just hard code some values. What you will learn from this example is how to build and provide a Web Service and how to consume it.

A Web Service source file is a plain text file with an `.asmx` extension. The `.asmx` file can be called from a browser just like a regular ASP.NET (.aspx) file. You can use any browser, although the formatting in IE is prettier.

Begin a plain text file with the following code:

```
<%@ WebService Language="VB" Class="StockTicker" %>
```

This line is a directive at the top of our file that indicates that it is a Web Service written in VB and it contains the class StockTicker. If you prefer, you could just as easily write the Web Service in other .NET languages such C# or JScript, but VB is used here, accessed from ASP pages.

Underneath, we can code for the class itself as follows:

```
Imports System
Imports System.Web.Services
Imports Microsoft.VisualBasic

Public Class StockTicker : Inherits WebService
    Public Function <WebMethod()> GetStockPrice(strSymbol  as String)_
                                                      as String

      Select Case strSymbol
         Case "MSFT"
             return "67"
         Case "YHOO"
             return "36 31/32"
         Case "CSCO"
             return "51"
         Case "AMZN"
             return "25 1/32"
         Case Else
             return "Unknown"
         End Select
    End Function
End Class
```

We begin the code by including all system level calls we will be making and the libraries where the compiler can find them. This is very similar to the #include files of C/C++. In our case, we are including the System and System.Web.Services libraries. In addition, we are also including the Microsoft.VisualBasic library since we will be using some VB constructs in our code. There are many more .NET classes that are available that you can use in your own Web Services.

Our class is defined beginning with the words Public Class. Within the class, we define one public function GetStockPrice. Notice that the code we have written till now is standard VB-like code. The new addition is the custom attribute <WebMethod()> in front of the function name. This custom attribute indicates that this function is a method that can be invoked from the web – that it can be called across the Internet – there could be other function calls within the class that are private and not callable across the Net. Within our function, all we do is simply check the value of the company symbol sent to us and based on that return some dummy stock price values.

Save your file as StockTicker.asmx within your .NET Framework enabled web server. Then browse to the page using your browser. You will be amazed at what comes up. With absolutely no coding, you get an entire web page that explains what this Web Service does and what method it exposes.

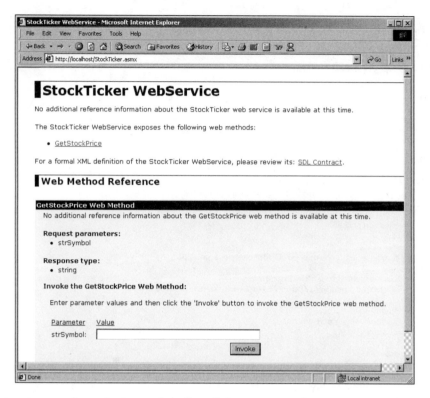

The page is quite appealing to look at and also has all the pertinent information. For example, it has identified the fact that there is a single method call exposed within our Web Service called `GetStockPrice`. It also knows that this method accepts one parameter `strSymbol` and that it returns a string.

At the bottom of the page is a sample area where you can actually test your Web Service by invoking its method. Type MSFT (remember that this is case sensitive) in the text box and click the Invoke button. You will get an XML rendering of the result sent back from the Web Service: 67.

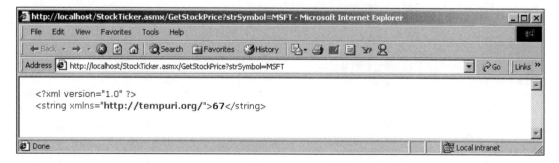

You can also request the Service Description Language (SDL) for this page using your browser. Simply browse to the .asmx file and append the text ?SDL to the query string. This returns the entire SDL, in XML format, which is the formal XML definition of the Web Service, or its SDL contract.

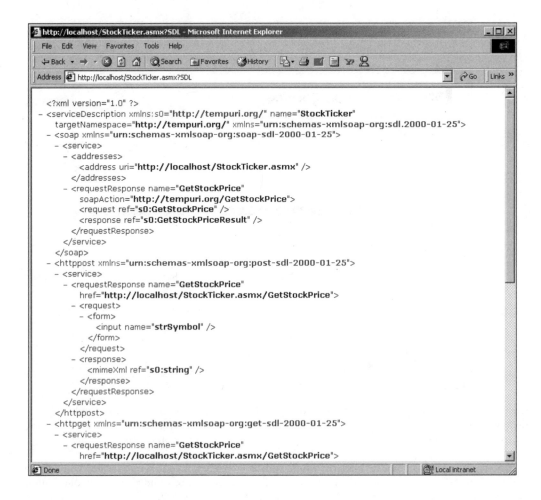

Compiling the Web Service

Once you have written and tested a Web Service, you can either leave it in its original .asmx format or you can compile it. If you wish to call the Web Service from an ASP.NET page, you need to create a Proxy Class DLL. This proxy class DLL wraps all the code and calls in the Web Service into a simple method call, similar to a COM object. We can then use this within our ASP.NET pages, or rich client. To compile the .asmx file into a DLL, you use the WebServiceUtil.exe utility that ships with the Framework SDK. This utility is simple to use, but has an arcane command line interface that is not easy to understand. I prefer to create a batch file and run the batch file to compile the .asmx file into a DLL. The SDK is also particular about wanting the DLL to reside in a \Bin directory so that's where we are going to place it.

Create a batch file called MakeStockTicker.bat with the following lines of code and then execute it.

```
WebServiceUtil.exe /c:proxy /pa:http://localhost/StockTicker.asmx?sdl /l:_
                                            VB /n:nsStockTicker

VBC /out:bin\StockTicker.dll /t:library /r:system.data.dll_
  /r:system.web.services.dll /r:system.xml.serialization.dll stockticker.vb
```

The first line converts the `.asmx` file from its location (`http://localhost/StockTicker.asmx`) to a VB file called `StockTicker.vb`.

The `/c:proxy` argument indicates that we want to create a stub or a proxy class of the Web Service from an SDL document specified in the `/pa` argument. The `/l:VB` signifies that the Web Service uses the VB language while the `/n` argument identifies the namespace to be used to refer to the Web Service. We have used the namespace `nsStockTicker`.

The second line takes the output of the first line (the `Stockticker.vb` file) and converts it into a DLL using the run time libraries that we use within our Web Service along the way. When you run the batch file it will compile and create a DLL in the `\Bin` directory you specified.

Consuming the Web Service

In order to consume the Web Service from an ASP.NET page, you will need to import the DLL namespace within an .aspx file and invoke the method call within your page. Use the following code to create a .aspx file and save it as `ConsumeStockTicker.aspx`.

```
<%@ Import Namespace="nsStockTicker" %>
<HTML>
<SCRIPT LANGUAGE="VB" RUNAT="server">
Sub GetPrice(Src as Object,E as EventArgs)
    Dim ST as New StockTicker
    Dim strPrice = ST.GetStockPrice(strSymbol.SelectedItem.Value)

    lblPrice.InnerText = strPrice
End Sub

</SCRIPT>

<BODY STYLE="font-family: Tahoma, Arial, Helvetica, Sans Serif; font-size: 10pt
verdana; background-color:#FFFFCC">

<DIV ALIGN="CENTER">
```

```
<H2><B>Check Stock Prices</B></H2>

<P />
<FORM RUNAT="server">
<TABLE WIDTH="450">
    <TR>
        <TD ALIGN="right">
            <B>Select Company :</B>
        </TD>
        <TD>
            <ASP:DROPDOWNLIST ID="strSymbol" RUNAT="server">
            <ASP:LISTITEM VALUE="MSFT">Microsoft</ASP:LISTITEM>
            <ASP:LISTITEM VALUE="YHOO">Yahoo</ASP:LISTITEM>
            <ASP:LISTITEM VALUE="CSCO">Cisco</ASP:LISTITEM>
            <ASP:LISTITEM VALUE="AMZN">Amazon</ASP:LISTITEM>
            </ASP:DROPDOWNLIST>
        </TD>
    </TR>
</TABLE>
<P />
<ASP:BUTTON RUNAT="server" TEXT="Get Stock Price" onclick="GetPrice" />

<P />

<H2 ID="lblPrice" RUNAT="server" />
</FORM>
</CENTER>

</BODY>
```

The first line imports our Web Service proxy DLL using the name space we defined.

```
<%@ Import Namespace="nsStockTicker" %>
```

The body of the page deals with displaying a drop down box of company names that, when selected, will return a company symbol (in reality, this would need to be a free form text box allowing the user to enter any company's symbol). Underneath the button that submits the form, there is an <H2> tag named lblPrice where we will be displaying the results of our Web Service method call.

The actual call to the Web Service happens in this piece of the code.

```
Sub GetPrice(Src as Object, E as EventArgs)
    Dim ST as New StockTicker
    Dim strPrice = ST.GetStockPrice(strSymbol.SelectedItem.Value)

    lblPrice.InnerText = strPrice
End Sub
```

As you can see, we first declare a variable of type `StockTicker`. We then invoke the method call `GetStockPrice` on the object passing the symbol of the company selected by the user. The result is placed in the variable `strPrice` which is then used to populate the `<H2>` tag. COM programmers will find the syntax of the method call very familiar. You instantiate an object and then invoke its method just like any COM component. Under the scenes, the proxy DLL is packaging our method call within a SOAP request and transferring it over the wire using XML. The resultant XML is also received and parsed back by our proxy DLL, transparent to both the web developer and the end user. When you run this page, you can check the stock prices for the four companies we listed.

Developing a Weather Information Web Service

Now that you have seen what a simple Web Service can do, let's take a look at a real-world example. There are a few real time information services that make ideal use of the Web Service model. Real time stock quotes for instance, or real time information on news and current events. One more example is real time weather. Let us see how we can build a real time weather Web Service and also take a look at how a consumer can utilise the Web Service.

SearchWho.com is a "Mega Portal" on the Internet with numerous links to search engines, and hundreds of pages of useful information. SearchWho.com also provides free weather information and in addition provides you with the ability to add local weather information to your own home page for free. You can view the details of how to add local weather to your own Web Site at:

http://weather.searchwho.com/sample_weather.html

SearchWho.com has been kind enough to give us permission to use their weather information display to demonstrate this Web Service in this book. In return, we will retain the link to their home page from the results that are returned to our application.

According to SearchWho.com, when you place the following lines of code on your own Web Site, they will provide you with dramatic, graphic weather information and forecast for any US based city, state and zip code. We will concentrate on zip code for our example.

```
<script language="Javascript"
   src="http://weather.searchwho.com/cgi-
   in/myweather.pl?loc=atlanta,ga">
</script>
```

If we substitute a zip code in the above Script's SRC tag at the very end, as part of the query string, we will obtain weather information for the corresponding US City.

```
<script language="Javascript"
src="http://weather.searchwho.com/cgi-bin/myweather.pl?loc=06905">
</script>
```

Since we know the format of the data that is returned by the above code, (you can execute it in your own local web page and check the results using View | Source, from the toolbar) we can build a Web Service that uses the above code and displays the resultant information. In essence, we are building a Web Service for SearchWho.com that, if they wished, they could use on their Web Site in place of the above `script` code. Let us see how we can build a Web Service to do this.

This time, instead of using a plain text editor, we will be using the Visual Studio.NET environment to build our Web Service. Here is our plan. We will have a Web Service called `CityWeather`. This will have one method called `GetWeather` that accepts a single zip code value. Based on the zip code value, the Web Service displays current and future weather information.

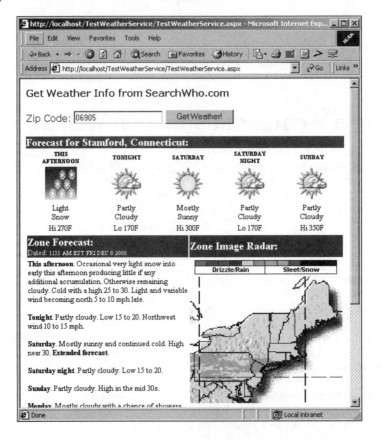

Writing our Web Service with Visual Studio.NET

Visual Studio.NET makes writing Web Services very easy. Some of the steps that we undertook previously (compiling the Web Service and importing its namespace) are done automatically by the Visual Studio.NET environment.

If you have successfully installed Visual Studio.NET, start the Visual Studio.NET development environment. VB developers will find this environment new and strange, because the familiar menus and toolbars have changed, but VC++ developers will be right at home. From the File menu, choose New | Project. Click on the Visual Basic Projects project type and then choose the Web Service template. At the bottom, make sure you name your Web Service as CityWeather and remember to check that it is being developed against a web server that has the .NET Framework SDK installed. Preferably, try to develop it on your local (development) machine (`http://localhost`).

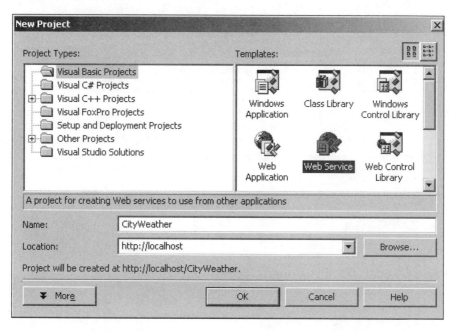

The beta one of Visual Studio.NET (VS.NET) has a quirk when it comes to Web Services. It automatically names the class declared within your Web Service as Service1. This forces you to call your Web Service Service1 all the time. I could not find any easy technique to change this class name completely (although superficially it may appear that you can change the name by simply renaming the file or renaming the Class, this does not work, as you will find out at runtime). I assume Microsoft will be fixing this issue in future releases prior to the final Visual Studio.NET release. For now, the only way to rename the Web Service is to delete the default Web Service that VS.NET provides and add a brand new one with the name of your choice. To do this, close all the windows that have opened up, so that no files are visible in the main development area. Right click on the file Service1.asmx and delete it. Then, from the Project menu, choose Add Web Service. In the Add New Item dialog box that pops up, click on the Web Service icon and change the name at the bottom to CityWeather.asmx and click the Open button.

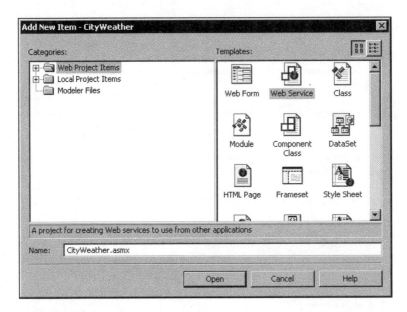

This action creates a new file CityWeather.asmx within your Solution Explorer. Right click on CityWeather.asmx and choose View Code from the context menu. Alternatively, you can click once on the CityWeather.asmx file in the Solution Explorer and click on the View Code button within the Solution Explorer toolbar. This brings up the code behind the object. You will see a commented area in the code where you will be inserting your new code.

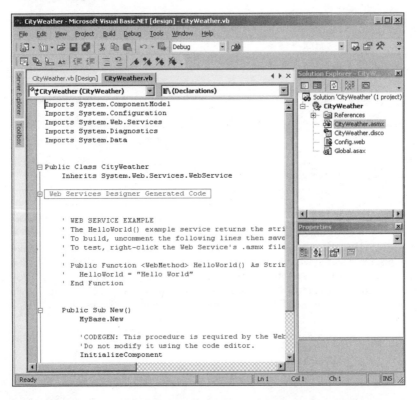

Also, make sure that the line that declares the class has the name CityWeather:

```
Public Class CityWeather
```

Under the green commented code under the section ' WEB SERVICE EXAMPLE, type in this code to begin a new method:

```
Public Function <WebMethod> GetWeather(byval strZipCode as String) as String

End Function
```

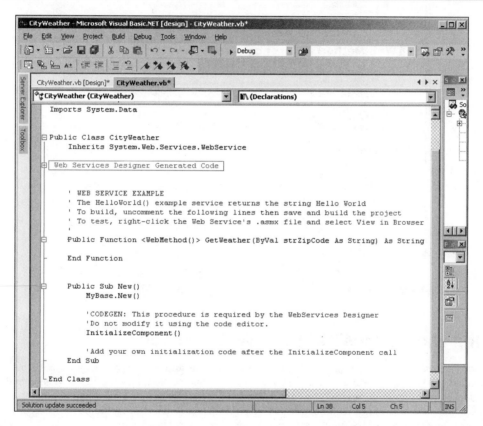

At this point, we do not have any code within our Web Service. Still, it is better to see if we are on the right path by compiling and testing our code. To begin this process, first, choose Build, from the Build menu. Make sure that the build process executes successfully with no errors.

To test the Web Service right click on the CityWeather.asmx file in the Solution Explorer and choose Set as Start Page. Then right click again and choose Preview in Browser. You will either view the preview within the built in browser or you can preview it in an external browser. To change the default from an internal to an external browser, right click on the .asmx file and choose Browse With from the context menu. This allows you to set your preview preferences. When a browser requests this file, it fetches back the Web Service description and its parameters. You should get a page that explains that the Web Service has one method called GetWeather that accepts one string called strZipCode.

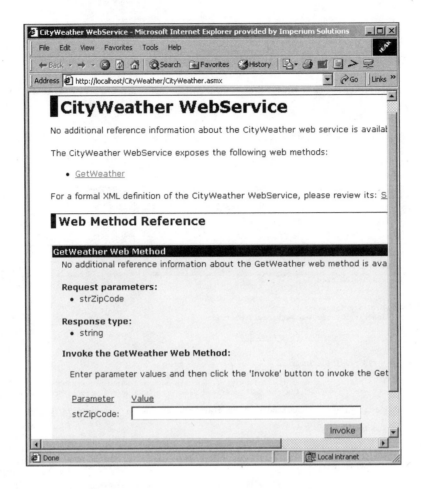

Writing the Code Within the Web Service

Let's take a break to see what we are trying to accomplish here, and how. In reality, if SearchWho.com was producing this Web Service as a means to provide weather information, I, as the SearchWho.com developer, would be able to access the SearchWho.com database to extract the weather information and return the values to the consumer of my Web Service. So, given the zip code 06905, I would be able to return the weather values for Stamford, Connecticut.

However, we do not have direct access to the SearchWho.com database. Instead, we are going to extract this information from results sent back by the `script` code provided to us by SearchWho.com. In order for us to accomplish this, we need to be able to access the SearchWho.com URL from within our Web Service. So we need server-side HTTP access. Luckily for us, one of the built-in namespaces of the .NET Framework (`System.NET`) allows us to do precisely that. Once we obtain the results back from SearchWho.com, we need to do some creative string manipulation to be able to present the information accurately. We will extract only the HTML tags within the results and present this as the output from our Web Service. The `System.NET` namespace allows us to perform server side HTTP-POST and HTTP-GET actions and enable browser/server communication. In addition it exposes the `WebRequest` class that we use to send a request and the `WebResponse` class that provides us with the response that came back from the server.

To add the namespace to our Web Service so that we can use it, we need to add references to the namespace in a manner very similar to the **Project References** dialog box in the current version of Visual Basic.

In the Solution Explorer in Visual Studio.NET, expand the **References** tree and check to see if `System.Net` is present in the list of references. If not, you can add it by right clicking on the **References** tree and choosing **Add Reference**. In the **Add Reference** dialog box that pops up, scroll down and select `System.net.dll` and choose **Select**. Then hit the **OK** button to add these references to your project. If the reference you are trying to add already exists in the Solution Explorer, VS.NET simply ignores it.

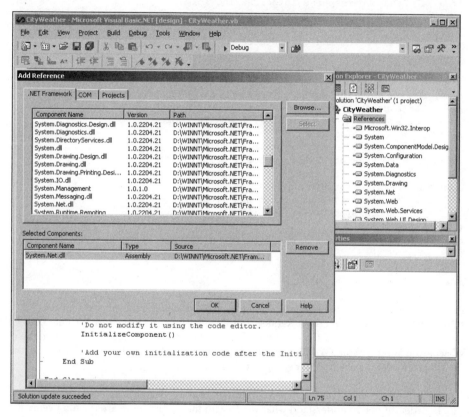

Use the following code within the method `GetWeather` to obtain the Weather information.

```vb
Public Function <WebMethod()> GetWeather(ByVal strZipCode As String) _
                                                         As String
    ' -- Declare variables
    Dim strResult As String     ' Our result
    Dim strHTML As String       ' The HTML we expect back
    Dim strURI As String        ' The URL/URI we are going to hit
    Dim objWRQ As System.Net.WebRequest    ' The Request object
    Dim objWRS As System.Net.WebResponse       ' The Response object
    Dim objWRF As System.Net.WebRequestFactory ' The Request object creator
    Dim objStream As System.IO.StreamReader  ' The stream of data coming back

    ' -- SearchWho.com URL to access
    Const WEATHER_URI As String = "http://weather.searchwho.com/" &_
```

```
                                              "cgi-bin/myweather.pl"
    ' -- 1. Build our URL using the Zip code sent in
    strURI = WEATHER_URI & "?loc=" & strZipCode
    ' -- 2. Create a Request object based on our URI,
    'and call the remote server
    objWRQ = objWRF.Create(strURI)
    ' -- 3. Get the response back from the remote server
    objWRS = objWRQ.GetResponse()
    ' -- 4. Read the response into a String format
    objStream = New System.IO.StreamReader(objWrs.GetResponseStream(), _
                                          System.Text.Encoding.ASCII)

    ' -- 5. Read to the end of the stream
    strHTML = objStream.ReadToEnd()


    ' --
    ' -- Now we have the entire HTML from SearchWho.com within our variable,
    ' -- Let's parse it
    ' -- Replace all double quotes with single quotes
    strHTML = Replace(strHTML, """", "'")
    ' -- Remove all "document.writeln('" text
    strHTML = Replace(strHTML, "document.writeln('", "")
    ' -- Remove all "');" text
    strHTML = Replace(strHTML, "');", "")
    ' -- Replae all "\n" text with a new line
    strHTML = Replace(strHTML, "\n", chr(13) & chr(10))
    ' --
    ' -- We now have just the Weather info within our string, return it
    Return strHTML

End Function
```

As you can see from the code, we first declare some variables including the constant for the SearchWho.com URL. We then create Request and Response objects using our Weather.com URL and concatenate the zip code sent in by the consumer. We use the `StreamReader` class to read the response coming back from Weather.com. We then use the `ReadToEnd` method of the `StreamReader` class to suck the entire HTML from the page into our string variable.

At this point, we have the entire output that was returned back by SearchWho.com within our string variable `strHTML`. In order for you to understand what we do with this output, here are the top twenty lines returned by the SearchWho.com URL when a zip code of 06905 is sent:

```
<!-- 11301: 16261 -->
document.writeln('<sw-zonecast-start>\n');
document.writeln('<table border="0" width="100%" cellspacing=0 cellpadding=0>\n');
document.writeln('        <tr>\n');
document.writeln('            <td width="100%">\n');
document.writeln('<!--\n');
document.writeln('<table cellspacing=2 cellpadding=0 border=0>\n');
document.writeln('<tr><td><form method="POST"
action="http://weather.searchwho.com/cgi-bin/weather/weather.cgi"><input
type="hidden" name="theme" value="default"><input type="hidden" name="user"
value="default"><input type="hidden" name="forecast" value="zandh"></td>\n');
document.writeln('<td><font face=helvetica size=2><b>&quot;City, State&quot;</b>,
<b>State</b> or <b>Zipcode</b>:</td>\n');
```

```
document.writeln('<td><input type="text" name="pands" size="15"
value="06905">\n');
document.writeln('</td>\n');
document.writeln('<td><input type="submit" value="Local Forecast"
name="Submit"></td>\n');
document.writeln('</td>\n');
document.writeln('<td></form></td>\n');
document.writeln('</tr>\n');
document.writeln('</table>\n');
document.writeln('-->\n');
document.writeln('            </td>\n');
document.writeln('            </tr>\n');
```

As you can see, the SearchWho.com Web site returns code that gets inserted into the HTML rendered by the browser and displays weather information. This is good for its original purpose – placing free weather information on your own homepage. However, we need to extract out only the HTML text and send them back to our Web Service consumer. If you look at the code, it is relatively easy. We need to remove all occurrences of the text document.writeln("*and its corresponding ending* ");. That, and a little more is what we do in the next few lines of code within our Web Service.

```
' -- Replace all double quotes with single quotes
strHTML = Replace(strHTML, """", "'")
' -- Remove all "document.writeln('" text
strHTML = Replace(strHTML, "document.writeln('", "")
' -- Remove all "');" text
strHTML = Replace(strHTML, "');", "")
' -- Replace all "\n" text with a new line
strHTML = Replace(strHTML, "\n", chr(13) & chr(10))
' --
```

Once we "massage" the output returned from SearchWho.com, we can simply return the entire HTML text back to the consumer:

```
' -- We now have just the Weather info within our string, return it
Return strHTML
```

Once we have the entire HTML for the page within our string, we can manipulate it any way we want before returning it back to the consumer. In our case, we are looking for two comment blocks that Weather.com has providentially placed within the HTML to identify the weather block. We use the string functions Left, Mid, Instr and InstrRev to chop off the block of text we need. Finally, we send this block of HTML text back to the consumer.

```
' -- We now have just the Weather info within our string, return it
Return strHTML
```

We are now ready to deploy our Web Service. All we need to do is to build it from the Build menu and we are all set. The Web Service is now available on the development machine's web server. If you notice, Visual Studio.NET has created a CityWeather.DLL file within the \Bin directory of our Web Service.

Writing a Web Service Consumer Application with Visual Studio.Net

It is now time for us to consume the Web Service we just created. Let us use the new Web Forms functionality in Visual Studio.NET to create a web application that will consume this Web Service.

To do so, begin Visual Studio.NET and select File | New Project. This time, choose the Web Application from the Templates section template and call it TestWeatherService within your local web server.

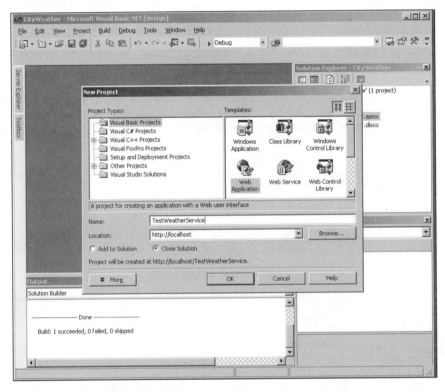

Close any open windows, then rename the WebForm1.aspx that Visual Studio.NET automatically creates as TestWeatherService.aspx. Double click TestWeatherService.aspx to open it up in the designer.

Before we proceed to test the Web Service, we need to reference it within our code. Remember how we had to compile the Web Service into a DLL and import it manually when we were creating the simple Web Service? With Visual Studio.NET we can do all that visually. The compilation to a DLL has already been taken care of when we built the Web Service. Now we need to add a reference to it within our web application. Right click the Project Name in the Solution Explorer and choose Add Web Reference (or you can do the same thing from the Project menu). We are trying to set a reference to the SOAP Discovery file for our Web Service. This will be a file with a .disco extension. If you know the name of the Web Service file, (.asmx), you can type it in the address box, or you can ask Visual Studio.NET to examine all available Web Services on the local machine by clicking the link Web references on local web server. This link will examine all available Web Services on the local web server and bring up a list from which you can select the one you want, which in our case is likely to be http://localhost/CityWeather/CityWeather.disco

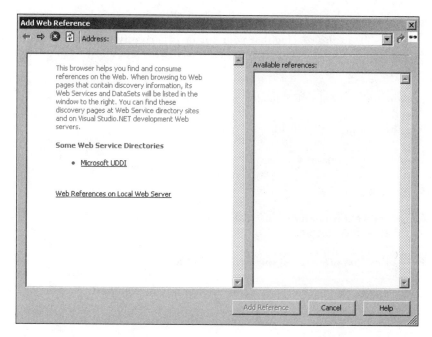

Once you choose the discovery file for the Web Service you just created, you can view its contract (SDL) and documentation. Finally click the **Add Reference** button to add a reference to this Web Service within your application. You will see a new **Web References** section added in the Solution Explorer, underneath the **References** in the Solution Explorer section. Within **Web References** you will notice localhost as the newly added Web Service Reference. Right click on localhost and rename it as **CityWeather**. This allows you to reference the Web Service by its name, `CityWeather`.

We are now ready to build our web application. Remember, our Web Form, `TestWeatherService.aspx`, is now open in the designer. Using the **Toolbox**, drag a label on to the form and then press *Return*. This creates a new label control on the top of the page and the cursor is now underneath it. Then drag another label, a text box and a button, one after the other from the toolbox to the form. You will now have a total of two labels, one text box and one button on the screen. Press *Return* again. Notice that when you press *Return* after dragging the button, your cursor moves underneath the button on the next paragraph. Hit *Return* again and you will see that you are on a new paragraph (`<P>`) tag (look in the **Properties** window).

Use the Properties window to set some properties, following these steps.

1. Change the ID of the <P> tag that your cursor is currently on, (at the bottom of the label, text box and the button) and set it to pWeather. This will allow us to reference the Paragraph within our code by its name.

2. Then change the font of the labels to Verdana.

3. Make the first label (the heading), bold.

4. Rename the text box as txtZip.

5. Rename the button as cmdGetWeather.

6. Change the Text property of the first label to Get Weather Info from WeatherSearchWho.com.

7. Change the Text property of the second label to Zip Code:

8. Finally change the text property of the button to Get Weather!

When you are done, your screen should look more or less like this:

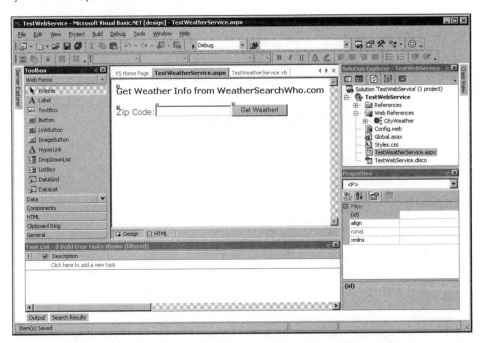

There is one more trick that needs to be done. We need to access the <P> tag, pWeather, through our server–side code. So we need to set the runat property to server. For some reason, the beta version does not let us do it from the Visual Studio Designer GUI (a bug that may be resolved in future releases). However, we can change the property by accessing the underlying HTML code for the <P> tag. To overcome this, click on the HTML tab at the bottom of the designer to view the HTML. Change the code near the bottom of the page from:

```
<p id=pWeather> </p>
```

to:

```
<p id=pWeather runat="server"> </p>
```

Switch back to the **Design** view by clicking on the **Design** tab. Double click the command button to start writing code for the button. Visual Studio.NET automatically takes you to the `cmdGetWeather_Click` event for the button. Add the following code for this event between the `Public Sub` and `End Sub` lines:

```
Public Sub cmdGetWeather_Click(ByVal sender As Object, ByVal e As_
                                            System.EventArgs)
    Dim strZip As String
    Dim strResult As String
    strZip = txtZip.Text
    If strZip = "" Or (Not IsNumeric(strZip)) Or Len(strZip) <> 5 Then
       pWeather.InnerText = "Invalid Zip Entered. Please Try again."
       Exit Sub
    End If

    '-- Create an instance of our Web Service
    Dim objWeather As New CityWeather.CityWeather()
    strResult = objWeather.GetWeather(strZip)
    objWeather = Nothing

    pWeather.InnerHtml = strResult

End Sub
```

When the button is clicked, and the form submitted, the code runs. Let's have a look at the code.

First we obtain the value of the text box and store it in a string variable:

```
    Dim strZip As String
    Dim strResult As String
    strZip = txtZip.Text
```

We then examine this string to make sure that the user has typed in a valid zip code. This is defined as a number exactly 5 digits long. If not, we display an error message and exit the sub-routine.

```
    If strZip = "" Or (Not IsNumeric(strZip)) Or Len(strZip) <> 5 Then
       pWeather.InnerText = "Invalid Zip Entered. Please Try again."
       Exit Sub
    End If
```

If the zip code is valid, then we create a new instance of our Web Service and invoke its method, very much like using a COM component.

```
    '-- Create an instance of our Web Service
    Dim objWeather As New WeatherTicker.CityWeather()
    strResult = objWeather.GetWeather(strZip)
    objWeather = Nothing
```

We obtain the result in a string variable that we then display as the HTML of our <P> tag.

```
pWeather.InnerHtml = strResult
```

To run this project, choose **Build** from the Build menu. Then right click the `TestWeatherService.aspx` file and select **Set as Start Page** from the context menu. Finally, right click the `TestWeatherService.aspx` file and select **View in Browser** from the context menu.

Enter any valid 5–digit US Zip code, for example, 06905 and click the **Get Weather!** button.

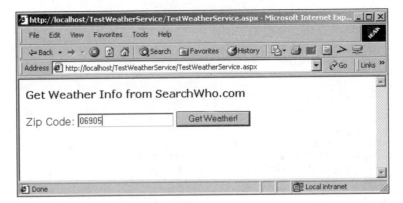

When you click the **Get Weather!** button, our server–side code invokes the method within the Web Service that in turn fetches the data from the SearchWho.com Web Site. *Et voilà*, you have real time weather information across the Internet!

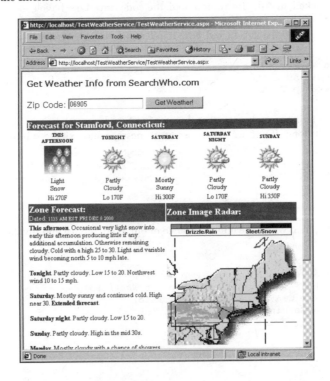

Remember, that while in our case the Web Service was on the same machine as the web page that was accessing it, it doesn't need to be. You can just as easily add references to a remote Web Service across the Internet. The very act of adding a Web Reference within Visual Studio to a remote Web Service creates a proxy DLL on your machine that can be used to access that remote Web Service.

Under the covers a lot of XML translation has taken place as the consumer's request has been converted into a SOAP request and the Web Service's response has been converted back. However, Visual Studio shields us from all of this and enables us to treat a Web Service as a remote COM component that we can instantiate.

Designing Web Services

When designing Web Services you need to keep a few things in mind. Web Services will be consumed by applications across the Net and multiple requests from different applications using your Web Service can use up your server resources very quickly. For this reason performance is a key issue and you should keep it top of your design goals when developing the service. A second goal for your Web Service is security of the information being handled as it crosses the Internet or your intranet. This is doubly important if it is sensitive, proprietary information.

Basically, your design aims should be to create Web Services that are secure, nimble and quick, without consuming a great deal of server resources.

Design for Stateless Environments

When developing Web Services, you should always design for a stateless environment. Most web applications should not require stateful objects or distributed transactions because they use enormous server resources. The functionality exposed by a Web Service should be **Stateless** and **Atomic**:

- ❑ **Stateless**: All the information required to perform the service should either be passed in with the request message or should be retrievable from a persistent data store (a database) based on some information provided with the request.

- ❑ **Atomic**: Each service request should be a complete unit of work that leaves databases and data stores in a consistent state. A Web Service should not expose two methods that perform complementary tasks that logically make up a single transaction. Instead, it should expose a single method that carries out the two tasks within the transaction. For example, a bank Web Service should not have separate `Debit` and `Credit` methods to transfer funds from one account to the other. Instead, it should have a single `TransferFunds` method that performs a debit and a credit nested within a single transaction. Within the transaction, the Web Service may call separate private Debit and Credit methods or may combine the two methods. In this way, if one task fails, the entire transaction fails and, assuming you have error handling in place which rolls back failed transactions, the data integrity is maintained.

Security Issues with Web Services

A key benefit of Web Services is the ease with which they can be accessed and used over the Internet. However, businesses that provide them would not want to make these services freely available to everybody. Access to Web Services can be restricted to authorized clients in the same way that Web Sites restrict access to authorized users. In addition to restricting access, a Web Service may need to ensure the privacy of data transmitted to and from clients, as well as protect internal business logic and data stores used to implement the service. Securing a Web Service is no different to securing a web page. You can use Internet Protocol Security (IPSec) or firewalls to protect your Web Service page if you know the IP address of the computers that are going to be consuming the Web Services. For example, a Web Service for use on an intranet can be set up to only accept requests from IP addresses belonging to the organization. However, when that is not possible, as in the case of a public consumption Web Service, you can specify SSL as a security mechanism. Instead of accepting SOAP requests over HTTP protocol, you can use HTTPS protocol. This will not only ensure authentication of the client, but also make sure that the data being sent back and forth is encrypted and secure. Using HTTPS however, will cause a severe performance hit, the impact of which you should consider carefully.

A third technique is to use a custom authentication scheme within your method call itself. You can code your method call so that it always requires an additional coded parameter that you and your consumer have agreed upon. The absence of a valid coded parameter would signify an invalid consumer and you could take necessary action. Another simple, but not really secure mechanism for protecting method calls could be to use encryption using public and private **keys**. You could send this coded information back and forth over HTTPS if you are further concerned with people sniffing the traffic on the Internet. You should choose the method that suits your needs.

Summary

In this chapter we have seen what Web Services are and how they form a major portion of Microsoft's .NET Framework. By utilizing the open Internet standards of XML and HTTP, Web Services allow programming and business logic to be provided by "black boxes" across the Internet that can be accessed and plugged into web applications. We also saw how the .NET framework handles most of the underlying XML plumbing when it comes to consuming and creating Web Services, allowing the web developer to focus on solving the business problem, rather than worrying about the infrastructure.

INTRODUCING.NET

9

Windows Forms

There is a great deal of development going on with Web based applications these days. The .NET Framework will make this development much easier; however, not all applications will run on the Web. This is where WinForms (or Windows Forms) comes in. WinForms is the forms package that .NET uses to build these Windows based applications. WinForms are a set of classes in the .NET framework and so incorporate the .NET platform's technologies, including object-oriented design, security, and managed execution, as well as support for building data-aware applications based on ADO.NET.

For those of you who have been developing VB applications for a while, WinForms will feel right at home. After creating the new form in the VS.NET IDE, you are presented with an empty frame. You then drag controls from the toolbox and drop them onto the form. You can then set the various properties of the controls, and add code to the methods and events of the controls and of the form. Sound familiar? We'll go through these steps in detail later in the chapter.

If you come from a C++/MFC background, then WinForms will take some of the pain away from writing Windows based applications. Window messages are handled for you, no more mapping messages. Events are based on **Delegates**, which are similar to function pointers. However if you feel that you need to implement your own WndProc(), you may do so.

One of the more exciting features of WinForms (and .NET in general) is visual inheritance. Since a Windows Form is really nothing more then a class, you can inherit that class to create other forms. The new form will contain all of the property settings for both the form and the controls on the form, and will contain any code that you may have implemented in the base form class. If another control is added to the base form, or a property value is changed, these changes will appear on the forms that are inherited from that base form. This can be a very powerful feature if used correctly. Imagine building a standard form, and then inheriting it for all of the forms in the application. The first benefit is that a lot of work only has to be done once, but also all of the forms will have, for example, the same look and feel or contain the same base menu structure.

In the rest of the chapter we will look at:

❑ Class hierarchy

❑ The event model

❑ Changes and additions to form properties and methods

❑ Layout enhancements

❑ GDI+

❑ Menus

❑ Inheritance

We will be looking at WinForms from a Visual Basic developer's standpoint; however, keep in mind that all of the code samples that you will see can be done just as easily in C#, Jscript, or any other CLR–enabled language.

Class Hierarchy

As we know, all classes in .NET are derived from the `System.Object` class. In Visual Basic versions prior to .NET, the forms package was a closed door; most developers really didn't understand how forms worked. WinForms is different. The object hierarchy is laid out in the documentation, and you can see which class is responsible for which functionality. You could go along, build some wonderful applications, and not ever really care what the class hierarchy is for WinForms. However, by understanding it, you can take advantage of some of the individual class features. The following diagram shows the class hierarchy and offers a short explanation of what each class is responsible for:

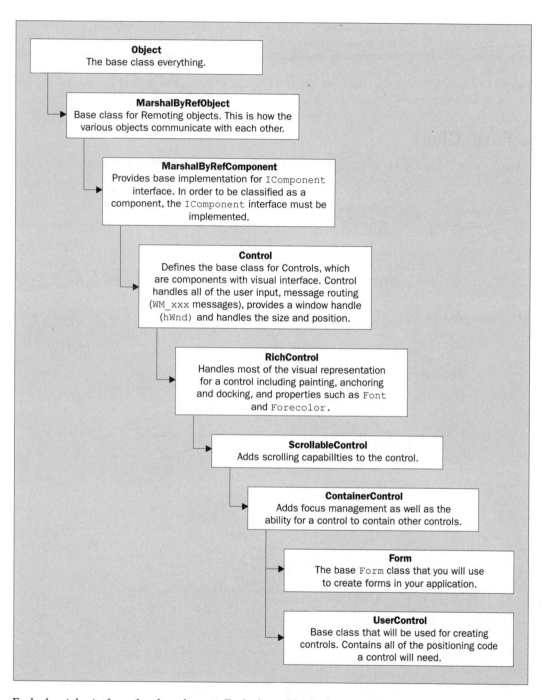

Each class inherits from the class above it. Each class adds a little more functionality until you finally end up with the complete forms class. UserControl is also derived from ContainerControl. UserControl will be the base class that you will most likely use to create your own user controls.

You could conceivably inherit from any of these classes in your application; however, `RichControl`, `ContainerControl` and, as mentioned, `UserControl` will be the ones you will most likely use. The SDK documentation lists and explains all of the events, methods, and properties that each of these classes expose.

Now that we have seen what the class hierarchy looks like, let's take a closer look at a form class and see how everything fits together.

The Form Class

Below is a code listing that you will get by selecting the Project I Add Windows Form menu option in Visual Studio.NET.

```
Imports System.ComponentModel
Imports System.Drawing
Imports System.WinForms


Public Class Form1
    Inherits System.WinForms.Form

'   Public Sub New()
        MyBase.New

        Form1 = Me

        'This call is required by the Win Form Designer.
        InitializeComponent

        'TODO: Add any initialization after the InitializeComponent() call
    End Sub

    'Form overrides dispose to clean up the component list.
    Overrides Public Sub Dispose()
        MyBase.Dispose
        components.Dispose
    End Sub

'#Region " Windows Form Designer generated code "

    'Required by the Windows Form Designer
    Private components As System.ComponentModel.Container

    Dim WithEvents Form1 As System.WinForms.Form

    'NOTE: The following procedure is required by the Windows Form Designer
    'It can be modified using the Windows Form Designer.
    'Do not modify it using the code editor.
    Private Sub InitializeComponent()
        components = New System.ComponentModel.Container
        Me.Text = "Form1"
    End Sub

#End Region

End Class
```

Let's quickly run over what we're looking at here.

The `Imports` statements are importing the various namespaces of referenced components in the project. By default VS.NET includes a reference to the following components:

- ❑ `Microsoft.Win32.Interop`
- ❑ `System`
- ❑ `System.Data`
- ❑ `System.Configuration`
- ❑ `System.Diagnostics`
- ❑ `System.Drawing`
- ❑ `System.WinForms`
- ❑ `System.WinForms.Design`
- ❑ `System.XML.Serialization`

Not all of the components in this list are needed by every project. `System.Configuration` and `System.XML.Serialization` could be removed for this example. You need to be careful when you remove referenced components however. In beta one, VS.NET becomes very unstable if you remove the `System.Data` component. You can also remove the Imports for namespaces that are not referenced in the project. For the current example, `System.ComponentModel` and `System.Drawing` would not be needed and could be deleted for this example, but it doesn't hurt anything to keep them included.

Next we see this:

```
Public Class Form1
    Inherits System.WinForms.Form
```

This is telling us that we are declaring a new class named `Form1` that is inheriting from `System.WinForms.Form`. Our form (`Form1`) has all of the functionality that the `System.WinForms.Form` exposes. It should be noted that you could also inherit from any form. We could have just as easily said to inherit from `Form1` or `MyCoolForm` or any other form that is available to the project. We will look at visual inheritance a little bit later in the chapter.

The next section is where initialization takes place. The `Public Sub New()` method is the constructor of the form. In prior versions of Visual Basic this would be analogous to the `Form.Initialize` event. The `MyBase.New` call is actually calling the constructor of the base class, in this case `System.WinForms.Form`. The `InitializeComponent` call is added by the environment and is part of all WinForms.

> It is where all of the components that you seat on your form will be initialized.

```
Public Sub New()
    MyBase.New

    Form1 = Me

    'This call is required by the Win Form Designer.
    InitializeComponent

    'TODO: Add any initialization after the InitializeComponent() call
End Sub
```

> The next section is wrapped in a **#Region / #EndRegion** block. This is the VS.NET editor's outlining feature. This section will be hidden from you by default. The reason is that you do not want to make any code changes in this section. Anytime you add or remove a control from the form, this section is re-written by the forms designer. Any code that you add to this section will disappear.

```
'Required by the Windows Form Designer
Private components As System.ComponentModel.Container

Dim WithEvents Form1 As System.WinForms.Form

'NOTE: The following procedure is required by the Windows Form Designer
'It can be modified using the Windows Form Designer.
'Do not modify it using the code editor.
Private Sub InitializeComponent()
    components = New System.ComponentModel.Container
    Me.Text = "Form1"
End Sub
```

The object variable components is declared as `System.ComponentModel.Container`. This is the default implementation of the `IContainer` interface, which has its base implementation provided by `System.ComponentModel.MarshalByRefComponent` class. Containers are objects that, well, contain other objects. A form is a container of other controls and the `System.ComponentModel.Container` class implements the adding, removing and retrieving of components.

The next declaration is to define `Form1` as `System.WinForms.Form`. This is creating an object variable of type `Form`. In the constructor there is a line `Form1 = Me`. Since this is being declared at the module level with the `Dim` keyword, `Form1` is now available to all code that is included in this module.

Every Windows Form should contain the following code, which is generated by the forms designer:

```
'Form overrides dispose to clean up the component list.
    Overrides Public Sub Dispose()
        MyBase.Dispose
        components.Dispose
    End Sub
```

Notice that when we override the `Dispose()` method of the base class, we **should** make a call to the `Dispose()` of the base class as the first thing. This always has to be done. The `Components.Dispose` is called next. This will in turn call the `Dispose()` of each and every control and component that you have on the form. You don't have to call the `Dispose()` on a form. It is called automatically when the form is destroyed. If you had any database connections or files open, for example, you could release them in the `Dispose()` method. However, it would probably be a better design to not rely upon `Dispose()` to do these things. It would be better to release any external resources as soon as you are finished with them prior to having the `Dispose()` method called.

If `Form1` is set as the Startup Object for your project, it will be shown when the application is started. To call this form from another part of the code you would need to write something like this:

```
Dim frmNewForm as Form1
frmNewForm = New Form
frmNewForm.Show
```

You could also create and instantiate the `Form1` object on one line.

```
Dim frmNewForm as New Form1
FrmNewForm.Show
```

Keep in mind that the constructor of `Form1` (`Sub New()`) is executed when the object is instantiated (in this case, when the `New` keyword is used) and not when the form is shown.

Now let's see what happens when we start adding controls, and setting the properties and making method calls.

Adding Controls

Adding controls to a WinForm in the forms designer is the same process that you used in previous versions of Visual Basic. You drag a control from the toolbox and drop it on the form. You can also double click on the control and it will appear on the form. You can then drag the control around on the form to get it to the position that you want. By adding two button controls and one textbox control, the designer generates the following code (highlighted in gray):

```
Imports System.ComponentModel
Imports System.Drawing
Imports System.WinForms

Public Class Form1
    Inherits System.WinForms.Form

    Public Sub New()
        MyBase.New

        Form1 = Me

        'This call is required by the Win Form Designer.
        InitializeComponent

        'TODO: Add any initialization after the InitializeComponent() call
    End Sub

    'Form overrides dispose to clean up the component list.
    Overrides Public Sub Dispose()
        MyBase.Dispose
        components.Dispose
    End Sub

#Region " Windows Form Designer generated code "

    'Required by the Windows Form Designer
    Private components As System.ComponentModel.Container
    Private WithEvents TextBox1 As System.WinForms.TextBox
    Private WithEvents Button2 As System.WinForms.Button
```

```
    Private WithEvents Button1 As System.WinForms.Button

    Dim WithEvents Form1 As System.WinForms.Form

    'NOTE: The following procedure is required by the Windows Form Designer
    'It can be modified using the Windows Form Designer.
    'Do not modify it using the code editor.
    Private Sub InitializeComponent()
        Me.components = New System.ComponentModel.Container()
        Me.Button1 = New System.WinForms.Button()
        Me.Button2 = New System.WinForms.Button()
        Me.TextBox1 = New System.WinForms.TextBox()

        '@design Me.TrayHeight = 0
        '@design Me.TrayLargeIcon = False
        '@design Me.TrayAutoArrange = True
        Button1.Location = New System.Drawing.Point(32, 80)
        Button1.Size = New System.Drawing.Size(75, 23)
        Button1.TabIndex = 0
        Button1.Text = "Button1"

        Button2.Location = New System.Drawing.Point(136, 80)
        Button2.Size = New System.Drawing.Size(75, 23)
        Button2.TabIndex = 1
        Button2.Text = "Button2"

        TextBox1.Location = New System.Drawing.Point(72, 40)
        TextBox1.Text = "TextBox1"
        TextBox1.TabIndex = 2
        TextBox1.Size = New System.Drawing.Size(100, 20)

        Me.Text = "Form1"
        Me.AutoScaleBaseSize = New System.Drawing.Size(5, 13)

        Me.Controls.Add(TextBox1)
        Me.Controls.Add(Button2)
        Me.Controls.Add(Button1)
    End Sub

#End Region

End Class
```

That's a lot of code – and it's great that you don't have to add this manually. Notice that all of the new code is actually in the #Region / #End Region block. If you had this block collapsed (the default) you wouldn't see any of this code. So let's look at what the designer generated and see if we can figure out what's going on here.

The class declaration hasn't changed, but there are a couple of new object variables being declared:

```
    Private WithEvents TextBox1 As System.WinForms.TextBox
    Private WithEvents Button2 As System.WinForms.Button
    Private WithEvents Button1 As System.WinForms.Button
```

As we might have imagined, they're for the two buttons (**Button1** and **Button2**) and for the textbox (**TextBox1**).

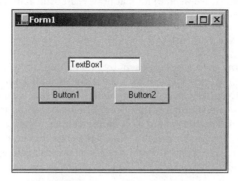

The constructor (`Sub New()`) and `Dispose()` methods are the same, so we won't bother with them; however, the `InitializeComponent` method has changed quite a bit. Now, instead of instantiating just the components object it also instantiates all of the controls on the form.

```
Me.Button1 = New System.WinForms.Button()
Me.Button2 = New System.WinForms.Button()
Me.TextBox1 = New System.WinForms.TextBox()
```

After the controls are created, properties for each control are set. If you had changed any of the default properties in the property browser on the forms designer, those changes would be seen here. Remember we said that you should not add code to the `InitializeComponent()` method; you can, however, change the code that the designer has added. Below are the changes for one of the button controls.

```
Button1.Location = New System.Drawing.Point(32, 80)
Button1.Size = New System.Drawing.Size(75, 23)
Button1.TabIndex = 0
Button1.Text = "Button1"
```

The first line is instantiating a new `System.Drawing.Point` structure and assigning it to the `Button1.Location` property. The second line is creating a new `System.Drawing.Size` structure and assigning it to the `Button1.Size` property. We could change either of the parameters to the structures and it would be reflected in the designer.

Finally, the controls are added to the controls collection of the form.

```
Me.Controls.Add(TextBox1)
Me.Controls.Add(Button2)
Me.Controls.Add(Button1)
```

A quick note on definition. A component is a class that implements or derives from a class that implements the `System.ComponentModel.IComponent` interface. A control is a component with user interface capabilities. That is why the controls on this form are added to the Controls collection. If we were to add a component from the Components tab of the Toolbox, we would see that the component does not get added to the Controls collection. The distinction between component and control is important in the .NET framework.

Now this is all well and good, but what if you want to add controls to your form dynamically. Let's say that we want to add another textbox to the form, but only when the user clicks on Button2. Well before we can add the code for the new textbox, we need to look at how WinForms handles events.

Events

An event is really nothing more then a message sent by "something" to let whatever is listening know that something has happened. In .NET, the object that triggers the event is known as the Event Sender and the object that is listening is the Event Receiver. The problem with events is making sure that the receiver knows what to listen for. It shouldn't care where it comes from. The sender shouldn't really care who is listening; it just needs to raise the event. A delegate is used to communicate the message between the source and the listener. A delegate is a type-safe function pointer, which is a class that holds a reference to a method that will perform the event handling functionality. A receiver registers the delegate with the sender in order to process the events. Another rather cool feature of the .NET event model is that delegates have multicast functionality. What this means is that an event sender can be dispatched to several receivers. This all is beginning to sound a lot more complicated than it really is, so let's look at how events work with controls on WinForms.

In order to see what the event process looks like, we are going to switch to C# for this example. We won't go over the complete form: functionally it is very much like the VB example we have been looking at. This form (Form2) was created in the VS.NET forms designer in the same way as Form1. We have 2 buttons and a text box. The code you will see first is what the designer gives you in the InitializeComponent() after double clicking on Button1 in the forms designer.

```
/// <summary>
///     Required method for Designer support - do not modify
///     the contents of this method with the code editor.
/// </summary>
private void InitializeComponent()
    {
        this.components = new System.ComponentModel.Container ();
        this.button1 = new System.WinForms.Button ();
        this.button2 = new System.WinForms.Button ();
        this.textBox1 = new System.WinForms.TextBox ();
        //@this.TrayHeight = 0;
        //@this.TrayLargeIcon = false;
        //@this.TrayAutoArrange = true;
        button1.Location = new System.Drawing.Point (32, 80);
        button1.Size = new System.Drawing.Size (75, 23);
        button1.TabIndex = 0;
        button1.Text = "button1";
        button1.Click += new System.EventHandler (this.button1_Click);
        button2.Location = new System.Drawing.Point (136, 80);
        button2.Size = new System.Drawing.Size (75, 23);
        button2.TabIndex = 1;
        button2.Text = "button2";
        textBox1.Location = new System.Drawing.Point (72, 40);
        textBox1.Text = "textBox1";
        textBox1.TabIndex = 2;
        textBox1.Size = new System.Drawing.Size (100, 20);
        this.Text = "Form1";
        this.AutoScaleBaseSize = new System.Drawing.Size (5, 13);
        this.Controls.Add (this.textBox1);
        this.Controls.Add (this.button2);
        this.Controls.Add (this.button1);
    }
```

With the exception of curly braces and semicolons, it looks familiar. An object variable is being created for components, button1, button2 and textbox1. Size and Point structures are being created and assigned to the Size and Location properties. Then we come across this line of code:

```
button1.Click += new System.EventHandler (this.button1_Click);
```

There are a couple of things happening here. First we are creating a new System.EventHandler() which is a delegate defined in the System namespace. It is used to handle events on controls. The parameter passed in this call is the method that you have defined as the event receiver. Now, by using the += assignment operator the sender (button1.Click) has been registered with the receiver (button1_Click()) using the delegate System.EventHandler().

this.Button1_Click() is the code that will deal with the click event of the button. This is the reference to the current form or class, similar to the Me keyword in VB, and Button1_Click is just a method with a specific signature that you write to respond to the event. This could have been called anything such as "SomeoneJustClickedThisButton", but the .NET documentation has naming standard suggestions for events and event handlers. The important thing about this method is the signature. If you look at the declaration:

```
protected void button1_Click (object sender, System.EventArgs e)
    {
        //code for the click event goes here
    }
```

Sender is the object that raised the event, Button1 in this case, and e would contain any other data that can be associated with an event. This could contain cursor location, which mouse button was pressed, and so on. The SDK documentation lists what is included with each event.

Something that you can't do easily in Visual Basic 6 is to remove the event handler from a control. How many times have you had to add some type of flag variable to track if you want to execute the code in an event handler, especially during control initialization or a form load? Not only does += assign the event handler, -= removes the event handler. This gives you the ability to assign and remove event handlers from a control at runtime. You can even assign a handler, remove it and then assign a different handler based on application or system state, or on some type of application data. So to remove the event handler from out example you would write:

```
button1.Click -= new System.EventHandler (this.button1_Click);
```

This would remove the event receiver button1_Click from the button1.Click event. If the button1.Click is raised, unless another event receiver is registered, nothing will happen.

Another interesting feature is that you can assign multiple handlers to an event. For example, we could have written:

```
button1.Click += new System.EventHandler (this.button1_Click1);
button1.Click += new System.EventHandler (this.button1_Click2);
button1.Click += new System.EventHandler (this.button1_Click3);
```

We would have to implement a button1_Click1, button1_Click2 and a button1_Click3, and when Button1 is clicked, all three handlers are executed in the sequence that they are added.

Now we were going to add a new textbox when the user clicked on Button1. The code to do this would look something like this:

```
protected void button1_Click (object sender, System.EventArgs e)
   {
       System.WinForms.TextBox textBox2=new System.WinForms.TextBox();
       textBox2.Location=new System.Drawing.Point(72,10);
       textBox2.Size=new System.Drawing.Size(100,20);
       textBox2.Text="New TextBox";
       this.Controls.Add (textBox2);

   }
```

Now when the user clicks on Button1, a new textbox (textBox2) will appear just above textBox1 with the text New TextBox in it. You could also add event handling to textBox2.

Visual Basic 6 allows you to dynamically add controls to a form; however the way the .NET platform and WinForms allows you to do this is so much cleaner and easier to implement. The event model gives you a great deal of flexibility when it comes to hooking up the events. You can have a form handle data entry for several different types of conditions just by adding and removing controls and events. Again, this isn't necessarily a new idea, however, as we have seen, this is a much better implementation of this feature.

VB.NET has these capabilities as well. Currently to add the click event to Button1, you would double click Button1. In the code window you would now have this code skeleton:

```
Protected Sub Button1_Click(ByVal sender As Object, ByVal e As System.EventArgs)

End Sub
```

You would add what ever code you need to have happen in the `Button1_Click()` method. If you wanted to remove the event from the `Button1.Click` event, you would use the `RemoveHandle` function. The call would look like this:

```
RemoveHandler Button1.Click, AddressOf Me.Button1_Click
```

If you needed to add the click event receiver back to Button1, here is what you would do:

```
AddHandler Button1.Click, AddressOf Me.Button1_Click
```

> **It should be noted that at the present time (beta one), the syntax for event handling in VB.NET is in a state of transition. Please be sure to review the SDK documentation for the correct syntax when the .NET framework is released.**

Events should not be overlooked in the .NET platform. Due to the way that events have been implemented in .NET, they can really provide power and flexibility to not only WinForm controls, but to any component or class that you develop.

Layout Enhancements

In earlier versions of Visual Basic, if you wanted to have the controls on your form resize properly when the form resized, you either wrote a fair amount of code in the `Paint` event, or you used a third party control that did it for you. Now you no longer have to do either. WinForms controls (controls derived from `RichControl`) contain two properties, `Dock` and `Anchor`.

The `Dock` property sets where the control will fasten itself to on the parent control. The possible values are `Right`, `Left`, `Top`, `Bottom`, `Fill` and `None`. If you select `Left`, for example, the control will fasten itself to the left side of the parent control, filling the edge from top to bottom, and will remain there when the parent is resized. An example of this would be Windows Explorer. It docks the TreeView to the left side and the ListView to the right side of the window.

The `Anchor` property sets an anchor position of the control on the parent control. The `Anchor` property is set using the `AnchorStyles` enumeration, which has values such as `All`, `BottomLeft`, `BottomLeftRight`, `LeftRight`, etc. The values would be the sides of the parent control that the control would maintain a constant distance. If you set the Anchored property of a control to `AnchorStyles.TopLeft`, then when the parent is resized, the distance between the left and top edges of the child control would maintain a constant distance from the left and top edges of the parent container.

These properties can be set at runtime. The following listing is an example of setting the `Anchor` property of Button1 to resize in all directions. This code would be in the `InitializeComponent()` method.

```
Button1.Location = New System.Drawing.Point(160, 64)
Button1.Size = New System.Drawing.Size(75, 23)
Button1.TabIndex = 1
Button1.Anchor = System.WinForms.AnchorStyles.All
Button1.Text = "Button1"
```

With this code, if you resize the form, Button1 would grow and shrink accordingly, always maintaining the constant distance from the parent's (in this case `Form1`) edges. By adding the following code to `Button1_Click`, we can change the way the button responds to form resizing.

```
Button1.Anchor = WinForms.AnchorStyles.None
Button1.Dock = WinForms.DockStyle.Left
```

Now `Button1` will be docked to the left edge of `Form1`, and will remain there regardless of how you resize the form.

This is a welcome feature that you will have to experiment with to fully understand the possibilities. It will allow you to have professional looking forms that will resize properly, without having to rely on third party controls, or messy resize code.

Changes and Additions

There have been a lot of change to the properties and methods of the form class from prior versions of Visual Basic to Visual Basic.NET. We won't go through all of them, but we do need to look at a few of the more interesting changes.

Properties Changes

There are some property changes that are worth mentioning. The first one is a change to how you assign what was once known as the Default and Cancel button. The Default button is the button that would raise its click event when the *Enter* key was pressed. The Cancel button would raise its click event when someone pressed the *ESC* key. In Visual Basic 6, these were properties of the buttons. Each button had a Default and Cancel property that you would set to either `True` or `False`. In WinForms, these properties are part of the form class and are called `AcceptButton` and `CancelButton`. Instead of telling the button that it is a Default button, you now set the `AcceptButton` property on the form to the proper button.

There are several changes to the various properties that control where a form is located and what size the form is. Instead of having the Top – Left and Height – Width combinations, there is now `DesktopBounds`, `DesktopLocation`, `MaxTrackSize` and `MinTrackSize`. Note that these properties are for forms only, not controls. These properties also use three structures located in the `System.Drawing` namespace. They are `Point`, `Size` and `Rectangle`.

The `DesktopLocation` property sets and gets a `Point` structure that contains the location of the form on the desktop. The `Size` property sets and gets the form's current size, returning a `Size` structure. `DesktopBounds` returns or sets a Rectangle that determines the size and location of the form on the current desktop. As you can see, `DesktopBounds` is `Size` and `DesktopLocation` combined into one property.

`MaxTrackSize` and `MinTrackSize` both get or set a `Size` structure. These properties have the effect of limiting the size that a form can be. If you want to have a form that can only be up to 200 x 200 pixels, and not any larger, then you would create an object of type `Size`, set the `Height` and `Width` property of that object and set it to the form's `MaxTrackSize` property. Now the form can be sized smaller than 200 x 200 pixels, but it cannot be set any larger. The `MinTrackSize` property sets the minimum size of a form.

MDI properties have changed somewhat as well. Now instead of setting the `MDIChild` property to `True`, you tell the form who the `MDIParent` is. There are `IsMDIChild` and `IsMDIContainer` properties. These return `True` or `False` whether the form is an `MDIChild` or `MDIParent` respectively. `MDIChildren` returns an array containing the `MDIChild` forms that are owned by the current form.

You can now set a form to be an owner of another form. To do this you set the `Owner` property of a form to another form that will become the Parent. If, for example, `Form1` owns `Form2`, whenever you minimize `Form1`, `Form2` gets minimized as well. If you close `Form1`, `Form2` gets closed also. Owned forms are never displayed behind the owner. If you close `Form2`, `Form1` will stay displayed in the current position and will receive focus. The only way to do this in Visual Basic before was when the form was first displayed. The `Show` method has the optional `OwnerForm` argument. You can change the owner of a form dynamically by setting the `Owner` property or by using the `AddOwnedForm` and `RemoveOwnedForm` methods. The `OwnedForms` property returns an array of `Form` objects of all forms that are owned by the form. You have to rely on Win32 API calls in order to accomplish this in previous versions of Visual Basic. A good example of owning a form is if your application had three different forms, such as a main form and two data entry forms. By making the main form the owner of the data entry forms, when the main form is minimized, the data entry form disappears. The user doesn't need to minimize multiple windows. When the main form is restored, the data entry form would be restored as well.

Method Changes

The single biggest change from Visual Basic 6 is the addition of the WndProc() method. You now have the ability of intercepting and reacting to messages without having to resort to third party controls or impossible to debug AddressOf hacks. And since the WndProc() method is implemented in the System.Control class, you have this feature not only at the form level, but for almost every control that you would ever use or build.

The .NET platform handles Windows messages pretty well; however, there is always a time when you need to get the extra little something. For a rather contrived example, let's monitor for the WM_RBUTTONDOWN and WM_LBUTTONDOWN messages, which are sent when someone clicks the right or left mouse button. We will post a message box with all of the parameter info from the message. Not overly useful, but it serves to demonstrate the functionality.

Here is the start of the Form1 class:

```
Imports System.ComponentModel
Imports System.Drawing
Imports System.WinForms


Public Class Form1
   Inherits System.WinForms.Form

   Public Sub New()
      MyBase.New

      Form1 = Me

      'This call is required by the Win Form Designer.
      InitializeComponent

      'TODO: Add any initialization after the InitializeComponent() call
   End Sub

   'Form overrides dispose to clean up the component list.
   Overrides Public Sub Dispose()
      MyBase.Dispose
      components.Dispose
   End Sub

#Region " Windows Form Designer generated code "

   'Required by the Windows Form Designer
   Private components As System.ComponentModel.Container

   Dim WithEvents Form1 As System.WinForms.Form

   'NOTE: The following procedure is required by the Windows Form Designer
   'It can be modified using the Windows Form Designer.
   'Do not modify it using the code editor.

   Private Sub InitializeComponent()
      components = New System.ComponentModel.Container
      Me.Text = "Form1"
   End Sub
```

```
#End Region

Protected Overrides Sub WndProc(ByRef m As Message)

    Select Case m.msg

        Case Microsoft.Win32.Interop.win.WM_RBUTTONDOWN
            MessageBox.Show("Right Button  " & m.wParam)

        Case Microsoft.Win32.Interop.win.WM_LBUTTONDOWN
            MessageBox.Show("Left Button   " & m.wParam)

    End Select

    MyBase.WndProc(m)

    End Sub
End Class
```

Notice the line `Protected Overrides Sub WndProc(ByRef m As Message). Overrides` tells us that although this method is implemented in the base class, we want to execute code that is not part of the base class implementation. After our code executes, then we call the base class implementation to execute. `WndProc()` is the method that we are overriding. The parameter `m as Message` is the message that will be passed in. Note that every message that the form will process will be passed into this method. So you don't really want to do this unless you have a need, because there will be a slight performance hit.

The `Select Case` will look for the messages that you want to handle, in this case WM_RBUTTONDOWN and WM_LBUTTONDOWN. When they are found, display the `MessageBox` (note the new syntax) and finally pass the message to the base class `WndProc()` so that it may be processed. If you have a situation where you don't want certain messages processed, then don't pass them to `MyBase.WndProc()`. To do this you would put the final call to `MyBase.WndProc()` inside an `if` construct or a `Select Case` statement.

If you come from a C++/MFC background, you're probably thinking "So what. What's the big deal!" If you come from a Visual Basic background, then you know what the big deal is. VB programmers have never been able to get to the message pump very easily without help from third party controls, and now you can.

GDI+

GDI+ is what is used to take advantage of the Windows graphics library. To utilize GDI+ you will need to include the `System.Drawing` and `System.Drawing.Drawing2D`. You will recognize some of the members of the `Drawing` class as being encapsulations of Win32 GDI functions. All of the basics are there, pens and brushes, rectangles etc. GDI+ however, is a snap to use compared to calling the Win32 GDI functions, especially if you were programming in Visual Basic.

Some of the things that are including in the `System.Drawing` class are:

❑ Bitmap manipulation

❑ Cursors class, contain all of the various cursors that you would need to set in your application (hourglasss, I-beam, etc.)

- ❑   Font class

- ❑   Graphics class, contain all of the drawing (line, curve, ellipse, etc.) and fill methods

- ❑   Icon class

- ❑   Various structures for dealing with graphics, including Point, Size, Color and Rectangle

- ❑   The Pen and Brush classes

There are many more, but this gives you an idea of what's in there. The `System.Drawing2D` namespace contains things like the `LinearGradientBrush` and `ColorBlend` class. Let's take a look at a couple of examples.

In the first example, we're going to display some text, but instead of a solid color, we will use a `TextureBrush` and use a bitmap to color the text. Here is the complete code for the form:

```
Imports System.ComponentModel
Imports System.Drawing
Imports System.Drawing.Drawing2D
Imports System.WinForms


Public Class Form1
    Inherits System.WinForms.Form

    Public Sub New()
        MyBase.New

        Form1 = Me

        'This call is required by the Win Form Designer.
        InitializeComponent

        'TODO: Add any initialization after the InitializeComponent() call
        Me.SetStyle(ControlStyles.ResizeRedraw, True)
    End Sub

    'Form overrides dispose to clean up the component list.
    Overrides Public Sub Dispose()
        MyBase.Dispose
        components.Dispose
    End Sub

#Region " Windows Form Designer generated code "

    'Required by the Windows Form Designer
    Private components As System.ComponentModel.Container
    Dim WithEvents Form1 As System.WinForms.Form

    'NOTE: The following procedure is required by the Windows Form Designer
    'It can be modified using the Windows Form Designer.
    'Do not modify it using the code editor.
    Private Sub InitializeComponent()
        Me.components = New System.ComponentModel.Container()
```

```
        '@design Me.TrayHeight = 90
        '@design Me.TrayLargeIcon = False
        '@design Me.TrayAutoArrange = True
        Me.Text = "Form1"
        Me.AutoScaleBaseSize = New System.Drawing.Size(5, 13)
        Me.ClientSize = New System.Drawing.Size(344, 213)

    End Sub

#End Region

    Protected Overrides Sub OnPaint(ByVal e As PaintEventArgs)
    Dim TextBrush As Brush
    Dim MyFont As Font
    Dim g As Graphics = e.Graphics

    'Change the next line as necessary for different paths
    TextBrush = New TextureBrush(New Bitmap("c:\winnt\Santa Fe Stucco.bmp"))
    MyFont = New Font("Comic Sans MS", 60, FontStyle.Bold)
    g.FillRectangle(New SolidBrush(Color.LightGray), e.ClipRectangle)
    g.DrawString("GDI Sample", myFont, TextBrush, 10, 20)

    End Sub

End Class
```

It should look familiar for the most part. It is, after all just a form. In the form constructor we added the
`Me.SetStyle(ControlStyles.ResizeRedraw, True)` statement. This tells the form to completely
redraw itself when it is resized. The other big difference is that we have overridden the `OnPaint()` event
from the base class. Anytime the window needs to be redrawn, this event is raised to do it. Here is what the
form looks like.

So what do we do in `OnPaint()`? First thing is to declare a couple of variables.

```
Protected Overrides Sub OnPaint(ByVal e As PaintEventArgs)
    Dim TextBrush As Brush
    Dim MyFont As Font
    Dim g As Graphics = e.Graphics
```

The first variable, `TextBrush`, is the Brush that we will be using to paint the text. `MyFont` is the Font that our text will be using. Notice that since we have included the `Drawing` namespace, we don't have to use the complete name – `System.Drawing.Brush` and `System.Drawing.Font`.

The next line may need a little explaining. The parameter passed into the `OnPaint` event is a `PaintEventArgs`, which is in the `System.WinForms` namespace. This class is derived from `System.EventArgs`, and, if you remember, this parameter is part of every event call. In this case it contains two properties, the `ClipRectangle` of what is to be painted and the `Graphics` object to use to do the painting. We are setting the local variable g to be the `Graphics` object that is passed in as part of e. In this case it is really just a shortcut, we could have just as easily written the method like this:

```
Protected Overrides Sub OnPaint(ByVal e As PaintEventArgs)
    Dim TextBrush As Brush
    Dim MyFont As Font

    TextBrush = New TextureBrush(New Bitmap("c:\winnt\Santa Fe Stucco.bmp"))
    MyFont = New Font("Comic Sans MS", 60, FontStyle.Bold)
    With e.Graphics
        .FillRectangle(New SolidBrush(Color.LightGray), e.ClipRectangle)
        .DrawString("GDI Sample", myFont, TextBrush, 10, 20)
    End With
End Sub
```

The next couple of lines do the real work here.

```
TextBrush = New TextureBrush(New Bitmap("c:\winnt\Santa Fe Stucco.bmp"))
MyFont = New Font("Comic Sans MS", 60, FontStyle.Bold)
""g.FillRectangle(New SolidBrush(Color.LightGray), e.ClipRectangle)
g.DrawString("GDI Sample", myFont, TextBrush, 10, 20)
```

The first line just sets the font to use for our example. The first parameter is the font name, next is size and finally is the font style. You need to use the `FontStyle` enum here. `FontStyle` is part of the `System.Drawing` namespace.

The next line is filling the background of the form. Here we are using the Graphics object g in order to call the `FillRectangle()` method. Notice that we actually create the new `SolidBrush()` in the call to `FillRectangle()`. We could have created another object variable of type `SolidBrush()` and passed in the variable if we wanted to. We set the color of the brush and tell it to paint the `e.ClipRectangle`, which is the area that needs repainting.

`TextBrush()` is created by instantiating a new `TextureBrush()`. We are using the `Sante Fe Stucco` bitmap that is in the `WinNT` folder. You could use just about any bitmap or jpeg that you want.

The last line actually draws the string that we want displayed. The string is the first parameter. Then we have the font variable that we just set up. Next is the brush that we created, and finally there are two points that represent the top left corner, relative to the client area of the form, to start drawing the text.

It should be noted that all of the method calls that we are looking at have many different overloads that can be called. For instance, the `Graphics.DrawString` class has six overloads with six different signatures, each passing in a different set of parameters. We are looking at but one of these signatures.

If we want to add a little pizzazz to the form, we can change the line:

```
g.FillRectangle(New SolidBrush(Color.LightGray), e.ClipRectangle)
```

to the following:

```
g.FillRectangle(New LinearGradientBrush(e.ClipRectangle, Color.DarkGray,
Color.White, 45, True), e.ClipRectangle)
```

By changing the brush to LinearGradientBrush, we get the effect of a gradient color change on the screen. The first parameter is the region to paint. The next two parameters are the colors that the gradient will blend. The next parameter is the angle of the gradient, in this case 45 says to go from the top left to the bottom right.

The resulting form looks like this:

Now let's say you want to rotate the text: this is easy enough to do by adding just two lines of code. All you need to do is add g.RotateTransform(10) before the DrawString() method and a g.ResetTransform() after the DrawString() method. Now the text will be at a 10 degree slant from the top left to the bottom right.

We can add shapes to the form rather easily as well. To add in an ellipse for instance, we can add just one line of code, g.FillEllipse(TextBrush, 150, 150, 200, 100). This will add an ellipse at location 150, 150 with a width of 200, and a height of 100 using the same brush that we used on our text. Notice that the ellipse is also at the same 10 degree angle. If the FillEllipse method call is added after the ResetTransform() call, the ellipse would be not be angled.

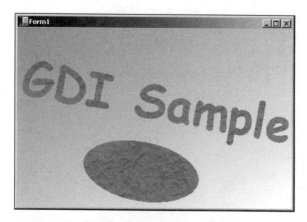

This is just scratching the surface of what GDI+ can actually do. If you have done GDI programming in C++/MFC or even in Visual Basic, you will find GDI+ to be a little more friendly but no less capable. If you haven't done any GDI programming because the API may have intimidated you, then you will be able to jump into GDI+ without any problem. The best way to learn is to experiment, and the .NET platform makes this easy.

Menus

Visual Studio.NET has included a new menu designer that is a big step up from previous versions. You can now edit the menus on the form, so you can see the structure and how they look as you design. You can also do a complete menu structure in code, if that is your preference.

To create a menu using the designer you first have to drag the MainMenu control from the toolbar to the form. You will now see a menu bar on the form, and you can start to type in menu names on the menu bar. If we were to enter File and then add an Exit to the File menu, then add a Help top line menu, and About to the Help menu, we would end up with something that looked similar to this:

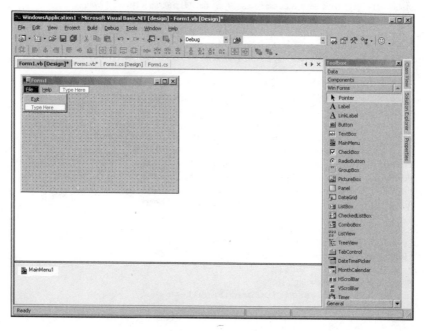

Let's take a look at the code that makes up the menus.

```vbnet
Imports System.ComponentModel
Imports System.Drawing
Imports System.WinForms


Public Class Form1
    Inherits System.WinForms.Form

    Public Sub New()
        MyBase.New

        Form1 = Me

        'This call is required by the Win Form Designer.
        InitializeComponent

        'TODO: Add any initialization after the InitializeComponent() call
    End Sub

    'Form overrides dispose to clean up the component list.
    Overrides Public Sub Dispose()
        MyBase.Dispose
        components.Dispose
    End Sub

#Region " Windows Form Designer generated code "

    'Required by the Windows Form Designer
    Private components As System.ComponentModel.Container
    Private WithEvents MenuItem4 As System.WinForms.MenuItem
    Private WithEvents MenuItem3 As System.WinForms.MenuItem
    Private WithEvents MenuItem2 As System.WinForms.MenuItem
    Private WithEvents MenuItem1 As System.WinForms.MenuItem
    Private MainMenu1 As System.WinForms.MainMenu
    Dim WithEvents Form1 As System.WinForms.Form

    'NOTE: The following procedure is required by the Windows Form Designer
    'It can be modified using the Windows Form Designer.
    'Do not modify it using the code editor.
    Private Sub InitializeComponent()
        Me.components = New System.ComponentModel.Container()
        Me.MenuItem1 = New System.WinForms.MenuItem()
        Me.MenuItem2 = New System.WinForms.MenuItem()
        Me.MainMenu1 = New System.WinForms.MainMenu()
        Me.MenuItem4 = New System.WinForms.MenuItem()
        Me.MenuItem3 = New System.WinForms.MenuItem()

        '@design Me.TrayHeight = 90
        '@design Me.TrayLargeIcon = False
        '@design Me.TrayAutoArrange = True
        MenuItem1.Text = "&File"
        MenuItem1.Index = 0
        Dim a__1(1) As System.WinForms.MenuItem
        a__1(0) = MenuItem2
```

```
        MenuItem1.MenuItems.All = a__1

        MenuItem2.Text = "E&xit"
        MenuItem2.Index = 0

        '@design MainMenu1.SetLocation(New System.Drawing.Point(7, 7))
        Dim a__2(2) As System.WinForms.MenuItem
        a__2(0) = MenuItem1
        a__2(1) = MenuItem3
        MainMenu1.MenuItems.All = a__2

        MenuItem4.Text = "About"
        MenuItem4.Index = 0

        MenuItem3.Text = "&Help"
        MenuItem3.Index = 1
        Dim a__3(1) As System.WinForms.MenuItem
        a__3(0) = MenuItem4
        MenuItem3.MenuItems.All = a__3
        Me.Text = "Form1"
        Me.AutoScaleBaseSize = New System.Drawing.Size(5, 13)
        Me.Menu = MainMenu1
        Me.ClientSize = New System.Drawing.Size(344, 213)

    End Sub

#End Region

End Class
```

This code was done completely in the designer. If you entered the menu names in a different order to that seen here, your code may look a little different, but should function the same. You'll notice that it's a basic form with the addition of some object variables and some extra code in the `InitializeComponent()`. First the object variable declarations:

```
Private WithEvents MenuItem4 As System.WinForms.MenuItem
Private WithEvents MenuItem3 As System.WinForms.MenuItem
Private WithEvents MenuItem2 As System.WinForms.MenuItem
Private WithEvents MenuItem1 As System.WinForms.MenuItem
Private MainMenu1 As System.WinForms.MainMenu
```

For a menu structure to work you need one `MainMenu` object (**MainMenu1**). To this `MainMenu` you add `MenuItem` objects. The `MenuItem` objects are what the user selects. Each `MenuItem` has several properties that can be set. For instance, there is a `Checked` property, a `DefaultItem` property and the `Text` property. Setting these properties can give you the effects and menu types that you want.

In the `InitializeComponent()` method we instantiate the `Menu` classes, and then we start setting up the menu structure. The `MainMenu` object has a `MenuItems` property, which is a collection of `MenuItem` objects. The `MenuItem` object has the same property. The top level menus are added to the `MainMenu.MenuItems()` collection. Each top level has the submenus added to its `MenuItems` collection and so on. You can look at the code and see how this works.

```
MenuItem1.Text = "&File"
MenuItem1.Index = 0
Dim a__1(1) As System.WinForms.MenuItem
a__1(0) = MenuItem2
MenuItem1.MenuItems.All = a__1
```

The way the designer does this is to create a temporary array of type `MenuItem`, in this case `a__1()`, and add each submenu entry into the array. You notice that the `MenuItem.Index` property is set. This determines the order in which menus are displayed. If you look at where `MenuItem3` is added, you can see that it is getting the index value of 1. In this example we are adding only one submenu (MenuItem2) to the top-level menu (MenuItem1). After all of the submenus are added to the array, the array is set to the `MenuItem.MenuItems.All` property. This is continued until the complete menu structure is built.

As our code sits right now, we have a menu system that does absolutely nothing. We need to add some event handlers. You do this the same way you would add event handlers for buttons or anything else. In the designer you can double click the menu option and you will be taken to the event automatically. If we double click the File/Exit menu in the designer, we get this code skeleton generated for us:

```
Protected Sub MenuItem2_Click(ByVal sender As System.Object, ByVal e As
System.EventArgs)
    'Event code goes here
End Sub
```

Remember that, because of the event model's flexibility, this can be the same handler that another control or another event uses. In other words, a command button and the menu can use the same method to respond to an event. This can really improve on code re-use and improve maintainability. This could be accomplished in Visual Basic 6, however the difference is that you would have to make a subroutine or function, and then call that code from inside the event handlers of you, button and menu. Now you can just make the method the event receiver.

Notice the line of code towards the bottom of `InitializeComponent();`

```
Me.Menu=MainMenu1
```

This is where MainMenu1 gets hooked up with the form. What you can do with this is actually change the menu structure of your program during execution. You could design two or three menu structures, and can then implement them at runtime, depending on what menu functionality is needed at the time.

Menus in .NET have definitely received some attention from the framework designers. The class hierarchy that the menu structure uses allows for a powerful and flexible toolset that you can use to design and implement professional menus in your application.

Inheritance

Inheritance is something that Visual Basic developers have been after for years. Now that it's here, we need to learn how to take advantage of the power and flexibility that it can offer. If you're not careful, however, it can turn into a confusing nightmare. When it comes to WinForms, inheritance can really cut down the amount of code that you will need to write. It can come in especially handy if you are building a framework for the rest of your group or organization to use. The best way to see how this works is to look at some code, so let's build an application that will contain three forms. There will be a base form, and two other forms that inherit from the base form. In addition, just to show that .NET does have cross-language inheritance, we will make the base form in C# and the two derived forms will be in Visual Basic.

First, the base form. Let's say we will be developing an application that has requirements for two data entry screens. One would be for businesses and the other would be for individuals. The data required for the business would be:

- ❏ Company Name
- ❏ Address Line 1
- ❏ Address Line2
- ❏ City
- ❏ State Zip
- ❏ Phone
- ❏ Fax

The individual data requirements are:

- ❏ Name
- ❏ Address Line 1
- ❏ Address Line2
- ❏ City
- ❏ State Zip
- ❏ Phone
- ❏ Cell Phone
- ❏ E-Mail

Now as you can see, there is some overlap in data requirements. It's the overlap that we will be including on the base form. Here is what our base form will look like – nothing fancy, we just want to prove a point.

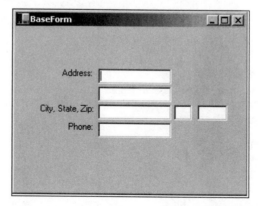

As you can see, we have included all of the data elements that overlapped on the requirements. We'll start by creating a new C# Class Library project, called Base. Add a form to this project, and call it BaseForm. The code for this form is as follows:

```
namespace Base
{
```

```csharp
using System;
using System.Drawing;
using System.Collections;
using System.ComponentModel;
using System.WinForms;
using System.Data;

/// <summary>
///     Summary description for Form1.
/// </summary>
public class BaseForm : System.WinForms.Form
{
    /// <summary>
    ///     Required designer variable.
    /// </summary>
private System.ComponentModel.Container components;
private System.WinForms.TextBox textBox6;
private System.WinForms.TextBox textBox5;
private System.WinForms.TextBox textBox4;
private System.WinForms.TextBox textBox3;
private System.WinForms.TextBox textBox2;
private System.WinForms.TextBox textBox1;
private System.WinForms.Label label3;
private System.WinForms.Label label2;
private System.WinForms.Label label1;

public BaseForm()
{
    //
    // Required for Windows Form Designer support
    //
    InitializeComponent();

    //
    // TODO: Add any constructor code after InitializeComponent call
    //
}

/// <summary>
///     Clean up any resources being used.
/// </summary>
public override void Dispose()
{
    base.Dispose();
    components.Dispose();
}

/// <summary>
///     Required method for Designer support - do not modify
///     the contents of this method with the code editor.
/// </summary>
private void InitializeComponent()
{
    this.components = new System.ComponentModel.Container ();
    this.textBox5 = new System.WinForms.TextBox ();
```

```
this.textBox4 = new System.WinForms.TextBox ();
this.label1 = new System.WinForms.Label ();
this.label3 = new System.WinForms.Label ();
this.label2 = new System.WinForms.Label ();
this.textBox2 = new System.WinForms.TextBox ();
this.textBox3 = new System.WinForms.TextBox ();
this.textBox6 = new System.WinForms.TextBox ();
this.textBox1 = new System.WinForms.TextBox ();
//@this.TrayHeight = 0;
//@this.TrayLargeIcon = false;
//@this.TrayAutoArrange = true;
textBox5.Location = new System.Drawing.Point (248, 104);
textBox5.Text = "textBox5";
textBox5.TabIndex = 7;
textBox5.Size = new System.Drawing.Size (40, 20);
textBox4.Location = new System.Drawing.Point (216, 104);
textBox4.Text = "textBox4";
textBox4.TabIndex = 6;
textBox4.Size = new System.Drawing.Size (24, 20);
label1.Location = new System.Drawing.Point (8, 56);
label1.Text = "Address:";
label1.Size = new System.Drawing.Size (100, 23);
label1.TabIndex = 0;
label1.TextAlign = System.WinForms.HorizontalAlignment.Right;
label3.Location = new System.Drawing.Point (8, 128);
label3.Text = "Phone:";
label3.Size = new System.Drawing.Size (100, 23);
label3.TabIndex = 2;
label3.TextAlign = System.WinForms.HorizontalAlignment.Right;
label2.Location = new System.Drawing.Point (8, 104);
label2.Text = "City, State, Zip:";
label2.Size = new System.Drawing.Size (100, 23);
label2.TabIndex = 1;
label2.TextAlign = System.WinForms.HorizontalAlignment.Right;
textBox2.Location = new System.Drawing.Point (112, 80);
textBox2.Text = "textBox2";
textBox2.TabIndex = 4;
textBox2.Size = new System.Drawing.Size (100, 20);
textBox3.Location = new System.Drawing.Point (112, 104);
textBox3.Text = "textBox3";
textBox3.TabIndex = 5;
textBox3.Size = new System.Drawing.Size (100, 20);
textBox6.Location = new System.Drawing.Point (112, 128);
textBox6.Text = "textBox6";
textBox6.TabIndex = 8;
textBox6.Size = new System.Drawing.Size (100, 20);
textBox1.Location = new System.Drawing.Point (112, 56);
textBox1.Text = "textBox1";
textBox1.TabIndex = 3;
textBox1.Size = new System.Drawing.Size (100, 20);
this.Text = "BaseForm";
this.AutoScaleBaseSize = new System.Drawing.Size (5, 13);
this.ClientSize = new System.Drawing.Size (312, 221);
this.Controls.Add (this.textBox6);
this.Controls.Add (this.textBox5);
```

```
        this.Controls.Add (this.textBox4);
        this.Controls.Add (this.textBox3);
        this.Controls.Add (this.textBox2);
        this.Controls.Add (this.textBox1);
        this.Controls.Add (this.label13);
        this.Controls.Add (this.label12);
        this.Controls.Add (this.label11);
    }


  }
}
```

There's nothing really new here, just a few labels and a few textbox controls. We could have added validation code or formatted the phone number field, but let's keep the example as short as we can. The only changes to this form is that we set the output of the project to be a class library and we removed the following code:

```
/// <summary>
/// The main entry point for the application.
/// </summary>
public static void Main(string[] args)
{
    Application.Run(new BaseForm());
}
```

Make sure you save the project. Now you will need to create a new Visual Basic Windows Application. In the Solutions window, add Base to the solution. You can also do this from the File | Add Project menu. Next you have to add a reference to the Base project in the Visual Basic project (Project | Properties, or right click on the references tab in the Solutions window). Now open Form1 of the Visual Basic project in code view and change the class declaration from this:

```
Public Class Form1
    Inherits System.WinForms.Form
```

to the following:

```
Public Class Form1
    Inherits Base.BaseForm
```

Save the form and redisplay it in the Forms Designer. You should see the controls that you added to the C# form grayed out in the designer. You can add controls, write additional code or do whatever you would normally do to a form. When you run the project, the address data fields from the C# form will be included in the new form. Any validation or business rule code that we would have had in the C# form would also be part of the new form.

Here is the code for the individual Visual Basic form:

```
Imports System.ComponentModel
Imports System.Drawing
Imports System.WinForms
```

```
Public Class Form1
    Inherits Base.BaseForm

    Public Sub New()
        MyBase.New

        Form1 = Me

        'This call is required by the Win Form Designer.
        InitializeComponent

        'TODO: Add any initialization after the InitializeComponent() call
    End Sub

    'Form overrides dispose to clean up the component list.
    Overrides Public Sub Dispose()
        MyBase.Dispose
        components.Dispose
    End Sub

#Region " Windows Form Designer generated code "

    'Required by the Windows Form Designer
    Private components As System.ComponentModel.Container
        Private WithEvents Label6 As System.WinForms.Label
        Private WithEvents Label5 As System.WinForms.Label
        Private WithEvents TextBox9 As System.WinForms.TextBox
        Private WithEvents TextBox8 As System.WinForms.TextBox
        Private WithEvents Label4 As System.WinForms.Label
        Private WithEvents TextBox7 As System.WinForms.TextBox

    Dim WithEvents Form1 As System.WinForms.Form

    'NOTE: The following procedure is required by the Windows Form Designer
    'It can be modified using the Windows Form Designer.
    'Do not modify it using the code editor.
    Private Sub InitializeComponent()
        Me.components = New System.ComponentModel.Container()
        Me.Label5 = New System.WinForms.Label()
        Me.Label6 = New System.WinForms.Label()
        Me.TextBox7 = New System.WinForms.TextBox()
        Me.Label4 = New System.WinForms.Label()
        Me.TextBox8 = New System.WinForms.TextBox()
        Me.TextBox9 = New System.WinForms.TextBox()

        '@design Me.TrayHeight = 0
        '@design Me.TrayLargeIcon = False
        '@design Me.TrayAutoArrange = True
        Label5.Location = New System.Drawing.Point(8, 152)
        Label5.Text = "Cell Phone:"
        Label5.Size = New System.Drawing.Size(100, 23)
        Label5.TabIndex = 13
        Label5.TextAlign = System.WinForms.HorizontalAlignment.Right
```

```
            Label16.Location = New System.Drawing.Point(8, 176)
            Label16.Text = "E-Mail:"
            Label16.Size = New System.Drawing.Size(100, 23)
            Label16.TabIndex = 14
            Label16.TextAlign = System.WinForms.HorizontalAlignment.Right

            TextBox7.Location = New System.Drawing.Point(112, 32)
            TextBox7.TabIndex = 9
            TextBox7.Size = New System.Drawing.Size(100, 20)

            Label4.Location = New System.Drawing.Point(8, 32)
            Label4.Text = "Name:"
            Label4.Size = New System.Drawing.Size(100, 23)
            Label4.TabIndex = 10
            Label4.TextAlign = System.WinForms.HorizontalAlignment.Right

            TextBox8.Location = New System.Drawing.Point(112, 152)
            TextBox8.TabIndex = 11
            TextBox8.Size = New System.Drawing.Size(100, 20)

            TextBox9.Location = New System.Drawing.Point(112, 176)
            TextBox9.TabIndex = 12
            TextBox9.Size = New System.Drawing.Size(100, 20)

            Me.Text = "Form1"
            Me.AutoScaleBaseSize = New System.Drawing.Size(5, 13)
            Me.ClientSize = New System.Drawing.Size(344, 269)

            Me.Controls.Add(Label16)
            Me.Controls.Add(Label15)
            Me.Controls.Add(TextBox9)
            Me.Controls.Add(TextBox8)
            Me.Controls.Add(Label14)
            Me.Controls.Add(TextBox7)
        End Sub

    #End Region

    End Class
```

The only difference in this form and any other form that we have is the class declaration. We added the controls for Name, Cell Phone and E-Mail, and that's it. Here is what the individual form looks like:

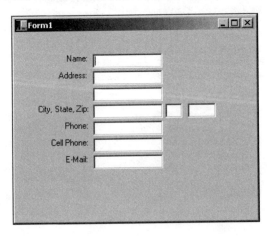

For the Company form, we would do the same process, except instead of adding the **Name**, **Cell Phone** and **E-Mail** fields, we would add **Company Name** and **Fax**. This is obviously a very contrived example, but it does prove that Visual Basic now does have visual inheritance. With a good design, you can take advantage of inheritance and make the applications that you develop robust and significantly easier to enhance than you could with Visual Basic 6's version of interface inheritance. Another thing that you can do is to inherit one of the base controls in the WinForms namespace. You could for example, inherit the `TextBox` class, set up your own `WndProc()` method, and trap all of the `WM_CHAR` messages that come in, rejecting the illegal characters that your backend system may not be able to handle.

Summary

In this chapter we took a brief look at WinForms. We looked from the perspective of the Visual Basic programmer who without question will gain the most out of the power and flexibility. C++/MFC programmers moving to Visual Basic or C# have something to gain as well, and that's ease of use and RAD (Rapid Application Development) capabilities. Everyone gains with features such as Visual Inheritance.

We looked at the event model, and how that has changed from Visual Basic 6, and what you will need to do in order to take advantage of the power. A study of delegates and how they work is a requirement to fully grasp what events can do for you.

The layout enhancements, Docking and Anchoring, were discussed. These are a long-awaited feature for Visual Basic programmers, since they will reduce ugly resizing code to nothing.

We also took a look at inheritance, the most anticipated feature of the .NET platform for VB programmers. Unfortunately it will also be the most abused and misused feature for a while. Good object-oriented design skills are not easy to develop. It will take a lot of trial and error before some developers will be able to master the OO concepts that are now part of the .NET platform.

Migration of existing Visual Basic applications should be mentioned here. As you may have noticed, there are some substantial differences between VB.NET and Visual Basic 5 and 6. Migrating an application will not be an easy task. There are many syntax changes, data types changes, and architectural changes to deal with. Microsoft has added a compatibility namespace (`Microsoft.VisualBasic`) to help in migration, as well as a migration tool to run your projects through, but it still will not be an easy task, especially a Visual Basic form to a Windows Form. You will need to look at your applications and decide which ones will benefit from being in the .NET framework. VB.NET and C# will work along side Visual Basic 6 and this may be the best migration path to take. It is safe to say however, that all of the new development that takes place will be in the .NET framework, and we all will benefit from that.

ODUCING.NETINTRODUCING.NETINTRODUCING.NETINTRODUCI
ETINTRODUCING.NETINTRODUCING.NETINTRODUCING.NETINT
CING.NETINTRODUCING.NETINTRODUCING.NETINTRODUCING.
NTRODUCING.NETINTRODUCING.NETINTRODUCING.NETINTROD
G.NETINTRODUCING.NETINTRODUCING.NETINTRODUCING.NET
ODUCING.NETINTRODUCING.NETINTRODUCING.NETINTRODUCI
ETINTRODUCING.NETINTRODUCING.NETINTRODUCING.NETINT
CING.NETINTRODUCING.NETINTRODUCING.NETINTRODUCING.
NTRODUCING.NETINTRODUCING.NETINTRODUCING.NETINTROD
G.NETINTRODUCING.NETINTRODUCING.NETINTRODUCING.NET
ODUCING.NETINTRODUCING.NETINTRODUCING.NETINTRODUCI
ETINTRODUCING.NETINTRODUCING.NETINTRODUCING.NETINT
CING.NETINTRODUCING.NETINTRODUCING.NETINTRODUCING.
NTRODUCING.NETINTRODUCING.NETINTRODUCING.NETINTROD
G.NETINTRODUCING.NETINTRODUCING.NETINTRODUCING.NET
ODUCING.NETINTRODUCING.NETINTRODUCING.NETINTRODUCI
ETINTRODUCING.NETINTRODUCING.NETINTRODUCING.NETINT
CING.NETINTRODUCING.NETINTRODUCING.NETINTRODUCING.
NTRODUCING.NETINTRODUCING.NETINTRODUCING.NETINTROD
G.NETINTRODUCING.NETINTRODUCING.NETINTRODUCING.NET
ODUCING.NETINTRODUCING.NETINTRODUCING.NETINTRODUCI
ETINTRODUCING.NETINTRODUCING.NETINTRODUCING.NETINT
CING.NETINTRODUCING.NETINTRODUCING.NETINTRODUCING.
NTRODUCING.NETINTRODUCING.NETINTRODUCING.NETINTROD
G.NETINTRODUCING.NETINTRODUCING.NETINTRODUCING.NET
ODUCING.NETINTRODUCING.NETINTRODUCING.NETINTRODUCI
ETINTRODUCING.NETINTRODUCING.NETINTRODUCING.NETINT
CING.NETINTRODUCING.NETINTRODUCING.NETINTRODUCING.
NTRODUCING.NETINTRODUCING.NETINTRODUCING.NETINTROD
G.NETINTRODUCING.NETINTRODUCING.NETINTRODUCING.NET
ODUCING.NETINTRODUCING.NETINTRODUCING.NETINTRODUCI
ETINTRODUCING.NETINTRODUCING.NETINTRODUCING.NETINT

10

Building .NET Components

Before beginning to build components using the new .NET Framework we need to look at how we will use these components as building blocks for applications. In the past, we have created applications out of COM components, compiled those COM components into DLLs, and then relied on the setup program of the application to make sure everything was installed properly. If we wanted to assemble all of the related DLLs for an application in one place, the only option would have been to use the file system. All the DLLs for an application could be put into one directory, registered within that directory, and then called from there when needed by the application.

The DLL allowed us to host our COM components in a set of files, but it was only good for holding executable code or compiled-in resources. While we could store icons directly in a DLL, there was no efficient way to store resources such as bitmaps or other images. As applications have progressively become more and more graphically rich, other resources needed a way to be included with them in a manageable way.

COM also gave us our first standard way to potentially reuse code between applications. By defining interfaces to interact with components, COM provided a defined way in which a component could be used. Because of this a single component could be used by multiple applications, even across process or machine boundaries. However, each COM component needed to have a complex plumbing arrangement attached to it in order for this to work. While advanced tools took care of a lot of the management of this plumbing, it still introduced a pretty sizeable overhead to the execution of the code. And if you were working with a less-capable tool, you were left having to write a lot of this plumbing yourself.

The external plumbing also meant that components couldn't interact directly with each other without going through it. Terms such as "Aggregating on the Free-Threaded Marshaller" became the words by which many a COM developer would perish. There was no explicit, simple way to provide direct interaction between components. You could not take an existing compiled COM component and subclass it to create a new component, without having access to the source code for the base component.

Under the .NET Framework, .NET components are all built upon a common infrastructure called the Common Language Runtime (which we looked at in Chapter 2). This replaces all of the COM plumbing that in the past we had to bolt on ourselves. Now components can interact as true objects with one another, while the hidden underlying code takes care of making it work.

In this chapter, we will be looking at building .NET components for use within both ASP.NET and WinForms applications. Specifically, we will be looking at:

❑   How Assemblies function as the primary unit of packaging and reuse in the .NET Framework

❑   Writing a Business Object using the .NET Framework

❑   Creating a class in one language and then inheriting from that class in a different language

❑   Working with unmanaged components and applications

❑   Assemblies

In Chapter 2, we looked at the concept of "managed code". Basically any code that is executed by the Common Language Runtime, regardless of the language it was written in, is considered to be managed code. Managed code supports things such as cross-language inheritance, cross-language exception handling, security boundaries, versioning and deployment support, and a simplified model for component interaction. Once we have written our managed code, we need a way to package that code so our applications, and possibly others, can take advantage of the services offered by it.

Assemblies are used by the .NET Framework to support the sharing and reuse of code. All classes must exist within in an assembly in order to be functional under the Common Language Runtime. The assembly contains the metadata that the Common Language Runtime uses to allow an object to function. Without an assembly, the component cannot function.

What are Assemblies

There is no concept of an assembly as a file. There is no such thing as an xxx.asb file that we need to worry about now. Rather an assembly is a collection of files that work together, and must all reside in the same directory on the disk. In fact, an assembly can contain more than just code, you can now add any resource files, such as bitmaps, which are needed for your code to function, into the assembly. The Common Language Runtime treats all these files as a single unit.

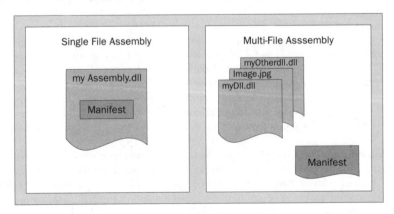

The assembly can be thought of as a logical DLL. In the past, we would have distributed components or resources through the deployment of a DLL. Now we distribute the pieces of an assembly in the same way. The main difference is that the DLL needed some other information somewhere – usually in the registry – to tell the system that it was available and ready to run. With an assembly, it carries that information along with it in its metadata.

An assembly is **not** an application. An application is built from one or more assemblies. The assemblies that make up an application can be deployed in a number of different ways. As an assembly contains its own metadata it is capable of telling the operating system all about itself. It does not rely on entries in the system registry to announce its existence.

Due to this, the easiest way to deploy an application is simply to copy all of its assemblies to a directory on the disk. This is known as XCOPY deployment, since the only tool required to deploy the files to disk is the XCOPY console command. When the application is first executed, the metadata within the assemblies will tell the system all that it needs to know in order to execute the application.

You can also use more traditional installation mechanisms to distribute applications built out of assemblies. For example you could build an `.msi` file and use the Windows Installer to deploy the files into the correct location. Likewise, you could build a `.cab` file and have a browser download the file to the system and then execute the application. In either event, all that the installation mechanism is responsible for is getting the proper files into the proper location on the destination system. No information about the assemblies needs to be added to the registry of the target system. This won't mean the registry will immediately disappear in future versions of the Windows OS, as it will be required to support legacy applications, but its role in application deployment under .NET is removed.

The End of DLL Hell

There are currently two problems with the Win32 architecture that have combined to give us what is known as DLL Hell. In DLL Hell, there is no control entity that is responsible for the management of all of the DLL files installed onto a system. Since the information about a COM DLL is only held in the registry, it can easily be over written by another application. Further an application can partially install over another, overwriting its DLL's. This can play havoc with any existing application that was relying on that particular DLL performing a specific function when a method is called.

One way that developers have tried to get around this is installing all of the DLLs needed by an application into the application's directory. This wasn't always a foolproof solution, as the registration of that DLL could cause changes to the registry that would affect other programs. However, what if an application relied on system DLLs, and, even worse, *specific versions* of system DLLs? How do developers deal with that?

One of the major problems with Win32 is that there is no system-level enforcement of versioning rules between components. It is left up to developers adhering to **best practices** coding, which says that once an interface is published it can never be changed. But there is nothing in the operating system that **explicitly** prevents changes from taking place. The other problem is that there is no way for an application to say that it needs version 1.2.1.1234 of a particular component. If the version that it finds is different, even if the interface is still intact, the code that it is relying on may no longer be there, or may not perform in the way expected. To try to combat this, Windows 2000 added **System File Protection**. This is an OS feature that can stop an installation program from overwriting system DLLs.

The Common Language Runtime extends this support by allowing developers to specify the specific version of a component that they want their application to use. It provides a means to make sure that the proper version is located and used by the requesting application. In doing this, it also allows for the execution of code from two similar components, that only differ in version. This is known as side-by-side execution and we will look at that a bit later in the chapter.

Assembly Manifest

In order for an assembly to describe itself to the Common Language Runtime it must contain a set of metadata. This metadata is contained in the assembly's manifest and specifies:

- ❑ The assembly version
- ❑ The security information for the assembly
- ❑ The scope of the assembly
- ❑ Information to resolve references to the resources and classes of the assembly

The manifest for an assembly can be stored in an EXE, a DLL, or a stand-alone file. You should remember that the assembly could be made up of one or more files, and there needn't be a specific file that contains it in its entirety. In a single-file assembly, the manifest is part of the file that comprises the assembly.

The manifest of an assembly lists all of the file and resources that make it up. It also lists all of the classes and types defined within it and specifies which resources or files they map onto. The manifest also identifies any other assemblies on which this assembly may be dependent.

Metadata

The manifest will specifically contain these pieces of metadata:

- ❑ **Assembly Name** – this is a textual string name that identifies the assembly. The name has a big impact on the scope of an assembly and how it can be used by multiple applications. When an assembly is used by only one application, the developer can generally enforce a unique name for it, thus preventing name collisions. However, when an assembly is shared, a more unique naming method must be used. This is called a **shared name**, and creating one allows the assembly to be stored in the **global assembly cache** that is used to store assemblies that can be used by several applications on a machine.

- ❑ **Version Information** – the components of the version number are the major and minor version numbers, a revision number, and a build number. This is represented as a set of four numbers with the format:

  ```
  <major version>.<minor version>.<build number>.<revision>
  ```

  When the Common Language Runtime is checking to see if an assembly is the proper version it first checks the major and minor version numbers. These **must** match in order for the assembly to be compatible. If these two numbers match but the build number is different, then as long as the build number of the assembly is greater than the build required by the application, it can be assumed to be compatible with the version expected by the application.

- ❑ **Assembly File List** – lists each file contained in the assembly, along with the relative path to the file. For version 1b of the .NET Framework, all files in an assembly must be in the same directory as the manifest file.

❑ **Type reference information** – maps all of the types included in the assembly to the specific file within it where they are contained. This is necessary so that the Runtime can resolve any types referenced within the classes contained in the assembly.

❑ **Referenced Assemblies** – lists all of the other assemblies that are statically referenced within the types contained in this assembly. Each entry contains the assembly name along with the required version information.

There is also custom metadata that can be included by the developer. Only the developer can use this information – the Common Language Runtime does not reference it in any way. In the first release of the .NET Framework, there are two sets of custom assembly metadata. The first set is made up of nine classes from the `System.Reflection` namespace. You can use this namespace to query the values for this metadata at runtime. It contains:

❑ Company information

❑ Build information, such as "Retail" or "Debug"

❑ Copyright information

❑ Additional naming and version information

❑ Assembly Title and Description

❑ Product and Trademark Information

The second set is made up of classes from the `System.Runtime.CompilerServices` namespace. This metadata includes:

❑ Cultures or languages supported by the assembly

❑ A Flag to indicated the assembly will be signed after compilation

❑ OS and Processors the assembly has been built to support. (Version 1 of the Common Language Runtime does not use this information)

Self-Describing Components

With other application architectures, the only way for components to communicate is through a binary interface. If these components were written in different languages, then there is a good chance that they will store data differently as well. This leads to problems with communication between the two components. In the .NET Framework, the metadata that is presented by each assembly helps to alleviate this confusion, as does the Common Language Runtime.

Since the components within an assembly are so thoroughly defined by the metadata, you can even define a new class that inherits from an existing class directly from the source code, without accessing it. In fact, the components don't even need to be in the same language, provided both are managed components. We will see an example of this later in this chapter.

The assemblies and the components within them are said to be "self-describing." This means that they carry all the information that other components need to know in order to interact with them. This information is all carried within the metadata of the assembly. There are no more IDL files in the .NET Framework, nor are there public header files that get out of sync with the executables. You are always ensured that the metadata information being used by the runtime is the proper metadata for the code being executed since they are held together within the assembly.

Side-by-Side Execution

The ability to run multiple versions of the same component at the same time is a very valuable feature of the Common Language Runtime. It can even execute two versions of a component within the same process. The ability to do this is called side-by-side execution. By allowing this, the .NET Framework offers the developer a substantial advantage over COM architectures.

When creating new versions of a component, a developer doesn't have to worry much about maintaining compatibility with previous versions, since the older component can run alongside the new one. The application using the component knows which version to use and both can coexist peacefully on the same machine. There are some precautions that the developer should take into account when having components that will run side-by-side with previous versions, though. For example, if the component is relying on a physical file as a data cache, then two components executing side-by-side will try to access that same file. For this to work the components would need to be written such that they keep the file in a location that is dependent on the version of the component being executed.

There are two ways that components can be side-by-side executed on the same machine either running in separate processes or running in the same process. When running components side-by-side in the same process, even more precautions should be taken, as the risk of overlap is substantially increased. These precautions involve how the components deal with process-wide resources to make sure that there are no conflicts or resource contention.

Writing Business Objects

Now that we understand the packaging concepts of the .NET Framework, we can turn our attention to using that knowledge to creating business objects that can be used by .NET applications. These business objects will perform the same types of functions that business objects in COM or other objects models do. But they will also be able to take advantage of all of the benefits offered by the .NET Framework and the Common Language Runtime.

In this section, we will look at how to create an object, and how we can utilize some of the COM+ component services within this .NET object. After creating the object, we will then compile it and place it in an assembly. Once the assembly is created, we can create a .NET application to test our new object. Finally, we will look at how we can take a class developed in one language and inherit from it in another language.

Throughout this section, we will be creating two example components. These components will perform exactly the same functions. The only difference will be that one will be written using C# and the other will be written using VB.NET. We will test these objects from an ASP.NET page, but you could just as easily test them from a WinForms or Command Line Application. We will be using a simple text editor to create the file, and using the command line compilers and tools to create the assemblies.

Creating the Object

When we begin to create our object, there are a couple of things that we need to look at. First, we need to acquaint ourselves with various guidelines for creating a component. Then, before getting started, we need to look at the various attributes that can be set to describe a component. Once we've done that we can move on to actually creating the design components.

Class Design Guidelines

As we begin to write components for this new application paradigm, some of our old, trusted design guidelines can continue to be used. However, just as the application paradigm has shifted under the .NET Framework, so some of the design guidelines we have used in the past are now implemented in a different way. For example where once guideline implementation differed between languages, now they are all aligned under the .NET Framework, and implemented in the same manner.

Error Handling

Now that robust error handling, including structured exception handling, is part of the .NET Framework it is available to all languages supported by the Framework and you should use it wherever possible. The former practice of using error codes and checking return values has been replaced with catching exceptions and handling the errors at that point. However, that doesn't mean you should use exceptions everywhere. Exceptions are designed to handle **errors** and consequently are something you should not expect to happen. That being said, however, there are instances where error codes can come in handy. For example, if you are trying to open a file and the file doesn't exist, then return a null value, since that error could be expected in normal use, but if the File System returns an I/O error, then throw an exception, since that condition isn't one normally expected.

Properties versus Methods

One of the most difficult choices in designing a component is choosing the type of interface to use. This holds true for all component-based architectures, not just the .NET platform. When to use a property as opposed to using a method and vice-versa is as much a matter of personal taste as it is the following of design guidelines, but for completeness the guidelines are:

❑ If there is an internal data member being exposed outside the component, then use a property.

❑ If the execution of the code causes some measurable side effect to the component or the environment, then use a method.

❑ If the order of code execution is important, then use a method. Since the Common Language Runtime has the ability to short-circuit expression testing, a property may not be accessed when you expect it will.

Memory Management

Memory management has to be one of the most difficult things that many programmers have to face. Actually the memory portion is rather easy to deal with – it is the management that seems to drive most developers crazy! Happily, with the Common Language Runtime, handling most of the memory management for our .NET components, there are only a few things that we need to do differently when dealing with memory than we did in the past.

The Common Language Runtime has the ability to create small, short-lived objects very quickly and cheaply. This means you shouldn't worry about creating objects that will make your development easier to follow. In fact, the runtime can allocate nearly 10 million objects per second on a moderately fast machine. Also an object running in the Common Language Runtime will be Garbage Collected once it is no longer being referenced. This will happen automatically, and keeps the developer from having to deal with memory leaks from improperly freed objects.

Using Attributes

Attributes in the Common Language Runtime allow developers to add additional information to the classes they have created. These are then available to the application using the component through the `System.Reflection` classes. You can use attributes to provide hints or flags to a number of different systems that may be using your component. Attributes can be used as compiler flags to tell the compiler how to handle the compilation of a class. A tool like Visual Studio.NET can use them to provide more information about the usage of the component at design time. Attributes can also be used to identify the transaction characteristics of a class when interacting with the component services of the operating system.

There are a set of standard attributes for properties and events that are defined in the `System.ComponentModel` class in the Common Language Runtime. As these attributes are already defined, they can be used by the developer without having to create a corresponding class for a custom attribute.

Attributes for Events and Properties

Attribute	Used for	Usage
BrowsableAttribute	Declares if this property should appear in the property window of a design tool.	[Browsable (false/true)]
CategoryAttribute	Used to group properties when being displayed by a design tool.	[Category (categoryName)]
DescriptionAttribute	Help text displayed by the design tool when this property or event is selected.	[Description (descriptionString)]

Attributes for Properties

Attribute	Used for	Usage
BindableAttribute	Declares if data should be bound to this property.	[Bindable (false/true)]
DefaultPropertyAttribute	Indicates that this is the default property for the class.	[DefaultProperty]
DefaultValueAttribute	Sets a default value for the property.	[DefaultValue (value)]
LocalizableAttribute	Indicates that a property can be localized. The compiler will cause all properties with this attribute to store the property in a resource file. You can then localize the resource file without having to modify any code.	[Localizable (false/true)]
PersistableAttribute	Indicates that a property should be saved when the object is persisted.	[Persistable (false/true)]

Attributes for Events

Attribute	Used for	Usage
DefaultEventAttribute	Specifies the default event for the class.	[DefaultEvent]

Our Sample Object

In this chapter, we will be creating a sample object. The sample object will be used to encapsulate business and data access functionality – this is the typical usage for objects in the applications that most developers are creating. Our business object will encapsulate the interaction with the Pubs sample database that is provided with SQL Server 7 or 2000. Since this more an example of how to build components, rather than a full case study on a business and data component, our component will have limited functionality.

The component will have one property:

Property Name	Type	Usage
DatabaseConnection	String	The DSN that will be used to connect to the database

The component will have three methods:

Method Name	Returns	Parameters	Usage
GetAuthors	DataSet	*none*	Returns a DataSet containing the names and IDs of all of the authors contained in the database
GetTitlesForAuthor	StringCollection	authorID	Returns an array containing the titles for the specified author
TotalSalesForAuthor	Integer	authorID	Returns the total sales for an author

Now that we know what the interface to our component is going to be, we can set about writing it. As we stated earlier, we will show how to develop the component in both Visual Basic.NET and in C#. We will start with the C# version.

C# Class Example

Here is how the final class looks when written in C#. We will then break down each part and describe what it does and how.

```
using System;
using System.Data;
using System.Data.SQL;
using System.Collections;


namespace BusObjectCS {

    public class PubsAccess {
```

```
private string m_DSN;

public PubsAccess () { }

public PubsAccess (string DSN) {
   m_DSN = DSN;
}

public string DatabaseConnection {
   set { m_DSN = value; }
   get { return m_DSN; }
}

public DataSet GetAuthors () {
   SQLConnection dbConnection = new SQLConnection(m_DSN);
   dbConnection.Open();

   SQLDataSetCommand sqlCommand = new SQLDataSetCommand(
"SELECT au_id, au_fname + ' ' + au_lname AS au_name FROM authors",
                                                dbConnection);
   DataSet authors = new DataSet();
   sqlCommand.FillDataSet(authors, "authors");
   dbConnection.Close();
   return authors;
}

public StringCollection GetTitlesForAuthor (string authorID) {

   StringCollection collTitles = new StringCollection();

   SQLConnection dbConnection = new SQLConnection(m_DSN);
   dbConnection.Open();

   SQLDataSetCommand sqlCommand = new SQLDataSetCommand(
"SELECT title FROM titles INNER JOIN titleauthor ON titles.title_id
      = titleauthor.title_id WHERE (au_id = '" + authorID + "')",
         dbConnection);

   DataSet titles = new DataSet();
   sqlCommand.FillDataSet(titles, "titles");

   DataRow[] titleRows;
   titleRows = titles.Tables["titles"].Select();

   for (int i=0; i <= titleRows.Length - 1; i++){
      collTitles.Add (titleRows[i]["title"].ToString());
   }
   return collTitles;
}

   public int TotalSalesForAuthor (string authorID) {
   SQLConnection dbConnection = new SQLConnection(m_DSN);
   dbConnection.Open();
```

```
            SQLDataSetCommand sqlCommand = new SQLDataSetCommand(
            "SELECT SUM(ytd_sales) AS TotalSales FROM titles INNER JOIN
                titleauthor ON titles.title_id = titleauthor.title_id WHERE
                (au_id = '" + authorID + "')", dbConnection);

            DataSet SalesTotal = new DataSet();
            sqlCommand.FillDataSet(SalesTotal, "SalesTotal");

            DataTable titleTable;
            titleTable = SalesTotal.Tables["SalesTotal"];
            if (titleTable.Rows.Count > 0)
            {
                return (int)titleTable.Rows[0]["TotalSales"];
                }
            else
                return 0;
        }
    }
}
```

Now, let's take a look at the object in detail. The first thing we do in the file is state which parts of the **System Frameworks** we will be using in this object.

```
using System;
using System.Data;
using System.Data.SQL;
using System.Collections;
```

We can actually use any part of the System Frameworks at any time in our code by simply referencing the full path to it, `System.Data.SQL.DataTable`, but that would begin to make our code cumbersome and unnecessarily long. By explicit stating which parts of the System Frameworks we will be using, we can refer to the particular class without having to state the full path.

In this object, we will be using the `System` namespace, which contains the necessary base classes to build our object. The `System.Data` namespace contains the classes that make up the ADO.NET data access architecture. Since our data will be accessed from a SQL Server 2000 database, we will also include the `System.Data.SQL` namespace. This namespace contains the classes to access the SQL Server managed provider. Finally, we will also be using a collection to move our data around, so we need the `System.Collections` namespace included as well.

```
namespace BusObjectCS {

    public class PubsAccess {
```

We will be encapsulating our object within its own unique namespace, `BusObjectCS`, so we need to declare all of the classes that make up our object within that namespace. Our business component is defined as a class – when we actually create an instance of it in our program we will then have an object.

```
        private string m_DSN;

        public PubsAccess () { }

        public PubsAccess (string DSN) {
            m_DSN = DSN;
        }
```

Within our object, there will be one private variable, which will be used to hold the database connection string. The next two methods are the constructors for the class. The constructor is automatically called by the runtime when an object is instantiated. We have actually created two constructors. The first one takes no parameters and is therefore called the default constructor. The second constructor takes a parameter, DSN, and will set the database connection string when the object is created.

```
public string DatabaseConnection {
    set { m_DSN = value; }
    get { return m_DSN; }
}
```

The second constructor allows us to set the database connection string when the object is created we also need to provide a way to set and read it at other times. Since the member variable holding this data is marked as `private`, we need to provide a property function to set and retrieve the value. The external name of the property is DatabaseConnection. Next, we will look at the methods that allow us to work with the information in the database.

```
public DataSet GetAuthors () {
    SQLConnection dbConnection = new SQLConnection(m_DSN);
    dbConnection.Open();
```

The first method, GetAuthors, will let us retrieve a listing of the authors stored in the database. We will return the listing to the calling program in a DataSet. A DataSet represents an in-memory cache of data. This means that it is a *copy* of the data in the database, so there is no underlying connection to the stored data. To access the database, we will first need to connect to it. The SQLConnection object provides this functionality and when its Open method is called, it will connect to the database using the connection string that was stored in the private member variable m_DSN.

```
SQLDataSetCommand sqlCommand = new SQLDataSetCommand(
"SELECT au_id, au_fname + ' ' + au_lname AS au_name FROM authors",
                                            dbConnection);
```

To retrieve the desired information from the database, we will be using an SQL Query. To process the query, we will be using the SQLDataSetCommand object. When we create the object, we will pass in the text of the SQL Query that will be executed by this object. We also tell the object which database connection object to use to access the data. That is the object that was created and opened in the previous steps.

```
DataSet authors = new DataSet();
sqlCommand.FillDataSet(authors, "authors");
return authors;
}
```

Now that we have the mechanism for retrieving the data from the database, we need a place to store it to pass it back to the caller. This will be in a DataSet object. We will create a new instance of this class and call it authors. The data will be placed in this object by using the FillDataSet method of the SQLDataSetCommand class. This method takes the destination DataSet object as well as a name to represent the data within the data set. To send the data back to the caller, we will return the DataSet object authors.

```
public StringCollection GetTitlesForAuthor (string authorID) {

    StringCollection collTitles = new StringCollection();
```

The next method will allow us to retrieve the list of titles for a specified author. We will specify the author by passing in the author ID string. The list of titles will be returned as a collection of strings, defined by the `StringCollection` class. To hold the results of our search, we will first create an instance of the class and call it `collTitles`. The next part of the method is the same as the previous method, in that we connect to the database and fill up a `DataSet` object with the information we want. However, instead of passing that `DataSet` back to the caller, we will fill up our string collection with the data.

```
DataRow[] titleRows;
titleRows = titles.Tables["titles"].Select();
```

There is no Framework method to copy from a `DataSet` to a `StringCollection`, so we will need to take a bit more of a brute force approach. We will want to move through each row in the `DataSet` and then take the value we want from each row and add that to the `StringCollection`. To be able to move through the `DataSet` row by row, we need to first create an array of `DataRow` objects. Then we use the `Select` method to copy the rows from the table named `titles` in the `DataSet` to the array.

```
for (int i=0; i <= titleRows.Length - 1; i++){
    collTitles.Add (titleRows[i]["title"].ToString());
}
return collTitles;
}
```

With the data we want now copied to the array, we can iterate through the array and add each entry to the `StringCollection` using the `Add` method. The resulting filled `collTitles` object can then be returned to the calling application. Next, we will look at the method to calculate the total sales for a specified author.

```
public int TotalSalesForAuthor (string authorID) {
```

The method to calculate the total sales for an author will pass that value back as an integer return value. Just as with the previous method, the one parameter for this method will be the author ID of the desired author. The database access code is again very similar, the primary difference being that the SQL statement will be calculating a **sum** rather than returning a set of rows from the database.

```
DataTable titleTable;
titleTable = SalesTotal.Tables["SalesTotal"];
if (titleTable.Rows.Count > 0)
{
    return (int)titleTable.Rows[0]["TotalSales"];
}
else
    return 0;
}
}
}
```

With the results of the database query in the `DataSet` object, we will want to take a look at the contents of the data to see what the total sales were. If there was no data returned, we will have a table with no rows in it. If this is the case, then we can return the total sales as 0. If there is one row in the table an SQL statement to calculate a sum will return at most one row; if this is the case we will look at the value contained in the field named `TotalSales` and return that value as the total sales for the author. The field named `TotalSales` does not exist in the physical database, but is rather an alias that we created with the SQL SELECT statement to hold the results of the `Sum()` function.

This brings us to the end of our C# class. Before we look at how to compile and test it, we will look at the exact same component coded in Visual Basic.NET.

VB.NET Class Example

Here is a look at the same class when written in Visual Basic.NET. We will then look at the differences between this version and the C# version that we have just coded.

```
Option Explicit
Option Strict

Imports System
Imports System.Data
Imports System.Data.SQL
Imports System.Collections


namespace BusObjectVB

   public class PubsAccess

      private m_DSN as String

         public overloads Sub New()
         MyBase.New
      end Sub

      public overloads Sub New(DSN as string)
         MyBase.New
         m_DSN = DSN
      end sub

      public Property DatabaseConnection as string
         set
            m_DSN = value
         end set
         get
            return m_DSN
         end get
      end Property

      public function GetAuthors () as DataSet
         dim dbConnection as new SQLConnection(m_DSN)
         dbConnection.Open()

         dim sqlCommand as new SQLDataSetCommand("SELECT au_id, au_fname + _
                        ' ' + au_lname AS au_name FROM authors", dbConnection)
         dim authors as new DataSet()
         sqlCommand.FillDataSet(authors, "authors")
         return authors
      end Function

      public Function GetTitlesForAuthor (authorID as string) as _
                                          StringCollection
```

```
        Dim collTitles as new StringCollection()

        dim dbConnection as new SQLConnection(m_DSN)
        dbConnection.Open()

        dim sqlCommand as new SQLDataSetCommand("SELECT title FROM titles _
                INNER JOIN titleauthor ON titles.title_id = _
                titleauthor.title_id WHERE (au_id = '" + authorID + _
                "')", dbConnection)

        dim titles as new DataSet()
        sqlCommand.FillDataSet(titles, "titles")

        dim titleRows() as DataRow
        titleRows = titles.Tables("titles").Select()

        dim i as integer

        for i=0 to titleRows.Length - 1
           collTitles.Add (titleRows(i)("title").ToString())
           next i
        return collTitles
    end Function

    public Function TotalSalesForAuthor (authorID as string) as integer
        dim dbConnection as new SQLConnection(m_DSN)
        dbConnection.Open()

        dim sqlCommand as new SQLDataSetCommand("SELECT SUM(ytd_sales) AS _
                TotalSales FROM titles INNER JOIN titleauthor ON _
                titles.title_id = titleauthor.title_id WHERE (au_id = _
                '" + authorID + "')", dbConnection)

        dim SalesTotal as new DataSet()
        sqlCommand.FillDataSet(SalesTotal, "SalesTotal")

        dim titleTable as DataTable
        titleTable = SalesTotal.Tables("SalesTotal")
        if not titleTable.Rows(0).IsNull("TotalSales") then
           return CInt(titleTable.Rows(0)("TotalSales"))
        else
           return 0
        end if
    end Function

  end Class
end Namespace
```

Let's now look at this object in detail. We will be focusing on the differences in the Visual Basic.NET version over the C# version. The functionality is exactly the same.

```
Option Explicit
Option Strict

Imports System
Imports System.Data
Imports System.Data.SQL
Imports System.Collections
```

The first two statements are unique to Visual Basic. With its roots as a loosely-typed language, Visual Basic.NET has had some directives added to it to tell the compiler that it should do some level of type checking when compiling the application. The Option Explicit statement is familiar to Visual Basic.NET programmers. It forces the declaration of all variables before they are used, and will generate a compiler error if a variable is used before it is declared. The Option Strict statement is new to Visual Basic.NET. It greatly limits the implicit data type conversions that VB has been able to do in the past. Option Strict also disallows any late binding.

The next set of statements is used to specify the System Framework namespaces that will be used by this class. Rather than using the C# keyword Using, Visual Basic.NET uses the keyword Imports. As mentioned earlier, we will be using the same four namespaces as we did in the C# version.

```
namespace BusObjectVB

    public class PubsAccess
```

The next step is to declare the namespace and the class that we will be creating. Note that the name of the class is exactly the same as in the previous C# version. This is OK, and we can even run both at the same time, because class names only need to be unique within a namespace, and the namespaces differ from the C# (BusObjectCS) to VB (BusObjectVB) versions.

```
public overloads Sub New()
    MyBase.New
end Sub

public overloads Sub New(DSN as string)
    MyBase.New
    m_DSN = DSN
end sub
```

The next major difference between the two implementations is in the way that constructors are defined. In C#, a constructor is defined with a method that has the same name as the class. In Visual Basic, the constructor for a class is always named New(). And since a constructor cannot return any values, it is declared as a Sub rather than a Function. Next, we need to tell Visual Basic.NET that we are creating multiple versions of this method with different parameter lists. To do this, we add the keyword Overloads to the method declaration. Finally, in Visual Basic, we must *explicitly* call the constructor for our base class – using the MyBase.New statement. In C#, the base class constructor is called automatically by the compiler.

```
public Property DatabaseConnection as string
    set
        m_DSN = value
    end set
    get
        return m_DSN
    end get
end Property
```

A property is defined in a similar way to C#, but just using a different syntax to declare the accessor methods. Whereas in C# you use a set or get statement followed by a block delimited by braces ({...}), in Visual Basic.NET you use a specific set...end set or get...end get block to denote the accessor methods.

The remainder of the component is identical to the C# version, except for the language syntax differences. With both of our components created, we can move on to the next step, compilation.

Compiling the Classes

As we saw in the early chapters of the book, the .NET Framework executes code stored in the MSIL format. This intermediate language is created from the source code of the various languages supported by the Common Language Runtime. We have already created the source code for our components. The next step is to compile this source code into the MSIL version. This is done by executing the appropriate compiler, with the proper arguments based on the language and destination.

Compiling the C# Class

For the C# component, we will be using the C# compiler. The C# compiler is `csc.exe`, and in beta one of the .NET Framework it can be found in the directory:

C:\WINNT\Microsoft.NET\Framework\v1.0.2204.

> *As newer builds of the .NET Framework are released, the directory name will change. The version number of the build is also the name of the directory. So in future builds, the path will be:*
>
> *C:\WINNT\Microsoft.NET\Framework\v1.0.<version>*

To make it easier to execute the compiler, the installation of the .NET Framework will place this directory in the system path. Therefore, all we need to do to execute the compiler is type `csc` at the command prompt.

In this chapter we will only be using the command line versions of the compilers. Many of you will be using Visual Studio.NET to create your .NET components, which will automatically call the compiler for you. However, by first learning the command line versions, you will have a better understanding of what Visual Studio.NET is doing under the covers for you.

To make it easier to run the compiler during development, we will be creating a batch file that will execute the compiler with all of the proper parameters. This file will be called `makecs.bat` and look like this:

```
csc /out:bin\BusObjectcs.dll /t:library BusObjectCS.cs /r:System.Data.dll
/r:System.dll
```

Next, let's take a look at the parameters that we pass to the compiler. The first parameter, `/out`, defines the output filename that the MSIL code will be placed in. In this example, the compiled output will be placed in the file named `BusObjectcs.dll`, and will be stored in the subdirectory named `bin` below the directory where the source file resides. If we did not include an `/out` parameter, then the compiler would have automatically created the filename based on the name of the source file and the target type and placed it in the current directory.

The next parameter, `/t`, is used to specify the type of output file format the compiler should create. This is a shortened version of the `/target` parameter, and either version can be legally used. There are four possible values for this parameter:

- ❑ **/target:exe** – this tells the compiler to create a command line executable program. This is the default value, so if the `/target` parameter is not included, an `.exe` file will be created.

- ❑ **/target:library** – this tells the compiler to create a DLL file that will contain an assembly that consists of all of the source files passed to the compiler. The compiler will also automatically create the manifest for this assembly.

- ❑ **/target:module** – this tells the compiler to create a DLL, but not to create a manifest for it. This means that in order for the module to be used by the .NET Framework, it will need to be manually added to an assembly by the developer.

- ❑ **/target:winexe** – this tells the compiler to create a WinForms application.

The next parameter is the name of the file to be compiled. In our example, the source file is named `BusObjectCS.cs`. The file extension is not critical, but it does make it easier to recognize the type of source file it is without having to open it up. If there are multiple source files, you can specify multiple source files on the same command line. They will be combined into the file type specified by the `/target` parameter.

The final set of parameters indicates the other assemblies that are referenced from within our component. Since the compiler will need to access the metadata within these assemblies in order to properly build our class, we have to tell the compiler which ones to include. For this example class, we are using the data access classes stored in the `System.Data` assembly and the collection classes stored in the `System` assembly.

When we execute the `makecs.bat` file, we will get the following output:

Since everything worked properly, at least there were no compile-time bugs in the code anyway, no errors were generated. If we change the `makecs.bat` file to not include the references to the other assemblies that we need and then execute it, here is what the output would look like:

As you can see, when we remove the reference to the assemblies that we have used in our component, error messages are generated as soon as the using statements are compiled. The numbers (2, 14) indicate the line number and character position where the compiler encountered the error. You can use this to quickly locate where the errors are in your code.

A new feature in Windows 2000 is the fact that Notepad now has the ability to jump to specified line numbers. Just press Ctrl-G and enter the line number you want to jump to. Be careful, if you have word wrap turned on, this can mess up your line number count.

Compiling the VB.NET Class

To compile our Visual Basic.NET component, we will use a similar batch file. This file is named makevb.bat.

```
vbc /out:bin\BusObjectvb.dll /t:library BusObjectVB.vb /r:System.Data.dll
/r:System.dll
```

As you can see, it is identical to the makecs.bat file except for three small changes. First, since we are calling the Visual Basic.NET compiler rather than the C# compiler, the file to execute is vbc instead of csc. The second difference is the name of the output file. Since we are creating a separate assembly for the Visual Basic.NET component, we gave it a different name of BusObjectvb.dll. Finally, the source file that contains the Visual Basic.NET code is called BusObjectVB.vb.

The output from running the makevb.bat file looks like:

You can see that the output from the Visual Basic.NET compiler is almost identical to the output from the C# compiler, except for its name. There is one additional important piece of information that you can take from the results of the compiler. As Microsoft develops the .NET Frameworks and the Common Language Runtime, they will be releasing new versions of it prior to the final release. As of now, we are working with the beta one release of the Frameworks. Microsoft has stated that it will try to maintain compatibility moving forward, but will not guarantee it. However, the information that we can gather from the compiler is the version number of the .NET Frameworks that are installed on our machine. You can see from above that the .NET Framework Common Language Runtime version is 1.00.2204.21. We know that this version number is the version number for the beta one release. This is the case with all compilers in the .NET Framework.

Testing the Class

Now that we have created our two identical objects, we need a way to test them. We can use these components from any application that is supported by the Common Language Runtime. This means that we could create a console application that uses the components, a WinForms application, another component, or perhaps an ASP.NET page. For the purposes of our test, we will access these components from within an ASP.NET page. We saw in Chapter 7 how to create ASP.NET pages, so we will focus on how to use our components from within a page.

Our first page will test the `GetAuthors()` method. This page will simply be used to display the results of a call to this method. The source code for the page looks like this:

```
<%@ Page Language="C#" Description="Component Test Program" %>
<%@ Import Namespace="System.Data" %>
<%@ Import Namespace="System.Data.ADO" %>
<%@ Import Namespace="BusObjectCS" %>
<%@ Import Namespace="BusObjectVB" %>
<html>
<script language="C#" runat="server" >

void Page_Load(Object sender, EventArgs evArgs){
    BusObjectCS.PubsAccess objPubs = new BusObjectCS.PubsAccess();
//    BusObjectVB.PubsAccess objPubs = new BusObjectVB.PubsAccess();

    String dsn = "server=localhost;uid=sa;pwd=;database=pubs";
    objPubs.DatabaseConnection = dsn;

    DataSet authors = objPubs.GetAuthors();

    DataView authorView = new DataView (authors.Tables[0]);
    dgAuthors.DataSource = authorView;
    dgAuthors.DataBind();

}

</script>

<body>
<h3><font face="Verdana">List of Authors</font></h3>

<asp:DataList id="dgAuthors" runat="server">

<template name="HeaderTemplate">
<table border=1>
    <tr><th>Click to Display list of titles</th><th>Author Name</th></tr>
</template>

<template name="ItemTemplate">
<tr>
<td align=center>
    <a href="displayTitles.aspx?auid=<%# DataBinder.Eval(Container.DataItem,
        "au_id", "{0:c}") %>"><%# DataBinder.Eval(Container.DataItem, "au_id",
                                                    "{0:c}") %></a>
</td>
```

```
<td>
<%# DataBinder.Eval(Container.DataItem, "au_name", "{0:c}") %>
</td>
</tr>
</template>

<template name="FooterTemplate">
</table>
</template>

</asp:DataList>

</body>
</html>
```

The first part of the page sets up the language we will be using, as well as the namespaces of the assemblies that will be used on the page.

```
<%@ Page Language="C#" Description="Component Test Program" %>
<%@ Import Namespace="System.Data" %>
<%@ Import Namespace="System.Data.ADO" %>
<%@ Import Namespace="BusObjectCS" %>
<%@ Import Namespace="BusObjectVB" %>
```

The code in this page will be written using C#. Remember that under .NET the language we use in our ASP.NET page does not have to correlate to the language we used in our business components. Since both the page and the components will be compiled to MSIL before they are executed.

We will also need to include the namespaces of the assemblies we are using. Even though we are not calling any of the methods from the `System.Data` namespace, we are using one of the classes (`DataSet`) as a return value from the method in our component. In order for the page to understand how to deal with this class, we have to add the namespace that contains it as an @Import to the page. Since this page will be used to test both the C# and VB versions of our component, we need to import the namespaces for both. We could comment out the one that we are not using, but since this statement is simply a compiler directive, no additional code gets added if we don't use the class in our page.

```
void Page_Load(Object sender, EventArgs evArgs){
    BusObjectCS.PubsAccess objPubs = new BusObjectCS.PubsAccess();
//   BusObjectVB.PubsAccess objPubs = new BusObjectVB.PubsAccess();
```

Within our `Page_Load` method, we will be working with the data provided by our business component. This test page will be used to test both components. Since each component has **exactly** the same interface (properties and methods), we can use the same local variable to represent the one we want. We simply will have two lines in the page (one of which will be commented out) that create the object in the language that we want to test. In our test page, the first line will create the C# version of the component, and the second the VB version.

```
String dsn = "server=localhost;uid=sa;pwd=;database=pubs";
objPubs.DatabaseConnection = dsn;
```

The component needs to know where to retrieve its data. We will pass in a database connection string as the `DatabaseConnection` property of the object. This value is simply stored in the page as a string. In a production environment, values like database connection strings are usually stored in the `config.web` file for the ASP.NET application.

```
DataSet authors = objPubs.GetAuthors();

DataView authorView = new DataView (authors.Tables[0]);
dgAuthors.DataSource = authorView;
dgAuthors.DataBind();
```

Once the instance of our class has been created and initialized with the proper database connection string, we can call the `GetAuthors()` method to return the list of authors. This data will be passed back as a `DataSet` and store in the local variable name `authors`. From this data set, we will be selecting the `DataView` that corresponds to the only table in the `DataSet`. This `DataView` will serve as the data source for the `asp:DataList` element named `dgAuthors` that will actually display the data for us. By calling the `DataBind()` method, the values in the `DataView` will be rendered out into the `DataList` element.

```
<template name="ItemTemplate">
<tr>
<td align=center>
    <a href="displayTitles.aspx?auid=<%# DataBinder.Eval(Container.DataItem,
        "au_id", "{0:c}") %>"><%# DataBinder.Eval(Container.DataItem,
        "au_id", "{0:c}") %></a>
</td>

<td>
<%# DataBinder.Eval(Container.DataItem, "au_name", "{0:c}") %>
</td>
</tr>
</template>
```

Our `asp:DataList` will use a template to add some formatting to the data. The header and footer will simply begin and end the `TABLE` element being used to display the data. The `ItemTemplate` template sets up the format for each row in the table. In this row, there will be two columns. The first will be the author ID string as a hyperlink to the page named `displayTitles.aspx`. The value of the author ID will be passed to this page as part of the Query String. The second column will contain the author's name.

When we display this page in our browser, the following is displayed:

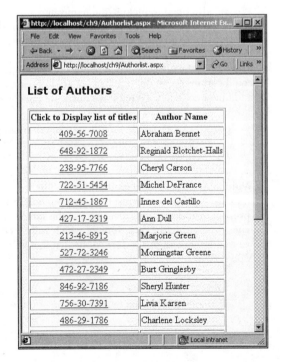

When the user clicks on any of the hyperlinks, they will be taken to the details test page that we have created called `displayTitles.aspx`. This page's source code looks like this:

```
<%@ Page Language="C#" Description="Component Test Program - Title List"
Debug="True" %>
<%@ Import Namespace="System.Collections" %>
<%@ Import Namespace="BusObjectCS" %>
<%@ Import Namespace="BusObjectVB" %>

<html>
<script language="C#" runat=server>
void Page_Load(Object sender, EventArgs evArgs){
//    BusObjectCS.PubsAccess objPubs = new BusObjectCS.PubsAccess();
    BusObjectVB.PubsAccess objPubs = new BusObjectVB.PubsAccess();

    String dsn = "server=localhost;uid=sa;pwd=;database=pubs";
    objPubs.DatabaseConnection = dsn;

    StringCollection titles =
        objPubs.GetTitlesForAuthor(Request.QueryString["auid"]);
    titlegrid.DataSource = titles;
    titlegrid.DataBind();

    totalSales.Text =
        objPubs.TotalSalesForAuthor(Request.QueryString["auid"]).Format(
        "c", null );
}

</script>

<body>

<h2>Total Sales for this author = <asp:Label runat="server" id=totalSales /></h2>

<h3><font face="Verdana">List of Titles</font></h3>

<asp:DataGrid id="titlegrid" runat="server" ShowHeader="False">
</asp:DataGrid>

</body>
</html>
```

In this page, we will be using the final two methods of our business component. The first thing we need to do in the page, however, is to make sure that the proper namespaces are included with the page.

```
<%@ Page Language="C#" Description="Component Test Program - Title List"
                                        Debug="True" %>
<%@ Import Namespace="System.Collections" %>
<%@ Import Namespace="BusObjectCS" %>
<%@ Import Namespace="BusObjectVB" %>
```

From the methods that we will be using in this page, we will be returning an integer from one and a `StringCollection` object from the other. In order for the code on this page to understand how to work with the `StringCollection` class, we need to import the `System.Collections` namespace into the page. As we did in the previous page, we will be importing both the C# and VB versions of the components.

```
void Page_Load(Object sender, EventArgs evArgs){
//    BusObjectCS.PubsAccess objPubs = new BusObjectCS.PubsAccess();
    BusObjectVB.PubsAccess objPubs = new BusObjectVB.PubsAccess();

    String dsn = "server=localhost;uid=sa;pwd=;database=pubs";
    objPubs.DatabaseConnection = dsn;
```

The first part of the `Page_Load` method is the same as the previous page. We have statements to create the object in both VB and in C#, but only one of these will be active when the page is run – the other will be commented out. In fact, if for some reason both lines were left in the page when it was executed, the C# object will be created first. Then the VB object will be created and assigned to the same variable name. When that happens the C# object will be marked for disposal, and will be destroyed the next time the Common Language Runtime Garbage Collector is run. So we will end up with a VB component!

```
    StringCollection titles =
            objPubs.GetTitlesForAuthor(Request.QueryString["auid"]);
    titlegrid.DataSource = titles;
    titlegrid.DataBind();
```

We will retrieve the list of titles for the requested author by using the `GetTitlesForAuthor` method of our class. The author ID has been passed in on the URL, and can be retrieved from the `Request.QueryString` collection. The information is returned as a `StringCollection` object. We want to use the values in this collection as the source to populate our `DataGrid`. The `DataGrid` requires that its data source object support the `System.Collections.ICollections` interface. Since the `StringCollection` class implements this interface directly, the object that we get back from our method call can be directly used as the `DataSource` property for the `asp:DataList` object.

```
    totalSales.Text=objPubs.TotalSalesForAuthor(Request.QueryString["auid"])
                                            .Format( "c", null );
```

The other piece of information that we want to display on the page will be the total sales for the author. This is retrieved by calling the `TotalSalesForAuthor()` function of our business component. When we call this method, it will return an integer value. We want to make the value display as a currency on our page, so we will use the `Format` method, to convert the integer into a string formatted as a monetary value.

```
    <h2>Total Sales for this author = <asp:Label runat="server"
                                            id=totalSales /></h2>

    <h3><font face="Verdana">List of Titles</font></h3>

    <asp:DataGrid id="titlegrid" runat="server" ShowHeader="False">
    </asp:DataGrid>
```

All of the difficult work in our page is done in the `Page_Load()` method. All that we need to do in the display portion is provide the proper server-side controls to display the information. The `asp:Label` element is a server-side control that we use to display the total sales value for the author. The `asp:DataGrid` element will display a simple table that contains the list of books for that author.

When we select one of the hyperlinks from the previous page, the browser will show the following:

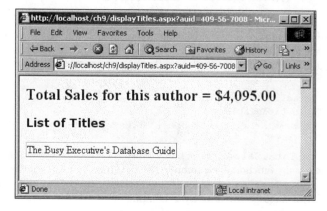

Cross-Language Inheritance

In the past, it has quite difficult (nearly impossible, actually) to have components written in one language subclass and extend a component written in another. You couldn't take a class written in C++ and inherit from it in Visual Basic to create a new object. Things like that just weren't possible. You also had no way of taking a compiled binary component, even if it was written in the same language, and deriving a new object from it without having the source code for the parent object, or at least a header file. It came down to the fact that there just wasn't enough information about the compiled components embedded in them to allow you to derive a new object from it.

However now, with the Common Language Runtime and the .NET Framework, we have the ability to do this. Earlier in this chapter, we looked at the concept of assembly manifests (the metadata about a class). Not only does this metadata contain enough information about a class to allow the Common Language Runtime to work with it, but it also has enough information to allow the component to be used as a base class in a new object that we create.

Cross-language inheritance, as this is known, also makes debugging much easier. It doesn't matter what language the code was written in when we are debugging. We simply run the debugger, and then the Common Language Runtime will allow us to trace from one language to the next **automatically** and **transparently** to the developer. We can even handle exceptions across languages and not have to worry about translating or modifying the information as it switches languages; the Common Language Runtime makes that all transparent to us.

The other key advantage to cross-language inheritance is that it makes a great way to create class libraries. If you remember back a few years to the Microsoft Foundation Classes (MFC) that were introduced by Microsoft to build Windows applications, you have a good example of a class library. MFC was written in C++, so they could be used to create C++ Windows applications. But because there was no capability for cross-language inheritance, Visual Basic.NET developers could not use any bit of MFC in their applications. With the .NET Frameworks, Microsoft has written the classes in C#, but the cross-language inheritance capabilities of the Common Language Runtime allow for any supported language to both use the Frameworks as well as create new classes that inherit from classes within the Framework.

Cross-Language Inheritance Example

To show how cross-language inheritance works, we will look at a quick example component. In this example, we will be taking the C# class that was created earlier in the chapter and we will derive another class from it. This class will be written in Visual Basic.NET and will override the function that calculates the total sales of the author. The first step is to modify the C# class so that we can override the function that we need to.

```
public virtual int TotalSalesForAuthor (string authorID) {
    DataTable titleTable;
    titleTable = SalesTotal.Tables["SalesTotal"];
```

We will be overriding the `TotalSalesForAuthor()` method in our new class. In order to do this, we must add the virtual modifier to the function declaration in the C# class. By default in C#, properties and methods are non-virtual meaning they can't be overridden in any derived classes. If we didn't add the virtual keyword, then we would get an error message when we try to compile our derived class saying that it was trying to override this method. Next, we can look at the new class, written in VB, that is derived from this C# class.

```
Option Explicit
Option Strict

Imports BusObjectCS

namespace SubBusinessClass
    public class SubPubsAccess
    Inherits PubsAccess
        public Overrides Function TotalSalesForAuthor (authorID as string)_
                                                            as integer

        dim iSaleTotal as Integer

        iSaleTotal = MyBase.TotalSalesForAuthor(authorID)

        return CInt(iSaleTotal * 0.65)
    end Function
    end Class
end Namespace
```

As with all Visual Basic.NET components, we should set both `Option Explicit` and `Option Strict` so that the compiler takes care of a lot of the error checking and code validation. These will greatly help to reduce any runtime errors that may occur.

```
Imports BusObjectCS
```

Since this class will be derived from the C# version of our business component, we need to import the namespace for that class so that the compiler will understand the references to that class that are made in our new component.

```
namespace SubBusinessClass
    public class SubPubsAccess
    Inherits PubsAccess
```

The next two lines are nearly identical to the VB component that we created earlier. We are defining a namespace called `SubBusinessClass` and then within that namespace we are creating a public class called `SubPubsAccess`. Remember that class names only have to be unique within the same namespace. This means that we could have named our class `PubsAccess`, as we did in both original classes, and still no naming conflicts would have occurred. The key line in this class is the next line. The `Inherits` statement defines the class that the class we are defining is inheriting from. It must be the **first** line in the class definition after the class declaration.

```
public Overrides Function TotalSalesForAuthor (authorID as string) as
                                                            integer
    dim iSaleTotal as Integer
    iSaleTotal = MyBase.TotalSalesForAuthor(authorID)
    return CInt(iSaleTotal * 0.65)
end Function
```

The only method in the derived class will be the one that we want to override. When we are defining a derived class, any public properties and methods from the parent class automatically become public properties or methods of the derived class. This means that we automatically get the two constructors of the parent class, along with the one property and three methods.

However, we want to change the implementation of the third method. This is why in the base class we added the virtual keyword to the method declaration – so that we can change its implementation. The new implementation will not have the `virtual` keyword (unless we want to further derive from this class and override the method again) but rather an `overrides` keyword. This keyword means that the function we are declaring here will replace the base class version of this function. In order to override a function in a base class, the overriding function must have the same declaration – function name, parameter list, and return type.

In the body of the function, we want to utilize some of the functionality of the base class implementation. To do this, we can actually call the base class version of the function directly. To do that, we use the `MyBase` keyword as a preface to the function call, so that the compiler knows which version to call. The value that is returned from the function is then modified and returned as the new return value for this function. There is no requirement that we use any of the base class implementation – we just want to leverage the code that is in there rather than having to rewrite it ourselves.

To test this component, we will first compile it, and then modify the test ASP.NET page so that this component is used instead of the original component. When we execute the page, we can see that the new value for total sales is now displayed.

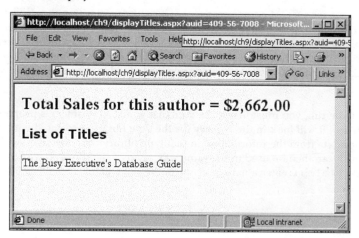

Working with Unmanaged Components

All this talk up to this point has revolved around creating new applications and components that work within the .NET Framework; but what about all of the existing code that is out there that uses the now-passé Component Object Model, or COM? How can we work with applications written for COM instead of .NET, and how can components written for COM work with .NET applications?

When a .NET application is executing, the Common Language Runtime is managing it. Remember that the various language compilers only create MSIL code, not executable code. The Common Language Runtime executes this code at runtime. Any code that is run in this manner is known as managed code. On the other hand, any code that runs outside of the Common Language Runtime is known as unmanaged code. This includes all COM components, ActiveX controls, and any calls to the native Win32 API – all are considered to be unmanaged code.

So how can we allow managed and unmanaged code to interoperate within the same application. We need to look at those things that differentiate managed and unmanaged code, and make sure that we are consistent in the way that the managed code and the unmanaged code is implemented. The runtime will do a lot of the work to mask the differences, but there are few things that developers must do themselves.

Using COM Components in a .NET application

There are a great number of COM components that are already in use in business and applications today. The pervasiveness of the Win32 platform has had a great effect on the utilization of this component architecture. In order to use a COM component within a .NET application, there are a number of things that we need to look at in the implementation and deployment of the component.

As we have seen earlier in this chapter, anything that executes within the Common Language Runtime needs to have metadata associated with it. The components and applications that we create directly within the .NET Framework automatically have their metadata created and associated with it, but COM components have no concept of metadata associated with them. There is the separate type library file that functions like assembly metadata, but it is part of a separate file and not related in any way to the component itself.

Generating Metadata

To build the metadata for a COM component so that it can be used within the .NET framework, we will use a tool called the **Type Library Importer**. This tool is included with the .NET Framework SDK and will create an assembly containing the necessary metadata for the COM component. It uses the component's type library to create the metadata. Since the metadata is necessary for compile time as well as runtime, you must run TlbImp against any COM components being used in your application *before* you compile your application.

In order for this to be run, you must first make sure that your COM object is properly registered. When you execute TlbImp, it will look in the registry for the type library associated with the COM object and then build the metadata from the information in that type library. The metadata will be stored in a DLL assembly file, which can then be used in the same way as any assembly that was created directly in the .NET Framework. TlbImp creates a namespace with the same name as the type library the classes came from.

Using the COM Component

This is probably the easiest part of working with COM components in .NET applications. Once you have created the assembly using TlbImp, all you need to do is treat the COM component as you would any other .NET component in your application. You will use New to create a new instance of it. You will interact with the methods and properties of the component. The Common Language Runtime takes care of any translation or marshaling between .NET and COM that needs to take place. All of the parameters are converted automatically from COM data types to the Common Language Runtime data types.

Compiling and Deploying COM Components

When you compile your .NET application that uses COM components, you need to reference the COM components in the same way that you would reference any assemblies within the .NET Framework. When you call the compiler, you need to add a /r: parameter to the compiler call that points to the DLL that was created by TlbImp. When the application is deployed, you have to take one additional step beyond the XCOPY deployment that is supported by the .NET Framework. While .NET assemblies do not need to be registered in order to work, COM is still COM and is still bound by its restrictions. This means that any COM components that are part of your .NET application must be properly registered when the application is installed onto the destination computer.

Using .NET Components in a COM Application

Just as we can use COM components within our .NET application, we can use .NET components within COM applications. In fact, any instance of a public class that includes a default constructor created in the .NET Framework can also be created and used within the COM environment. Just as a COM component being used in .NET needs to have metadata created for it, a .NET component being used within COM needs to be properly registered in order to work.

In the previous section, we looked at the TlbImp utility, which allowed COM components to be used in a .NET application. The reverse of that utility is RegAsm.exe. This utility adds information about a .NET assembly to the registry so that COM can access it. In essence, it makes a .NET component look like an old-fashioned COM component. The utility will add the CLSID of the .NET class to the registry and will configure the registry settings so that when the COM application tries to access the component, the Common Language Runtime will automatically be executed to handle the processing for the .NET component.

Once the class is registered to look like a COM object, it can be used as if it were natively created. The application using the object can create instances of it as well as request services from it. From the point of view of both the .NET component and the COM application, the Common Language Runtime hides the differences between COM and .NET.

Summary

The flexibility and power of the .NET Framework extends beyond just creating applications, web services, and ASP.NET pages. We can create powerful business components using the .NET Frameworks and the Common Language Runtime that have just as much power and flexibility as COM objects. In some cases, the capabilities offered by the Common Language Runtime provide distinct advantages over COM. Now we can actually derive new objects from classes written in different languages. And we can do this even if all we have is the compiled version of the base class. However, that doesn't mean that we can't have COM and .NET work together in the same application.

In this chapter, we have specifically looked at.

- ❑ How assemblies and metadata provide a way to package both the executable code along with detailed descriptions of the code that is executing.

- ❑ How to write a business object in two different languages, and then use the same test program to work with both objects.

- ❑ How to take a class written in one language and extend its functionality by deriving a new class in a totally different language.

- ❑ How COM and .NET components and applications can interoperate in a manner that is transparent to both the application and to the developer.

In the next chapter, we will take a look at how to interact with data using the .NET Frameworks. We will also take a look at the next version of the ActiveX Data Objects known as ADO.NET.

NETINTRODUCING.NETINTRODUCING.NETINTRODUCING.NETINTRODUCI
ODUCING.NETINTRODUCING.NETINTRODUCING.NETINTRODUCI
ETINTRODUCING.NETINTRODUCING.NETINTRODUCING.NETINT
CING.NETINTRODUCING.NETINTRODUCING.NETINTRODUCING.
NTRODUCING.NETINTRODUCING.NETINTRODUCING.NETINTROD
G.NETINTRODUCING.NETINTRODUCING.NETINTRODUCING.NET
ODUCING.NETINTRODUCING.NETINTRODUCING.NETINTRODUCI
ETINTRODUCING.NETINTRODUCING.NETINTRODUCING.NETINT
CING.NETINTRODUCING.NETINTRODUCING.NETINTRODUCING.
NTRODUCING.NETINTRODUCING.NETINTRODUCING.NETINTROD
G.NETINTRODUCING.NETINTRODUCING.NETINTRODUCING.NET
ODUCING.NETINTRODUCING.NETINTRODUCING.NETINTRODUCI
ETINTRODUCING.NETINTRODUCING.NETINTRODUCING.NETINT
CING.NETINTRODUCING.NETINTRODUCING.NETINTRODUCING.
NTRODUCING.NETINTRODUCING.NETINTRODUCING.NETINTROD
G.NETINTRODUCING.NETINTRODUCING.NETINTRODUCING.NET
ODUCING.NETINTRODUCING.NETINTRODUCING.NETINTRODUCI
ETINTRODUCING.NETINTRODUCING.NETINTRODUCING.NETINT
CING.NETINTRODUCING.NETINTRODUCING.NETINTRODUCING.
NTRODUCING.NETINTRODUCING.NETINTRODUCING.NETINTROD
G.NETINTRODUCING.NETINTRODUCING.NETINTRODUCING.NET
ODUCING.NETINTRODUCING.NETINTRODUCING.NETINTRODUCI
ETINTRODUCING.NETINTRODUCING.NETINTRODUCING.NETINT
CING.NETINTRODUCING.NETINTRODUCING.NETINTRODUCING.
NTRODUCING.NETINTRODUCING.NETINTRODUCING.NETINTROD
G.NETINTRODUCING.NETINTRODUCING.NETINTRODUCING.NET
ODUCING.NETINTRODUCING.NETINTRODUCING.NETINTRODUCI
ETINTRODUCING.NETINTRODUCING.NETINTRODUCING.NETINT
CING.NETINTRODUCING.NETINTRODUCING.NETINTRODUCING.
NTRODUCING.NETINTRODUCING.NETINTRODUCING.NETINTROD
G.NETINTRODUCING.NETINTRODUCING.NETINTRODUCING.NET
ODUCING.NETINTRODUCING.NETINTRODUCING.NETINTRODUCI
ETINTRODUCING.NETINTRODUCING.NETINTRODUCING.NETINT
CING.NETINTRODUCING.NETINTRODUCING.NETINTRODUCING.
NTRODUCING.NETINTRODUCING.NETINTRODUCING.NETINTROD
G.NETINTRODUCING.NETINTRODUCING.NETINTRODUCING.NET
ODUCING.NETINTRODUCING.NETINTRODUCING.NETINTRODUCI
ETINTRODUCING.NETINTRODUCING.NETINTRODUCING.NETINT
ING.NETINTRODUCING.NETINTRODUCING.NETINTRODUCING.
NTRODUCING.NETINTRODUCING.NETINTRODUCING.NETINTROD
G.NETINTRODUCING.NETINTRODUCING.NETINTRODUCING.NET
ODUCING.NETINTRODUCING.NETINTRODUCING.NETINTRODUCI
ETINTRODUCING.NETINTRODUCING.NETINTRODUCING.NETINT

11

ADO.NET

ADO.NET is not engineered as a replacement for the ADO that we're all familiar with. It has been developed to enhance the creation of powerful and scalable web applications, by working with data in a disconnected way under the .NET Framework's stateless distributed web model. It has been specifically designed to operate in this 3-tier environment, although its properties and methods are efficient and readily useable when dealing with scenarios at the middle-tier web server level, as well. As ADO.NET operates in a disconnected way, no longer remaining connected to the data server whilst performing positional updates, for example, there is far greater scope for data manipulation. This mode of working suits large distributed web applications with data stored in more than one place at any given time.

ADO.NET's properties and methods are also extremely portable, via XML, to the outside world, increasing possibilities for data sharing between applications. There is greater standardization with support for XML and SQL, and using ADO's disconnected recordsets (or ADO.NET datasets), overall performance of applications can be improved.

The implementation of ADO.NET, however, means that some of the familiar ADO objects have taken on slightly different behaviors.

> According to Microsoft's **Universal Data Access Strategy** ADO.NET is considered the primary library for building solutions within the .NET Framework, while for COM based applications ADO and OLEDB are preferred. This is because, while you are be able to manipulate native COM based ADO code with ADO.NET objects, they do not support the COM variant datatype, and running type-conversions to counter this causes a performance hit.

This chapter aims to provide you with a very general understanding of how data-centric web techniques fit together under the .NET Framework and will then spend time previewing some of the main tools and features of Visual Studio.NET as it relates to ADO.NET. Specifically it will demonstrate:

❑   The creation of schemas from databases

❑   The concept of stateless data components

❑   How to publish information via XML

❑   Building an application that consumes a Web Service

ADO to ADO.NET

ADO.NET is very different from Microsoft's previous data handling technologies. It's true that some of the object designs in ADO.NET are based on previous ADO objects, and as such will be familiar to developers, but there are also many new objects that have no comparable entities in classic ADO. As we briefly mentioned in the first few lines of this chapter, this is principally due to Microsoft's desire for ADO.NET to provide full support for **disconnected data access.** This is data access where, most of the time, the data you're working with is not connected to a data source. Microsoft have committed to this **stateless** data model because it works very well for web-style applications, and also has the advantage of offering far easier scalability than the traditional ADO, OLEDB and ODBC, client/server models.

A typical use of ADO.NET across the web might go like this:

❑   A request for data arrives at a stateless Web Service as an HTTP posting (this post can either come locally from Windows, over the web, or from somewhere else – it doesn't matter so long as it conforms to HTTP standards).

❑   A public WebMethod is invoked, which opens a connection, executes one or more commands, and then returns the result in XML format to the sender.

❑   If the returning information is being consumed through the .NET Framework the returning information can be **typecast** into a special new Sytem.Data type called a DataSet, replacing the previous ADO Recordset.

❑   The information in the DataSet can then be accessed through its schema, which can either by dynamic, or may already have been fixed and published to consumers. We'll learn more on this later.

❑   Finally other objects within the architecture, such as Connection and DataSetCommand, are then used to move data in and out of the imported data source ready for manipulation by other program sequences.

It should be noted that in this new distributed web world the majority of components live almost exclusively on the web, or middle, tier. The DataSet, which we'll talk about in just a moment, is the object that moves around, and now the Command and Connection objects are used exclusively for talking directly to the database.

Under this new design, a component will allow data to flow in and out, and is easily controlled remotely from stored procedures, and the DataSet is an important part of this new architecture as you can see in the diagram:

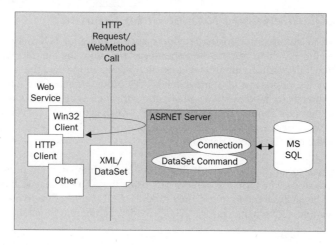

We'll take a look at datasets a little later. Before that we'll look briefly at the ADO.NET object model and see how it has altered.

The ADO.NET Object Model

Familiarizing ourselves with the ADO.NET object model will make more sense if we first understand the new namespaces that come with ADO.NET. In ASP.NET pages you have to tell ASP.NET that you wish to use a certain namespace; it's a bit like using References in a Visual Basic program. To do this you use the Import construct at the top of the page:

```
<%@ Import Namespace="System.Data.ADO" %>
```

This would import the ADO namespace into an ASP.NET page, allowing the objects to be used. The namespaces made available with ADO.NET are listed below:

Code Namespace	Contains
System.Data	Base objects and types for ADO+
System.Data.ADO	Managed OLEDB data store objects
System.Data.SQL	SQL Server specific implementations of ADO+ objects
System.Data.XML	XML objects
System.Data.SQLTypes	SQL data types

We said at the beginning of this chapter that ADO.NET is more standardized, supporting XML and SQL. As well as a System.Data XML, you'll notice a System.Data.ADO and a System.Data.SQL. System.Data.ADO and System.Data.SQL map pretty much one to one onto each other. The reason is that System.Data provides the code facilities, whilst System.Data.ADO and System.Data.SQL are the namespaces for the two managed providers.

So Why Has an SQL Managed Provider Been Created?

In traditional ADO we've got used to OLEDB Providers, such as those for SQL Server, Access, and Oracle. ADO leverages the features of these and provides a uniform programming interface; however, this isn't always the best solution. Supporting common features often means supporting the lowest common denominator. ADO.NET supports this idea, but extends it by providing managed data providers, which are optimized for talking directly to the data store without going through OLEDB. In the case of the managed SQL Server provider, this uses Tabular Data Stream (TDS), which is the SQL Server native communication protocol (as used by DBlib for those of you with long memories). For those sites that use SQL Server it's a great way to improve the performance of data access.

You now have the option of supporting multiple data stores or obtaining the best possible performance by targeting a specific data store. The former is achieved by using the ADO Managed Provider, which supports all ADO data stores. The latter, at the moment, only supports SQL Server. Future releases will contain a native Oracle provider and an Exchange Server 2000 provider, giving rich functionality and great performance.

The managed provider for ADO and the equivalent managed provider for SQL consist of:

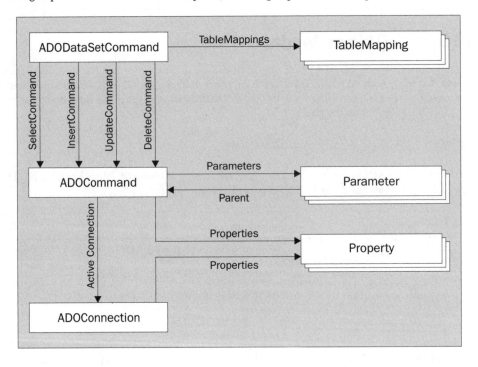

ADOConnection/SQLConnection

In ADO.NET, connection to the data source occurs through the ADOConnection object, which will be familiar to ADO developers as it mirrors the behavior of the Connection object in classic ADO. This object provides connectivity with .NET compliant OLEDB data sources using the same properties (ConnectionString), methods (Open) and events (InfoMessage) as before.

Other connection objects are being built that will ship with the final version, including the SQLConnection object, which aims to provide as pure a connection as possible when talking natively (and exclusively) to MS-SQL Server. Supplying different data-handling objects marks a significant shift in the ADO approach that will be apparent through all the remaining objects we are highlighting in this section. Rather than having one object that works with everything, ADO.NET will offer a range of better factored, more efficient objects that each focus on a different data source. This means that if you are creating an application that exclusively uses MS-SQL Server you have the benefit of using libraries that have been built exclusively for it.

*It is worth remembering that while the object itself is written in **managed code** it has the ability to access unmanaged COM-based OLEDB data sources to provide backward compatibility.*

ADOCommand/SQLCommand

To execute commands against a data source, you use the ADOCommand object. This mirrors the behavior of the Command object used in traditional ADO, but with one important exception. While it can apply changes through commands such as insert, update and delete, it is now limited to read-only, forward-only, access to the Results Set through the ADODataReader. Aside from this it has the same properties (CommandText, Parameters) and methods (Execute) as the classic Command object.

As mentioned already, when discussing ADOConnection, in the interests of better performance, different connection objects will be developed and shipped for different data sources.

ADODataReader/SQLDataReader

The ADODataReader, which we mentioned in the last paragraph, uses streaming methods such as Read() to fetch data in rows. It is a good lightweight object to use in scenarios where, for example, read-only results are going to be streamed to a report in a web page. The DataReader is returned from an Execute call on the Command (in fact the DataReader is a parameter of the Execute call). It is the closest you'll get to the classic ADO Recordset object (but using a Read-Only Forward-Only cursor) in ADO.NET. There is also a parallel SQLDataReader for working with SQL Server data.

ADODataSetCommand/SQLDataSetCommand

To better facilitate **stateless batch update** scenarios ADO.NET provides a composite object called the ADODataSetCommand. This object uses four ADOCommands to provide Insert, Update, Delete, and Select access to a data store. It does this by pulling data from a data source and retrieving it into **sets** using SelectCommand and then taking set changes and reconciling them with the data source (using InsertCommand, UpdateCommand, and DeleteCommand).

To help you visualize this complex operation, imagine if in classic ADO you had the ability to update, insert, and delete stored procedures to a Recordset, so that if an update is made it calls the update stored procedure, but if an insert occurs, the insert procedure would be called instead. ADO.NET achieves this by grouping the commands with one DataSetCommand. By doing this the ADO.NET object is able to execute the required command most efficiently.

This DataSetCommand uses two primary methods: FillDataSet and UpdateDataSource. The FillDataSet method takes an existing DataSet and pushes data into it. This is like a traditional Select command filling a Recordset.

There are many different scenarios in which data, as well as schema, will need to be changed within a `DataSet`. As these changes take place the `DataSet` tracks them and records whether they are deletes, updates (merges) or inserts. This means that later those changes can be applied back to the data source through the use of the `UpdateDataSource()` method.

Any further changes that result from applying the updates will then be returned from the data source back into `DataSet1`. Again, there is an equivalent `SQLDataSetCommand`.

The DataSet

As we mentioned earlier on in this section, ADO.NET introduces a new object, called a `DataSet`. This is a top level object which doesn't appear on the diagram you just saw. The `DataSet` deals with actual data from a data store and provides access to tables, rows and columns:

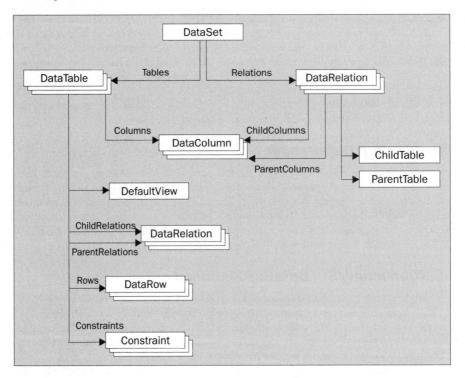

This object is technology neutral, so there is no specific version required for interacting with, for example, ADO or SQL data. For the same reason, it does not require a Command or Connection object either, as it was specifically designed not to take on the characteristics of a specific data source, but rather to store its data independently. The best way to think about a `DataSet` is as a small in-memory database within which there is no imposed structure of cursors, commands and connections. A useful analogy is to think of it as an off-line copy of a data store. The whole thing is very XML compliant in line with the .NET Framework's ideals of cross-platform, cross-Internet, communication. Once a schema for data storage has been established within a `DataSet` it can be manipulated and changed throughout the `DataSet`'s life. The `DataSet` will also take on other elements defined within the schema, such as its relationship and constraints. As we already pointed out, within the schema the `DataSet` is comprised of a series of tables that are in turn comprised of a series of columns. Data is stored in rows across the columns in an open structure that allows adding, editing, filtering and updating of the information when required.

It contains a great deal of the XML compatibility, and also oversees the conversion of other data types to and from XML when working with non-.NET clients allowing them easy interaction with .NET components.

A good example of a `DataSet` would be a purchase order submitted from a web page. It could contain details of the customer, their order, and how they want to be billed. As your business logic worked through the information submitted the `DataSet` could be changed to incorporate the new information and its Tables and schema would be updated accordingly.

The other top-level object, which isn't featured in our object model, is the `DataView`. This is a custom view of a data table (similar to the old ADO `Recordset`). It contains a single view on top of table data. The primary purpose of the `Dataview` is to assist with data binding.

ADO.NET's Capabilities, using VS.NET

As an example of using ADO.NET's data-centric web techniques in Visual Studio.NET we will build a component to run on a web server that returns purchase orders for processing. To do this we will:

❑   Create a data component that both gets and sets data to an SQL Server data source.

❑   Create a publishable XML schema that represents the data.

❑   Create a Web Service to expose the schema and data on the Internet.

For simplicity we will use the Northwind database, which is installed by default with SQL Server, for our data store and assume that it is local.

An illustration of the architecture of the application we are going to build is shown below.

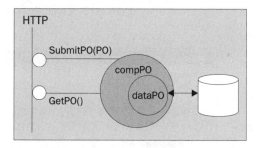

At first sight the architecture outlined may look a bit complex for the simple component that we are going to build, but in ADO.NET the tools are designed in such a way that they actually encourage the building of standard structures. Building well-factored applications in this way takes full advantages of the tool's capabilities and leads to more efficient, more easily maintainable applications. The section labelled `dataPO` will contain our data-access connections and commands, while `compPO` will wrap around it, conduct our computations, and expose more friendly signatures to the outside world. Additionally it will provide another layer of abstraction to improve the code's readability, usability and maintainability by separating the computational from data-access code.

Creating the Data Component

To create the data component we should create a new Visual Basic Web Application in Visual Studio.NET. We'll refer to it in this discussion as PurchaseOrders.

We can use the **Add Item** menu option to create the `dataPO` component class. To do this right click Purchase Orders in the **Solution Explorer**, then select **Add Item**. Select **New Component Class** and name it `dataPO`. This object will contain methods that will pass data from a `DataSet` to the Database, and vice-versa. This is the section of the component that will deal with data-handling and integrity that is not part of the component's business logic.

With the **Component Designer** open, we can select the **Data** tab on the **Toolbox**, and drag and drop an `SQLDataSetCommand` object onto the class surface. The `DataSet` that we create is going to contain our `Customer` information table. This will automatically launch the **DataSetCommand Configuration Wizard**. This helps us set up the properties for the `DataSetCommand`:

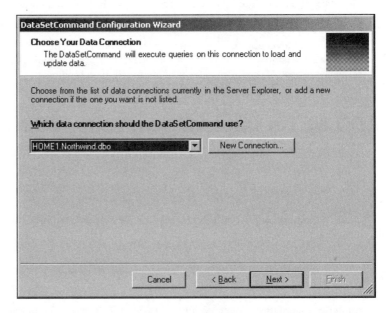

The wizard asks users to select, or create, a connection. We can do this against a local SQL Server for the purpose of this example. Creating this connection creates an **SQLConnection** object in our component, and places a link to it on the **Server Explorer**.

Next we configure the commands that we will use to talk through the connection to SQL Server. There are three options for setting up these commands in the wizard: **Use SQL statement**, **Use newly created stored procedures** and **Use existing stored procedures**:

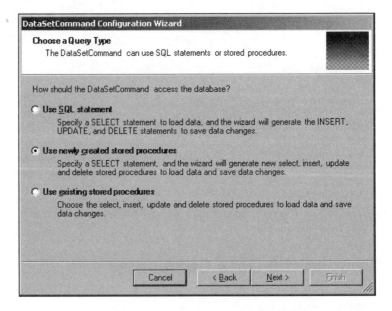

As we are creating a stateless model we choose the **second** option, that automatically generates newly created insert, update, and delete statements once we specify a SELECT statement. This way the statements will be created at design time and compiled as part of the object, which will help to improve overall system performance later.

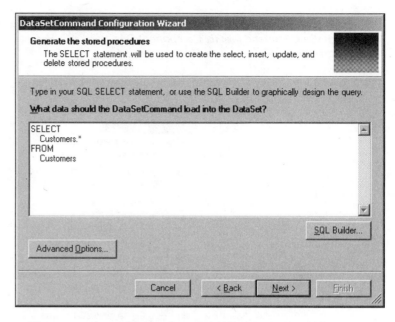

The next screen asks for the SELECT statements that will be used to get the data. In the textbox we put Select Customers.* FROM Customers or we could use the **SQL Builder** button to design the statement.

For proficient ADO users, the Advanced Options button allows you to set further preferences, such as to return the row after an insert, or to use Optimistic Concurrency. For this example leave them as the defaults.

The final screen of the wizard allows the naming of the four stored procedures (INSERT, UPDATE, DELETE, and GET) that will be created in our DataSet: sp_getCustomers; sp_insertCustomers; sp_updateCustomers, and sp_deleteCustomers.

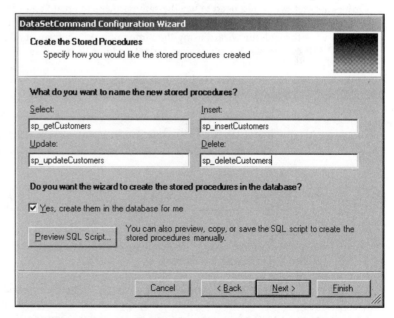

If we inspect the **Data Connections** node in the **Server Explorer** for the connection (created by the wizard), we find that we can expand the **Stored Procedures** node and view the new stored procedures that have been created in the database.

Should we wish to re-launch the wizard at another time, we can do so by selecting the
DataSetCommand *from the* Component Designer, *and using the* Configure DataSet
Command *hyperlink from the* Properties *window.*

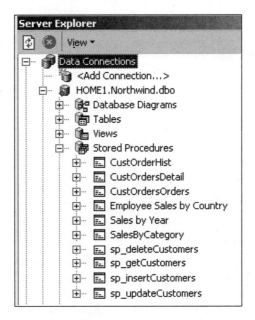

As we want our customers orders to come alongside their customer information, we can create a purchase
Orders data set, we would need to use the same process to create an orders table. We can drag a new
`SQLDataSetCommand` to the surface, and select the existing SQLConnection1 that we have already set up.
We can work through the wizard using the same options as before, but for the statement we type SELECT
Orders.* FROM Orders. We give the stored procedures the same names as before.

At this stage the component would now look like the following screenshot, showing one `SQLConnection`
and two `SQLDataSetCommands`:

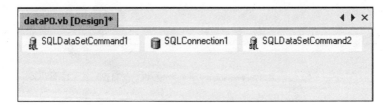

We have now completed adding the main data object instances and setting their appropriate properties.
Now we need to write some code to invoke these objects. We do this by selecting the Component Designer
surface and then right clicking the mouse:

Clicking the View Code option on the menu opens the code-editing window. Here we write a function called
`FillPurchaseOrderDataSet()` that will operate on our class. It will open a connection, invoke the
`FillDataSet()` method on both the `Customers` and the `Orders` `SQLDataSetCommands` and then
close the connection again.

The most important part of this code is `FillDataSet()`. This method executes the `SelectCommand` on `SQLDataSetCommand1` and pushes the results into a `DataSet`. There is one function for each, `Customers` (`SQLDataSetCommand1`) and `Orders` (`SQLDataSetCommand2`). With a little error trapping code, the function should look as follows:

```
Public Function FillPurchaseOrdersDataSet() As DataSet

Dim dataSet As New DataSet()

'Create an error handling block in case filldataset throws an exception
Try
    'Open The Connection
    SQLConnection1.Open()
    'Load the dataset from the DataSetCommand
    SQLDataSetCommand1.FillDataSet(dataSet, "Customers")
    SQLDataSetCommand2.FillDataSet(dataSet, "Orders")
    Catch eFillException As System.Exception
    'TODO: Handle errors here

Throw eFillException
Finally
    'Explicitly Close Connection
    SQLConnection1.Close()
End Try

Return (dataSet)

End Function
```

The data in these datasets, once filled by the `FillDataSet` method, can then be accessed through the `Tables` collection. As we've mentioned previously a dataset contains a collection of tables. Our dataset currently contains the `Customers` table and `Orders` table that we created with the `DataSetCommands`.

```
dataSet.Tables("Customers").Rows(0)("FirstName")
```

This code will give us the first customer's `FirstName`. As this is a collection you can access the tables and columns either by name, or by index and, unless otherwise specified, they are read/write. Iterating through the collection of customers to return each customer's first name can be done as follows:

```
Dim rowCustomer As System.Data.DataRow
    For Each rowCustomer In dataSet.Tables("Customer").Rows
    Response.Write(rowCustomer("FirstName").ToString)
Next
```

However, we have yet to establish a relation. We cannot see how `Customers` relate to their `Orders`. We can give the `DataSet` relational characteristics by adding a relation to the **Relations** collection. Here we will create a relation between the `CustomerId` column in the `Customers` table and the `CustomerId` column in the `Orders` table.

```
dataSet.Relations.Add("CustomerOrders", _
dataSet.Tables("Customers").Columns("CustomerID"), _
dataSet.Tables("Orders").Columns("CustomerId"))
```

Now we can iterate through both the `Customers` and their `Orders` in the following way.

```
For Each rowCustomer In dataSet.Tables("Customer").Rows
    Response.Write(rowCustomer("FirstName").ToString)
    For Each rowOrder In rowCustomer.GetChildRows("CustomerOrders")
        Response.Write(rowOrder("OrderDate").ToString)
    Next
Next
```

The above code would output each customer's first name, and the dates of their orders, in turn. The relation allows us to see orders for a given customer using the `GetChildRows()` function, which returns the collection of the `Orders` rows.

This is the data-handling section of the component. Next we will look into how we can describe the schema that we have created to potential customers. For, example if we were exposing this data to a third party we'd need a way to describe the data they would receive so that they could make use of it.

Creating the Publishable XML

We can describe data very easily in ADO.NET by making use of XML. Visual Studio.NET allows the easy creation of an XML schema from the existing results returned by `DataSetCommand`.

We can select the **DataClass** menu from the **Component Designer** of the `dataPO` component, and then select **Generate Dataset**. A dialog appears, and in this we type **dsPurchaseOrder** for the name of the `DataSet` class.

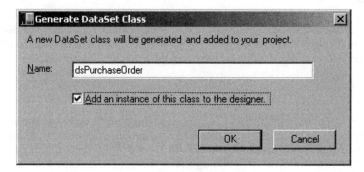

We also check the box to add an instance of the class to the designer.

An instance of `dsPurchaseOrder` (`dsPurchaseOrder1`) appears on the class surface, and a new file, `dsPurchaseOrder.xsd`, appears in the **Project** window. A tool, called `xsd.exe`, takes XML schemas and compiles them into a subclassed `DataSet`.

Now we'll examine the schema that was created by opening `dsPurchaseOrder.xsd`. This will invoke the **XML Designer**, which will allow us to design both schemas and data. In this instance we are working with schemas; the designer allows a hybrid approach to schema design, geared both towards the relational world (the typical database world) as well as the hierarchical world (the typical XML world). The illustration below shows the schema that would be generated from the **Customers** and **Orders** tables.

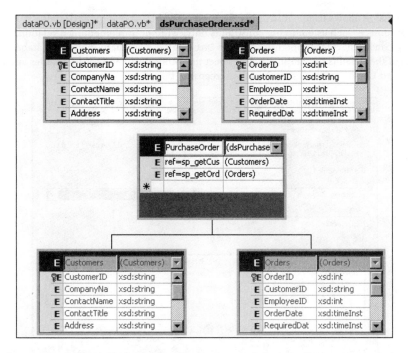

The XML schema creates two **complex types**, Customers and Orders, that are contained within the parent type, PurchaseOrder. Notice, however, that the schema does not note that the Customers and Orders tables were related (though this may be fixed in the final shipping version). To correct this we could take advantage of the fact that the XML designer also allows for text editing of the schema. To switch from the Graphical to Text modes, we can select the **XML** button at the bottom of the designer window.

```
Form1.vb   WebForm1.aspx   dataPO.vb [Design]*   dataPO.vb*   dsPurchaseOrder.xsd   ◄ ► ×
<xsd:schema id="dsPurchaseOrder" targetNamespace="http://ww
    <xsd:element name="Customers">
        <xsd:complexType content="elementOnly">
            <xsd:all>
                <xsd:element name="CustomerID" type="xsd:st
                <xsd:element name="CompanyName" type="xsd:s
                <xsd:element name="ContactName" minOccurs="
                <xsd:element name="ContactTitle" minOccurs=
                <xsd:element name="Address" minOccurs="0" t
                <xsd:element name="City" minOccurs="0" type
                <xsd:element name="Region" minOccurs="0" ty
                <xsd:element name="PostalCode" minOccurs="0
                <xsd:element name="Country" minOccurs="0" t
                <xsd:element name="Phone" minOccurs="0" typ
                <xsd:element name="Fax" minOccurs="0" type=
            </xsd:all>
        </xsd:complexType>
```

This text design view allows for fairly complete manipulation of the schema. To add the same relationship that was added in the code (CustomerOrders) we switch back to the Visual Designer (by pressing the Schema button), select the Customers complex type, right click, and select Add | New Relation.

The Relation dialog allows us to construct a relation between `Customers` and `Orders`. It also allows more complex operations – such as enforcing constraints only, without implementing a relation, as well as implementing constraint rules (remember that the `DataSet` is a small, in memory, database). In this example we accept all of the defaults for simplicity. We select the **Customers** and **Orders** tables and the **CustomerId** as the Parent and Child Fields, as shown in the screenshot below.

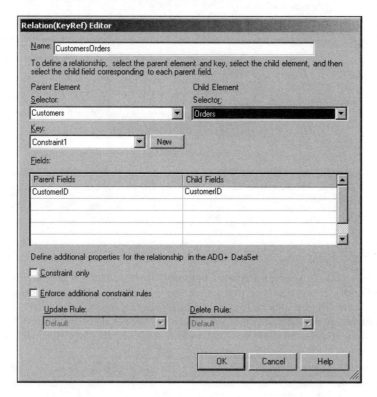

The following is the XML representing the schema:

```
<xsd:schema id="dsPurchaseOrder"
targetNamespace="http://home1/PurchaseOrders/dsPurchaseOrder.xsd"
xmlns="http://home1/PurchaseOrders/dsPurchaseOrder.xsd"
xmlns:xsd="http://www.w3.org/1999/XMLSchema" xmlns:msdata="urn:schemas-microsoft-
com:xml-msdata">
  <xsd:element name="Customers">
    <xsd:complexType content="elementOnly">
      <xsd:all>
        <xsd:element name="CustomerID" type="xsd:string"/>
        <xsd:element name="CompanyName" type="xsd:string"/>
        <xsd:element name="ContactName" minOccurs="0" type="xsd:string"/>
        <xsd:element name="ContactTitle" minOccurs="0" type="xsd:string"/>
        <xsd:element name="Address" minOccurs="0" type="xsd:string"/>
        <xsd:element name="City" minOccurs="0" type="xsd:string"/>
        <xsd:element name="Region" minOccurs="0" type="xsd:string"/>
        <xsd:element name="PostalCode" minOccurs="0" type="xsd:string"/>
        <xsd:element name="Country" minOccurs="0" type="xsd:string"/>
```

```
            <xsd:element name="Phone" minOccurs="0" type="xsd:string"/>
            <xsd:element name="Fax" minOccurs="0" type="xsd:string"/>
          </xsd:all>
        </xsd:complexType>
        <xsd:key name="Constraint1" msdata:PrimaryKey="True">
          <xsd:selector>.</xsd:selector>
          <xsd:field>CustomerID</xsd:field>
        </xsd:key>
      </xsd:element>
      <xsd:element name="Orders">
        <xsd:complexType content="elementOnly">
          <xsd:all>
            <xsd:element name="OrderID" msdata:ReadOnly="True" type="xsd:int"/>
            <xsd:element name="CustomerID" minOccurs="0" type="xsd:string"/>
            <xsd:element name="EmployeeID" minOccurs="0" type="xsd:int"/>
            <xsd:element name="OrderDate" minOccurs="0" type="xsd:timeInstant"/>
            <xsd:element name="RequiredDate" minOccurs="0" type="xsd:timeInstant"/>
            <xsd:element name="ShippedDate" minOccurs="0" type="xsd:timeInstant"/>
            <xsd:element name="ShipVia" minOccurs="0" type="xsd:int"/>
            <xsd:element name="Freight" minOccurs="0" type="xsd:decimal"/>
            <xsd:element name="ShipName" minOccurs="0" type="xsd:string"/>
            <xsd:element name="ShipAddress" minOccurs="0" type="xsd:string"/>
            <xsd:element name="ShipCity" minOccurs="0" type="xsd:string"/>
            <xsd:element name="ShipRegion" minOccurs="0" type="xsd:string"/>
            <xsd:element name="ShipPostalCode" minOccurs="0" type="xsd:string"/>
            <xsd:element name="ShipCountry" minOccurs="0" type="xsd:string"/>
          </xsd:all>
        </xsd:complexType>
        <xsd:key name="sp_getOrders_Constraint1"
                 msdata:ConstraintName="Constraint1" msdata:PrimaryKey="True">
          <xsd:selector>.</xsd:selector>
          <xsd:field>OrderID</xsd:field>
        </xsd:key>
        <xsd:keyref name="CustomersOrders" refer="Constraint1">
          <xsd:selector>.</xsd:selector>
          <xsd:field>CustomerID</xsd:field>
        </xsd:keyref>
      </xsd:element>
      <xsd:element name="dsPurchaseOrder" msdata:IsDataSet="True">
        <xsd:complexType>
          <xsd:choice maxOccurs="unbounded">
            <xsd:element ref="Customers"/>
            <xsd:element ref="Orders"/>
          </xsd:choice>
        </xsd:complexType>
      </xsd:element>
    </xsd:schema>
```

This is an XML Schema that will describe the data being fetched. If we were to close the **Schema Designer**, and select the `dsPurchaseOrders.xsd` file in the **Project window** we could inspect the properties sheet. Notice the **CustomTool** property:

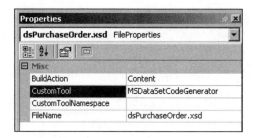

This file-level property indicates to the build process that the file will need some pre- or post-processing. In this case, the `MSDataSetCodeGenerator` creates a subclassed `DataSet` for this schema. This property was set earlier, when we used the **Create DataSet** option from the **DataClass** menu.

> *If we had selected the Show All Files option in the Project window, we could expand the*
> `dsPurchaseOrder.xsd` *file, open the* `dsPurchaseOrder.vb` *and view the code that*
> *was generated.*

This sub classed dataset is known as a **typed** dataset and serves two primary purposes. Firstly it encourages more efficient and accurate coding by providing typed accessors to the data through tables, columns and relations. These reduce coding errors that would previously have been exposed as run-time errors.

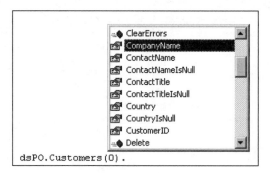

Secondly, because the accessors are typed, we can have compile time, as opposed to run-time, type-checking. This yields an additional performance advantage over and above the efficiencies gained through the storing and moving of typed, rather than variant, data.

Taking advantage of this, our code now has a much more intuitive way to navigate the orders for a given customer:

```
myDate = ds.Customers(0).OrdersByCustomersOrders(0).OrderDate
```

Notice that we can easily get the orders for a given customer by following the `OrdersByCustomersOrders` property.

At this point we have a data component (`dataPO`) with instances of appropriate objects and properties set, and code written to return the data. We also have a schema to describe the result set.

UpdateDataSource

When changes are made to a `DataSet`, it records those changes. It is these changes that can then be applied to the database using the `DataSetCommand`. This will map appropriate inserts, updates, and deletes from the `DataSet` to the appropriate database command. It will also take any results from updates and deletes (via output parameters, or a result row) and update the `DataSet` from these. For example, if I added a row to the `DataSet`, and then submitted it to a stored procedure in which the database assigned an identity, that identity could then be returned to the `DataSet`. This returning of data is usually only necessary when you are updating, as a client may want to see the `Order` number as confirmation that the update has occurred successfully.

Next, we will create a function in `dataPO()` to take `PurchaseOrder` changes (in the form of XML or a `DataSet`) and submit them to the database. The function will take changes either in the form of the original dataset, a dataset with a subset of changes (for example, using `GetChanges()`), or in XML format (since `DataSets` are compatible with XML this is an acceptable form of input).

The function we write here, `MaintainPO()`, will allow for the updating, inserting and deleting of customers and orders. We will simply execute `UpdateDataSource()` on the Customers `DataSetCommand` (called `SQLDataSetCommand1`) and then `UpdateDataSource()` on the Orders `DataSetCommand` (called `SQLDataSetCommand2`).

```
Public Function MaintainPO(ByVal updatedDataSet As DataSet) As DataSet

    Try
        SQLDataSetCommand1.Update(updatedDataSet)
        SQLDataSetCommand2.Update(updatedDataSet)
    Catch eUpdateException As System.Exception
    Throw eUpdateException
    End Try

End Function
```

Due to the relational nature of the data, you may have to control when data gets inserted and deleted. For example, assume our database assigns identities to Customers and Orders. This means that if we are submitting a new customer and a new order, we need to insert the customer first, so that the `CustomerId` can then be assigned to the Order (in this case, because of the relationship we created, the `DataSet` will handle this). However, in the case of deleting information, there may exist a cascading delete trigger in the database that automatically deletes all orders, or there may be a constraint that disallows the deleting of a customer unless all his orders are deleted first.

To handle these difficulties, we can filter out different rows from the changes and update them accordingly. For example, to delete just the orders, and ignore any update or insert commands waiting to be applied:

```
SQLDataSetCommand2.Update(updatedDataSet.GetChanges_
(System.Data.DataRowState.Deleted))
```

By applying the filter `DataRowState.Deleted`, only the `DeleteRows` are passed to the `Update`.

The `DataRowStates` (`Deleted`, `New`, `Modified` (updated),`Original` (unchanged)) are available for filtering.

Creating the Web Service

Finally, we will expose our data component (dataPO) as a Web Service. This will allow subscribers to invoke functions over HTTP regardless of their local platform. As we outlined in our architecture plan at the beginning, we create a wrapper component for the dataPO component called compo. This component has two functions: GetPO() and SubmitPO(dsUpdate). These functions would ordinarily implement any business rules, such as validating zip codes, or credit card details. As our component is only a simple example we don't have any business rules, so we will pass straight on to our two dataPO components FillPurchaseOrdersDataSet() and MaintainPO() functions.

Within the existing project, we added a **New Web Service** and called it compPO. This Web Service template allows us to expose our functions to the world! A function exposed as a Web Service has the attribute <WebMethod>. This attribute on a function will create contracts (WSDLs) for the Web Service and also cause the project to update SOAP Discovery (.disco) files. We can add the following code to the project.

```
Public Function <WebMethod()> GetPO() As PurchaseOrders.dsPurchaseOrder
Dim dsPO As New PurchaseOrders. dsPurchaseOrder
Dim dataPO As New PurchaseOrders.dataPO()

dsPO = dataPO.FillPurchaseOrdersDataSet()
Return (dsPO)
End Function

Public Function <WebMethod()> SubmitPO(dsUpdate As_
        PurchaseOrders.dsPurchaseOrder) As PurchaseOrders.dsPurchaseOrder

Dim dataPO As New PurchaseOrders.dataPO()

dsUpdate = dataPO.MaintainPO(dsUpdate)
Return (dsUpdate)

End Function
```

Once the project is built we have a Web Service that returns XML, invokable through HTTP! For example, the GetPO is:

http://(yourcomputer)/PurchaseOrders/compPO.asmx/GetPO?

If we preview compPO.asmx we would see the description and a link to the WSDL contract.

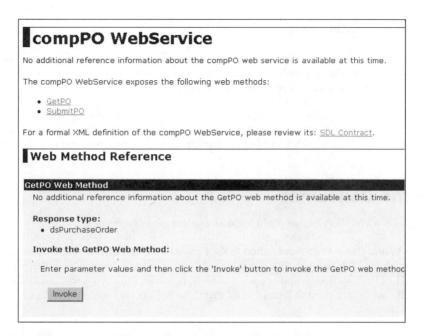

The SDL Contract describes in XML how the function can be invoked over HTTP. Invoking the function shows the XML representing the results:

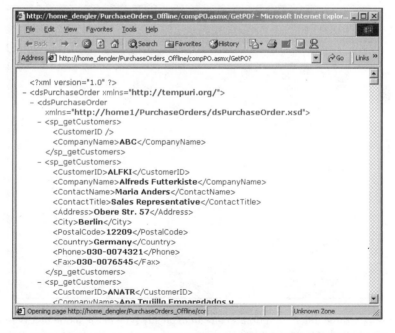

The element names currently happen to be the same as the stored procedures, but if this is undesirable it can easily be adjusted in the schema designer, as we've mentioned earlier. In this result set we are getting Customers and Orders in their own elements. This is because the XML Schema allows us to describe the elements of relationships in such a way that they do not have to be nested. Nested relationships are possible by changing the properties of the relationship, but the beta-one edition of the designer does not currently allow for this.

```
dsPO.Relations(0).Nested = True
```

We have now created a Web Service component that is wrapping a data component. Our data component in turn receives and submits data through stored procedures to an SQL Database, as well as exposing that data as XML and describing the data's schema through an XML Schema.

However, for others to discover and access our schema, we need to add a discovery file to the project (if you created a Web Service project initially, this file will already be there). Otherwise, simply select Add Item and select the Dynamic Discovery File. Once this is done our Web Service is discoverable through Visual Studio and other means.

Building the Consumer

Now that we have a Web Service, we could build an application to consume it.

We can add a Visual Basic Web Application to the Project – we've called it WebConsumer1. Then we can add a reference to the Web Service. This is just like adding any other reference, only that the methods are invoked over HTTP. From the developer's point of view, however, the objects will feel as though they are local objects. We would just need to bear in mind that these objects are stateless components, and that each method call is unique.

To add the references we select Add Web Reference, from the Project menu. This brings up the following dialog box:

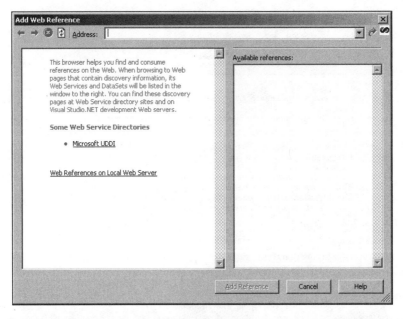

This dialog allows for three different options. You can explicitly type in the name of a Web Reference (for example, http://www.dedicatedradio.com), or discover references on the local server (using the hyperlink), or search through Microsoft UDDI (http://uddi.microsoft.com/, http://www.uddi.org) published Web Services. (UDDI is in beta, currently, but is a registry of published services for use in your application. You can also publish your own.)

The dialog also allows for navigating descriptions and contracts. To do this we select the local server, and then select **Add Reference**.

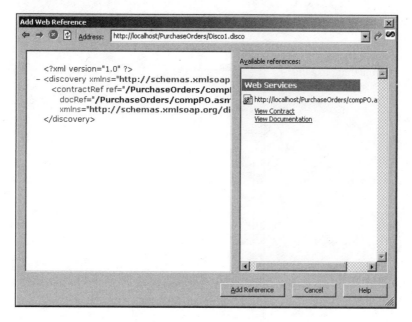

The project window displays a new folder, **Web References**, as well as the Local node (for the local web reference) and some other files whose functions we will quickly explain.

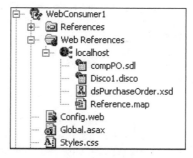

comPO.sdl is the Service Description File, similar to a Web Service Type Library(WSTL). It describes the WebMethods available together with their parameters and types. For the most part when using Visual Studio.NET, you needn't worry about this file as the environment uses this information to build proxy classes for talking to these objects. Also, notice that the dsPurchaseOrder.xsd file is also in this **WebReference** folder. This is because the environment specifically understands typed datasets, and knows that the schema needs to be instantiated on the consuming side as well. As our **WebMethod** returned a dsPurchaseOrder our consumer can now instance that same type.

We open up the WebForm1.aspx and in the designer we can add a **button** and a **textbox** control. Double clicking on the button control will create a shell function for the Click event. Within the click event we instantiate the Web Service, invoke the GetPO function, and show the results in the label control.

```
Public Sub Button1_Click(ByVal sender As Object, ByVal e As
                                         System.EventArgs)
Dim ds As New localhost.dsPurchaseOrder()
```

```
Dim webService As New localhost.CompPO()

ds = webService.GetPO()
Label1.Text = ds.xmldata

End Sub
```

The results look something like this:

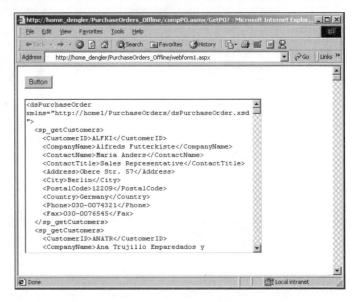

However, there are better ways to show the results. One is using the **DataGrid** control. The databound controls in Visual Studio.NET are not technology specific; they will bind to arrays, collections, etc. Since the data in the `DataSet` is simply a collection, we can bind directly to the `DataSet`. However, in order to allow for cursoring, such as movement through the `DataSet` a `DataView` object is provided. Multiple `DataViews` can be associated with one table, and `DataViews` can be related to each other (like a `CustomerOrders DataView`). Each table in the `DataSet` has a property called `DefaultView`, which manufactures a `DataView` on demand for databinding.

A binding to a **DataGrid** can be set up by removing the **Text** control, adding a **DataGrid** and then adding a **DataSet** (from the **Data** tab on the **Toolbox**). When a `DataSet` is added a dialog is provided to select a typed or untyped dataset. We would select the **typed** dataset, and then select the **PurchaseOrders** dataset, as in the screenshot below.

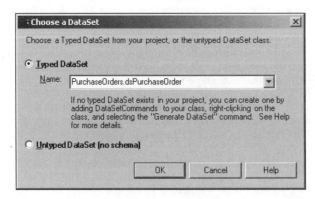

We can also use the development environment to set up the databindings, by adding a **DataView** to the surface, as well. Add a **DataView** control, and set the **Table** property to the **Customer** table in the `DataSet`. This means that the `DataView` is cursoring over the Customer table in the `DataSet`. Once we've done that, we then set the `DataSource` property of the grid to point at the `DataView`. This will cause the grid to bind to the `DataView`. Note at this point, the grid will autoformat to the schema of the `DataSet`.

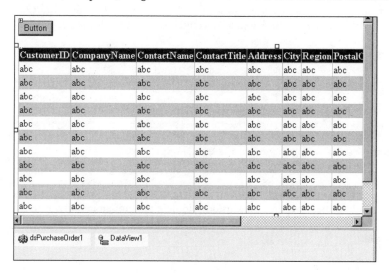

To preview the page, you would simply push the **Button**.

Updating Data

Let's move on to take a quick look at how we could update some data.

We add a new **Web Form** to the **Application**. Then, within the designer, we add two textbox controls, two labels and one button from the toolbox. We name the text controls txtCustomerId and txtCompanyName and give them appropriate labels:

We then have to write some underlying code that will perform our updating.

Having built the typed dataset there are two ways to add a Customer row. The first is instancing a Customer row object, setting the columns, and adding it to the rows collection using the `AddCustomersRow` method. The second is an override that is provided for `AddCustomersRow` that takes each of the columns of data as parameters. For this example we grab the values from the textboxes to pass into `CustomerId` and `CompanyName`, and set the others to " " for now, as shown in the code on the next page.

```
Dim dsPO As New WebConsumer1.localhost.dsPurchaseOrder()

    dsPO.Customers.AddCustomersRow(txtCustomerId.Text, txtCompanyName.Text, _
                                   "", "", "", "", "", "", "", "", "")
```

In the statement completion help text you can see that the parameters list of the AddCustomersRow method is also typed rather than being variant based as it would have been in classic ADO.

Once this is done we enter code to instance the Web Service, and send off the DataSet.

```
Public Sub Button1_Click(ByVal sender As Object, ByVal e As_
                                              System.EventArgs)
Dim dsPO As New WebConsumer1.localhost.dsPurchaseOrder()
dsPO.Customers.AddCustomersRow(txtCustomerId.Text, txtCompanyNaText, _
                               "", "", "", "", "", "", "", "", "")
Dim webService As New WebConsumer1.localhost.CompPO()
    webService.SubmitPO(dsPO)
End Sub
```

Since the Northwind database requires the CustomerId field and not an identity, when we run the code, we need to enter actual information. Once this is done we use the Button to submit it. The underlying code then does the following:

❑   Instances a new dsPurchaseOrders

❑   Adds a Customer to the order

❑   Instances the Web Service

❑   Submits the PurchaseOrder

In reality, of course, this would be far more complex, but this serves well as an illustration.

If we were to try this out we could check that the insert has taken place by going to the Customers table in the DataView.

Summary

In the walkthrough above we created a Web Service that allows data to flow in and out using XML and HTTP. This service is stateless and uses stored procedures to get data in and out of a database. Its Web Service can be discovered, and invoked, by any computer that has HTTP access regardless of platform. The architecture is properly factored to allow for data integrity rules to be implemented in the data component (dataPO) and business rules to be implemented at the service (compPO).

This was intended to give you a brief overview of just some of the objects, functions, tools and features of ADO.NET and Visual Studio.NET, as it is not possible to give a complete explanation of this area within one small chapter. It is also worth remembering that these examples were constructed with beta software that may be subject to change in the final release.

ODUCING.NETINTRODUCING.NETINTRODUCING.NETINTRODUCI
ETINTRODUCING.NETINTRODUCING.NETINTRODUCING.NETINT
CING.NETINTRODUCING.NETINTRODUCING.NETINTRODUCING.
NTRODUCING.NETINTRODUCING.NETINTRODUCING.NETINTROD
G.NETINTRODUCING.NETINTRODUCING.NETINTRODUCING.NET
ODUCING.NETINTRODUCING.NETINTRODUCING.NETINTRODUCI
ETINTRODUCING.NETINTRODUCING.NETINTRODUCING.NETINT
CING.NETINTRODUCING.NETINTRODUCING.NETINTRODUCING.
NTRODUCING.NETINTRODUCING.NETINTRODUCING.NETINTROD
G.NETINTRODUCING.NETINTRODUCING.NETINTRODUCING.NET
ODUCING.NETINTRODUCING.NETINTRODUCING.NETINTRODUCI
ETINTRODUCING.NETINTRODUCING.NETINTRODUCING.NETINT
CING.NETINTRODUCING.NETINTRODUCING.NETINTRODUCING.
NTRODUCING.NETINTRODUCING.NETINTRODUCING.NETINTROD
G.NETINTRODUCING.NETINTRODUCING.NETINTRODUCING.NET
ODUCING.NETINTRODUCING.NETINTRODUCING.NETINTRODUCI
ETINTRODUCING.NETINTRODUCING.NETINTRODUCING.NETINT
CING.NETINTRODUCING.NETINTRODUCING.NETINTRODUCING.
NTRODUCING.NETINTRODUCING.NETINTRODUCING.NETINTROD
G.NETINTRODUCING.NETINTRODUCING.NETINTRODUCING.NET
ODUCING.NETINTRODUCING.NETINTRODUCING.NETINTRODUCI
ETINTRODUCING.NETINTRODUCING.NETINTRODUCING.NETINT
CING.NETINTRODUCING.NETINTRODUCING.NETINTRODUCING.
NTRODUCING.NETINTRODUCING.NETINTRODUCING.NETINTROD
G.NETINTRODUCING.NETINTRODUCING.NETINTRODUCING.NET
ODUCING.NETINTRODUCING.NETINTRODUCING.NETINTRODUCI
ETINTRODUCING.NETINTRODUCING.NETINTRODUCING.NETINT
CING.NETINTRODUCING.NETINTRODUCING.NETINTRODUCING.
NTRODUCING.NETINTRODUCING.NETINTRODUCING.NETINTROD
G.NETINTRODUCING.NETINTRODUCING.NETINTRODUCING.NET
ODUCING.NETINTRODUCING.NETINTRODUCING.NETINTRODUCI
ETINTRODUCING.NETINTRODUCING.NETINTRODUCING.NETINT
CING.NETINTRODUCING.NETINTRODUCING.NETINTRODUCING.
NTRODUCING.NETINTRODUCING.NETINTRODUCING.NETINTROD
G.NETINTRODUCING.NETINTRODUCING.NETINTRODUCING.NET
ODUCING.NETINTRODUCING.NETINTRODUCING.NETINTRODUCI
ETINTRODUCING.NETINTRODUCING.NETINTRODUCING.NETINT

12

Enterprise Servers

The .NET Enterprise Server Family

Microsoft is promoting its new .NET initiative to businesses as a way to "make information available any time, any place, and on any device". For this to work they've had to come up with a plethora of operating system and software changes to handle the new requirements. These have moved development away from traditional client-server paradigms, where information was managed locally, in favour of a Web Services Model. With this model, while the central business elements of a solution will still be managed locally, services can be subscribed to seamlessly from remote locations.

These changes have brought about Microsoft's range of Enterprise Servers. These are servers founded on COM+ technology, combined with a strong support for XML. This support allows tight integration, both between the servers in the family and also with any other system that can interface through XML. It makes no difference to the server if that system is local, or accessed over the Internet. This chapter will focus on these new Enterprise Servers, which have been branded by Microsoft as **.NET Enabled,** and aims to provide an overview of how they fit together within the .NET Framework.

The .NET Enterprise Servers, along with the Microsoft Windows 2000, supply the foundation for developing and managing applications for the .NET platform. Under the .NET Framework, software is seen as a service to be delivered and should fully programmable, customisable and accessible. Microsoft has designed the .NET Enterprise Servers specifically to help companies rapidly integrate and orchestrate services and applications into a single comprehensive solution. The .NET Framework consists of a complementary set of development tools and libraries used to create applications that run on the .NET family of server products. Together, they form Microsoft's .NET initiative.

The .NET Enterprise Servers consist of:

- ❏ **Application Center 2000** – an integral component of the Microsoft .NET platform, Microsoft Application Center 2000 contains server side components as well as client side tools that enable you to deploy and maintain Web Applications and Services built on the Windows 2000 platform; its focus is on scalability, availability and ease-of-deployment.

- ❏ **BizTalk Server 2000** – enables the development and management of application integration within, and between, organizations using the universal standard of XML. BizTalk Server 2000 provides comprehensive process management and is a platform for reliable business document interchange and business processes integration.

- ❏ **Commerce Server 2000** – a complementary product to Microsoft's Internet Information Server (IIS), Commerce Server 2000 enables a business to get online fast. It provides all of the personalization, closed loop analysis, and electronic-store infrastructure necessary for business-to-business and business-to-consumer e-commerce. It is designed for quickly building tailored, scalable e-commerce solutions that optimize the user experience and provide business managers with real time analysis and control of their online business.

- ❏ **Exchange 2000 Server** – builds on the powerful messaging and collaboration features that have made Exchange Server a leader in today's market. Exchange 2000 Server will significantly advance messaging and collaboration technology by introducing several important new features (chief among them, the Web Storage system), further increasing the reliability, scalability and performance of its core architecture. These will also enhance the integration of Exchange 2000 Server with Microsoft Windows 2000, Microsoft Office 2000 and the Internet.

- ❏ **SQL Server 2000** – Microsoft's premier database platform has been improved to provide additional ease-of-use, scalability, and greater performance – especially for Web Applications. SQL Server 2000 includes rich support for XML and HTTP; also performance and availability features to partition load and ensure uptime. Together with advanced management and tuning functionality to automate routine tasks and lower the total cost of ownership. Additionally, SQL Server 2000 takes full advantage of Windows 2000, including support for the Active Directory service, up to 32 processors and 64 GB of RAM.

- ❏ **Host Integration Server 2000** – a comprehensive integration platform that provides the best way to embrace Internet, intranet and client/server technologies while preserving investments in existing AS/400 and mainframe-based legacy systems. Host Integration Server 2000 extends the Microsoft Windows operating system to other systems by providing application, data and network integration. This is Microsoft's next release of SNA Server.

- ❏ **Internet Security and Acceleration Server 2000** – provides secure, fast, manageable Internet connectivity. ISA Server includes an extensible, multilevel, enterprise firewall and a scalable high-performance web cache. It builds on Microsoft Windows 2000's security directory for policy-based security, acceleration and management of Internet working.

- ❏ **Mobile Information 2001 Server**– Due for release slightly later than the rest of the Enterprise Servers, Mobile Information Server is designed for the mobile community. It acts as an application server that specifically targets mobile devices, allowing users to perform tasks such as check their e-mail, consult their calendars, and look through their contact database. It essentially extends the capabilities of Exchange to reach this specialized audience.

What's Common Between All the .NET Enterprise Servers

Microsoft has offered the .NET Enterprise Servers as a family of products that work together and therefore can be leveraged to build and deploy scalable, integrated, web-based solutions. They have been specifically designed for mission-critical applications, high demand applications and applications where high availability (low downtime) is very important. Although the core of some of these products remains the same, they have all been significantly re-built from the ground up for interoperability both with each other and with other Web Services (including other platforms and products from other companies) using open web standards such as XML. Here is a list of common features among all the .NET Enterprise Servers. Some of the servers support these features more cohesively than the others.

Support for XML and other Internet Protocols/Standards

All the .NET Enterprise Servers now use XML as their underlying data format as well as the format for interoperability. While this may be to some extent "marketing hype" (they didn't throw away SQL Server's internal data storage and convert it into an XML based relational database structure), what is true is that you can use XML to pump data into, and pull data out of, all these products. To the end user (or the developer), that's what's ultimately important. Internally, the server products may be translating XML data into their own native formats, but they expose the ability to communicate using XML. The big advantage of supporting Internet standards such as XML, HTTP, HTML, FTP, and XPath is that data can be efficiently exchanged across the Internet, including through firewalls.

Software Scaling and Availability

One of the design goals of the .NET Enterprise Servers has been scalability. Enterprises right now are achieving high availability by deploying web applications simultaneously on multiple servers and using a load-balancing mechanism to distribute the incoming requests. This approach is called **software scaling**. Many large web sites use this technique. A single URL for a large well-known web site could point to one of 50 different web servers. The incoming request for a web page is re-routed to any one of those 50 servers according to its current load. Each server is capable of supporting over 1,000 concurrent users. The entire web site therefore, is capable of supporting 50,000 concurrent users. By scaling out, the web site can keep adding web servers and use Application Center to adjust its load-balancing mechanism to meet the demands of additional users, (as opposed to Scaling up, which is where individual server hardware is upgraded instead). In this scenario, even if one or more servers are taken offline for maintenance or if a server goes down, the other servers will pick up the demand, which is something that Application Center handles very well. To the web site's visitor, all of this is transparent.

Using the .NET Enterprise Servers, server **farms** or clusters can be created using a bank of inexpensive, off-the-shelf PC servers rather than using an expensive, hardware scalability solution. Further by adding additional servers in a software scaling deployment downtime also is intrinsically reduced. In addition, the .NET Enterprise Servers provide tools to monitor the health of the system and take pro-active action when needed.

Interoperability

Real world web applications are built using a collection of disparate systems to connect customers, partners and suppliers. Web site analysis, customer analysis, customer relationship management, supply chain management, order processing, and logistics: all of these functions are supplied, by different providers, using different systems. The .NET Enterprise Servers allow developers to build solutions that integrate all these varied environments into one homogeneous solution.

Focus on Business Logic, not on Deployment

The .NET Enterprise Servers offer in-built access to a lot of the "plumbing" functionality that developers had to deal with when deploying large scale web applications. Where previously a lot of work would have gone into developing cluster applications, caching, and component load balancing, these are now dealt with at an operating system level. This frees up the developer to focus on the business logic within their application, rather than on developing custom infrastructure and components for its deployment.

Ease of Management

The .NET Enterprise Servers provide management tools that ease deployment, administration and management. They allow you to manage multiple servers from a single management console and handle administration of all tiers (presentation tier, application tier and data tier) from a single point.

Application Center 2000

Application Center 2000 is Microsoft's deployment and management tool for high-availability web applications built on the Windows 2000 operating system. AC2000 enables you to deploy large e-commerce web sites as well as mission-critical web applications on one or multiple servers and yet have the ease of managing and monitoring all the servers from a central location.

Product Availability

At the time of writing, Application Center is in Release Candidate phase.

A pre-requisite for installing the Application Center Server components is the presence of a Windows 2000 Server, Windows 2000 Advanced Server or Windows 2000 DataCenter operating system with Service Pack 1, although you'll need to use either Advanced Server or DataCenter Server to take advantage of Network Load Balancing.

What's the Focus?

Pieces of Application Center were available earlier in the form of the Network Load Balancing Services (NLBS) as well as enhancements to the COM+ packaging model (COM+ Applications) in the Windows 2000 Server products. Application Center, however, is billed as a separate, brand new, set of components and services that were primarily developed by the Internet Information Server (IIS) team based on extensive customer visits. Based on feedback from customers, Microsoft learned that Web application developers and IT professionals were using IIS/NT and Windows 2000 for deploying large-scale Web applications (Web sites, internal Web applications, extranet applications, B2B exchanges, and portal sites). The key requirement for these Web applications was high availability (an uptime of nearly 100%) and high scalability (the ability to handle an excess load of users without degradation in performance). Developers and IT professionals were making do with whatever facilities IIS/Win2K was providing at that time – this included creating Web server farms by combining multiple server machines and using NLBS for load balancing. In addition, clusters of machines were being created to handle database as well as middle-tier logic related applications. However, creating these clusters and maintaining multiple machines was not easy and was creating a great "barrier-to-entry". Microsoft identified the difficulties that its customers were facing in moving their Web applications to a software-scaled architecture using multiple Win2K machines clustered together. These common problems included the following:

❏   Keeping copies of applications synchronized with each other was labor intensive

❏   Scaling applications was too complex

❏   Managing and monitoring clusters was hard

Application Center has been introduced to solve these problems. The team's design focus has been on three areas:

❏   Application Management

❏   Software Scaling

❏   Mission-Critical Availability

What's New?

Everything! Application Center 2000 is a brand new product and provides a glut of wizards, technologies, and management tools that sit on top of Windows 2000 Server products. Specifically, Application Center provides the following features:

Cluster Services: Application Center makes it easy to set up and maintain a cluster of servers. A Cluster Wizard walks you through the steps to create a cluster. The wizard analyses your server to determine if it has the necessary hardware and software configuration to serve as a cluster controller and if so, proceeds to build a cluster for you. You can add and delete servers in the cluster and determine what kind of content the cluster will serve. You can also determine the load-balancing scheme to be used – either the integrated Network Load Balancing (NLB) service or an external application. The wizard also sets up default and general monitoring services for the cluster. At the end of the process, you have a cluster that contains one member server – the cluster controller. You can then add additional members to the cluster and manage all the servers via a single **MMC** window.

Load Balancing: Application Center provides an enhanced management view of the Network Load Balancing Service that ships with Windows 2000 Advanced Server and DataCenter Server. This enables you to monitor and deploy Load Balancing on multiple servers from a single point. The main advantage of this is that a wizard helps you set up the load balancing and examines your hardware and software for its capability. You can then specify the load-balancing algorithm to use. In addition, Application Center adds a new kind of load balancing that was previously unavailable called Component Load Balancing. This allows you to manage the load on the Application Layer running within COM+ components. The COM+ components do not need to be on the same machine as the Web server, so can be offloaded to a separate server or set of servers. At run time, the load for requests to these COM+ components is distributed among the machines that are being balanced by Component Load Balancing. Using this technique, a single cluster can use multiple servers running COM+ applications to service component requests.

Synchronization and Deployment: When deploying web applications to multiple servers, synchronizing the content between them is either fairly simple or overly complex depending on the kind of Web site you are developing. For static web pages, it is a simple matter to copy the pages from one machine to the other, thereby making sure that all the servers are in synch. However, when you need to manage and deploy components and IIS settings these have to be done individually on each web server machine in a server cluster or **server farm**.

In Application Center 2000, a cluster can be synchronized by replicating either configuration or application settings. A replication engine that uses custom drivers makes the links to the various configuration stores on the controller machine and copies their settings to the target servers. The replication of configuration settings is transparent to the user and done automatically.

Web application deployment is synchronized by using the Application Deployment Wizard that mirrors the web application's image from the controlling machine to all other machines within the cluster. In addition, the following items are also replicated during synchronization:

❑   COM+ settings

❑   CAPI settings

❑   Registry keys

❑   WMI settings

❑   File system information

❑   Metabase settings

Monitoring: Application Center 2000 provides new tools for monitoring the performance and health (condition) of a server system. The performance monitoring has been enhanced by the addition of events that can be monitored and evaluated. Numerous objects and applications will generate events, or actions, that take place on your server. A new concept, Health Monitor, includes several sets of data collectors, with predefined thresholds that monitor server and cluster health. You can either use the predefined health monitors or create your own using an MMC snap-in.

You can evaluate the health of your system and web applications by monitoring data collectors such as:

❑   Request execution time

❑   Request wait time

❑   Thread count

❑   Processor queue length

❑   Number of deadlocks in SQL Server

❑   COM+ object creations per second

❑   Total committed transactions

The performance monitor and health monitor can also be controlled programmatically. Within your web applications you can generate code to install additional performance counters as well as query the Application Center database of performance monitors – you can therefore check the health of the system programmatically and take proactive action when needed.

BizTalk Server 2000

Microsoft's BizTalk Server is used to manipulate and manage business processes between Web Services within, and beyond, the enterprise using the Internet and its protocols as a communications medium. Using BizTalk, enterprises can exchange data with their suppliers and vendors quickly and efficiently. To do this BizTalk relies heavily on XML.

Product Availability

BizTalk Server 2000 Enterprise Edition is available as a beta at this time. You can download the beta version at:

http://www.microsoft.com/biztalk/productinfo/evaluate.htm.

This beta download requires that you already have SQL Server version 7.0, with Service Pack 2 (SP2) or later, Visio 2000 Standard Edition, and Office 2000 Web Components. If you do not already have Windows Advanced Server installed on your computer, you can order a 120-day evaluation edition from the Windows 2000 Web site. Pricing information for the full product is not available at this time.

What's the Focus?

BizTalk Server provides a single tool that allows enterprises to build processes that exchange data between applications across the Internet. BizTalk Server helps enterprises build processes that span not only applications, but also businesses. A typical example would be the interaction required between a web application within an enterprise and that enterprise's supplier. The format of a purchase order or invoice may differ between different companies and different industries. But using XML as a common format, it is possible to exchange data between them over the Internet. However, the XML schema needs to match in order for both entities to process the information. BizTalk Server eases this process by establishing a set of guidelines for XML data-transfer. In addition, BizTalk Server provides a GUI interface to build XML schemas, perform schema translations or transformations and establish partnerships between businesses over the Internet. Instead of trading hard copy XML schemas that need to be programmatically or manually translated, the server automatically synchronizes the XML data from two disparate organizations. BizTalk Server relies on XML, HTTP and SMTP protocols for data transfer and is probably the best example of the .NET Framework among the .NET Enterprise Servers.

What's New

BizTalk Server has a number of tools, wizards and guidelines that make it easy for an enterprise to standardize on XML schemas for data exchange. The success of BizTalk will depend on the acceptance in the market of its guidelines and its penetration. If two companies both use BizTalk Server, they will be able to seamlessly exchange XML data related to their business processes.

Tools: BizTalk Orchestration Designer is a tool that enables you to visually build workflow operations between business analysts, IT professionals, and developers. The BizTalk Editor allows you to rapidly generate XML schemas while the BizTalk Mapper allows you to transfer one XML schema to another using a drag and drop visual metaphor. While you work visually, the BizTalk Mapper generates XSLT files in the background for transforming documents.

Support for Internet standards: All BizTalk Server document exchanges are done using XML. All document transformation is done using W3C-standard XSLT. In addition, BizTalk Server supports EDI, HTTP, HTTPS, SMTP, FTP and Flat files.

Document Delivery and Tracking: BizTalk Server provides a framework for document exchange and routing. This BizTalk Framework Version 2.0 is built around SOAP and provides guaranteed delivery of documents. BizTalk Server 2000 sends, receives and queues messages with exactly-once semantics. BizTalk Server 2000 also offers easy tracking of documents and it integrates with MS SQL Server for online analytical processing of data and document progress. In addition, BizTalk has the Messaging Manager that automates the exchange of trading profiles and business agreements through a graphical UI.

Microsoft is trying very hard to get industry acceptance of BizTalk. They have set up a Web site located at www.biztalk.org where companies can share information and publish their BizTalk schemas in the hope of accelerating electronic commerce and application integration using BizTalk.

Commerce Server 2000

Commerce Server 2000 is the next incarnation of Site Server Commerce Edition. It allows a company to set up an online business quickly and easily. Commerce Server 2000 provides an integrated e-commerce solution combined with extensive personalization and decision support tools to target content for users and react to market changes. Commerce Server 2000 also ships with pre-built B2C (business-to-customer) and B2B (business-to-business) sites that an enterprise can use to be up and running very quickly.

Product Availability

At this time, the Commerce Server 2000 Evaluation Edition is available for download from:

http://www.microsoft.com/commerceserver/downloads/evaledition.htm.

This download is for trial and evaluation purposes only and will expire on February 28, 2001. Pricing for Commerce Server 2000 is on a per-processor basis. Details of pricing are available at:

http://www.microsoft.com/commerceserver/productinfo/pricing.htm.

The download is also available if you are an MSDN Universal subscriber from the MSDN Web site.

What's the Focus

Commerce Server 2000 offers an easy and quick way to build tailored, effective e-commerce solutions that incorporate targeting, feedback and analytical capabilities. It tightly integrates with MS SQL Server, and includes User Profiling, Product, and Service Management tools; as well as tools for Transaction Processing, Targeted Marketing, and Merchandizing Solutions. In addition, it provides "out-of-the-box" pre-built B2C and B2B sites that can be customized. These include a Retail Solution site for B2C applications, a Supplier Solution site for B2B applications and an Auction site.

What's New

Commerce Server has been developed with several links into the .NET framework to justify its label as a .NET enabled Enterprise server.

At the application-tier level, Commerce Server 2000 integrates with Active Directory and its security features. It also takes advantage of the multiprocessor support, component and network load balancing services of Windows 2000 and Windows Application Server 2000.

At the data-tier level, Commerce Server integrates with MS SQL Server 2000 for data and analysis capabilities.

At the back-end processing level Commerce Server tightly integrates with BizTalk Server 2000 and Host Integration Server 2000. Together they provide data interchange for offering Web promotions, handling Web marketplace transactions and back-end interactions between vendors, suppliers and partner systems. Commerce Server is the successor to Site Server 3.0 Commerce Edition. This product was a complete rewrite and many of the features are completely new.

Exchange 2000

Exchange 2000 is Microsoft's messaging and collaboration platform. Exchange 2000 has been vastly improved with lots of new features and capabilities. Engineered from the ground up to take advantage of Windows 2000, Exchange 2000's primary promise is the delivery of unified management for all messaging, collaboration and networked capabilities and resources.

Product Availability

Exchange 2000 is a shipping product. You can obtain the details of how to purchase this system in its various configurations at:

http://www.microsoft.com/exchange/productinfo/howtobuy.htm .

The download is also available if you are an MSDN Universal subscriber from the MSDN Web site.

What's the Focus

Messaging used to mean communication by e-mail messages and was similar to communication using phone, paper, or fax. Today, however, with digital processing and the Internet, enterprises have discovered the power of messaging systems that can manage all aspects of information and workflow within and beyond an organization. This is the target audience that Exchange 2000 is focusing on. By providing support for Web standard protocols, XML and HTTP, Exchange provides a hosting solution for web applications that automate day-to-day business tasks.

What's New

The key to the major changes in Exchange 2000 is its new Web Storage System, the updated version of the Exchange Information Store, which serves as a single database, not only for messaging, but also for documents and web applications.

Web Storage System: This single database has been built from the ground up to support XML and HTTP protocols. In addition, the Web Storage System provides tight integration with Microsoft Office applications enabling any Office document to be stored in the Web Storage System and efficiently retrieved. This means that enterprises can now streamline the business processes that revolve around a collaboration workflow, for example following the path of a document from its initial preparation through reviews, edits and approvals to final action. A user can generate a document, have it e-mailed to a manager who can review and edit it, and then forward it to their peers for approval and action. All this can take place without the document ever leaving the confines of the Web Storage System within Exchange, so the chance of multiple older versions of a document is eliminated. Besides, the workflow need not be confined to the enterprise itself, because through the support for Web Distributed Authoring and Versioning (WebDAV) collaboration can take place among users spread across the Internet.

New Development Tools: Exchange 2000 exposes the Web Storage System to developers for programmatic manipulation. Also, significant improvements have been made to the Collaboration Data Objects (CDO) model to make it easier to incorporate Exchange 2000 features, such as calendaring, contact management, messaging and system management, within Web and workflow applications. Web Forms allow the developer to add business logic to web applications and then transmit the form using HTTP to a browser. Finally, the Web Storage System incorporates OLEDB and ADO interfaces directly into Exchange 2000 so that developers can query the contents of Exchange 2000 for use in their own applications.

Anytime, anywhere communication: Exchange 2000 includes upgrades and enhancements to existing client applications to ensure that users can access the rich functionality of Exchange 2000 from any location using a wide variety of client access tools. A significantly enhanced Outlook Web Access (OWA – a browser-based version of Outlook) now looks and operates so much like the desktop Outlook client that it is hard to tell the difference from the interfaces. In fact OWA now provides the same user interface as Outlook but in HTML format so that users can access it via a browser. Functionality in OWA has also been increased; you can now use OWA to access e-mail, scheduling, contacts, and collaborative information. URL Addressing allows end users to provide HTTP URL addresses to inboxes allowing them to access their inbox remotely from a web browser. On top of this, Exchange 2000 also includes Instant Messaging and Chat services.

Real-time Collaboration: A new product, Exchange 2000 Conferencing Server, is also available from Microsoft. This complementary software provides online conferencing capabilities, conference management tools, as well as support for clients on multiple platforms, be they NetMeeting clients, Linux clients, Unix clients, or Macintosh clients.

SQL Server 2000

SQL Server 2000 has finally come of age, not only as a robust relational database engine but also as a data analysis package with impressive data warehousing and data mining tools. The winner of numerous benchmark records for scalability, speed and cost per transaction, SQL Server 2000 is among Microsoft's premier Enterprise Server products. MS SQL Server is a relational database management system (RDBMS) for building business applications.

Product Availability

The release version of SQL Server 2000 is now available from Microsoft. Pricing and Licensing information is available from:

http://www.microsoft.com/sql/productinfo/pricing.htm.

while instructions on how to purchase is available at:

http://www.microsoft.com/sql/productinfo/howtobuy.htm.

The information is also available if you are an MSDN Universal subscriber from the MSDN Web site.

What's the Focus

Microsoft has focused SQL Server 2000 on three major areas, Data Warehousing, e-Commerce, and Line-of-Business (LOB). In addition, its tight integration with other .NET Enterprise Servers means that SQL Server is the database platform of choice when working with the other .NET Enterprise Servers.

What's New

SQL Server 2000 has a host of new features, aimed specifically at the developer.

Rich XML Support: Recognizing the fact that XML is quickly becoming the standard for data interchange on the Internet, Microsoft has enabled developers to quickly convert database information into XML format by simply adding a few keywords to the end of their SQL SELECT statements. OpenXML, a T-SQL keyword, provides a relational view of XML data that can be used to query data from XML, join XML data with existing relational tables, and update the database. SQL Server enables queries to return data as XML (rather than a standard rowset) from a SELECT statement through the FOR XML clause.

For example, the SQL Statement:

```
SELECT firstname,lastname FROM employees FOR XML AUTO
```

when used against the Northwind database, returns the following output (in XML):

```
<?xml version="1.0" encoding="UTF-8" ?>
<root>
    <row firstname="Nancy" lastname="Davolio" />
    <row firstname="Andrew" lastname="Fuller" />
    <row firstname="Janet" lastname="Leverling" />
    <row firstname="Margaret" lastname="Peacock" />
    <row firstname="Steven" lastname="Buchanan" />
    <row firstname="Michael" lastname="Suyama" />
    <row firstname="Robert" lastname="King" />
    <row firstname="Laura" lastname="Callahan" />
    <row firstname="Anne" lastname="Dodsworth" />
</root>
```

You can even run this SQL Query across the Internet using the HTTP protocol. If your database was exposed to the Net, you could simply access this URL to get the same identical output:

http://localhost/Northwind?sql=SELECT+firstname,lastname+FROM+employees+FOR+XML+AUTO.

Besides retrieving data as XML, it is important to be able to store data efficiently in XML format, maintaining the relationships and hierarchy of data while taking full advantage of the speed offered by a high-performance database like SQL Server. SQL Server 2000 can provide an XML View of relational data as well as mapping XML into relational tables. Whereas XML Views enable relational tables to be accessed as if they were XML documents (as we saw in the above code example), OpenXML allows XML documents to be addressed with relational SQL syntax. OpenXML is a T-SQL keyword that provides an updateable rowset over in-memory XML documents. The records in XML can be stored in database tables, similar to the rowsets provided by tables and views. OpenXML can be used in SELECT, and SELECT INTO statements wherever rowset providers such as table, view, or OPENROWSET can appear. Two XML features in SQL Server 2000 that are now available as beta one versions, are the XML Updategrams (commands sent to the server that allow Web developers to use XML to insert, update, and delete data from SQL Server 2000 tables) and the XML bulk load facility (that enables bulk loads of data packaged with XML).

Access SQL Server data over the Internet: SQL Server 2000 delivers features for accessing data stored in SQL Server databases and OLAP cubes through the Web. SQL Server 2000 enables access using a Uniform Resource Locator (URL) by several different mechanisms that are associated with an instance of SQL Server 2000. Among other actions, the URL can do the following:

❑ Execute SQL Queries directly using http://servername/virtualroot?sql="SELECT statement" syntax (as shown earlier).

❑   Access Database Objects (for example, for tables) by using
http://servername/virtualroot/dbobject/xpath syntax. The xpath syntax treats tables and views
as elements and columns as attributes.

❑   Execute template files by using the http://servername/virtualroot/virtualname?params syntax
to directly reference a template file. A template file is a valid XML file containing one or more
SQL Statements. When a template file is specified, all the SQL statements within it are
executed and the entire results sent back.

❑   Execute XPath queries through an XML View.

Enhanced Data Warehousing tools: SQL Server 2000 features the Analysis Services for SQL Server
2000, formerly called OLAP Services. This provides a complete end-to-end platform for analysis, data
warehousing and data mining. You can mix-and-match algorithms and tools from Microsoft and other
third party providers. DTS packages can now be created to extract, transform, and load heterogeneous
data using OLEDB, ODBC, and text-files into the database or into a multidimensional store. DTS has
been improved from previous releases in terms of usability and programmability. DTS packages can be
stored as Visual Basic-based code simplifying its development and manipulation.

Indexed views: SQL Server has always supported the ability to create virtual persistent tables (or **views**)
out of data in the database. These views provide a mechanism for the developer or administrator to
create a custom look from a table, or a set of tables joined together for a specific reason.

Views in SQL Server prior to the 2000 version were aggregates of the underlying SELECT statements.
At run time, the SELECT statement was parsed, compiled, and an execution plan chosen. SQL Server
2000 now has performance enhancements to Views, allowing you to specify a clustered index for a
view. In SQL Server, a view that has a clustered index is called an **Indexed View**. This view improves
performance by allowing SQL Server to reference the indexed view directly, or by allowing the query
optimizer to make a decision on whether to use the index or its underlying low-cost query plan. Because
of this, aggregations in the view can be pre-computed and stored in the index to minimize expensive
computations during query execution. Tables can be pre-joined and the resulting data set can be stored.
One obvious use for indexed views is for Online Analytical Processing (OLAP) applications or Data
Warehousing Applications.

Other .NET Enterprise Servers

There is not much information available on the remaining servers in the .NET Framework, as they
have yet to be launched in retail versions. Here are the scheduled features for the remaining .NET
Enterprise Servers.

Host Integration Server 2000

Host Integration Server is the follow-up server product to SNA server providing Microsoft Windows
access to other systems and enabling application, data and network integration.

Product Availability

You can obtain evaluation editions of the different Host Integration Server 2000 components from:

http://www.microsoft.com/hiserver/productinfo/downloads/default.htm.

What's the Focus

Host Integration Server 2000 extends Microsoft Windows to other systems by providing application, data and network interoperability.

Internet Security and Acceleration Server 2000

Internet Security and Acceleration (ISA) Server 2000 provides secure, fast, and manageable Internet connectivity. ISA Server integrates an extensible, multilayer enterprise firewall and a scalable high performance Web cache.

Product Availability

At this time, Release Candidate 1 of the ISA is available for download from:

http://www.microsoft.com/isaserver/productinfo/evaledition.htm.

ISA Server requires Windows 2000 Advanced Server.

What's the Focus

ISA Server provides secure Internet connectivity. It includes a multi-layer firewall featuring security traffic screening at the packet, circuit, and application level, together with integrated Virtual Private Networking (VPN), Intrusion Detection, and Smart Filters.

ISA also features a web cache that improves performance for enterprise Internet access. The ISA web cache is aimed at minimizing performance bottlenecks and saving network bandwidth.

ISA Server boasts a unified and simplified management interface, but from tests conducted on the Release Candidate version, I found that the management interface is not very easy and takes a while to get used to.

Mobile Information Server 2001

Mobile Information Server 2001 is an application server for mobile devices, opening up access to applications to a specific set of users who have strict requirements about protocols, size of applications, and screen size.

Product Availability

At this time, Mobile Information Server is at an early stage of development, but it scheduled to hit the shelves in 2001. For more information, you can look at:

http://www.microsoft.com/servers/miserver/default.htm.

Mobile Information Server will be available in two versions – Mobile Information Server Enterprise Edition, and Mobile Information Server Carrier Edition.

What's the Focus

Mobile Information Server incorporates modules that support HTML, WAP 1.1, and Phone.com's HDML browsers, to ensure compatibility with a wide range of devices from mobile phones, to PDAs. The product also contains Outlook Mobile Access, which is designed to integrate with Exchange 2000 to allow mobile users to access their e-mail, contact information, tasks, and calendar.

Mobile Information Server also supports SMTP and SMS (and potentially WAP-Push), to notify users of events, such as a meeting reminder, without the need to be connected constantly to a network.

Mobile Information Server takes full advantage of the Windows 2000 Active Directory. You can manage Mobile Information Server from an MMC snap-in, from the Mobile Information Server support of Windows Management Instrumentation, or through a programming interface that can be used to build customized management applications.

Summary

This chapter gave a brief look at the .Net Enterprise Servers from Microsoft. All of the servers in the .NET platform are built on an open architecture. Meaning that much of the functionality of a particular server is exposed through a set of COM+ interfaces that allow the developer to access them and to program against them. This is available today and using the new Visual Studio.NET is not required to do so. A developer can create scripts to automate the server, or can program against the interfaces using VB, VC or any language of their choice, that can access COM+ components.

The level of support for the .NET Framework among the different servers varies currently but it will steadily converge as Microsoft adds enhancements to them. The .NET servers provide support for open Internet standards, chiefly XML and HTTP as well as tight integration both with each other and with the Win2K Server operating systems.

INTRODUCING·NETINTRODUCING·NETINTRODUCING·NETINTRODUCI
ODUCING·NETINTRODUCING·NETINTRODUCING·NETINTRODUCI
ETINTRODUCING·NETINTRODUCING·NETINTRODUCING·NETINT
CING·NETINTRODUCING·NETINTRODUCING·NETINTRODUCING·
NTRODUCING·NETINTRODUCING·NETINTRODUCING·NETINTROD
G·NETINTRODUCING·NETINTRODUCING·NETINTRODUCING·NET
ODUCING·NETINTRODUCING·NETINTRODUCING·NETINTRODUCI
ETINTRODUCING·NETINTRODUCING·NETINTRODUCING·NETINT
CING·NETINTRODUCING·NETINTRODUCING·NETINTRODUCING·
NTRODUCING·NETINTRODUCING·NETINTRODUCING·NETINTROD
G·NETINTRODUCING·NETINTRODUCING·NETINTRODUCING·NET
ODUCING·NETINTRODUCING·NETINTRODUCING·NETINTRODUCI
ETINTRODUCING·NETINTRODUCING·NETINTRODUCING·NETINT
CING·NETINTRODUCING·NETINTRODUCING·NETINTRODUCING·
NTRODUCING·NETINTRODUCING·NETINTRODUCING·NETINTROD
G·NETINTRODUCING·NETINTRODUCING·NETINTRODUCING·NET
ODUCING·NETINTRODUCING·NETINTRODUCING·NETINTRODUCI
ETINTRODUCING·NETINTRODUCING·NETINTRODUCING·NETINT
CING·NETINTRODUCING·NETINTRODUCING·NETINTRODUCING·
NTRODUCING·NETINTRODUCING·NETINTRODUCING·NETINTROD
G·NETINTRODUCING·NETINTRODUCING·NETINTRODUCING·NET
ODUCING·NETINTRODUCING·NETINTRODUCING·NETINTRODUCI
ETINTRODUCING·NETINTRODUCING·NETINTRODUCING·NETINT
CING·NETINTRODUCING·NETINTRODUCING·NETINTRODUCING·
NTRODUCING·NETINTRODUCING·NETINTRODUCING·NETINTROD
G·NETINTRODUCING·NETINTRODUCING·NETINTRODUCING·NET
ODUCING·NETINTRODUCING·NETINTRODUCING·NETINTRODUCI
ETINTRODUCING·NETINTRODUCING·NETINTRODUCING·NETINT
CING·NETINTRODUCING·NETINTRODUCING·NETINTRODUCING·
NTRODUCING·NETINTRODUCING·NETINTRODUCING·NETINTROD
G·NETINTRODUCING·NETINTRODUCING·NETINTRODUCING·NET
ODUCING·NETINTRODUCING·NETINTRODUCING·NETINTRODUCI
ETINTRODUCING·NETINTRODUCING·NETINTRODUCING·NETINT

13

ASP.NET Case Study

In the preceding chapters of this book we have conceptually covered the ideals, approaches, and components used for developing .NET applications. In this chapter we will focus more on the actual implementation of a real-world application – an e-commerce website. Although this is a sample that has been used many times before, it's time to look at how we build this type of application using the .NET components and services.

Normally you would refer to an example as an application. However, in our case, the far more fitting description is a solution. The example is composed of four different applications or projects which, when combined, create the e-commerce solution that will be detailed in this chapter. After we have explained the purpose of each application we will then detail its implementation. Once we have covered each of the parts of the application we will see how they all work together to provide the solution.

Building a .NET Solution

The question that will most likely be on your mind is: What are these different applications that we will be building and using? In order to explain what parts are being used, we must first understand what is the intended use of the solution.

In this chapter, we are going to explore the development of an e-commerce solution. This solution will allow end users to view inventory for a company, view details on specific items, add items to their shopping cart, and be able to checkout and submit their order. For the user interface, we will be creating a web-based front end using the capabilities of .NET. Users will need to login to the application in order to see a listing of the current inventory. Then, they should be able to select items and add them to a shopping cart. After the user has finished their selections they will then proceed to the checkout. Once the order is submitted, the user does not see any of the work done behind the scenes by the solution. Instead, the user will get a confirmation page that their order was submitted. Meanwhile, upon submission, the solution will need to send the order to processing. Once the processing is completed, the order will need to be billed and shipped.

So, knowing the function of the solution, how should the parts be broken down? What applications must be built to create the solution? The most obvious is the web application. This is the only part of the solution with which the user will interact. Another application that will need to be provided is the submitting of the order for processing. In order to then process that order, it will be necessary to build an order processing application. The solution would also require the implementation of billing and shipping processes, but those will not be fully implemented in this chapter, as they do not provide any situations that will not already be covered in the other applications.

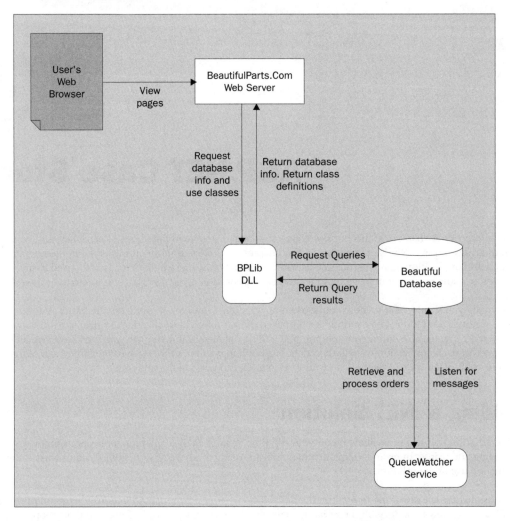

It is not immediately apparent from looking at the design, but an important part of the solution is the transfer and exchange of data between the multiple applications. In order to accomplish this data transfer, we will be creating a separate application (DLL) that provides the data structures and supporting database functionality that will be needed in the solution. The separate DLL is preferable as it centralizes the management of the data formats as well as the data retrieval functionality. One downside of using a DLL is that it introduces another dependency to the solution. The added cost of this file is offset by the reduced maintenance cost of handling changes and updates to the data structures or backend database.

The first step in creating the solution is to have a name. For this solution we will be creating BeautifulParts.Com. In examining the remainder of the solution, we will be working a bit backwards. Instead of starting with the web application and then drilling down into each part involved, we will start from the smallest part and make our way back to the web application. For this solution, the applications that will be built are:

- ❑ **Beautiful Database** – the back-end database

- ❑ **BPLib** – a Library (DLL) containing data structures and database support utilities

- ❑ **QueueWatcherService** – Windows NT Service to "listen" the message queue and process the incoming orders

- ❑ **OrderSubmitService** – a Web Service used to submit orders to the Orders message queue

- ❑ **BeautifulParts.Com** – the web application that a user will interact with in order to select and order car parts

BeautifulParts.Com Requirements

This chapter, and the building of the solution, make a number of assumptions about the system on which the solution is developed. For our purposes, we will assume that the development machine and the server machine are the same – this approach works for developing applications, but dedicated server machines should be used for any production web sites. The machine needs to have Visual Studio.NET (VS.NET), SQL Server (or MSDE), and MSMQ installed. The full solution source, downloadable from the Wrox web site, www.wrox.com, includes scripts to run to create the necessary database and tables on the server. In addition to the database, the server needs to have the following private queues created: Orders, Billing, and Shipping. The permissions on these queues must be set so that Everyone can send and receive on the queue.

> As this application was developed on the beta one release of Visual Studio.NET, it is certain that there will be programming model changes before Visual Studio.NET is released.

BeautifulParts Database

As with any solution these days, this one will involve a database. Since the solution will be listing inventory and tracking customers, the database should be structured to store all the necessary information. However, our solution is not intended to show e-commerce development as much as it is to show .NET development. Due to that, this solution will not store as much information as would be stored for a real-world e-commerce solution. In a more product ready solution, we would be interested in storing more information and details for customers and their orders, but, for the purpose of demonstrating .NET applications, that information would be extraneous. Instead, this solution will only be concerned with limited customer and inventory information. As such, we will be creating/using two tables in the database: Products and Customers.

The `Products` table design is:

Field Name	Type	Length	Allow Null	Description
ProductID	int	4	No	Unique ID for product. (Identity field)
Description	varchar	50	No	Sales description for product
Price	float	8	No	Unit price of product
PhotoURL	varchar	100	Yes	URL to photo of product

The `Customers` table design is:

Field Name	Type	Length	Allow Null	Description
CustomerID	int	4	No	Unique ID for customer (Identity Field)
FirstName	varchar	50	No	Customer's First Name
LastName	varchar	50	No	Customer's Last Name
Address1	varchar	50	Yes	Street Address #1
Address2	varchar	50	Yes	Street Address #2
City	varchar	50	Yes	City
State	varchar	2	Yes	State
Zip	varchar	10	Yes	Zip
Phone	varchar	12	Yes	Phone Number
Password	varchar	15	No	Password

For implementing and testing the application, the `Customers` and `Products` tables have been filled with some test data.

BPLib.DLL

As the data structure is core to any solution, the first thing we will be implementing will be the BPLib DLL. It is in this DLL that we will define the data structure used for customer orders, inventory items, and billing information. The DLL will also provide a class to be used for retrieving data from the backend database. We will be implementing this DLL using C#, though you could use any supported .NET language for its creation.

In order to create this DLL, we first need to launch VS.NET and create a new project, then click on the **Visual C# Projects** node in the **Project Types** pane, and on **Class Library** in the **Templates** pane. This will present the user with the following dialog:

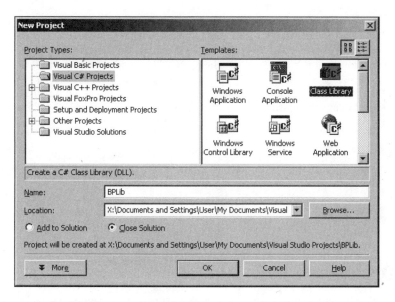

From this dialog we will select to create a new C# Class Library (DLL) and give it the name of BPLib. Once the user clicks OK the project will be created and a new class1.cs will be added. In this case we want to right click on the file in the Solution explorer, select **Rename**, and rename the file to be BPLib.cs.

The last step before beginning to implement the class is to add the necessary references. Since the project is using early binding and the System.Data assemblies we need to add a new reference to the System.Data.Dll. References can be added by right clicking on the **References** folder in the **Solution Explorer** and selecting **Add Reference**. That will bring up the **Add Reference** dialog:

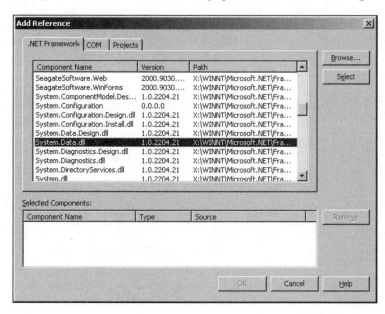

In this dialog we need to scroll down and select System.Data.Dll, click **Select**, and then click the OK button. Once we have done that we are then ready to begin implementing the BPLib classes.

One of the features of C# (and the other .NET languages) is that multiple class definitions can be contained within a single file. Finally, with VB.NET, this capability is available to Visual Basic programmers. That means that we only have to create BPLib.cs, which will contain the class definitions for all of the classes we will create. Instead of listing the full file contents here, we will instead only list parts of the code.

The first part of the file will declare the namespace for the classes; in this case it is BPLib. Also, the using directive will be used to import information from a number of other namespaces, as those will be used within this DLL.

```
namespace BPLib
{
    using System;
    using System.Collections;
    using System.Data;
    using System.Data.SQL;
    using System.Diagnostics;
```

BeautifulDatabase Class

Once the namespace has been defined and the necessary namespaces included, we will define the BeautifulDatabase class. This class will provide methods that can be used to retrieve data from the database. The code for the class is:

```
/// <summary>
///     The BeautifulDatabase class is used to simplify querying
///     data from the backend database
/// </summary>
public class BeautifulDatabase
{
    // Retrieve the inventory items from the database
    public static DataSet GetItemListing()
    {
        return GetDataSet("Select * from products","Products");
    }

    // Retrieve the formatted customer name from the database
    public static string GetCustomerName(string CustomerID)
    {
        DataRow  tmpDR = GetCustomerInfo(CustomerID);
        return (tmpDR["FirstName"] + " " + tmpDR["LastName"]);
    }

    // Retrieve the Item's information from the database
    public static DataSet GetItemInfo(string productID)
    {
    return GetDataSet("Select * from Products where productID=" +
                                        productID,"Products");
    }

    // Retrieve the Customers's information from the database
    public static DataRow GetCustomerInfo(string CustomerID)
    {
    return GetResults("Select * from Customers where CustomerID=" +
```

```
                                          CustomerID, "Customers");
    }

    // Retrieve the Customer's Billing information from the database
    public static DataRow GetBillingInfo(string CustomerID)
    {
    return GetResults("Select * from BillingInfo where CustomerID=" +
                                          CustomerID, "BillingInfo");
    }

    // Retrieve the results of a SQL Query
    protected static DataRow GetResults(string strQuery, string
                                                  strTblName)
    {
        DataSet Results = GetDataSet(strQuery,strTblName);
        return Results.Tables[0].Rows[0];
    }

    // Retrieve the Dataset from a SQL Query
    protected static DataSet GetDataSet(string strQuery,string
                                              strTblName)
    {
        SQLConnection sqlConnection = GetDBConnection();
        SQLDataSetCommand sqlAdapter1 = new SQLDataSetCommand(strQuery,
        sqlConnection);
        DataSet Results = new DataSet();
        sqlAdapter1.FillDataSet(Results,strTblName);

        return Results;
    }

    // Retrieve the Item's information from the database
    protected static SQLConnection GetDBConnection()
    {
    return (new
        SQLConnection("server=jsdev1;uid=sa;pwd=;database=Store_DB"));
    }
}
```

In looking at this source code there are a couple of functions that are very similar, all of which are publicly exposed methods. The GetCustomerInfo, GetItemInfo, GetItemListing and GetBillingInfo functions are very simple functions that are used to retrieve specific datasets from the database. The GetCustomerInfo and GetBillingInfo function both take a CustomerID as a parameter. The GetCustomerInfo method will return all of the customer's information from the database. The GetBillingInfo will return all of the customer's billing information from the database. The GetItemInfo method takes an ItemID as parameter and returns all of the details for that specific item. The GetItemListing method will return all items that currently exist in the database. The GetCustomerName method is used to return the customer's full name. Since the database stores the first and last name separately, this method is used to concatenate the two.

In addition to the public methods there are also a couple of private methods that are only available within the class. The most utilized method of these is the GetDataSet method. It is this method that is the workhorse of the class. This method will take a specific SQL query, execute it against the database, and then return the results of the query as an SQL DataSet.

The GetResults method is used for the cases where it is preferable to return a DataRow instead of a DataSet. This method will return the first DataRow object that results from the specified SQL query.

Lastly, there is the GetDBConnection method. This method serves as the single location for specifying the database connection that will be used by the library. The method creates an SQLConnection to the database and returns the SQLConnection object.

As none of the methods are very involved methods, we will not cover them in any greater depth. Instead we will move on to the other classes contained within BPLib.cs.

OrderItem Class

The next class needing definition is the OrderItem class. This class provides the data structure for storing the necessary details on a specific item in an order. An instance of this class will represent a line item in the customer's order. There will never be more than one instance of this class for any individual item. The instance contains all of the items details as well as the quantity to be ordered.

```
///    <summary>
///    The OrderItem class is used to represent
///    each line item on a customer's order.
///    Only the ItemNumber & Quantity are needed,
///    as the price and description are
///    looked up from the database
///  </summary>
public class OrderItem
{
    protected string m_ItemNumber;
    protected long m_ItemQty;
    protected float m_ItemPrice;
    protected string m_ItemDescription;
```

The first part of the class is the declaration of the private variables that will be used internally in the class to store the information about the item. Though the class could have been implemented using public data members on the class, using Get / Set methods allows for easy updates in the event that any properties need more work done. For example, if we wanted to add a check that the item was in stock before setting the quantity, we would write some additional logic code in the ItemQty set method. For the ItemNumber, ItemDescription, ItemQty, and ItemPrice properties the get and set methods are very simple:

```
public string ItemNumber
{
   get {return m_ItemNumber;}
   set {m_ItemNumber = value;}
}

public long ItemQty
{
   get {return m_ItemQty;}
   set {m_ItemQty = value;}
}

public float ItemPrice
```

```
        {
            get {return m_ItemPrice;}
            set {m_ItemPrice = value;}
        }

        public string ItemDescription
        {
            get {return m_ItemDescription;}
            set {m_ItemDescription = value;}
        }
```

The only property of the class that does not have a direct mapping to a single property is the
`ItemTotalPrice` property. This property is used to get the total price for this line item entry. Instead of
tracking the `ItemTotalPrice` with each change in quantity, it is much easier to provide this property that
will only do the calculation when necessary.

```
        public float ItemTotalPrice
        {
            get {return (m_ItemQty * m_ItemPrice);}
        }
    }
```

You will notice that the `ItemTotalPrice` property does not have a `set` method defined. This is because
the property is calculated, and the user setting the property introduces the chance of an error. Using a read-
only property is a much preferable approach.

As you can see, this class is primarily a data structure. The only property that is anything other than a simple
`get` / `set` property is the `ItemTotalPrice` property.

OrderInfo Class

The primary class used in this solution will be the `OrderInfo` class. It is this class that contains all of the
required information for a complete customer order. For this application a complete customer's order would
contain the customer's ID, their billing info, and a collection of the items contained in the order. All of this
information is contained within a single instance of the `OrderInfo` class.

First up in the `OrderInfo` class is the declarations of the variables for the class. The `CustomerID` and
`BillingDetails` variables are simple public variables of the class. They are both read / write
properties and since they are public properties of the class it is not necessary to define a `get` / `set` block for
them. Next is the private `hashtable` object that is only accessible from within the class. This `hashtable` is
used to store the different `OrderItem` objects for the order. The use of this object will become clearer when
we cover the `AddItem` method below.

```
        /// <summary>
        /// The OrderInfo class is used to contain all
        /// of the information for a customer's order
        /// from the web site.
        /// </summary>
        public class OrderInfo
        {
            public string CustomerID;
            public BillingInfo BillingDetails;
            private Hashtable orderDetails = new Hashtable();
```

Since this class contains private variables, and the state/value of those variables must be maintained, using this class requires the developer to create an instance of the class. In order to do that, we must implement a constructor for the class. If necessary, any initialisation code for the class would be placed in this method. In this case, there is no initialisation required for the class.

```
// Simple non-parameterized constructor
public OrderInfo()
{
}
```

The next part of the class provides some public properties allowing for the retrieval of specific order items or the full collection of order items. The `Values` property will return a collection containing all of the `OrderItem` objects.

```
public ICollection Values
{
   get
   {
       return orderDetails.Values;
   }        }
```

The implementation of this property is such that it retrieves the specified item from the `orderDetails` hashtable:

```
public OrderItem this[string name]
{
   get
   {
       return (OrderItem) orderDetails[name];
   }
}
```

Before we can even consider retrieving an item from the `hashtable`, we must be able to first add an item. This is handled by the `AddItem` method. In this class the method is overloaded such that it can accept either an `ItemID` or a valid `OrderItem` instance.

For the overload that accepts an `ItemID`, it is necessary to construct a complete `OrderItem` object to be added to the `orderDetails` hashtable. Once the object has been created, a database query is used to retrieve the Items details from the `BeautifulDatabase`. Those details are used to set the properties of the `OrderItem` object. Once the valid object is created, it is passed to the `AddItem` overload which accepts an `OrderItem` object.

```
// Add an Item by its ID
public void AddItem(string ItemID)
{
    DataRow prodInfo;
    EventLog tmpLog = new EventLog("Application",".","Orders_Class");
    tmpLog.WriteEntry("Adding item #" + ItemID);

    OrderItem tmpItem = new OrderItem();
    tmpItem.ItemNumber=ItemID;
    prodInfo = BeautifulDatabase.GetItemInfo(ItemID).Tables[0].Rows[0];
```

```
        tmpItem.ItemQty=1;
        tmpItem.ItemPrice = float.Parse(prodInfo["Price"].ToString());
        tmpItem.ItemDescription = prodInfo["Description"].ToString();

        AddItem(tmpItem);
    }
```

It is this overload of the AddItem method that actually does the adding of the OrderItem object to the hashtable. The method will first check to see if the item already exists in the hashtable. If the item exists, then the quantity of the item will be incremented by 1. If the item does not exist then it is added to the hashtable.

```
    // Add an item if already have the OrderItem object
    public void AddItem(OrderItem tmpItem)
    {
        if (orderDetails[tmpItem.ItemNumber] == null)
        {
            orderDetails.Add(tmpItem.ItemNumber, tmpItem);
        }
        else
        {
            OrderItem oI = (OrderItem)orderDetails[tmpItem.ItemNumber];
            oI.ItemQty += 1;
        }
    }
}
```

In looking at the code it will be apparent that there isn't a method to remove all the items from the order. This would be useful functionality in a shopping application, but the implementation of the method is left as a programming exercise.

BillingInfo Class

The last class in the library is the BillingInfo class. This is the simplest of the BPLib classes as it is purely a data structure used to store the customer's credit card number and expiration date.

```
    /// <summary>
    ///The BillingInfo class is used to represent the
    ///credit card information that the customer
    ///is using to pay for a specific order.
    /// </summary>
    public class BillingInfo
    {
        public string CardNumber;
        public string CardExpDate;
    }
}
```

As you can see the class consists of two properties: CardNumber and CardExpDate. These represent the credit card number and its expiration date, respectively. The problem with this approach is that the types of cards that can be used are limited. In order to support other types of cards it would be necessary to create a CardType property on the class. This property could be set to "AMEX", "MC", "VISA", and so on.

BPLib.DLL Summary

At this point we have created a library (DLL) that will be used by all of the applications in the solution that is being built. This library will allow for multiple applications to centralize the location and maintenance of data structures and database queries, resulting in lower administration costs as well as easier maintenance and updates. This DLL will be the core of the solution, and each application/project in the solution will include a reference to the BPLib.DLL.

QueueWatcherService Application

The next application we will explore is the QueueWatcherService. This application is actually a Windows NT service. The service will act as a "listener" to the Orders message queue. When a new message (Order) arrives in the queue, the service will be notified and will receive and process the message. As we are building multiple applications as part of a solution, the easiest way to develop the solution is to create a Visual Studio Solution that contains all of the projects we are building.

To add a new project to the existing BPLib solution, right click on the solution node and select **Add New Project**. From the **New Project** dialog, we will want to select the C# Project node and then **Windows Service** application. As we did with the BPLib project, we will be using C# as the language for this application. The name of the project will be QueueWatcherService. Also, in this project will we need to add references to System.Messaging (since the service will be using the MSMQ component), and BPLib (since the service needs to understand the data structures for the orders). To add a reference to the BPLib project, you go to the **Projects** tab on the **Add Reference** dialog, select the BPLib project, and then click **OK**.

QueueWatcher.cs

Once the project is created and the references added, you are presented with WinService1.cs open in the designer. First we need to close that designer, and then we want to rename the file to be QueueWatcher.cs.

Next, we will then want to re-open the QueueWatcher.cs file in both the **designer** and the **code editor** views. We will be using both editor views to make changes to the service. The first changes to be made are in the code editor. We need to change any references to occurrences of WinService1 to be QueueWatcher. This will apply to both the class name and the constructor. Also, we want to declare the private MessageQueue object that will reference the Orders queue and the TraceSwitch object that will be used for the Trace capabilities of VS.NET. After the changes, the code should look like this:

```
namespace QueueWatcherService
{
    using System;
    using System.Collections;
    using System.Core;
    using System.ComponentModel;
    using System.Configuration;
    using System.Data;
    using System.Web.Services;
    using System.Diagnostics;
    using System.ServiceProcess;
```

```
using System.Configuration.Install;
using System.Messaging;
using BPLib;

public class QueueWatcher : System.ServiceProcess.ServiceBase
{
    private void InitializeComponent ()
    {
    }

    private MessageQueue tmpQ;
    private TraceSwitch traceSwitch;
```

Once we have changed the name correctly, we will then want to set some of the properties of the service. To do this we need to change back to the designer view and show the property grid.

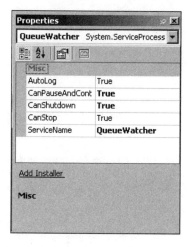

In the grid, we need to set the `CanStop`, `CanPauseAndContinue`, and `CanShutdown` properties to be `True`, and we need to specify the `ServiceName` property to be `QueueWatcher`. You will notice there is a hotlink for **Add Installer**. We will come back to this in the next section on `ProjectInstaller.cs`

Before we get to implement the different service event handlers, the service constructor needs to be implemented. When the service starts, it will need to perform all initialisation necessary.

```
public QueueWatcher()
{
    /// Set the information for the service
    ServiceName = "Queue Watcher Service";
    CanPauseAndContinue = true;
    CanShutdown = true;
    CanStop = true;
```

This code will instantiate the private `MessageQueue` object and set it to reference the correct message queue.

```
            // Create the MessageQueue object to reference the orders queue
            tmpQ = new MessageQueue(".\\Private$\\Orders",true);
```

One of the features of this service is that it will use a performance counter to keep track of the number of orders that it has processed. The service will be using a custom counter. This code will determine if the counter is already created on the system. If the counter does not exist, it will be created.

```
        // For this service, we will use a performance
        // counter to track the orders that
        // have been processed. When the service
        //starts we will verify that the counter does exist

        if (!PerformanceCounter.CategoryExists("OrderService"))
        {
            PerformanceCounter.CreateCategory("OrderService","","Orders
                            Processed","Count of orders processed");
        }
```

For debugging purposes, the service will also be using the `Trace` capabilities of VS.NET. This code will instantiate and initialise the private `TraceSwitch` object that will be used.

```
        traceSwitch = new TraceSwitch("ATraceSwitch",
                        "Queue Watcher Service Trace Switch");
    }
```

Looking at the code, the next part we will see is the `Main` method. This method is the entry point for the service application. It is here that we need to define the services that will run in this process. Though it is possible for multiple services to run in the process, our application will only be running the `QueueWatcher` service.

```
    // The main entry point for the process
    static void Main()
    {
        // Though it is possible to run more than one service in the process,
        // this application will only run the QueueWatcher service
        System.ServiceProcess.ServiceBase[] ServicesToRun;
        ServicesToRun = new System.ServiceProcess.ServiceBase[]
        {
            new QueueWatcher()
        };
        System.ServiceProcess.ServiceBase.Run(ServicesToRun);
    }
```

By default, the code for `QueueWatcher` creates empty functions to handle the `OnStart` and `OnStop` events of the service. We will need to write the code to be executed for these events. Additionally, we also want to implement the handlers for the `OnContinue` and `OnPause` events.

Conceptually, the `OnStart` and `OnContinue` events are very similar. The methods will need to set a `ReceiveCompleted` event handler on the message queue so that the service is notified of messages arriving in the queue. Since they both have the same purpose, both will call the `AddMQListener` method.

```
/// <summary>
/// Set things in motion so your service can do its work.
/// </summary>
protected override void OnStart(string[] args)
{
    AddMQListener();
}


/// <summary>
///     Continue this service.
/// </summary>
protected override void OnContinue()
{
    AddMQListener();
}
```

The `AddMQListener` method will create a new `ReceiveCompleted` event handler specifying the `QueueProcessor.OnMessageReceived` method (defined in the next section) as the method to be executed when a message arrives in the queue. After the event handler has been set up, the `BeginReceive` method is called to actually start listening for received messages.

```
/// <summary>
/// Hook up the event handler so that we can
/// receive notification of new messages
/// </summary>
protected void AddMQListener()
{
    tmpQ.ReceiveCompleted += new
        ReceiveCompletedEventHandler(QueueProcessor.OnMessageReceived);
    tmpQ.BeginReceive();
}
```

For the `OnStop` and `OnPause` events, the service should stop listening to the message queue. To do this, the service needs to remove the event handler from the message queue. As with the `OnStart` and `OnContinue` methods, the `OnStop` and `OnPause` methods will both call the `RemoveMQListener` method.

```
/// <summary>
///     Stop this service.
/// </summary>
protected override void OnStop()
{
    RemoveMQListener();
}


/// <summary>
///     Pause this service.
/// </summary>
protected override void OnPause()
{
    RemoveMQListener();
}
```

The `RemoveMQListener` method will simply remove the event handler from the message queues list of handlers. This will mean that the handler will not be called when messages arrive in the queue.

```
/// <summary>
/// Remove up the event handler so that we stop
/// receive notification of new messages
/// </summary>
protected void RemoveMQListener()
{
tmpQ.ReceiveCompleted -= new
        ReceiveCompletedEventHandler(QueueProcessor.OnMessageReceived);

}
```

QueueProcessor Class

In the above section we were creating the NT Service to be used for watching the orders message queue. Though the service handles setting and removing the event handlers, a separate class – QueueProcessor, will perform the actual processing of messages. This class only has one public method: OnMessageReceived. The AddMQListener method in the QueueWatcherService sets up the QueueProcessor.OnMessageReceived method as the method to be executed when a message arrives in the queue.

As we mentioned in the QueueWatcherService section, we want to use a performance counter to track the number of orders processed by the service. In order to increment this counter from the OnMessageReceived method we have declared a private PerformanceCounter object in the QueueProcessor class.

```
public class QueueProcessor
{
    private static PerformanceCounter pcCounter = new
                PerformanceCounter("OrderService","Orders Processed");
```

Next there is the code to handle the messages arriving in the queue. Since we are using Trace to provide some debugging of the application it is necessary to declare and instantiate a TraceSwitch object.

```
public static void OnMessageReceived(Object source,
                ReceiveAsyncEventArgs asyncResult)
{
    TraceSwitch traceSwitch = new
        TraceSwitch("ATraceSwitch","QueueProcessorTrace Switch");
```

Once the TraceSwitch object is created, the next step is to receive the message from the queue and perform the processing. We will wrap that processing in a try...catch statement so that we can have some error reporting in case there is any error.

```
        try
        {
```

The first step is to get the MessageQueue object from which the message will be received.

```
        // Get the queue object
        Trace.WriteLineIf(traceSwitch.TraceVerbose ,"Getting the Queue
                                                Object");
        MessageQueue RecQueue = (MessageQueue)source;
```

Using the .NET MSMQ component, there are different ways that you can serialize objects into a message body. The serialization is provided by message formatters. The .NET SDK includes three of these formatters: ActiveX, XML, and Binary. For the most part, the XML formatter is preferred. For serializing ActiveX objects you will need to use the ActiveX formatter. The catch to using a formatter is that the specified formatter must be told which types of objects can be serialized and de-serialized. For this message queue, we need to set the types of objects that the queue's formatter can understand. In this case we want to be able to read/write `BPLib.OrderInfo` objects.

```
// Set the formatter so it can read this type
Trace.WriteLineIf(traceSwitch.TraceVerbose ,"Setting the
                                             formatter");
(XmlMessageFormatter)RecQueue.Formatter).TargetTypeNames=
                    new string[]{"BPLib.OrderInfo"};
```

Then it is possible to declare a `Message` object (`RecMsg`) and set it to reference the message received from the queue.

```
// Then get the message that arrived in the queue
Trace.WriteLineIf(traceSwitch.TraceVerbose ,"Calling
                                          EndReceive");
Message RecMsg = RecQueue.EndReceive(asyncResult.AsyncResult);
```

The `asyncResult` object contains the information specifying the result of the operation. The result can be successful, have an exception, or have timed out, among other possibilities.

At this point we also declare the `OrderReceived` object that will contain all the order information.

```
BPLib.OrderInfo OrderReceived;
```

Again, to be safe, we will set the formatter on the `Message` object so that it can read `BPLib.OrderInfo` objects. In theory, the `Message` object should get its formatter from the queue, but due to the beta nature of the component, that is not always the case.

```
Trace.WriteLineIf(traceSwitch.TraceVerbose ,"Setting Formatter
                                    on the Received message");

(XmlMessageFormatter)RecMsg.Formatter).TargetTypeNames = new
                                string[]{"BPLib.OrderInfo"};
```

To retrieve the actual `OrderInfo` object from the message we need to get the value of the `Body` property of the message. The .NET `MessageQueue` components will handle de-serializing the message body into an object, which we then cast into an `OrderInfo` instance.

```
Trace.WriteLineIf(traceSwitch.TraceVerbose ,"Getting the body of
                                               message");
OrderReceived = (BPLib.OrderInfo)RecMsg.Body;
```

At this point we have an `OrderInfo` object that contains all of the information for the customer's order. In this case there is no specific processing we want to do, so we will just use the trace functionality to list the `CustomerID` and the `CardNumber` used for the order. It is here that any other processing could occur for the order.

```
//    TODO : Process the message
//    As this is more of a sample of the framework/approach
//    rather than the application
//    the processing of the order will not be dealt with
//    in great detail and will
//    be left as an exercise for the reader
//

Trace.WriteLineIf(traceSwitch.TraceVerbose ,
                          OrderReceived.CustomerID.ToString());
Trace.WriteLineIf(traceSwitch.TraceVerbose ,
            OrderReceived.BillingDetails.CardNumber.ToString());
```

Next we will increment the performance counter to reflect that another order has been processed.

```
// Increment the counter to show we've processed another order
Trace.WriteLineIf(traceSwitch.TraceVerbose ,"Incrementing the
                                          perf counter");

pcCounter.IncrementBy(1);
```

And, in order to have the event handler keep receiving and processing messages we need to call BeginReceive on the message queue.

```
// Keep receiving messages from the queue
RecQueue.BeginReceive();
}
```

Next we implement the catch block. In the event that there is any exception thrown in the receiving and/or processing of the message we want to catch that exception and log it to the event log. We can also use the trace switch to write that exception to the debug console if specified.

```
catch (Exception E)
{
    // If we catch an exception we will then write it
    //   to the Application log and stop processing
    //   remaining messages in the queue.
    EventLog lgApp = new
            EventLog("Application",".","QueueProcessor");
    lgApp.WriteEntry("Unexpected exception  - " +
                    E.ToString(),EventLogEntryType.Error);

    Trace.WriteLineIf(traceSwitch.TraceError,
                              "Unexpected Exception");
    Trace.WriteLineIf(traceSwitch.TraceError,E.ToString());
}
}
}
}
```

QueueWatcher.cs Summary

In this project we have declared the class for the NT Service as well as the class containing the event handler that will process messages arriving in the Orders queue. However, how do we handle installing the application so that it runs as a Service in Windows NT/2000? The VS.NET product has provided a very simple way to handle that task – Installers.

ProjectInstaller.cs

Earlier, when looking at the property grid for the QueueWatcher service we noted that there was a hotlink of Add Installer. It is now that we get to see what this hotlink actually does for the developer. Change back to the design view on QueueWatcher.cs, show the Property grid, and then click on the Add Installer hotlink. Clicking this link will cause a new file (ProjectInstaller.cs) to be created and added to the project. This file will then be opened in the designer. On the design surface you will note there are two components: ServiceProcessInstaller1 and ServiceInstaller1.

Select the ServiceProcessInstaller1 object and you will note that in the Property grid you can set the details on the service process. You can specify whether the process runs as a system account or a user account. And, if it is as a user account, you can specify the Username and Password to run under. For this case, we will want to run under the system account.

When you select the ServiceInstaller1 object, the Property grid will show the properties that can be set on the service. It is here that you can specify the DisplayName, ServiceName, and StartType for the service. Also, if desired, you can specify which services your service is dependent on. For now, we want to set the properties as:

Property	Value
DisplayName	.NETBeautifulParts Queue Watcher Service
ServiceName	QueueWatcher
StartType	Automatic

Once these changes have been made and saved, the source code for the ProjectInstaller.cs file will look like this:

```
using System;
using System.Collections;
using System.Configuration.Install;
using System.ServiceProcess;
using System.ComponentModel;

[RunInstallerAttribute(true)]
public class ProjectInstaller: Installer
{
    private void InitializeComponent ()
    {
    }

    private ServiceInstaller serviceInstaller;
    private ServiceProcessInstaller processInstaller;
```

```
public ProjectInstaller()
{
    processInstaller = new ServiceProcessInstaller();
    serviceInstaller = new ServiceInstaller();

    // Service will run under system account
    processInstaller.RunUnderSystemAccount = true;

    // Service will have Start Type of Manual
    serviceInstaller.StartType = ServiceStart.Manual;

    serviceInstaller.ServiceName = "Queue Watcher Service";

    Installers.Add(serviceInstaller);
    Installers.Add(processInstaller);
}
}
}
```

What has actually been done at this point? Creating this installer has only created a file. The next step is to run the installer and install the service. In order to do this, we must first build the `QueueWatcherService` project. Once the project is built we then will run `InstallUtil / QueueWatcherService.exe`. `InstallUtil.exe` is a utility that is included with the .NET SDK and provides installation capabilities for Visual Studio .NET projects. Executing `InstallUtil.Exe` will install the service and configure the service according the properties that we set on the objects in the `ProjectInstaller` designer. Once the service is installed, it will be recognized by Windows as a service and shown in the Service controller dialog of Windows 2000.

QueueWatcherService Summary

After installing, we are done with the service. In the solution being built, two of the parts are now completed. We have created the `BPLib.Dll` and the `QueueWatcherService` applications. The service that we have just created will be able to listen to the `Orders` message queue and respond to messages arriving in the queue. The service will also be able to correctly handle `Start`, `Stop`, `Pause`, `Continue`, and `Shutdown` events.

BPOrderService WebService

Moving backwards another step, we come to getting the order into the Orders message queue so that the `QueueProcessor` class can receive the messages. Here we will create a `WebService` that will be able to take an `OrderInfo` object and send it to the `orders` message queue. Although there are other options that could provide the same functionality, we have chosen a Web Service since it illustrates a key new feature of .NET applications.

The `WebService` concept is another new capability being introduced with VS.NET and the .NET Frameworks. The basic idea is that a method can be called through the **HTTP protocol** (utilizing SOAP) and act just like any method. In this application we will utilize a `WebService` for submitting orders to the Orders message queue. As such, there is only one method that is exposed, and it appears to be a simple one. That is the idea of `WebServices`, that there is no big change for the developer. All of the work is taken care of behind the scenes and the developer need not concern themselves with the details. Developers can treat any `WebService` as just another method call.

Once again we will be using C#. For this project, we will need to create a **Web Service C# project** in the New Project dialog. The name of the project will be BPOrderService. Again, this will bring up a file in the designer. Before continuing, we will need to add references for BPLib and the System.Messaging assembly. Once those references are added we can begin implementing the WebService. In this case it will be easier to create the WebService solely in code view, so we can close the designer. We will rename the file to be BPOrderService.cs.

Next we will open the file in the code editor to make our changes. First we will need to add using statements for BPLib and System.Messaging. Since this is a simple WebService, the majority of the code in the file will be left unchanged.

```
namespace BPOrderService
{
    using System;
    using System.Collections;
    using System.Configuration;
    using System.ComponentModel;
    using System.Data;
    using System.Diagnostics;
    using System.Web;
    using System.Web.Services;
    using System.Messaging;
    using BPLib;

    ///    <summary>
    ///    Summary description for BPOrderService
    ///    </summary>
    public class OrderSubmit : System.Web.Services.WebService
    {
        public OrderSubmit()
        {
        //CODEGEN: This call is required by the ASP.NET Web Services Designer
            InitializeComponent();
        }

        ///    <summary>
        ///    Required method for Designer support - do not modify
        ///    the contents of this method with the code editor.
        ///    </summary>
        private void InitializeComponent()
        {
        }

        ///    <summary>
        ///    Clean up any resources being used.
        ///    </summary>
        public override void Dispose()
        {
        }
```

We will only be adding new code to the file. In that case we will add the SendOrder method. In order to be accessible through a WebService, the method needs to have the [WebMethod] attribute. Other than that, the method is written just like any other method.

For this method, we need to

❑ Instantiate a `MessageQueue` object referencing the `Orders` queue

❑ Set the formatter of the queue so that it will be able to write `BPLib.OrderInfo` objects

❑ Send the `OrderInfo` object to the queue, specifying a message label of `Order Submission`

```
[WebMethod]
public void SendOrder(OrderInfo tmpOrder)
{
    MessageQueue OrderQ = new MessageQueue(".\\Private$\\Orders");

    ((XmlMessageFormatter) OrderQ.Formatter).TargetTypeNames =
                          new String[] {"BPLib.OrderInfo"};
    OrderQ.Send(tmpOrder,"Order Submission");
    }
  }
}
```

And that is it. We have now created a publicly accessibly `WebMethod` that will accept `OrderInfo` objects and send them to the `Orders` message queue where the `QueueWatcherService` will receive and process the orders. This is an extremely insecure method of ordering though, as anyone can call the service with any `OrderInfo` object, even if they have modified the prices or items. When the order is received, the `OrderInfo` object should verify the items in the order to ensure that the prices match the database prices.

BPOrderService Summary

As is apparent from the code, the creation of a `WebMethod` is not terribly complicated. The work involved is handled by the .NET framework, which frees the developer to focus on implementing the logic of the application.

At this point we have implemented all of the functionality that will not actually be seen by any users. All of the applications built so far have been behind the scenes applications that mean nothing to the user, except for the fact that they make the solution work better. If any of these applications had problems then the user would see them, but that would not be a good situation.

In our case, the behind the scenes applications are written and working, so we will now move on to creating the web site application.

BeautifulParts Web Site

Now, taking the final step back, we arrive at the user interface portion of the solution. As almost everything is web based these days, our UI will be a web application. The name of the web site will be `BeautifulParts.Com` and we will be using VB code for this application. The UI we create will need to perform the following tasks:

❑ Login and validate the user

❑ List inventory items

❑ List inventory item details and add items to the cart

❑ Show a checkout page and submit the final order via the BPOrderService WebMethod

User Login and Validation

For our web site, we want to have all shoppers login for each shopping session. In order to do this, this application will make use of the Cookie authentication capabilities provided by ASP.NET. By using this, the developer allows ASP.NET to handle the authentication and tracking of users. ASP.NET will handle the cookie creation behind the scenes. Additionally, ASP.NET will handle checking the cookie when a user requests a page from the solution. When a valid cookie is returned, the user is logged in to the solution automatically. If the cookie is not there, or has expired, the user will not be presented with the login page. In order to make use of the ASP.NET cookie authentication there are some web application settings that must be configured.

Config.Web

The Config.Web file contains all of the settings and configuration options that will be applied to the web application. Each ASP.NET web application contains a Config.Web file – if the web application was created in Visual Studio, a default Config.Web has been generated automatically. For the cookie authentication, the part that we care about is the security section. It is the security section that allows you to specify the authentication mode being used as well as which users, if any, to deny access.

For BeautifulParts.Com, we want to use the Cookie authentication mode and deny access to any anonymous users. In order to do this, the Security section in Config.web should look like this:

```
<!-- SECURITY
This section sets the security policies of the application.
Possible modes are "Windows", "Cookie", "Passport" and "None"
-->
<security>
   <authentication mode="Cookie">
      <cookie decryptionkey="autogenerate" loginurl="login.aspx"
                                   cookie="BeautifulParts_Login" />
   </authentication>

   <authorization>
      <deny users="?" />
   </authorization>
</security>
```

The first section, authentication mode, is where we specify to use the Cookie authentication mode. The cookie tag contains three attributes:

Attribute Name	Purpose
decryptionkey	Key to use when encrypting cookie for authentication
Loginurl	The URL to send users to when they are unvalidated
Cookie	The name of the cookie to use in authentication

In this case, we want the encryption/decryption key to be specified by ASP.NET. In the event that a user requests a page from the web site and they are not authorized, they will be sent to login.aspx page. Lastly, for this application we want to have the cookie be named "BeautifulParts_Login".

The section authorization allows you to specify which users are explicitly allowed or disallowed. For BeautifulParts.Com, we want to deny all anonymous users and require everyone to login. The deny tag and its attributes allow us to do so:

```
<deny users="?" />
```

Login.aspx

Now that we have configured the web setting correctly, we need to create the login.aspx page. On this page we will ask the users to specify their user names and passwords in order to login.

When viewed in the browser, the page will appear as:

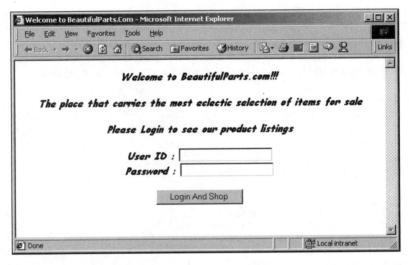

Looking at the UI, the page looks very similar to one that can be easily created using ASP 3.0. The difference will be more apparent when looking into the source that creates the page.

Just as in ASP 3.0, the top of the page has directives for the language of the page. In VB, the Import statement is equivalent to the using statement in C#.

```
<%@ Page Language="vb" %>
<%@ Import Namespace="System.Data" %>
<%@ Import Namespace="System.Data.SQL" %>
<%@ Import Namespace="System.Web.Security" %>
```

The next section of the page is the script block containing the logic to be executed when the user clicks the login button. In this case, if the Password and the UserID are identical then the user is validated.

```
<script language=vbscript runat=server ID=Script1>
    Public Sub btnLogin_Click(ByVal sender As Object, ByVal e As _
```

```
                                          System.EventArgs)
    '//For this Application very simple verification will suffice,
    '//for future applications you should rely on something more
    '//sophisticated.

    If (UserName.Value = Password.Value) Then
        Session("UserID") = UserName.Value

        '//   Verfified, so send them on.
        CookieAuthentication.RedirectFromLoginPage(UserName.Value, True)

    Else
        '//   Failed verification, back to login page
        Msg.Text = "Invalid Credentials: Please try again"
    End If
  End Sub
</script>
```

From here on, the rest of the page looks mostly as it did with ASP 3.0, with a few new additions.

```
<html>
<head>
<title> Welcome to Beautiful Parts.Com</title>
<meta name=vs_targetSchema content="HTML 4.0">
<meta name="CODE_LANGUAGE" content="Visual Basic 7.0">
</head>
<body bgcolor=white text=black style="FONT-STYLE: italic; FONT-FAMILY:
                                                'Comic Sans MS'">
    <form id="WebForm1" method="post" runat="server">
        <p align=center><strong><em>
Welcome to BeautifalParts.com!!!
        </font></em></strong></p>
        <p align=center><strong><em>
The place that carries the most eclectic selection of items for sale
        </font></em></strong></p>
        <p align=center><strong><em>
Please Login to see our product listings
        </font></em></strong></p>

        <p align=center><strong><em>
User ID : </font></em></strong>
        <input id=UserName type="text" runat=server />
        <ASP:RequiredFieldValidator ControlToValidate="UserName"
                        Display="Static" ErrorMessage="*" />
        <br>
        <strong><em><font face="Comic Sans MS" color=#ff0000>
Password :
        </font></em></strong>
        <input id=Password type="password" runat=server />
        <ASP:RequiredFieldValidator ControlToValidate="Password"
                            Display="Static" ErrorMessage="*"/>
        <p align=center>
        <asp:Button id=btnLogin runat="server" OnClick="btnLogin_Click"
                        Text="Login And Shop"></asp:Button></p>
        <ASP:label id=Msg runat=server />
    </form>
</body></html>
```

The noticeable change that we see is the <ASP: tag. It is these tags that denote an ASP Web control. In this page, three types of ASP Web controls are utilized: RequiredFieldValidator, Label, and Button. The RequiredFieldValidator control is used to ensure that any required fields have been filled in with data.

The Button control is just like an HTML button, except that it is generated on the server and its events are processed on the server. In the <asp:button tag, the attributes define the appearance and behaviour for the button. In this case, the btnLogin_Click method will be executed when the button is clicked.

The Label control is used for providing feedback to the user. In the event that the login failed, an error message of "Invalid Credentials: Please try again" will be shown as the text of the Msg label.

Login and Validation Summary

By making use of the ASP.NET Cookie authentication capabilities, we have been able to quickly and easily create a web application that requires customers to login. Additionally, we have easily created the Login page for the customers. We can now move on to the next step, listing the items in the inventory.

Listing Inventory Items

In order to sell anything from a web site, you must first be able to list the items that are available for sale. In the BeatifulParts.Com site, the InventoryList.aspx page handles this. This page, when viewed in the browser will look like this:

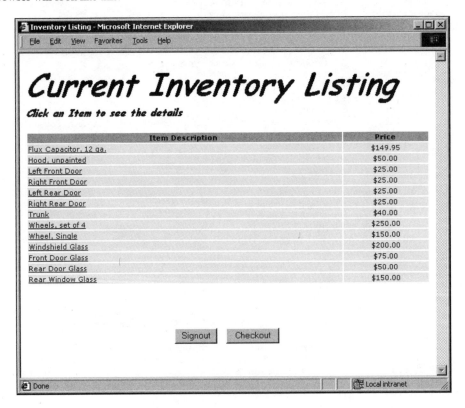

InventoryList.aspx

This page will retrieve the list of items in the Products table and show it as an HTML table. At the start of this page there are some page attributes that have not previously been seen in ASP 3 programming.

```
<%@ Page Language="vb" AutoEventWireup="false" Codebehind="InventoryList.vb"
                          Inherits="InventoryList.InventoryList"%>
```

The function of this statement is to specify page attributes. The two attributes that need the most explanation are the Codebehind and Inherits attributes. The Codebehind attribute is used to specify the name of the file that contains the code behind the ASPX page and object. In this case, and in most cases, the code-behind file has the same name as the ASPX page but a different extension. The Inherits attribute specifies that the ASPX page is to inherit objects and methods from the InventoryList class contained in the InventoryList.vb file. Since this class exists in the BeautifulParts namespace, it is fully referenced as InventoryList.InventoryList. We will look at the InventoryList.VB file in the next section.

The next section of the page is more general HTML code.

```
<html><head>
<title>Inventory Listing</title>
<META http-equiv=Content-Type content="text/html; charset=windows-1252">
<meta content="HTML 4.0" name=vs_targetSchema>
<meta content="Visual Basic 7.0" name=CODE_LANGUAGE></head>
<body bgColor=navy style="FONT-WEIGHT: bold; COLOR: red; FONT-STYLE: italic;
                FONT-FAMILY: 'Comic Sans MS'; BACKGROUND-COLOR: #000080">
<font size=+5>Current Inventory Listing</font><BR>
                                    Click an Item to see the details<br>

<form id=InventoryList method=post runat="server">
```

It is the <ASP: tag that denotes where ASP.NET controls are again being utilized. In this case, the repeater control is being used to loop through the dataset containing the items in inventory.

```
<ASP:REPEATER id=MyDataList runat="server">
```

The repeated control makes use of templates for generating HTML code. In this page the HeaderTemplate, ItemTemplate, and FooterTemplate are being used. The HeaderTemplate will generate the HTML for a table and the table headers.

```
<template name = "HeaderTemplate">
<table style="FONT: 8pt verdana" width="100%">
   <TBODY>
   <tr style="BACKGROUND-COLOR: #dfa894">
      <th>Item Description </th>
      <th>Price </th>
   </tr>
</TEMPLATE>
```

The next section is the ItemTemplate. This section will be repeated for each of the items in the dataset. In this case, there are two table cells that are generated. The first cell contains the name of the item. That name is also a link that will take the customer to the details for that item. The second cell is the individual price for the item.

```
<template name="ItemTemplate">
  <tr style="BACKGROUND-COLOR: #ffecd8">
    <td width="75%"><a href="InventoryDetail.aspx?ProductID=
    <%# Databinder.Eval(Container.DataItem,"ProductID") %>">
    <%# Databinder.Eval(Container.DataItem,"Description") %>
    </a></td>
    <td width="20%">
    <div align=center>
    <%# format(Databinder.Eval(Container.DataItem,"Price"),"$####.00")%>
    </div></td>
  </tr>
</TEMPLATE>
```

Then, once all of the items have been listed to the page, we want to close the TBody and Table tags.

```
<template name="FooterTemplate">
  </TBODY>
  </TABLE>
</TEMPLATE>
</ASP:REPEATER>
```

Lastly, the page will also generate two buttons. The first button, Checkout, will take the user to the checkout page for their shopping session. The second button, Signout, will sign the user out of their shopping session. The code for both of these events is actually contained in the code-behind file, InventoryList.VB.

```
<br><br>   
<div align=center>
<asp:Button id=btnCheckout runat="server" Text="Checkout"></asp:Button> 
<asp:Button id=btnSignout runat="server" onclick="Signout_Click"
                              Text="Signout"></asp:Button>
</div>
</form>
</body>
</html>
```

Contrasting to the way this would be coded with ASP 3.0, there is hardly any code in this aspx page. The only code really done in the page is the **databinding**. Other than that, all the code is contained in the **code-behind** page, InventoryList.VB.

InventoryList.VB

In ASP 3.0, any procedural methods would be placed in <Script></Script> blocks. In ASP.NET, these methods are instead located in the **code-behind** page. Although you could still place those methods in the .aspx page, the design guidelines are to place the code in the .vb file and the presentation in the .aspx file. When looking at the source of a code-behind page, it appears just like a VB class file. For InventoryList.VB, we will go through the file and explore the sections

First up are the Imports statements. As mentioned earlier, the Imports statement functions just as the using statement does in C#.

```
Imports System
Imports System.ComponentModel.Design
Imports System.Data
Imports System.Drawing
Imports System.Web
Imports System.Web.SessionState
Imports System.Web.UI
Imports System.Web.UI.WebControls
Imports System.Web.UI.HtmlControls
Imports Microsoft.VisualBasic
Imports System.Data.SQL
Imports System.Web.Security
Imports BPLib
```

Next is the declaration of the class, InventoryList, and the directive that the class is to inherit from System.Web.UI.Page.

```
Public Class InventoryList
    Inherits System.Web.UI.Page
```

The class then contains the protected declarations with events for the ASP Web controls that exist on the aspx page.

```
Protected WithEvents btnCheckout As System.Web.UI.WebControls.Button
Protected WithEvents btnSignout As System.Web.UI.WebControls.Button
Protected WithEvents MyDataList As System.Web.UI.WebControls.Repeater
```

The next section is the code that has been generated by the web forms designer. This code should not be modified in most cases.

```
#Region " Web Forms Designer Generated Code "

    Dim WithEvents InventoryList As System.Web.UI.Page

    Sub New()
        InventoryList = Me
    End Sub

    'CODEGEN: This procedure is required by the Web Form Designer
    'Do not modify it using the code editor.
    Private Sub InitializeComponent()
    End Sub

#End Region
```

Following the designer generated code come the **event handlers**. The first two handlers are for the click events on the Signout and Checkout buttons. The handler for the Signout button click will cause the user to be signed out of their shopping session and authentication. The Session.Abandon method will release any Session variables that were persisted for that user. The CookieAuthentication.SignOut method will invalidate the authentication cookie and force the user to login again in order to access the site. The handler for the Checkout button click will redirect the browser to the checkout.aspx page where they can proceed with their checkout.

```
      Public Sub btnSignout_Click(ByVal sender As Object, _
                                ByVal e As System.EventArgs)
         Session.Abandon()
         CookieAuthentication.SignOut()
         Response.Redirect("login.aspx")
      End Sub


      Public Sub btnCheckout_Click(ByVal sender As Object, _
                                ByVal e As System.EventArgs)
         Response.Redirect("Checkout.aspx")
      End Sub
```

The next handler is for the **page load event**. It is here that any initialisation for the page should occur. In this case, the code will utilize the `BPLib.OrdersDatabase` class to retrieve the dataset containing a listing of items in the `Products` table. Then, it will bind the `MyDataList` repeater control (of `InventoryList.aspx`) to that dataset.

```
      Protected Sub InventoryList_Load(ByVal Sender As System.Object, _
                                ByVal e As System.EventArgs)
         Dim DS As DataSet
         DS = BPLib.BeautifulDatabase.GetItemListing()
         MyDataList.DataSource = DS.Tables("GetItemList").DefaultView
         MyDataList.DataBind()
      End Sub
```

Lastly, there is the `Init` handler. This is another method that should not be modified by a developer. Any of the initialisation code required should be located in the page load event handler.

```
      Protected Sub InventoryList_Init(ByVal Sender As System.Object, _
                                ByVal e As System.EventArgs)
         'CODEGEN: This method call is required by the Web Form Designer
         'Do not modify it using the code editor.
         InitializeComponent()
      End Sub

   End Class
```

InventoryList Summary

It is from `InventoryList.aspx` that we first see examples of the code-behind web forms. We have seen the change from the mixing of HTML and code (ASP 3.0) to the separation of presentation and logic layers (ASP.NET). The code-behind approach distinctly separates the two layers into separate files. In this case we used VB language for the code-behind file, but we could just have easily used the C# language or any .NET language.

The `InventoryList` page will now display a table of the items contained in the inventory. When the user clicks on the hyper-linked description of one of the items they will be redirected to the `InventoryDetail.aspx` page. And, that is the next page we will create.

List Inventory Item Details

The `InventoryDetail.aspx` page will show the user all of the details on a specific item. For this application, those details are the item's description, price, and photo. The `InventoryDetail.aspx` page makes use of many of the same ASP.NET features and controls that were used in the `InventoryList.aspx` page. When viewed in the browser, the page will show the details for a specific item:

InventoryDetail.aspx

For the most part, this page is the same as the `InventoryDetail.aspx` page. The page makes use of the ASP `Repeater` control, `Templates`, `Databinding`, and ASP `buttons`. The noticeable difference is the handling of the `Photo` cell in the table.

```
<%@ Page Language="vb" AutoEventWireup="true" Codebehind="InventoryDetail.vb"
Inherits="BeautifulParts.InventoryDetail"%>
<html><head>
<title>Inventory Detail</title>
<meta content="HTML 4.0" name=vs_targetSchema>
```

```
<meta content="Microsoft Visual Studio.NET 7.0" name=GENERATOR>
<meta content="Visual Basic 7.0" name=CODE_LANGUAGE></head>
<body
style=" FONT-STYLE: italic; FONT-FAMILY: 'Comic Sans MS'">
<form id=frmInventoryDetail method=post runat="server">
<ASP:REPEATER id=MyDataList runat="server">
<template name="HeaderTemplate">
<font color=red> Detailed Item Listing</font><br><br>
<table cellspacing=1 cellpadding=1 width="60%" align=center
    border=0></TEMPLATE><template name="ItemTemplate">
    <TBODY>
        <td align=center style="WIDTH: 150px;HEIGHT:50px">Description</td>
        <td align=center style="COLOR: blue">
            <%# Databinder.Eval(Container.DataItem,"Description") %>
        </td></tr>
    <tr>
        <td align=center style="WIDTH: 150px;HEIGHT:50px">Price</td>
        <td align=center style="COLOR: blue">
            <%# Databinder.Eval(Container.DataItem,"Price","{0:c}") %>
        </td>
    </tr>
    <tr>
        <td align=center style="WIDTH: 150px">Photo</td>
        <td align=center style="COLOR: blue"><% =Me.strItemURL %></td>
    </tr>
</TEMPLATE>
```

Since it is possible for the Photo field to be a null value in the database, the page needs to handle both valid and empty values. The processing for determining what to display is performed in the Page Load event handler. That event handler will set the value of a page property, strItemURL, to contain the HTML to display. That HTML can be either the IMG tag to the photo, or the text "Photo Unavailable".

After that section is the **Add To Order** button. This button is used to add the item to the customer's shopping cart, which we will see in the InventoryDetail.vb page.

```
<template name="FooterTemplate">
</TBODY></table>
</template>
</ASP:REPEATER>

<div align=center>
<ASP:BUTTON id=btnAddToOrder runat="Server" text="Add To
                                               Order"></ASP:BUTTON>
<br><br><br>
<ASP:BUTTON id=btnPlaceOrder runat="Server" text="Checkout"></ASP:BUTTON>
</div>
</form>
</body></html>
```

InventoryDetail.vb

Again, in keeping with the separation of logic and presentation, the majority of the code for the InventoryDetail page is contained within InventoryDetail.vb.

The first part of the page contains the `Imports` statements and the protected variable declarations.

```
Option Strict Off

Imports System
Imports System.ComponentModel.Design
Imports System.Data
Imports System.Data.SQL
Imports BPLib
Imports System.Drawing
Imports System.Web
Imports System.Web.SessionState
Imports System.Web.UI
Imports System.Web.UI.WebControls
Imports System.Web.UI.HtmlControls
Imports Microsoft.VisualBasic

Public Class InventoryDetail
    Inherits System.Web.UI.Page
    Protected WithEvents btnPlaceOrder As System.Web.UI.WebControls.Button
    Protected WithEvents btnAddToOrder As System.Web.UI.WebControls.Button
    Protected WithEvents MyDataList As System.Web.UI.WebControls.Repeater
```

The next section of code declares a private variable that will be used for exposing a public property of the page. In the page load event we use the querystring to determine the `ItemID`. From then on, in the code, we can use the property instead of using `Request.QueryString` in each place the `ItemID` is needed.

```
Public strItemURL as String
Private m_ItemID As String

    Property ItemID() As String
        Get
            ItemID = m_ItemID
        End Get
        Set
            m_ItemID = value
        End Set
    End Property
```

Again, as with the `InventoryList.aspx`, there is the designer generated code that should not be modified by the developer.

```
#Region " Web Forms Designer Generated Code "

    Dim WithEvents InventoryDetail As System.Web.UI.Page

    Sub New()
        InventoryDetail = Me
    End Sub

    'CODEGEN: This procedure is required by the Web Form Designer
    'Do not modify it using the code editor.
    Private Sub InitializeComponent()
```

```
      End Sub

#End Region
    Protected Sub InventoryDetail_Init(ByVal Sender As System.Object, _
                                      ByVal e As System.EventArgs)
      'CODEGEN: This method call is required by the Web Form Designer
      'Do not modify it using the code editor.
      InitializeComponent()
    End Sub
```

For the remainder of the file, there are only event handlers. The event handler for the Checkout button click will redirect the browser to the checkout.aspx page so they can proceed with checkout.

```
    Public Sub btnPlaceOrder_Click(ByVal sender As Object, _
                                  ByVal e As System.EventArgs)
      Response.Redirect("Checkout.aspx")
    End Sub
```

The **Order Item** button click handler will just call the AddItemToOrder method and pass the ItemID as a parameter.

```
    Public Sub btnAddToOrder_Click(ByVal sender As Object, _
                                  ByVal e As System.EventArgs)
      AddItemToOrder(ItemID)
    End Sub
```

The AddItemToOrder method will:

1. Retrieve the OrderInfo object stored in the CurrentOrder session variable

2. Add the item to that order

3. Store the OrderInfo object back to the CurrentOrder session variable

4. Redirect the user back to the InventoryListing.aspx page

```
    Public Sub AddItemToOrder(ByVal tmpItemID As String)
      Dim CurOrder As OrderInfo

      CurOrder = CType(Session("CurrentOrder"), OrderInfo)

      Dim tmp As String
      tmp = CurOrder.CustomerID

      If CurOrder Is Nothing Then
         CurOrder = New BPLib.OrderInfo()
      End If
```

```
         CurOrder.AddItem(tmpItemID)
         Session("CurrentOrder") = curOrder
         Response.Redirect("InventoryList.aspx")

     End Sub
```

The event handler for the page load event first sets the `ItemID` property value and then queries the database for the details on the specific product. Next, the code checks the value of the `PhotoURL` field from the database result. If that field is empty, then the `strItemURL` property is set to display Photo Unavailable, otherwise a valid `IMG` tag is created using the value specified in the `PhotoURL` database field. Lastly, the `MyDataList` control is bound to the dataset with the product's information.

```
     Protected Sub InventoryDetail_Load(ByVal Sender As System.Object, _
                               ByVal e As System.EventArgs)
         Dim tmpURLString As String
         Dim DS As DataSet

         Session("CurItem") = Request.QueryString("ProductID")
         ItemID = Request.QueryString("ProductID")

         DS = BPLib.BeautifulDatabase.GetItemInfo(ItemID)

         Dim tmpTable As DataTable
         tmpTable = DS.Tables("Products")

         tmpURLString = tmpTable.Rows(0).Item(3).ToString
         If (tmpURLString = "") Then
             strItemURL = "Photo Unavailable"
         Else
             strItemURL = "<IMG SRC=" & tmpURLString & ">"
         End If

         MyDataList.DataSource = DS.Tables("Products").DefaultView
         MyDataList.DataBind()

     End Sub

 End Class
```

InventoryDetail Summary

At this point the solution is nearly complete. The web application allows the users to see the inventory listing, view individual item details, and add items to their order. The application also provides shopping cart functionality to the users by the storing of the `OrderInfo` instance in a session variable. The last step in this application is the checkout process.

Checkout.aspx

In the checkout process the user is shown the listing of items in their shopping cart. They are prompted to enter their billing information and then submit their order:

Again, the source code for the file is primarily HTML code with very little inline script.

```
<%@ Page Language="vb" AutoEventWireup="false" Codebehind="Checkout.vb"
Inherits="BeautifulParts.Checkout"%>
<%@ Import Namespace="Orders" %>
<html>
<body style="COLOR: red; FONT-STYLE: italic; FONT-FAMILY: 'Comic Sans MS';
                              BACKGROUND-COLOR: #000080" >

<form id="Checkout" method="post" runat="server">
```

The first location that script is used is in displaying the greeting to the user. Here the BPLib BeautifulDatabase object is being used to get the greeting name for the specific customer.

```
<p><font color=white>Welcome <%
Response.Write(BPLib.BeautifulDatabase.GetCustomerName(Session("UserID"))_
                                     .ToString())%>, <br><br>
```

Following that is the code to display the text controls for entering the credit card number and expiration date.

```
How would you like to pay for your order?<br></font>
</p>
<p><font color=white>Card Number</font>
<asp:TextBox id=txtCardNumber runat="server"></asp:TextBox><br>

<font color=white>Expiration Date</font>
<asp:TextBox id=txtExpirationDate runat="server"></asp:TextBox></p>
<br><br>
```

The user is then given a listing of all the items contained within their order and a button to submit the order.

```
<div align=center>
<asp:datalist id="ShoppingCartList" borderwidth=0 DataKeyField="ItemNumber"
                                                        runat="server">
<template name="headertemplate">
<table width="80%" align=center border=1>
    <TBODY>
    <tr>
        <th>Quantity</th>
        <th>Description</th>
        <th>Item Price</th>
        <th>Total Price</th></tr>
</TEMPLATE>
<template name="ItemTemplate">
    <tr>
        <td><%# DataBinder.Eval(Container.DataItem, "ItemQty") %></td>
        <td><%# DataBinder.Eval(Container.DataItem, "ItemDescription") %></td>
        <td><%# DataBinder.Eval(Container.DataItem, "ItemPrice", "{0:C}")%>
        </td>
        <td><%# DataBinder.Eval(Container.DataItem, "ItemTotalPrice", "{0:C}")
            %>
        </td>
    </tr>
</TEMPLATE>

<template name="FooterTemplate">
</TBODY>
</TABLE>
</TEMPLATE>
</asp:datalist>
</div>
<BR><BR>
<div align=center>
<asp:Button id=btnOrder runat="server" Text="Submit Order Now"></asp:Button>
</div>
</form>
</body>
</html>
```

Checkout.VB

It is in this file that the last steps of the application are performed. This file will handle the final processing of the order before it is submitted to the Orders message queue.

For the most part, this is not considerably different from the other code-behind files. The only difference lies in the two event handlers that are declared at the bottom of the file. For completeness we have included the whole file below with the important sections highlighted and annotated.

```
Option Strict Off

Imports System
Imports System.ComponentModel.Design
Imports System.Data
```

```
Imports System.Drawing
Imports System.Web
Imports System.Web.SessionState
Imports System.Web.UI
Imports System.Web.UI.WebControls
Imports System.Web.UI.HtmlControls
Imports Microsoft.VisualBasic

Public Class Checkout
    Inherits System.Web.UI.Page
    Protected WithEvents btnOrder As System.Web.UI.WebControls.Button
    Protected WithEvents ShoppingCartList As System.Web.UI.WebControls.DataList
    Protected WithEvents txtExpirationDate As System.Web.UI.WebControls.TextBox
    Protected WithEvents txtCardNumber As System.Web.UI.WebControls.TextBox

#Region " Web Forms Designer Generated Code "

    Dim WithEvents Checkout As System.Web.UI.Page

    Sub New()
        Checkout = Me
    End Sub

    'CODEGEN: This procedure is required by the Web Form Designer
    'Do not modify it using the code editor.
    Private Sub InitializeComponent()

    End Sub

#End Region

    Protected Sub Checkout_Init(ByVal Sender As System.Object, ByVal e As _
System.EventArgs)
        'CODEGEN: This method call is required by the Web Form Designer
        'Do not modify it using the code editor.
        InitializeComponent()
    End Sub
    Protected Sub Checkout_Load(ByVal Sender As System.Object, _
                            ByVal e As System.EventArgs)

        Dim shoppingCart As Orders.OrderInfo

        ShoppingCart = CType(Session("CurrentOrder"), Orders.OrderInfo)
        ShoppingCartList.DataSource = shoppingCart.Values
        ShoppingCartList.DataBind()

    End Sub
```

This event handler is the one fired when the page is loaded. It will retrieve the `OrderInfo` instance that is stored in the `CurrentOrder` session variable. The `.Values` property, which returns a collection of all the `OrderItem` objects in the order, is then used as the source to which the `ShoppingCartList` repeater is bound.

```
    Public Sub btnOrder_Click(ByVal sender As Object, _
                            ByVal e As System.EventArgs)

        Dim OrderSubmitter As New localhost.OrderService()
        Dim tmpOrderInfo As New localhost.OrderInfo()

        tmpOrderInfo = CType(Session("CurrentOrder"), localhost.OrderInfo)

        tmpOrderInfo.BillingDetails = New localhost.BillingInfo()
        tmpOrderInfo.BillingDetails.CardExpDate = txtExpirationDate.Text
        tmpOrderInfo.BillingDetails.CardNumber = txtCardNumber.Text
        tmpOrderInfo.CustomerID = Session("UserID")

        OrderSubmitter.EnterOrder(CType(tmpOrderInfo, localhost.OrderInfo))
        Session("CurrentOrder") = New Orders.OrderInfo()
        Response.Redirect("InventoryList.aspx")
    End Sub

End Class
```

The handler for the **Submit Order Now** button will fill in all the necessary details on the `OrderInfo` instance and then pass that instance to the `EnterOrder` WebMethod that we created in the `BPOrderService` WebService.

Once the order has been submitted, the `CurrentOrder` session variable is reset to an empty instance, and the user is redirected back to the `InventoryList` page.

Checkout Summary

With the submitting of the order, the web application has completed its purpose. The checkout page presents the user with the full listing of the items in their order and prompts them to enter their billing information. After all the information is entered and applied to the `OrderInfo` instance, that instance is passed to the web method we created earlier in the chapter.

Summary

In looking back at the solution that we have built, there are some areas for improvement in the application. Even so, this solution has provided some very good examples of building applications and solutions with Visual Studio .NET. We have been able to explore the use of some of the new components and features provided by the .NET frameworks. In this solution we have seen the use of:

❑   WebServices

❑   NT Services

❑   MSMQ Component

❑   EventLog Component

❑   PerformanceCounter Component

❑   Trace/Debug Capabilities

❑   WebMethods

In creating the applications we have also seen how there is a distinct separation between the logic and presentation layers of a web application. There are so many new capabilities in .NET that it would be impossible to cover all of them in a single chapter. As such, this chapter was intended to take a common example and show how that same solution could be written using Visual Studio .NET and the .NET Frameworks provided by Microsoft. This book serves as a great introduction to .NET and its capabilities, and a future book will provide more in depth coverage of all the features and capabilities that developers can utilize.

ODUCING.NETINTRODUCING.NETINTRODUCING.NETINTRODUCI
ETINTRODUCING.NETINTRODUCING.NETINTRODUCING.NETINT
CING.NETINTRODUCING.NETINTRODUCING.NETINTRODUCING.
NTRODUCING.NETINTRODUCING.NETINTRODUCING.NETINTROD
G.NETINTRODUCING.NETINTRODUCING.NETINTRODUCING.NET
ODUCING.NETINTRODUCING.NETINTRODUCING.NETINTRODUCI
ETINTRODUCING.NETINTRODUCING.NETINTRODUCING.NETINT
CING.NETINTRODUCING.NETINTRODUCING.NETINTRODUCING.
NTRODUCING.NETINTRODUCING.NETINTRODUCING.NETINTROD
G.NETINTRODUCING.NETINTRODUCING.NETINTRODUCING.NET
ODUCING.NETINTRODUCING.NETINTRODUCING.NETINTRODUCI
ETINTRODUCING.NETINTRODUCING.NETINTRODUCING.NETINT
CING.NETINTRODUCING.NETINTRODUCING.NETINTRODUCING.
NTRODUCING.NETINTRODUCING.NETINTRODUCING.NETINTROD
G.NETINTRODUCING.NETINTRODUCING.NETINTRODUCING.NET
ODUCING.NETINTRODUCING.NETINTRODUCING.NETINTRODUCI
ETINTRODUCING.NETINTRODUCING.NETINTRODUCING.NETINT
CING.NETINTRODUCING.NETINTRODUCING.NETINTRODUCING.
NTRODUCING.NETINTRODUCING.NETINTRODUCING.NETINTROD
G.NETINTRODUCING.NETINTRODUCING.NETINTRODUCING.NET
ODUCING.NETINTRODUCING.NETINTRODUCING.NETINTRODUCI
ETINTRODUCING.NETINTRODUCING.NETINTRODUCING.NETINT
CING.NETINTRODUCING.NETINTRODUCING.NETINTRODUCING.
NTRODUCING.NETINTRODUCING.NETINTRODUCING.NETINTROD
G.NETINTRODUCING.NETINTRODUCING.NETINTRODUCING.NET
ODUCING.NETINTRODUCING.NETINTRODUCING.NETINTRODUCI
NTRODUCING.NETINTRODUCING.NETINTRODUCING.NETINT
NETINTRODUCING.NETINTRODUCING.NETINTRODUCING.
DUCING.NETINTRODUCING.NETINTRODUCING.NETINTROD
NETINTRODUCING.NETINTRODUCING.NETINTRODUCING.NET
ODUCING.NETINTRODUCING.NETINTRODUCING.NETINTRODUCI
ETINTRODUCING.NETINTRODUCING.NETINTRODUCING.NETINT

.NET Framework Reference

This is a reference appendix listing all the .NET Framework namespaces, correct to beta one.

Namespace	Description
Microsoft.ComServices	This namespace provides access to COM+ applications, such as security details, object activation properties, and most details commonly found in the Component Services Management Console.
System	This namespace provides commonly-used types. It includes base types for everything (`Object`), Value Types (`ValueType`), Enums (`enums`), Exceptions (`Exception`), and Attributes (`Attribute`), and Event data (`EventArgs`).
	Other classes provide services supporting method parameter manipulation, supervision of managed and unmanaged applications, mathematics, remote and local program invocation, data type conversion, and application environment management.
System.CodeDOM	This namespace provides classes that can be used to represent the structure and elements of a source code document.
System.CodeDOM.Compiler	This namespace contains infrastructure for translating CodeDom trees into source code.
System.Collections	This namespace provides classes and interfaces that describe various collections of objects, such as arrays, lists, queues, and hashtables.

Table continued on following page

Namespace	Description
System.ComponentModel	This namespace contains classes and attributes useful for components designers (licensing, designer support ,etc.).
System.Configuration	This namespace provides application configuration classes, such as locations of configuration files, web server configuration, and so on.
System.Data	This namespace mainly consists of the classes that constitute the ADO.NET architecture, which allows you to build components that manage data efficiently from multiple data sources. ADO.NET provides the tools to request, update, and reconcile data in n-tier systems in a disconnected scenario. The ADO.NET architecture can also be used in client applications, such as HTML pages created by ASP.NET, or Windows Forms.
System.Data.ADO	This namespace contains the ADO.NET managed provider.
System.Data.SQL	This namespace contains the SQL Server managed provider.
System.Data.SQLTypes	This namespace contains classes for native data types in SQL Server.
System.Diagnostics	This namespace contains classes that allow you to trace the execution of your code and to debug your application. System.Diagnostics also provides classes that allow you to read and write to event logs, start system processes, and monitor system performance using performance counters.
System.DirectoryServices	This namespace facilitates access to the Active Directory from managed code. The classes in this namespace can be used with any of the Active Directory service providers. The current providers are: Internet Information Server (IIS), Lightweight Directory Access Protocol (LDAP), Novell NetWare Directory Service (NDS), and WinNT.
System.Drawing	This namespace enables access to GDI+ basic graphics functionality. More advanced functionality is provided in the System.Drawing.Drawing2D, System.Drawing.Imaging, and System.Drawing.Text namespaces.
System.Drawing.Design	This namespace provides classes that can be used to extend design-time user interface and drawing support.
System.Drawing.Drawing2D	This namespace provides advanced 2-dimensional and vector graphics functionality. It also includes the gradient brushes, the Matrix class (used to define geometric transforms), and the GraphicsPath class.
System.Drawing.Imaging	This namespace contains advanced GDI+ imaging functionality. The Encoder and Decoder classes allow users to extend GDI+ to support any image format. The PropertyItem class contains methods for storing and retrieving image file metadata. The Metafile class contains methods for recording and saving metafiles.
System.Drawing.Printing	This namespace allows you to specify how documents print.

Namespace	Description
System.Drawing.Text	This namespace contains advanced GDI+ typography functionality. The classes in this namespace enable users to create and use font collections.
System.Globalization	This namespace supplies classes that provide globalization features (such as calendars, date and number formatting and parsing, etc.) for writing multi-language applications.
System.IO	The IO namespace provides types that allow synchronous and asynchronous reading from and writing to data streams and files.
System.IO.IsolatedStorage	This namespaces provides untrusted code access persistent storage.
System.Management	This namespace provides access to the Windows Management and Instrumentation service (WMI).
System.Messaging	This namespace provides classes that allow you to connect to message queues on the network, send messages to queues, and receive or peek (read without removing) messages from queues. This is implemented using MSMQ.
System.Net	This namespace provides a simple programming interface to many of the protocols found on the net today, (web requests, etc.).
System.Net.Sockets	This namespace provides a managed implementation of the Windows Sockets interface for developers that need to tightly control access to the network.
System.Reflection	This namespace provides classes and interfaces that provide a managed view of loaded types, fields, methods, properties, and events with the ability to dynamically create and invoke types.
System.Reflection.Emit	This namespace provides a way of generating metadata that can be consumed by the System.Reflection namespace classes. As such it provides a way to generate managed libraries and executables.
System.Resources	This namespace provides management of localization resources, to aid in the development of multi-lingual applications.
System.Runtime.CompilerServices	This namespace provides custom attributes that are used at development time to describe various aspects of the assembly being built. For example, this namespace includes attributes for supplying a keyfile used to give the assembly a shared (strong) name, or for specifying the assembly's version number.
System.Runtime.InteropServices	This namespace provides a layer between managed code (that is .NET code) and unmanaged COM/COM+ code.
System.Runtime.Remoting	This namespace provides classes and interfaces that allow developers to create tightly- or loosely-coupled distributed applications.
System.Runtime.Remoting.Channels.HTTP	This namespace provides direct access to a remote HTTP stream.

Table continued on following page

Namespace	Description
System.Runtime.Remoting.Channels.SMTP	This namespace provides direct access to a remote SMTP stream.
System.Runtime.Remoting.Channels.TCP	This namespace provides direct access to a remote TCP stream.
System.Runtime.Serialization	This namespace provides support for the serialization of objects, allowing persistent storage, or remote transfer of objects.
System.Runtime.Serialization.Formatters	This namespace provides classes to format objects being serialized.
System.Runtime.Serialization.Formatters.Binary	This namespace provides the ability to format instances into a binary representation.
System.Runtime.Serialization.Formatters.Soap	This namespace provides serialization of instances into a SOAP representation.
System.Security	This namespace provides the underlying structure of the .NET Framework security system, including attributes, interfaces, exceptions, and base classes for permissions.
System.Security.Cryptography	This namespace provides cryptographic services, including secure encoding and decoding of data, as well as many other operations, such as random number generation, message authentication, creation of digital signatures, and hashing.
System.Security.Cryptography.X509Certificates	This namespace encapsulates the management of security certificates in the x509 standard.
System.Security.Permissions	This namespace defines classes that control access to operations and resources based on policy.
System.Security.Policy	This namespace defines classes that use a set of rules that can be configured to determine which permissions to grant to code, based on the user, domain, and assembly of the code.
System.Security.Principal	This namespace provides access to the security principle in place whilst running an application. This is useful for obtaining details such as the user name, authentication mode, and so on.
System.ServiceProcess	This namespace contains classes that allow you to install and run NT Services.
System.Text	This namespace provides classes representing ASCII, Unicode, UTF-7, and UTF-8 character encodings; abstract base classes for converting blocks of characters to and from blocks of bytes; and a helper class that manipulates and formats String objects without creating intermediate instances of String.
System.Text.RegularExpressions	This namespace provides classes that provide access to the .NET Framework regular expression engine.
System.Threading	This namespace provides classes and interfaces that enable multi-threaded programming.

Namespace	Description
System.Timers	This namespace provides two components which allow you to raise an event on an interval or more complex schedule, the Timer component, which is a server-based timer, which allows you to specify a recurring interval at which the Tick event is raised in your application, and the Schedule component, which allows the specification of a schedule on which to raise the EventOccurred event.
System.Web	This namespace contains classes and interfaces that enable browser/server communication.
System.Web.Caching	This namespace provides access to the ASP.NET Cache.
System.Web.Configuration	This namespace provides classes that are used to configure ASP.NET.
System.Web.Security	This namespace provides classes that are used to implement ASP.NET security in web server applications.
System.Web.Services	This namespace consists of the classes that enable you to build and use Web Services.
System.Web.Services.Description	This namespace consists of the classes that enable you to publicly describe a Web Service via Service Description Language(SDL).
System.Web.Services.Discovery	This namespace consists of the classes that enable you to publicly describe a Web Service via Service Description Language(SDL).
System.Web.Services.Protocols	This namespace consists of the classes that define the protocols used to transmit data during the communication between the Web Service and its clients.
System.Web.UI	This namespace implements the base classes used by the Web controls.
System.Web.UI.Design	This namespace provides classes that can be used to extend design-time support for Web Forms.
System.Web.UI.Design.WebControls	This namespace provides classes that can be used to extend design-time support for Web controls.
System.Web.UI.Design.WebControls.ListControls	This namespace provides classes that can be used to extend design-time support for list controls.
System.Web.UI.HtmlControls	This namespace provide the standard HTML controls.
System.Web.UI.WebControls	This namespace provides the extended ASP controls (such as DataGrid).
System.Web.Util	This namespace provide a mixed set of classes, such as SmtpMail for mail access, EventLog for Event Log access, and so on.
System.WinForms	This namespace provides classes for creating Windows-based applications, or WinForms.

Table continued on following page

Namespace	Description
`System.WinForms.ComponentModel`	This namespace provides the details used for installation of component types.
`System.WinForms.Design`	This namespace provides classes that can be used to extend design-time support for WinForms.
`System.XML`	This is the overall namespace for the XML classes that provide standards-based support for processing XML. The supported standards are:

For `System.XML`, the supported standards:

- ❑ XML 1.0: http://www.w3.org/TR/1998/REC-xml-19980210 – including DTD support (XmlTextReader)
- ❑ XML Namespaces: http://www.w3.org/TR/REC-xml-names/ – both stream level and DOM
- ❑ XML Schemas: http://www.w3.org/TR/xmlschema-1/ – supported for schema mapping, and serialization, but not yet for validation. (see also XmlSchemaCollection which currently provides XDR schema validation)
- ❑ XPath expressions: http://www.w3.org/TR/xpath (XmlNavigator)
- ❑ XSL/T transformations: http://www.w3.org/TR/xslt (XslTransform)
- ❑ DOM Level 2 Core: http://www.w3.org/TR/DOM-Level-2/ – for (XmlDocument)
- ❑ SOAP 1.1: http://msdn.microsoft.com/xml/general/soapspec.asp (including the Soap Contract Language and Soap Discovery) used in XML object serialization

Namespace	Description
`System.XML.Serialization`	This namespace provides classes that provide a higher level way to read and write XML. It allows a programmer to interact with an XML document as a set of objects rather than nodes and attributes.
`System.XML.Serialization.Schema`	This namespace provides the classes that define schema elements as in-memory objects. Each class represents logical groupings of standard XML elements, and they allow creation of schemas, loading, and saving to streams. The class abstractions insulate the developer from the syntax details of XSD.
`System.XML.XPath`	This namespace provides the XPath parser and evaluation engine.
`System.XML.XSL`	This namespace contains support for XSL/T transformations.

DUCING·NETINTRODUCING·NETINTRODUCING·NETINTRODUCI
ETINTRODUCING·NETINTRODUCING·NETINTRODUCING·NETINT
CING·NETINTRODUCING·NETINTRODUCING·NETINTRODUCING·N
NTRODUCING·NETINTRODUCING·NETINTRODUCING·NETINTROD
G·NETINTRODUCING·NETINTRODUCING·NETINTRODUCING·NETI
ODUCING·NETINTRODUCING·NETINTRODUCING·NETINTRODUCI
ETINTRODUCING·NETINTRODUCING·NETINTRODUCING·NETINT
CING·NETINTRODUCING·NETINTRODUCING·NETINTRODUCING·N
NTRODUCING·NETINTRODUCING·NETINTRODUCING·NETINTROD
G·NETINTRODUCING·NETINTRODUCING·NETINTRODUCING·NETI
ODUCING·NETINTRODUCING·NETINTRODUCING·NETINTRODUCI
ETINTRODUCING·NETINTRODUCING·NETINTRODUCING·NETINT
CING·NETINTRODUCING·NETINTRODUCING·NETINTRODUCING·N
NTRODUCING·NETINTRODUCING·NETINTRODUCING·NETINTROD
G·NETINTRODUCING·NETINTRODUCING·NETINTRODUCING·NETI
ODUCING·NETINTRODUCING·NETINTRODUCING·NETINTRODUCI
ETINTRODUCING·NETINTRODUCING·NETINTRODUCING·NETINT
CING·NETINTRODUCING·NETINTRODUCING·NETINTRODUCING·N
NTRODUCING·NETINTRODUCING·NETINTRODUCING·NETINTROD
G·NETINTRODUCING·NETINTRODUCING·NETINTRODUCING·NETI
ODUCING·NETINTRODUCING·NETINTRODUCING·NETINTRODUCI
ETINTRODUCING·NETINTRODUCING·NETINTRODUCING·NETINT
CING·NETINTRODUCING·NETINTRODUCING·NETINTRODUCING·
NTRODUCING·NETINTRODUCING·NETINTRODUCING·NETINTROD
G·NETINTRODUCING·NETINTRODUCING·NETINTRODUCING·NET
ODUCING·NETINTRODUCING·NETINTRODUCING·NETINTRODUCI
ETINTRODUCING·NETINTRODUCING·NETINTRODUCING·NETINT
CING·NETINTRODUCING·NETINTRODUCING·NETINTRODUCING·
NTRODUCING·NETINTRODUCING·NETINTRODUCING·NETINTROD
G·NETINTRODUCING·NETINTRODUCING·NETINTRODUCING·NET
ODUCING·NETINTRODUCING·NETINTRODUCING·NETINTRODUCI
ETINTRODUCING·NETINTRODUCING·NETINTRODUCING·NETINT
CING·NETINTRODUCING·NETINTRODUCING·NETINTRODUCING·
NTRODUCING·NETINTRODUCING·NETINTRODUCING·NETINTROD
G·NETINTRODUCING·NETINTRODUCING·NETINTRODUCING·NET
ODUCING·NETINTRODUCING·NETINTRODUCING·NETINTRODUCI
ETINTRODUCING·NETINTRODUCING·NETINTRODUCING·NETINT

Using Classic COM Components in ASP.NET

B

Components are a fundamental part of most Windows DNA applications. Many companies have followed the Window DNA blueprint laid out by Microsoft, and have subsequently benefited from the scalability and reliability it gives enterprise applications. However, this adoption means that a lot of time and money has been invested into component development that must be usable in the .NET Framework **without** change.

Realizing this component investment exists, and understanding that not everybody will instantly adopt the new runtime for various reasons, Microsoft have provided a sophisticated interoperability layer between the new .NET runtime and classic COM. This allows existing COM components to be in the new managed runtime, and for managed components to be used by classic COM applications.

In this appendix we are going to take a brief look at how a classic COM component can be used in an ASP.NET application, after which we'll discuss some of the implications of doing this.

Type Library Importer

The .NET Framework SDK ships with a utility called the Type Library Importer (**TlbImp** – `tlbimp.exe`). This takes a standard COM type library and creates an assembly that contains equivalent .NET metadata. This metadata can be used in managed code to create and use an instance of any unmanaged component that was defined in the original type library, seemingly as if they were managed components created by a managed language. Other definitions within the type library (such as enumerations) can also be accessed.

TlbImp is designed to enable managed code to **early bind** to unmanaged components and their interfaces. This results in excellent interop performance, but, if you just want to late bind to unmanaged components using `Server.CreateObject` and `CreateObject`, you do not need to use the `TlbImp` tool. The late binding syntax/code that worked in ASP will work without change in ASP.NET.

> All managed code requires metadata descriptions of the various types (classes, etc.) it uses. This is similar to metadata held in a traditional type library, but it is much richer and it is also extensible.

Using a VB6 Component in ASP.NET (Early Binding)

To see `TlbImp` in action I've created a simple VB6 ActiveX DLL project called `ClassicCOM` that contains one component called `myComponent`. This exposes its standard default VB interface (`_myComponent`) and a custom interface called `_myInterface`. The default interface has one method called `Add` that takes a number and adds a specified amount to it. The `_myInterface` interface has one method called `Subtract` that takes a number and subtracts a specified amount from it.

Both interfaces are implemented in the way you'd expect, and the component code *really* couldn't be much simpler:

```
Implements myInterface

Public Function Add(number As Long, valueToAdd As Long) As Long
    Add = number + valueToAdd
End Function

Public Function myInterface_Subtract(number As Long, _
                                valueToSubtract As Long) As Long

    myInterface_Subtract = number - valueToSubtract

End Function
```

> Although this component is very simple, the basic techniques we are showing should work for any COM server/type library including those published by Microsoft.

Once the project has been compiled and **registered**, we can use the TlbImp utility to create an assembly for our VB6 DLL:

```
TlbImp ClassicCOM.dll /out:Wrapper.DLL
```

To view the contents of the assembly we can use the ILDASM tool:

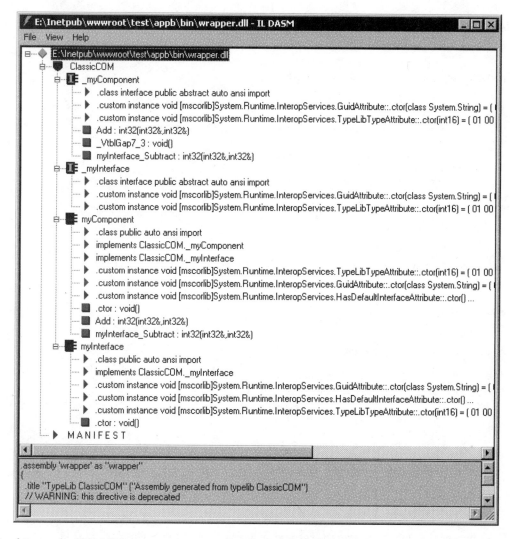

Looking at the ILDASM output we can see that the namespace ClassicCOM has been created, which matches the name of the DLL containing the type library. The first two definitions within this namespace match our VB6 definitions (remember VB adds the underscore behind the scenes), and the following definition for the component also matches. The final definition is slightly confusing, as our original VB6 COM server did not contain a component called myInterface. However, as VB6 hides the underscore and actually lets you type myInterface rather than _myInterface, the type library converter is working on the principle that it should also support both naming conventions.

Once the assembly is created we can copy it into the bin directory of an ASP.NET application and use it. The COM component must also be properly registered in order for the assembly to function. So if you move the COM component too, be sure to re-register it.

Using a TlbImp-created Assembly

Create a new web application, and in it create a page called `default.aspx` that looks like this:

```
<%@Import namespace="ClassicCOM" %>

<script language="VB" runat="server">

    protected Sub Page_Load( sender as object, e as EventArgs )

        ' First time through set current value to 100

        If (Page.IsPostBack = false ) Then
            currentValue.Text = "100"
        End If
    End Sub

    ' increment the value

    protected Sub DoAdd( sender as object, e as EventArgs )

        dim test as myComponent
        test = new myComponent()

        dim total as Int32
        dim value as Int32

        value = int32.Parse( change.Text )
        total = int32.Parse( currentValue.Text )

        total = test.Add( total, value )

        currentValue.Text = total.ToString()

    End Sub


    ' decrement the value

    protected Sub DoSubtract( sender as object, e as EventArgs )

        dim test as myComponent
        test = new myComponent()

        dim total as Int32
        dim value as Int32

        value = int32.Parse( change.Text )
        total = int32.Parse( currentValue.Text )

        total = test.myInterface_Subtract (total, value )

        currentValue.Text = total.ToString()

    End Sub
```

```
</script>

<h2>ASP.NET using a 'Classic COM' component</h2>

<form runat="server">

  <asp:TextBox id="change" runat="server" Text="10"/>
  <asp:Button Text="Add" OnClick="DoAdd" runat="server" />
  <asp:Button Text="Subtract" OnClick="DoSubtract" runat="server" />

<br>Current value is: <asp:label id="currentValue" runat="server" />

</form>
```

When viewed in the browser the pages will look like this:

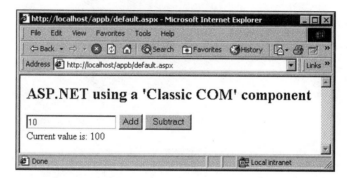

The ASP.NET code is relatively straight forward, so we'll just focus upon the important sections. The first point to note is that the namespace ClassicCOM has been imported into the page, which saves us having to prefix all of our declarations with ClassicCOM. :

```
<%@Import namespace="ClassicCOM" %>
```

The component within this namespace is then used within the DoAdd and DoSubtract functions. If we look at the DoAdd function we can see that there really is no special code needed to access and use the unmanaged component:

```
protected Sub DoAdd( sender as object, e as EventArgs )

    dim test as myComponent
    test = new myComponent()

    dim total as Int32
    dim value as Int32

    value = int32.Parse( change.Text )
    total = int32.Parse( currentValue.Text )

    total = test.Add( total, value )

    currentValue.Text = total.ToString()

  End Sub
```

We are just calling the Add function and the runtime is taking call of all the interop issues.

Late Binding

The .NET interop layer supports late binding in the same way as classic ASP, so we can still create and access unmanaged components using `Server.CreateObject` and `CreateObject` functions:

```
protected Sub DoAdd( sender as object, e as EventArgs )

    dim test as object

    test = Server.CreateObject("ClassicCOM.myComponent")

    dim total as Int32
    dim value as Int32

    value = int32.Parse( change.Text )
    total = int32.Parse( currentValue.Text )

    total = test.Add( total, value )

    currentValue.Text = total.ToString()

End Sub
```

Late bound code like this should be avoided in ASP.NET because it will not execute as quickly as early bound code, and it is more error prone – just like traditional ASP code. For example, if you mistyped a method name, the error will occur at runtime, and not compile time.

Error Handling

In the world of COM all methods return HRESULTs (although this is hidden in higher-level languages such as VB). Because the new runtime does not support HRESULTs directly, the interop layer automatically converts any errors (failed HRESULTs) returned from your components into `ComException` exceptions. These should be caught and processed in your code:

```
Try
   someClassCOMObject.SomeMethod()
Catch e As ComException
   ...
End Try
```

For some well-known error codes, other exceptions will be thrown, such as `ArgumentNullException` for `E_POINTER` and `NotImplementedException` for `E_NOTIMPL`.

Performance

Although we have showed you how to use classic COM components inside an ASP.NET page, **we must make it clear** that doing this incurs a number of performance penalties that you should consider from day one. Ideally, we recommend that you recompile your components using the new compilers where possible, and only use the interoperability where you really have no other choice (such as a dependency of a third party component).

Calling into Unmanaged Code from Managed Code

Calling from managed code into unmanaged code requires some special processing, so creating an instance of an unmanaged component and calling its methods from within a managed application such as an ASP.NET page is not as quick as creating and calling other managed components. The performance overhead will vary depending upon the complexity of the individual parameters used in component interfaces, as certain types require more conversion and processing (marshaling) than others.

Runtime Callable Wrapper (RCW)

As the new managed runtime is so radically different to classic COM, a **Runtime Callable Wrapper** (RCW) is used to bridge the communications between managed code and an unmanaged class COM component:

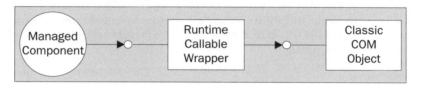

The RCW is a managed component with which managed code like ASP.NET interacts. The RCW consumes the interfaces exposed by a classic COM component and re-exposes them as if they were part of a native managed component. Each time an unmanaged component is created, or any of an unmanaged component's interfaces return an object reference, an RCW will be created to manage it. In many ways the RCW is like a standard COM proxy, except that it lives by the rules of the NGWS runtime and is therefore garbage collected.

Not all interfaces of unmanaged components are re-exposed by an RCW; no classic **standard** COM specific interfaces such as `IUnknown` and `IDispatch` are accessible, only custom interfaces.

> If you are a VB programmer the new managed runtime really isn't a radical concept as VB has primarily worked this way since its first incarnation (p-code). However, if you are a C/C++ programmer you'll appreciate that the RCW has to do a lot of tricks to enable the interop, such as lifetime management, identity management, etc.

Calling into Managed Code from Unmanaged Code

Although not the primary topic of this appendix, calling from unmanaged code into managed code also requires some special processing, and can affect ASP.NET developers. Like the RCW discussed earlier, classic COM objects use a COM Callable Wrapper (CCW) when accessing managed components to bridge the differences between them:

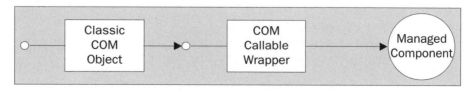

Like the RCW, the CCW is created each time a classic COM component interacts with a managed component. If you create an unmanaged component within an ASP.NET page and pass it a reference to a managed component via an interface method, a CCW will be created. However in theory, CCW are less of an overhead in real terms, as the new runtime promises to generate code that is more efficient and scalable than the existing range of unmanaged compilers (especially VB6), so the overhead is compensated for by the performance of the new runtime. Microsoft realizes that performance of the new runtime is the crucial key requirement for the new runtime to be accepted, so you can be sure that this interop layer and managed code in general will be **lightning** fast. Initial tests have already shown ASP.NET to be 2-4 times faster than ASP today.

ASP.NET is Built on an MTA Thread Pool

ASP.NET under the hood is built on top of a thread pool, where each thread is registered as a Multiple Threaded Apartment (MTA). Any calls to classic COM components that are apartment threaded (for example, All VB6 components) will always require proxy/stubs to be used when they are invoked. This overhead is quite significant and will dramatically reduce the performance of your unmanaged components in a managed application.

Index

A Guide to the Index

The index is arranged hierarchically, in alphabetical order, with symbols preceding the letter A. Most second-level entries and many third-level entries also occur as first-level entries. This is to ensure that users will find the information they require however they choose to search for it.

O

ODUCING.NETINTRODUCING.NETINTRODUCING.NETINTRODUCI
ETINTRODUCING.NETINTRODUCING.NETINTRODUCING.NETINT
CING.NETINTRODUCING.NETINTRODUCING.NETINTRODUCING.
NTRODUCING.NETINTRODUCING.NETINTRODUCING.NETINTROD
G.NETINTRODUCING.NETINTRODUCING.NETINTRODUCING.NET
ODUCING.NETINTRODUCING.NETINTRODUCING.NETINTRODUCI
ETINTRODUCING.NETINTRODUCING.NETINTRODUCING.NETINT
CING.NETINTRODUCING.NETINTRODUCING.NETINTRODUCING.
NTRODUCING.NETINTRODUCING.NETINTRODUCING.NETINTROD
G.NETINTRODUCING.NETINTRODUCING.NETINTRODUCING.NET
ODUCING.NETINTRODUCING.NETINTRODUCING.NETINTRODUCI
ETINTRODUCING.NETINTRODUCING.NETINTRODUCING.NETINT
CING.NETINTRODUCING.NETINTRODUCING.NETINTRODUCING.
NTRODUCING.NETINTRODUCING.NETINTRODUCING.NETINTROD
G.NETINTRODUCING.NETINTRODUCING.NETINTRODUCING.NET
ODUCING.NETINTRODUCING.NETINTRODUCING.NETINTRODUCI
ETINTRODUCING.NETINTRODUCING.NETINTRODUCING.NETINT
CING.NETINTRODUCING.NETINTRODUCING.NETINTRODUCING.
NTRODUCING.NETINTRODUCING.NETINTRODUCING.NETINTROD
G.NETINTRODUCING.NETINTRODUCING.NETINTRODUCING.NET
ODUCING.NETINTRODUCING.NETINTRODUCING.NETINTRODUCI
ETINTRODUCING.NETINTRODUCING.NETINTRODUCING.NETINT
CING.NETINTRODUCING.NETINTRODUCING.NETINTRODUCING.
NTRODUCING.NETINTRODUCING.NETINTRODUCING.NETINTROD
G.NETINTRODUCING.NETINTRODUCING.NETINTRODUCING.NET
ODUCING.NETINTRODUCING.NETINTRODUCING.NETINTRODUCI
ETINTRODUCING.NETINTRODUCING.NETINTRODUCING.NETINT
CING.NETINTRODUCING.NETINTRODUCING.NETINTRODUCING.
NTRODUCING.NETINTRODUCING.NETINTRODUCING.NETINTROD
G.NETINTRODUCING.NETINTRODUCING.NETINTRODUCING.NET
ODUCING.NETINTRODUCING.NETINTRODUCING.NETINTRODUCI
ETINTRODUCING.NETINTRODUCING.NETINTRODUCING.NETINT